THEORY
OF
ECONOMIC STATICS

THEORY

OF

ECONOMIC STATICS

Second Edition

Michael J. Brennan

Dean, Graduate School
Brown University

PRENTICE-HALL, INC., ENGLEWOOD CLIFFS, NEW JERSEY

13-913624-X
Library of Congress Catalog Card Number 73-99969

Current printing (last digit)
10 9 8 7 6 5 4 3 2 1

PRENTICE-HALL INTERNATIONAL, INC., *London*
PRENTICE HALL OF AUSTRALIA PTY. LTD., *Sydney*
PRENTICE-HALL OF CANADA, LTD., *Toronto*
PRENTICE-HALL OF INDIA PRIVATE LTD., *New Delhi*
PRENTICE-HALL OF JAPAN, INC., *Tokyo*

To Tommi, Mark, and Moira

Preface

Theory of Economic Statics is an exposition of contemporary microeconomic theory. Emphasis is laid upon theoretical analysis rather than descriptive material dealing with institutions or current events. And the treatment of theory is more intensive than is customary in an elementary presentation.

Presumably, the preface to a textbook allows an author to spell out his pedagogical biases. Some of mine are born of the discovery that many who have difficulty with economics know the buzz words and the fragments but don't know how they fit together. These students are mentally perspiring over the separate pieces of a jigsaw puzzle without a clear idea of the picture to be constructed. Consequently, I have included more introductory material than one usually finds at the intermediate level. The first four chapters, though short, are designed to provide at the outset an overall perspective on content and methodology—a guideline that demonstrates how the subjects covered in subsequent chapters are connected to form a body of theory.

Unlike most books on price theory, this one does not devote chapters to Marshallian diminishing marginal utility, Say's Law, the Giffin paradox, or other excursions into the economics of yesteryear. These are subjects that general readers and undergraduates (and graduate students who do not intend to become professional economists) forget within six months. Moreover, their inclusion serves to cloud over an exposition of contemporary theories actually utilized by economists in modern research.

The space saved by limiting the topics to contemporary theory permits a more thorough development of each concept, more treatment of related markets, and more applications—all without adding inches to the thickness of the volume. The book stresses theory as a tool of analysis. And the practicality of abstract models is illustrated by frequent applications and problem assignments. Applications are both theoretical and empirical. Since theoretical applications concentrate on the formulation of models aimed at interpreting and predicting observable market behavior, the empirical applications are oriented toward econometrics. Statistical estimation and tests of hypotheses are not explained in detail. But the description of econometric method should be sufficient to demonstrate the role of theory in the entire process of economic research.

Aside from simple algebra and two-dimensional geometry, no mathematics is required of the student. Functional notation is employed, however, in order to distinguish explicitly between movements along a curve and shifts in its position. In the future, economic theory may be expounded mathematically as, say, engineering is today. But as things stand, many students of economics find mathematics an obstacle rather than an aid to understanding. For readers with mathematical aptitude, a Mathematical Appendix has been included at the end of the book.

In revising *Theory of Economic Statics,* I have removed the entire section on macroeconomics. In fact, the book has found its greatest audience in courses on microeconomics or price theory. Deletion of the macroeconomic theory constitutes an adjustment to the revealed preferences of consumers and restores the book to its original structure, conceived over five years ago.

Chapter 9 on the production function has been revised. Returns to scale and the two-dimensional product curves are derived directly from the production isoquants. This exposition provides symmetry with the earlier derivation of the law of diminishing returns and the short-run product curves.

A second chapter on oligopoly (Chapter 17) has been added to provide more discussion of mutually interdependent decision making on the part of firms. Hypotheses alternative to profit maximization, simulation models, and game theory are outlined briefly. The intent is not a comprehensive treatment of the subjects but rather an introduction to methods of analysis to which the reader is not normally exposed.

In the area of resource pricing and allocation, a new chapter (Chapter 23) has been written on Human Capital. It was felt that this general approach, if carefully built upon the theory of investment in nonhuman capital, would provide a framework for discussion of many "relevant" applications.

Aside from these major revisions, the style has been improved in several places throughout the book, the number of applications has been increased, and material has been added on income distribution and the problem of poverty.

Thanks are due to professors W. Carl Biven, Edward C. Budd, Edwin S. Mills, James R. Nelson, Nathan Rosenberg, Menahem E. Yaari, and Stuart Altman, all of whom contributed constructive criticism and helpful suggestions. I also wish to express my gratitude to Miss Marion Anthony who typed the major portion of the manuscript.

MICHAEL J. BRENNAN

Contents

Part I

Introduction

1

The Why of Economics

Once upon a time, a man who owned a handsome pig lived in a province that was struck by a famine. Nearly all the people were starving, and they greedily eyed the pig, thinking of the delicious pork chops he would make. But the man loved that old pig, loved it so dearly that he was willing to do anything to protect its life. Fearing that the people would steal his pet, he took the pig into the house, barred the door, loaded his shotgun, and waited to see what would happen. When the hungry mob surrounded his house, he rushed about the room, firing from each window. But every time he ran across the room he stumbled over the pig. Finally, he opened the door, kicked out the pig, and continued to run from window to window, blasting away at the mob.

We are about to embark upon a study of economics. In the chapters that follow we shall be dealing with specific economic activities and a multitude of particular problems close to our everyday experience. Unless in the process we too should "kick out the pig," we must begin with a clear idea of *why* these activities are carried on—and then keep it in mind. Otherwise, like the defender of the pig, we may lose sight of our goal; from preoccupation with immediate problems we run the risk of blindness to the over-all objective.

Society faces many economic problems, each one characterized by the circumstances of the particular situation in which it arises. Underlying these specific problems, and common to them all, is a fundamental problem. Later in the book we will examine in detail some situations that demonstrate how the basic problem reveals itself in practice. For the present, however, in order to fix our bearings, let us take a broad perspective and survey the over-all background of economic activity.

THE BASIC ECONOMIC PROBLEM

If one were to ask "What does economics involve?" he could be sure of getting at least some answers like "Making a livelihood," "The study of wealth," "The study of business." Such answers are either too narrow or too broad to get at the roots of economic activity. It may be said without too much oversimplification that *economics is the study of the principles governing allocation of scarce means among alternative ends.*[1]

This is an abstract and very general definition. It applies to a primitive agricultural community no less than to a highly industrialized one. It does not depend upon the kind of political system or the legal sanctions and customs of society. Given this degree of generality, the meaning of the definition can be clarified by considering each of its components in turn.

Scarce Means

Suppose there were no scarcity in the world. Clearly, everything would be free (require no effort, have no cost). To obtain more of some goods or services—such as more oranges, medical advice, education, movies, or books—one would merely have to wish for them and they would appear. In this fairyland everything would be there for the asking. With no scarcity, no economic problem arises. But in our world we do not come by goods and services so easily. *Scarcity* forces us to distribute the means of production we have among the various alternative uses to which they may be put. People want more than can be produced of some goods, and they want less than can be produced of others. Thus, the necessity for *allocation* arises. Since society cannot have as much as it wants of everything, it must decide what goods to produce and how much of each to produce. The need to make this decision, however it may be made, is common to all societies.

Total wants are generally insatiable; when one want is satisfied, another develops. Our wants are directed toward goods and services. Yet when we come to examine the problem more closely, we see that what we ultimately want is services only. We want the service rendered to us by a piece of pastry (the nutrition and the palatable taste, though perhaps not the calories); we do not desire the pastry in and of itself. Likewise, we want the transportation, and perhaps the prestige, yielded by an automobile rather than the automobile itself.

Some services can be used directly—a massage or a haircut for example. Others must be obtained indirectly from the acquisition of some object that in a sense "contains within it" the desired service. The nutrition wanted can be obtained from oatmeal, the sartorial splendor from particular items of clothing, the taste sensation from a cigarette. The essential point is that human beings do possess *wants* that are satisfied by services or by goods yielding those services of want-satisfaction.

The world is endowed with a certain amount of resources, human and nonhuman, that can be used to produce goods and services. Nonhuman

[1] See F. H. Knight, *The Economic Organization* (Chicago: University of Chicago Press, 1933), pp. 1-4.

resources include land and raw materials, such as lakes, waterfalls, coal, and oil—sometimes called "natural" resources. There are also man-made nonhuman resources: factory buildings, machines, tools, and equipment. In addition, any society will have some human resources. Muscle and bone provide human energy that can be used for production; mental energy for scientific research or business management is no less useful for this purpose, and neither are the talents people possess for musical composition, acting, tailoring, etc. All these physical, intellectual, and artistic characteristics make up the human resources of any society.

Now, how does the economic problem arise? If no one wants a good or service, there is no need to produce it. It does not even matter if none is available, so there is no problem. On the other hand, if a good or service is desired but is already superabundant, then each person can have all he wants. Again there is no problem. But whenever there is scarcity of goods or services *relative to* the amounts wanted, not all wants can be completely satisfied. The reason a society does not have a superabundance of final goods and services is that it does not have a superabundance of the resources needed to produce them. Since any society does not have all it wants of every good and service, what it does have (what it can produce) must be distributed in some way among the members of society. The problem becomes one of allocating resources: if a given amount of resources are being used in production of X, Y, and Z, and if society wishes to have more of X, more resources must be devoted to the production of X, and consequently less can be devoted to the production of Y or Z.

Alternative Ends

The means to be allocated, then, are at bottom the productive resource services of a society. The immediate ends are productive uses, but the ultimate ends are want-satisfactions. More concretely, resources are to be used to produce the kinds of goods and services in the quantities demanded by society as a whole.

Allocation of the means implies that *alternative* ends rather than a single end are required, and these ends are in a sense competing for the scarce means. If there is but one end to be pursued, the problem can be called a technical one. To illustrate, assume a community decides that a bridge is to be erected. A certain amount of the community's resources is set aside for this purpose. The community further decides that from the given resources a bridge of the greatest durability shall be built. Only one end is specified, so the problem is a "technical" one that requires knowledge of engineering alone. But let the objective be to build the "best" bridge, where "best" includes not only considerations of durability but also size, weight, appearance, location, and traffic flow. There is no longer a single end. No amount of purely technical knowledge can yield a solution. The ends and means must be balanced and weighed in making choices. Technical knowledge alone cannot help the community decide how much traffic flow is worth giving up to obtain smaller size or what details of appearance ought to be sacrificed for the sake of a more convenient location.

The same sort of weighing and balancing of alternatives is an integral part of producing potatoes, constructing dormitories, changing jobs, and all the other activities we call economic. Indeed it is very difficult to think of any decision process that is a purely technical one, that is, that has only one end in view. As a consequence, the principles of economics have very widespread application.

Efficient Allocation

If means are not scarce, no economic problem exists. If the means are scarce but only one end is relevant, there is still no economic problem. An economic problem arises when there are *both* scarce means *and* alternative competing ends. Hence, the basic economic problem is one of allocating scarce means among alternative ends.

Obviously, society is not interested in just any allocation. Presumably it seeks the best allocation consistent with the ends dictated by its institutions. Efficiency is the prime consideration in this respect. Efficiency may be defined as the ratio of useful output to total input.[2] In concrete terms, from a given total input of resource services, the most efficient production yields the greatest possible total output of desired goods and services.

Society can combine units of labor, land, equipment, and other resources in several ways. The resulting types and quantities of goods and services will depend on how they are combined. Given the total amount of resources available, one kind of allocation will yield a given total output, but another allocation may yield a greater output. The second allocation is then said to be more efficient than the first. The most efficient allocation is the combination of resource services that produces as much as possible from the total amount of resources. We can append this to our definition of the basic economic problem. The basic economic problem of any society is the *efficient allocation* of scarce means among alternative ends.

Social and Individual Economizing

The fundamental economic problem posed in our discussion has been designated as a social or communal problem. This should not be taken to mean that individual problems of choice are not encompassed by the boundaries of economics. Like society, the individual must consider

[2] Knight, *The Economic Organization*, p. 8.

alternative ends and select means for satisfying the ends most efficiently. The allocation of my scarce (not unlimited) time between work and leisure is an economic problem. So is the allocation of my income between saving and spending, and then the allocation of my expenditures over the various goods and services I consume. The businessman allocates his given work force among a set of defined jobs, and the engineer allocates his resources to construct an engine of specified weight, size, and horsepower.

There are all kinds of individual economic activities. Of course, the choices made by individuals and the allocation of resources by society as a whole are closely interrelated. The behavior patterns of groups are the net result of a multitude of individual decisions. The science of economics is concerned primarily with the social effects of choice rather than the effects on this or that individual. Nevertheless, economics utilizes individual economic decisions in order to say something significant about their combined social effects.

ASSOCIATED ECONOMIC PROBLEMS

We have not yet exhausted the fruitful topic of ends and means. There remain some unanswered questions. The preceding discussion may seem to imply that the only economic problem is one of combining in the best way a *given* amount of resources, all of which are already employed. But what about changes in the total quantity of resources available to the economy? And what about business booms and depressions, or inflation? Do these phenomena fall outside the context of the basic economic problem?

Consider a depression involving mass unemployment of men and of nonhuman resources. From a broad viewpoint this state of affairs is one of inefficiency. It is a waste, and it entails human misery due to the loss of income. The economy has allocated resources in an inefficient (wasteful) way; some resources involuntarily stand idle. By reallocation of the means, in particular by reallocation from unproductive to productive activities, the total output of goods and services can be increased and misery can be alleviated. This sort of problem is encompassed within the meaning of the basic economic problem. Rather than something different, it is a special case of the basic problem with its own peculiarities.

Or take the problem of long-run growth in the standard of living. The total quantity of resources available to society is not static. Human resources change in size and composition with changes in population and education. The stock of factories and machines may grow or decline over long periods of time. These also are problems of ends and means. One of the ends of society is a greater amount of nonhuman resources than it currently possesses. Society has the means at hand to achieve the end, namely, the use of present resources to provide more in the future. In common-sense terms, some labor, machines, and factories are devoted to the production of more machines and factories. In the area of human resources, some skilled labor and physical plants are allocated to the training of more skilled labor. One of the social ends is the provision of more resources; other ends include the provision of goods and services for current consumption. The economic problem is the efficient allocation of the present means among all these ends.

Similar arguments can be advanced for the problems arising from other phenomena mentioned. However, it is certainly true that the special features surrounding these problems deserve careful scrutiny. This is why a student contemplating a catalog of course offerings in economics finds special courses devoted to Money and Banking, International Trade, and Labor Economics. Keeping in mind that these several topics follow the general form of the basic economic problem already outlined, we can list the specific kinds of economic problems that fall within its purview yet have characteristics distinctive enough to warrant special treatment.

(1) The problem of efficient resource allocation among particular industries and firms within the economy and the distribution of goods and services among particular households. This involves the social decisions of what to produce, how to produce it, in what quantities, and for whom. It implies the problem of the distribution of income among the members of society.

(2) The problem of overall stability for the economy as a whole. In contrast to the problems related to individual firms, industries, households, and individual goods and services, this problem refers to the entire economy considered as a unit. It centers around the avoidance of serious depressions and inflations. In a more positive sense it deals with the achievement of a stable level of prosperity and full employment in the short run.

(3) The problem of economic maintenance and long-run progress. The rate of economic growth is the rate of increase in the general living conditions of the community. The problem here is that of efficient provision of the means for sustained increase in the quantity and quality of the standard of living in society. It turns upon the rate of increase in the stock of human and nonhuman resources in the long run.

(4) The problem of international economic relations. The problems of resource, product, and income distribution among nations are identical in nature to Problem 1 above. Mutual overall stability and growth among nations are, of course, related to domestic stability and growth.

Though conceived of as distinct socioeconomic problems, all four are closely interrelated. It is easy to see, for example, that the third problem cuts across the other three.

This book is devoted to *microeconomics*: study of the principles governing the allocation of resources among industries, the production and consumption of particular commodities, and the consequent distribution of income. Microeconomics deals mainly with questions bearing on the first problem and certain aspects of the fourth, though it indirectly touches on questions of stability and growth.

Microeconomics is contrasted with *macroeconomics*, which treats aggregate relationships for the economy as a whole. National income, total employment, total consumption of all goods and services, and the general (average) price level are studied in this area of economics. The second and third problems are of direct importance, but again the first and fourth have some relevance.

Together, microeconomic and macroeconomic theories form the foundations for the analysis of all economic problems. In a sense the material covered in this volume may be called general microeconomic theory. The principles of analysis are presented in their broadest context. They can readily be applied, with suitable modifications, to the investigation of specific problems in labor economics, international trade, public finance, and other areas concerned with resource and/or product allocation.

SUGGESTED READING

F. H. Knight, *The Economic Organization*, pp. 1-30. Chicago: University of Chicago Press, 1933.

A. Marshall, *Principles of Economics*, 8th ed., Book I. London: Macmillan & Co., Ltd., 1925.

T. Scitovsky, *Welfare and Competition*, Chap. 1. Chicago: Richard D. Irwin, Inc., 1951.

2

The What of Economics

The basic economic problem is unavoidable. Recognition of the problem, and the subproblems it entails, is sufficient to appreciate *why* the study of economics is important. It is not sufficient to answer the question of *what* is studied in economics. A specific answer to this question requires a description of the economic institutions of society. Though the fundamental problem is the same for all societies, it is solved in different ways. The methods of solution give birth to a set of economic institutions, and these institutions are closely allied to the political structure of society.

THE ECONOMIC ORGANIZATION

Economic activity cannot be chaotic; it must be organized. The issue is not whether to organize or not, but how to organize. A primitive society might place total responsibility and authority for organization in the hands of a tribal chief, who would then decide who shall tend the sheep; who shall dig turnips and for how long; who shall be a minstrel; how much tobacco, beads, and eggs shall be produced; and who shall receive what amounts of each produced good or service.

Today, however, this form of economic organization persists only in small areas with strong traditions of status. If a modern society does vest authority for economic decisions in a central agency, it is almost certain to take the form of a military dictatorship or some system of socialism. In the former, a totalitarian political setup gives rise to centralized economic institutions that direct and control the allocation of resources. Socialism (the planning, control, and perhaps ownership of the means of production by the state) may be consistent with democracy, depending upon whether the central authority is accountable to the people for its decisions. Nevertheless, ultimate responsibility to the citizens by means of their free voting power does not necessarily demand forfeiture of immediate economic control. The state planning agency

could conceivably determine every detail of product and resource allocation.

The common feature of these kinds of economic organization is the
centralization of economic decision-making. They are contrasted with an
exchange economy, sometimes called a free enterprise or private enterprise economy. The distinguishing property of an exchange economy is
the decentralization of the majority of economic decisions. Instead of
being delegated to a central authority, the whole system of allocation is
worked out and controlled through exchange in an impersonal market.
No one assigns production duties to the labor force, dictates the technical
methods of production, or doles out the proceeds of production. Consumers are free to choose which goods and services they will consume
and in what amounts; individual enterprisers are free to enter into and
exit from the business of their choice; resource owners are free to place
their services in employment wherever it can be found.

This organization, like the others, gives rise to its own peculiar institutions. A politically democratic society does not need to have an
exchange economy. But an exchange economy, because it rests upon
institutions of private property, competition, and free exchange, cannot
prevail in a totalitarian political system. This is not to say that the state
in an exchange economy owns no property or makes no economic decisions. No such society ever existed! The government owns some property and makes some decisions, but it operates through the marketplace
subject to the same rules as any other economic unit—except for certain
delegated powers such as taxation, currency control, and police protection. Neither does an exchange economy imply the absence of planning.
Economic planning is decentralized, i.e., performed by many individual
private units and executed by competitive exchange.

A Simplified Model of an Exchange Economy

As a first approximation let us separate the institutions of the economy into households and business firms. Everyone is a member of a
household, and every member of a household who performs some productive service does so in a firm. Now, members of households may be looked
at in terms of the economic *functions* they perform. Notice that household members are classified by functions, not by personalities or individuals; a given individual may perform more than one function. First,
every person is a consumer. Second, most people engage in producing
some goods or services. Hence, members of society perform the functions
of consumption and production.

No modern economies, and few primitive ones, rely on barter to carry
out exchange. Because of specialization in production, money serves a
dual purpose: (1) a medium of exchange and (2) a standard or measure
of value. Consumers pay for goods and services with money and receive

money in exchange for the productive activities they carry on. Figure 2.1 depicts these real and monetary flows.

Let us first examine the real flows. Members of households are owners of resources in the form of labor, land, machines, and so on. The services of these resources flow into the firms to be used up in the production process. The final results of production flow out of the firms and into the households where they are consumed.

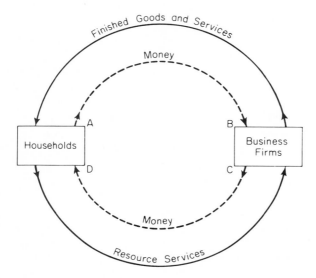

FIG. 2.1. The Circular Flow of Income and Expenditure

In a monetary economy these real flows are facilitated by the use of money exchanges. Households pay firms for the goods and services they receive, and they receive money for the resource services they sell to firms. Money circulates continuously from households to firms and back to households. At point A in Fig. 2.1 this money expenditure is regarded by the household as its cost of living. The same money flow at point B is regarded by firms as total receipts from sales. Firms use their sales receipts for the purchase of resource services to continue production. Thus, at point C the money flow is viewed by the firm as the cost of production. Finally, the cost of production is the money income of the households when received by them at point D.

A Somewhat Less Simplified Model

We can expand our bird's-eye view of the economy by introducing two additional institutions. We have the following five: (1) consumers, (2) firms, (3) factors of production, (4) markets, and (5) government. Notice that the classifications are still made according to economic functions rather than to individuals. Consumers have already been discussed. *Factors of production* is just another name for resource services; it is introduced here because both terms are used interchangeably in economics. At this point we have separated the two *functions* performed by household members, namely, consumption and production. The revised economic scheme is shown in Fig. 2.2, which is not very different from Fig. 2.1

The unbroken arrows denote real flows and the broken arrows denote

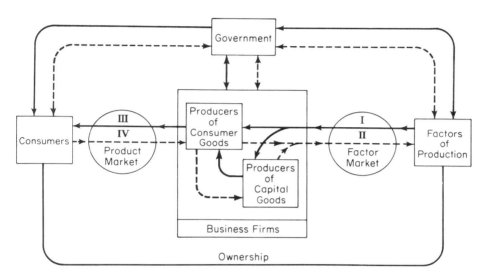

FIG. 2.2. The Circular Flow of Income by Functions

money flows. The unbroken horizontal arrow I, running from factors of production to business firms, represents the flow of factors or resource services. The money-income flow, broken arrow II, is payments by firms to factors of production: wages, salaries, interest, rent, dividends. The exchange of factors of production for money takes place in the factor market. Arrow III signifies the flow of final goods and services from firms to consumers, and arrow IV is the money given in exchange for these. This exchange occurs in the product market. The connecting link on the bottom of the diagram indicates that consumers are also the owners of factors of production.

Leaving aside firms and markets for the moment, the role of government remains to be explained. For the sake of simplicity, let us ignore the fact that the government may own some factors of production. The striking distinction of the role of government is the dual direction of some flows. Consider first the real flows from government to the rest of the economy. The government does dispense certain goods and services to citizens. These goods and services take the form of legislation and enforcement of pure food and drug acts, police protection, military defense, social welfare programs, and so forth. All three of the other sectors benefit. Real flows move also in the opposite direction. To carry out its functions the government uses human and nonhuman resources, which it obtains from firms and factors of production. Of course, the government purchases these in the factor market or the product market, but we shall overlook this to keep the diagram as simple as possible. Finally, there are the money flows to and from the government. Money flows from the government are (1) payments for products it buys or resources it hires and (2) transfer payments such as social security pensions or relief checks. Money flows to the government are mostly taxes, and these are collected from all three of the other sectors.

Business Firms. Like everything else, business firms have many facets and can be viewed from various angles. From the viewpoint of their legal organization, firms can be classified into three main types: the individual proprietorship, the partnership, and the corporation. An individual proprietorship is a business enterprise owned and operated by one person. He assumes full responsibility for directing the affairs of the firm and absorbs all profits or losses. He executes all contracts and makes all decisions on purchases, sales, and production techniques. As the owner, he is also personally liable for the debts of the firm. Many small businesses like dental offices, barbershops, gas stations, and farms are individual proprietorships.

Co-ownership is the predominant feature of a partnership. There may be two or more partners; each owns all the assets and each has unlimited personal liability for all the debts of the firm. Mutual agency provides that any one of the partners may legally represent the firm and all are bound by the conditions of such contracts. Profits and losses are shared according to some agreed-upon provision. Several firms supplying professional services are of this type: legal firms, brokerage houses, night clubs.

The most highly developed form of legal organization is the corporation. The corporation is a "legal person" that exists independently of the owners; it can own, sell, purchase, borrow, and lend in its own name, and it is taxed like any other person. The owners of the corporation are the shareholders—those who have title to certificates of ownership called shares of stock. Each owner has limited liability: he stands to lose only the amount of money he paid for his stock. In large corporations there is usually separation of ownership and management. Stockholders elect a board of directors that is responsible for corporation policy and the success or failure of the firm. The board of directors in turn appoints executives to manage the firm's affairs. Practically all large firms in the United States are corporations, for example, the United States Steel Corporation, the Columbia Broadcasting System, and the Metropolitan Opera Association.

Another angle from which firms can be viewed is their place in the marketing process. Marketing is the movement of goods and services from the place of manufacture to the place of consumption. In this connection, firms are distinguished according to manufacturing, wholesaling, and retailing. One of the factors bearing upon the problems of marketing is the nature of the good or service being marketed. Some, such as marital counseling, go through no marketing operations; others, for instance agricultural products, require many operations—storing, packaging, and transportation—to complete the marketing process.

The legal and marketing characteristics of a given firm offer two ways to look at it. An important economic characteristic is the distinction between production for consumers and production for other firms. In the former case the firm is called a producer of consumer goods or services; in the latter it is called a producer of capital goods. Since capital goods are those used in further production, producers of capital goods sell to other firms rather than to final consumers.

Figure 2.2 helps to bring out the relations that emerge from the distinction between capital and consumer goods. Factors of production flow into both kinds of firms. Likewise, money income moves from each type of firm to the owners of the factors. The flow of final goods and services proceeds from producers of consumer goods and services only, and all monetary receipts from sales to households come to them. A real flow of capital goods runs between firms, and corresponding money payments flow in the opposite direction.

So far the notion of a firm has been more or less intuitive. For economic analysis we shall find that a more rigorous definition is needed. In economics a firm is defined as an abstract entity, consisting of an entrepreneur and all the factors of production he purchases, engaged in the production of any good or service. Let us consider the components of the definition in more detail.

First, the firm is an *abstract* entity. The firm is not the owners of the assets; neither is it the physical plant and equipment nor the laborers who work for the firm. It is the intangible organization itself. Many difficulties students encounter in economic analysis can be traced to a confusion about the meaning of the word *firm*. Some tend to identify it with the tangible persons or things mentioned above, especially the physical plant. A little reflection, however, shows that the plant and the firm are not one and the same. General Motors, for example, has many plants throughout the country; some do research, some make automobiles, some do paper work. Common sense leads us to reject the idea that one of these plants, or even a combination of them, is General Motors. The earlier discussion of the corporation should also help to avoid confusion, for the corporation was seen to be something other than the plant or the owners. Moreover, the concept of the firm is not so strange when one reflects on the meaning of the household. This also is really an abstract entity. The household is not simply the house or the family or the furnishings. It is a combination of all these: an intangible organization as opposed to the concrete objects that contribute to its composition.

Second, the firm is comprised of an *entrepreneur* (enterpriser is the closest English translation) and the factors of production he purchases. The entrepreneur is defined according to function, not personality. He purchases factors of production, and as income he receives the difference between total sales receipts and total payments to factor owners. If any money is left over after he pays the factor owners, he receives it as profit. If not, if contractual payments for factors exceed sales receipts, he absorbs the loss.

Although the entrepreneur has been called *he* for convenience's sake, we must bear in mind that the entrepreneur need not be only one person. The function of entrepreneurship is performed by several persons at once if the firm has more than one residual income recipient. Similarly, a person may be partly a factor owner with contractual income and partly an entrepreneur with residual income.

In economics the legal organization of a firm is generally ignored. All firms, be they individual proprietorships, partnerships, or corporations, satisfy the economic definition. The number of persons who are partly or wholly entrepreneurs will differ according to the legal type, but this is not our main concern—nor does it alter the definition. Similarly, no distinction is made on a marketing basis. All firms are regarded as production firms regardless of whether they are manufacturers, wholesalers, retailers, or what not. In economics, marketing is treated as one stage in production, which includes every step from the extraction of raw materials to delivery to the consumer's door. All marketing functions can therefore be listed under the general heading *production*.

Markets.   A market is an area within which buyers and sellers come into contact and fix a common price. The market may be but a few miles in circumference or it may be worldwide. Its size depends on the prevalence of a single price for the commodity traded. When a farmer's daughter sets up a roadside stand far from town to sell fresh vegetables, she is selling in a very small market. Contact between buyer and seller is limited to firsthand physical exchange on the roadside, and prices are established on the spot. When a broker in New York City purchases bales of cotton on the New Orleans Cotton Exchange by long-distance telephone, he is buying in a very large market. He pays the same price (operates in the same market) as buyers located in New Orleans or Timbuktu. Here again there are buyers and sellers establishing an agreed-upon price at which cotton will exchange ownership.

The size or extent of the market is determined primarily by the cost of transportation and the existing state of communication. The extremely high cost of transporting concrete, for example, limits each market to a local area. At the other extreme the market for wheat is worldwide. Its money value per unit is so large relative to its weight and size that the transport cost is a very small percentage of its value. Thus wheat can be shipped long distances without appreciable addition to its price. Communication affects the distribution of information about the quality, quantity, and price of a commodity. Compare the case of the farmer's daughter with that of the New York broker. In the former, communication with potential customers is restricted. A person two miles away may be paying a much higher price for the same commodity (may be in a different market) because he is unaware of the existence of the roadside market. In the broker's market communication is organized, cheap, and rapid. As a result, buyers and sellers in all parts of the world are aware of the quality and price quotations in New Orleans. So traders on two different continents can enter into a contract to buy and sell New Orleans cotton at an agreed-upon price.

Given the state of communication and assuming no artificial barriers to spatial movement of a commodity, its quoted price will differ in different localities within the market by the transport cost per unit. That is, in a defined market the price is the same to all buyers at the point of production. In various geographical parts of the market, the cost of transportation per unit from the point of production to the point of utilization will be added to the price. This does not alter the actual price, for purchasers buy the product itself *and* the transportation service.

THE PRICE SYSTEM

The diagrammatic models of Figs. 2.1 and 2.2 describing the institutions in an exchange economy are simplified. They are abstracts of many details that tend to obscure the overall picture of economic activity. With minor exceptions this activity in the final analysis boils down to the flows depicted in Fig. 2.1. One should keep in mind, however, the vast complexity that lies beneath this simplified blueprint of the real world.

However complex the real world may be, the economic roles played by various institutions do not alter; neither does the fundamental economic problem change. The somewhat astonishing fact is that, in spite of complexity, the economic problems of society are solved with a tolerable degree of efficiency.

In an exchange economy prices are established by competitive exchange. *These prices perform the social function of product and resource allocation.* And they do so without the conscious personal intent of any one firm or household, any group of firms or households, or any central social agency. Within the limits set by law and custom, consumers spend their income on the things they want. Naturally, they will offer higher prices for the goods and services they desire greatly and lower prices for those they desire less. Owners of resources services are free to sell their services to the firm of their choice. They are inclined to sell where the price offered is most attractive, given certain other considerations. Entrepreneurs devote their efforts to producing things that bring the highest return. The consequent interaction of households and firms determines market prices. Considered from the viewpoint of the basic economic problem, prices serve two major purposes in an exchange economy: (1) they transmit information and (2) they provide incentives for economic units to be guided by this information.

Our everyday experience suggests the way in which prices convey information. When a price is quoted for French perfume in a department store, a lady has knowledge of the relative value of this perfume, that is, its value relative to other perfumes and all other commodities. This information facilitates her purchasing decisions, for in the absence of some such information no comparisons can be made. On the production side, the market price of a commodity informs a firm of the gross revenue to be expected from sales and permits the firm to compare returns with costs of production. It also allows the firm to contrast the price of its product with the prices of related products, such as those that compete with the product of the firm in question, or that are complementary to it.

In the factor market the prices of factors of production impart information to firms as users of factors and to households as owners of factors. Quoted market prices inform firms and households of the cost and income possibilities respectively existing in the market. By so doing they communicate information that is utilized by both institutions in arriving at decisions about where to sell or buy, how much to sell or buy, and so on.

A change in a price is new information transmitted to firms and households. At the new price, new decisions may be executed. A higher wage rate offered by firms for a particular kind of labor in a given market is a signal to workers that the firms put a higher value on this labor and want more of it. If consumers increase their preference for musical comedies, they will be willing to pay more for them. The higher price offered is a way of informing producers of musical comedy about the increased preference.

Prices do more than broadcast information, however. They also provide incentives to firms and households. Suppose firms in California want to hire more labor than is currently available. They can attract more labor into the area by offering higher wages. The higher wage rate is not only a signal to workers that a higher valuation is put upon labor; it is also an incentive to movement because of the prospect for greater income. An increased preference for medical services on the part of consumers is conveyed to medical firms (physicians) by a higher price offer. A higher price makes the profession more attractive and stimulates more entry into the profession. Hence, more medical services are forthcoming to satisfy the increased wants of consumers.

The price mechanism imparts information and provides the incentives to reallocate resources according to the wants of consumers. And this is done by competitive exchange without the conscious design of any central directing agency. It must be emphasized that the difference is not one of planning versus nonplanning. Planning is unavoidable under any form of economic organization. Different types of economic organizations are distinguished by *who does the planning*. In an exchange economy, planning is decentralized. Market prices communicate information that enables the individual to fit his decisions into the pattern of change going on in the larger economic system. In communicating information and providing incentives, prices act, more or less effectively, to coordinate the separate actions of different firms and households.

SUGGESTED READING

F. H. Knight, *The Economic Organization*, pp. 31-68. Chicago: University of Chicago Press, 1933.

F. A. Hayek, "The Use of Knowledge in Society," *American Economic Review* (September 1945).

E. T. Weiler and W. H. Martin, *The American Economic System*, Chaps. 1-4. New York: The Macmillan Company, 1957.

J. Schumpeter, "The Nature and Necessity of a Price System," in R. V. Clemens, ed., *Readings in Economic Analysis*, Vol. II. Cambridge: Addison-Wesley Press, 1950.

3

The How of Economics

This chapter is devoted to a brief survey of the scope and method of economics. These are important preliminary subjects if the more substantive chapters that follow are to be understood. A little extra time spent on the scope and methods of economics now will save time and avoid confusion later.

THE SCOPE OF ECONOMICS

The scope of economics, the subject matter it embraces, has two aspects. First is the question of how economics fits into the general scheme of knowledge, how it is related to other disciplines. Second is the question of how to distinguish the different kinds of economics.

Economics is a social science, so economists are interested in explaining group behavior. In particular, group behavior in the market is studied. When doing so, economists make explanatory statements about the behavior of individual units in society—individual laborers, business firms, or consumers. But this is done to establish logical connections between individual behavior and patterns of group behavior. For the effects on price and allocation determined by group action are in turn the net result of a multitude of individual actions. Economic behavior is based on decisions, and only individuals make decisions. Therefore, one must at some point refer to individual decision processes in order to explain their social consequences.

Any social event has various causes and effects, and economics centers on certain facets of the event. To illustrate, suppose there is large-scale migration from farms to cities. The social consequences of the movement are many, and they can be separated by the following fields of interest.

Field of Interest	*Phenomena to Be Explained*
(1) Economics	Effects on wage rates, product prices, income distribution, etc.
(2) Political Science	Effects on voting behavior, pressure-group activity, etc.
(3) Sociology	Effects on juvenile delinquency, family structure, etc.
(4) Military Science	Effects on readiness for defense, etc.

Any social change has, among others, certain effects that economics isolates for purposes of analysis and that define the boundaries of economics. Other effects produced by the same change bear upon the economic effects but lie outside the confines of economics proper.

Several decades ago John Neville Keynes distinguished between two kinds of economics: positive economics and normative economics. Positive economics is that branch of economics concerned with questions of "what is." Normative economics, on the other hand, is concerned with questions of "what ought to be."

Positive economics is a science. It consists of systematic knowledge of the determinants of prices, production, employment, income distribution, saving, and other magnitudes established by market forces. It seeks to explain the causes of changes in prices and other economic magnitudes, and the effects these changes have upon resource allocation. Notice that economics as a positive science does not say anything about the desirability or undesirability of existing prices, wage rates, unemployment, industrial structures, or any other economic variable. Nor is judgment passed on the human motives behind social change; one attempts merely to explain the consequences of these motives. In this sense, positive economics is like the natural sciences.

Economics is, however, more than a specialized branch of scientific learning. It is a source of continuous public controversy on issues of economic policy. Normative economics, therefore, consists of knowledge regarding the criteria of what ought to be: the norms or goals of economic behavior. Whereas positive economics takes as given data the legal system, customs, industrial organization, and the ethical value structure of society, normative economics may not. It enters into the question of what is best for society. As a consequence, this branch of economics necessarily shades into other disciplines such as political science and philosophy.

Many ambiguities can arise from the failure to distinguish economics as a positive scientific inquiry from economics as a set of public policy recommendations. The first can exist independently of the second. It is possible for one to examine the causes of social events while withholding judgment on their desirability. It is doubtful, however, that intelligent discussion of normative policy issues can be carried on without some knowledge of the causes operating, how they operate, and what effects they produce.

THE METHODS OF ECONOMICS

Positive economics applies general scientific method to economic problems. We shall therefore look briefly into the nature of scientific method.

Scientific Method

Science is knowledge that is both general and systematic. Rather than attempting to understand events in particular isolated instances, scientists relate various events one to another in a general scheme of knowledge. This scheme has an order and consistency that distinguishes it from casual speculation. The methods of science differ from one discipline to another. They even differ from one research worker to another within any given discipline, and from one problem to another in the hands of a single research worker.

Nevertheless, all these methods do have a common pattern. There are essentially five steps in any scientific investigation:

(1) Definition of the problem.
(2) Assembly of existing facts bearing upon the problem.
(3) Formulation of a general hypothesis or hypotheses to explain the facts.
(4) Deduction of specific predictions from the general hypothesis.
(5) Testing the validity and accuracy of the predictions by reference to the facts.

The choice of a problem to be studied is largely a matter of personal preference and good judgment. No general rules can be laid down—except perhaps that the problem should not be trivial. Because of some specialized scientific interest one person may decide to study a problem that has little direct practical applicability, while another selects a problem because of its pressing impact on the community. The problem under investigation may be very broad or very narrow in scope.

Once the problem is chosen and defined, the next step is to collect existing information. Previous studies often contain useful insights, and usually a set of empirical data must be collected. Biochemists may observe the growth of diseased cells in a culture. In economics the initial facts are often a statistical series of prices, outputs, incomes, migration flows, or other economic magnitudes. Regardless of the field of interest, these observations will show a certain behavior (change); the crux of the problem is to explain that behavior.

The mere collection and observation of facts will never explain their behavior. To provide the explanation of why blood cells deteriorate under given conditions or why the general price level rises when the total supply of money in the economy increases, the human mind must be brought into play. Consequently, the third step is to construct a tentative explanation of the observed phenomena, to discover what *general relations* exist among a multitude of events. The explanation is suggested by something in the subject matter or by previous knowledge and experience.

The explanation may begin by being vague or intuitive. Perhaps it is not more than a "feel" for the causes and effects operating. But if it is to be fruitful for widespread applications, the explanation must be codified into formal propositions. When this is done, the general explanation is called a hypothesis. The hypothesis is both general and systematic; it refers to a whole set or class of occurrences, not just to particular instances.

In formulating a hypothesis, assumptions must be made, and these assumptions serve the purpose of simplification. In an observed situation all the events that occur may be interrelated: each one affects all the others more or less; not all will exert an equal influence, however. To make the problem manageable it may be assumed that certain of the other events exert no influence on the event in question, or that they are random rather than systematic causes. Hence, the main problem in formulating a hypothesis is to make assumptions that reveal the important causal factors. These assumptions are by their very nature abstract and simplified. As such they permit the scientist to achieve generality.

The hypothesis, once formulated, is general. It applies to all cases of a given kind. Predictions are more specific, and are derived by deductive logic from the hypothesis. One might say they are the hypothesis when applied to particular cases. For example, the behavior of the solar system is explained by the general hypothesis of gravitational forces. A prediction derived from the hypothesis might be that Venus will be in such and such a location at such and such a time.

Prediction does not necessarily refer to future events; but it does necessarily refer to unobserved events, that is, events unknown previous to or at the time of prediction. The event predicted could have occurred in the past but be unobserved (not previously known) at the present time. For instance, one might offer as a hypothesis to explain business booms and depressions the argument that changes in the total money supply cause changes in national income and employment. This hypothesis would predict that the money supply decreased in the United States at the time when income and employment fell from 1929 to 1933. The prediction refers to a past event not previously known. Or again, the homeopathic hypothesis in medical research holds that diseases are cured by injecting into the patient small doses of cells infected with the same disease. A prediction of this hypothesis is that polio cases can be prevented by isolating the polio virus and injecting it into potential victims. Hence, predictions can refer to past, present, or future events so long as they are not known previous to or at the time of prediction. The special kind of prediction that refers to the future is sometimes called forecasting.

How do we know that the hypothesis offered to explain the behavior of facts is correct? The way to find out is to test the hypothesis against a new set of facts. Does it explain events in addition to those assembled to formulate the hypothesis? If so, we accept it; if not, we reject it. This means one has to go back to facts in order to judge the validity of a hypothesis.

More exactly, it is the predictions that are tested. Hypotheses are general, while facts are particular. We cannot physically observe generalities or universals; our sensory perceptions are geared to individual events. Since the predictions yielded by a hypothesis are specific statements about concrete cases, these can be compared with our observations. We can observe the actual position of the planet Venus but not gravitational forces. We can observe particular patients who have been injected with the Salk vaccine, but we cannot observe all cures to all diseases simultaneously. We can observe the records of the 1929-33 depression, but we cannot observe all past and future depressions.

If the hypothesis at hand repeatedly yields correct predictions (if the predictions are not contradicted by the facts), it is accepted—at least until a better one comes along. If the hypothesis yields incorrect predictions, it is rejected. In this case we must seek another explanation. The history of science is the story of true and false hypotheses. When one hypothesis is shown to be false, the search goes on until new ones are discovered, tested, and accepted.

When we accept a hypothesis we say it is verified. We do not say it is proved to be true. We have merely failed to disprove it; some future evidence may show it to be false. A careful scientist always maintains a mental reservation or healthy skepticism in the back of his mind, and he preserves an open mind toward newly discovered evidence.

This brief description of scientific method is not meant to imply that one always follows a neat five-step pattern in scientific investigations. There is continuous interaction among the five steps. Revisions and new applications are constantly being made. Fresh evidence may lead a scientist to revise his hypothesis, and original hypotheses may suggest new ways to look at and organize empirical evidence.

Steps 3 and 4 in the pattern of research are called *theory*. Scientific theory, therefore, is a set of abstract propositions designed to interpret and explain observable phenomena. It follows that economic theory is such a set of propositions used to interpret and explain economic behavior, including the formulation of hypotheses and the deduction of predictions from hypotheses. To illustrate, consider a typical economic hypothesis. Almost everyone is familiar with the statement "Prices are determined by supply and demand." The proposition does not state that only the price of cheese or only the price of iron ore is determined by supply and demand. The proposition is independent of the peculiarities of particular products and factors of production. A prediction yielded by the hypothesis will refer to the price of a particular product during some period of time in a given place. What is predicted is the price of this or that commodity, not all commodity prices simultaneously. The prediction, however, remains a theoretical statement.

General economic theory can be regarded as a set of tools—tools of analysis that are applicable to a wide variety of situations. In this text we shall be interested in economic theory at its broadest, and therefore its most abstract, level. These very broad hypotheses are sometimes called the *principles* of economic theory. Knowledge of principles is necessary but not sufficient for the analysis of concrete problems. Learning the principles of fly casting is essential to good game fishing. But it is not enough. A clever game fisherman will manipulate the principles and adjust to the circumstances of current, wind, and the habits of fish. Likewise, how successfully the principles of economics are applied to various kinds of economic problems depends largely on the ingenuity of the user.

General economic theory can be divided into *static theory* and *dynamic theory*. Static theory is timeless and assumes instantaneous adjustments to change in the economy. Its objective is to determine the direction in which economic variables will move in response to changes in other variables. But static theory does not attempt to establish how long adjustments will take. The economic theory presented in the chapters that follow is static. Dynamic theory, on the other hand, is specifically concerned with the time required for adjustments to change. Though it utilizes and builds upon the concepts of static theory, dynamic theory goes further to trace the time paths of economic variables and to investigate the conditions under which an economic system will show stability or instability over time.

Statistics

People tend to think of economics as synonymous with economic theory. We have seen, however, that theory comprises only two steps in a total scientific investigation. Theoretical reasoning is extremely important, but theory must eventually be tested to determine its empirical validity. In the theoretical realm one asks if the deductive logic is correct. Granted that the theory is logically correct, the next question is whether it is compatible with observed events or is refuted by them.

One of the classic research techniques used in the natural sciences is the laboratory experiment. Theories are tested and quantitative relations among events are measured by setting up a controlled environment. By experiment one can create a situation in which the events assumed to be irrelevant can be removed or held constant. Then the effects of those assumed relevant can be studied in isolation.

Imagine trying to do this in the social sciences! Experimentation is sometimes possible; usually, however, large social groups cannot be put into a laboratory and subjected to alternating stimuli in order to measure their reactions. Nevertheless, the situation is not hopeless. We can observe social groups at different times and under varying circumstances and record their reactions, even if we do not control the environment. Economists use these recorded reactions (changes in output, consumption, employment, capital investment) to compare them with what the theory predicts.

Statistical analysis is a powerful research method now widely used in economics. Since the concepts of economics are mostly quantitative, statistics is especially appropriate for testing economic theories and for measuring the relations among economic magnitudes. In its modern form, statistical inference is a newcomer to the field. In the past thirty years existing procedures have been improved, new ones forged, and explorations carried into uncharted areas.

In his empirical investigations the economist collects a sample of observations on the economic variables being studied. The sample most often consists of a set of data published by the government or some private agency. When the data wanted are not available from these sources, the economist may have to compile them himself from interviews or questionnaires answered by firms or households. Regardless of the source, the data will include empirical observations on the economic magnitude being predicted and on the economic magnitudes used to do the predicting. The statistical problem is to infer from the behavior of the sample data the probable truth or falsity of the economic hypothesis. Because the sample consists of a limited number of observations and because the hypothesis is general, the inference of the truth or falsity of the hypothesis is not certain; it is only probable. Decision rules, based upon probability theory, have been developed by statisticians. Under specified conditions these rules permit an inference from the observed sample data to the theoretical predictions, an inference regarding the probable truth or falsity of the predictions. The more closely the predictions of a hypothesis correspond with the sample observations in repeated tests, the more probable is the hypothesis.

SOME COMMON FALLACIES

In arriving at an explanation of product and resource allocation, economic theory adopts a logical structure of reasoning. Failure to understand the explanation can often be traced to a misunderstanding of the logical methods employed in economic analysis. Proper interpretation of method is no less important than knowledge of the substance of economics. Consequently, it is well worth noting some of the more common logical errors found in discussions of economic problems.

The Post Hoc Ergo Propter Hoc Fallacy

The literal translation of the Latin phrase is "after this, therefore because of this." Suppose it is observed that event x is followed by event y. Maybe x caused y, but maybe x had nothing whatever to do with y. Because one event precedes another does not *necessarily* mean that the first caused the second.

Let us assume there is a change in the income tax structure so it becomes more progressive (the percentage of income taxed is raised for higher incomes relative to lower incomes). Now suppose this is followed by a reduction in the number of hours per year worked by people with relatively high incomes. Can we immediately infer that the first event is the cause of the second so that the higher tax weakened personal incentive? Of course, the answer is no. Most social events have not one but a multitude of proximate causes. It is only by careful theoretical reasoning that we can hope to account for the various influences operating and to relate one to another.

The Fallacy of Misplaced Realism

Everyone agrees that a theory should be realistic. But not everyone agrees on what is meant by realism. We need not go into the philosophical issues of this difficult concept. It is sufficient to point out a common misinterpretation of method, namely, the unqualified assertion that a theory is wrong because its assumptions are not realistic. No doubt there is some truth to the argument that basic assumptions should have some correspondence to reality. But the point can be pushed too far. We have seen that all assumptions made by anyone about anything are more or less abstract and simplified. They never are *complete* descriptions of actual situations. As such, they are bound to be unrealistic if this is taken to mean that not all facets of complex events, indirectly and incompletely observed, are included in the assumption.

The realism of a theory is judged primarily by the realism of its predictions—not by the realism of its assumptions. If predictions explain or correspond to facts, they may be regarded as realistic; if they fail to explain facts, if they are refuted by facts, the predictions are unrealistic and the theory should be discarded. Whereas predictions are judged in terms of their correspondence to observable empirical phenomena, assumptions are usually judged by their fruitfulness in yielding widespread implications or predictions.

The significance of the fallacy will become apparent when we come to treat the key assumptions of economic theory. In brief, the basic assumption is that both firms and households maximize some economic magnitude: consumers maximize total utility and firms maximize total profit. This assumption is equivalent to the assumption that an entrepreneur, for instance, is not influenced by his cat's pregnancy, his wife's penchant for psychosomatic headaches, his subconscious drives for power or security, and so forth, *in arriving at his economic decisions*. At least these factors do not cause the facts to behave in a way that contradicts the predictions derived from the maximization assumption.

The abstract "unrealistic" assumptions of economic theory are similar to those employed in the natural sciences. For example, the mathematical assumptions underlying the quantum theory in physics are not statements that can be verified by observation. They are accepted because the deductions made from them (the predictions) describe the motion of heavenly bodies, the properties of crystals, the characteristics of light emitted by different substances, and the materialization of energy. These are the things the theory seeks to explain, not its abstract mathematical assumptions.

The Ceteris Paribus Fallacy

Here is another Latin term meaning "other things being equal" or "other things being held constant." Economists as well as physical scientists have to deal with complicated events. We saw earlier that laboratory experiments can in practice separate the elements of an event, hold some elements constant, and view the others in isolation. This is not so in economics. For the sake of clear step-by-step reasoning, however, it is convenient to handle the elements one or two at a time while *conceptually* holding the others constant.

An economist will analyze the relation of cost to the total output of a firm, assuming all resource prices and technological conditions are unchanged. Or he may examine theoretically the quantities of a commodity that consumers purchase at various prices while mentally holding constant other determinants of consumer purchases, such as consumer income.

There is danger that such theoretical propositions may be interpreted to mean all other things are *in fact* constant. Suppose events A, B, C, and D are all interrelated. The theorist merely assumes C and D are constant so he can establish the relation between variations in A and B. Then he can conceptually hold B and C constant while he looks at the mutual dependence between A and D, and so on. In the end he can put the four events together and let all of them vary. Had he attempted this at the outset, the probable result would have been confusion, whereas he can now do so with an orderly idea of their separate influences on each other.

But-the-Cat-Doesn't-Speak-French Fallacy

A theory, like anything else, should be judged by what it is designed to do. Since theories are used to interpret and predict certain events, they ought rightly to be evaluated by their ability to interpret and predict *those* events—not some other events. Suppose an economic theory is offered to explain the effects of devaluation of the pound sterling on American exports. It is hardly constructive criticism to argue that this theory does not explain the effects of unionization on employment in the American cement industry. Consider a less obvious example. A general theory purports to explain what determines market prices. To cite instances in which the theory fails to describe accurately the mental processes of businessmen is irrelevant. It is not intended to do this. Rather, it is intended to organize and relate the aggregate social forces that determine prices, and thereby to predict prices.

A pseudo-problem that often arises is that of theory versus practice. Who has not heard the accusation "It works in theory but not in practice"? This is a nonsense statement. What works in theory by definition works in practice. It is hard to see what *practice* means if not concrete factual or practical situations. Certainly, there are poor theories. These do not work; they cannot successfully be applied; they do not do what they intend, namely, to explain the behavior of certain phenomena. But a good theory will work in practice, for this is one of the things that makes it a good theory, i.e., it will explain what it is designed to explain. The existence of poor theories is no justification for a bias against all theory as somehow defective. For that matter, as we saw earlier, every "practical" explanation does explicitly or implicitly contain theory.

Conclusion

The description of common fallacies is not meant to stifle all disagreements. Progress in the acquisition of knowledge has often had its source in some challenge to an accepted body of hypotheses. First, questions of fact may be disputed. Empirical evidence is often elusive and incomplete. Discoveries of new data or new ways to view old data can lead us to suspect the validity of some previously accepted theories. Second, purely theoretical disagreements are not out of the question. Often, very subtle deductive reasoning from the assumptions is required to derive conclusions, and undetected errors are not unheard of. Sometimes new assumptions will prove to be simpler (less restrictive) than the old ones.

In the realm of theory an explanation should be complete and internally consistent. In the realm of observable phenomena it should be able to predict the events it is intended to predict. Innovations in both realms are possible and, if they are improvements, desirable. As one famous economist has put it:

> The object of our analysis is, not to provide a machine, or method of blind manipulation, which will furnish an infallible answer, but to provide ourselves with an organized and orderly method of thinking out particular problems; and after we have reached a provisional conclusion by isolating the complicating factors one by one, we then have to go back on ourselves and allow, as well as we can, for the probable interactions of the factors amongst themselves. This is the nature of economic thinking.[1]

SUGGESTED READING

M. R. Cohen and E. Nagel, *An Introduction to Logic and Scientific Method*, Chaps. X and XI. New York: Harcourt, Brace & Co., 1934.

J. M. Keynes, *The Scope and Method of Political Economy*, 4th ed., Chaps. I and II. London: Macmillan & Co., Ltd., 1930.

L. Robbins, *The Nature and Significance of Economic Science*, 2nd ed., Chaps. IV and V. New York: The Macmillan Company, 1952.

O. Lange, "The Scope and Method of Economics," *Review of Economic Studies*, XIII (1945-46), 19-32.

M. Friedman, "The Methodology of Positive Economics," Part I of *Essays in Positive Economics*. Chicago: The University of Chicago Press, 1953.

[1] John M. Keynes, *The General Theory of Employment, Interest and Money* (New York: Harcourt, Brace & Co., 1935), p. 297. Quoted by permission of Harcourt, Brace & World, Inc.

The Determination of Prices:
a preview

In a sense, everything said in the following chapters on micro theory is an elaboration and an extension of the ideas contained in this chapter. Since in an exchange economy resources and products are allocated by the price mechanism, we are naturally interested in what determines prices, both product and resource prices.

One of the main tasks of economic theory is to discover why products and factors of production have prices, why some are expensive and others cheap. For the sake of brevity and simplicity, in the following analysis only product prices will be discussed. But the methods of analysis apply equally to resource prices, as we shall see later in the book. Also, competitive conditions, i.e., the absence of any monopoly or government control over prices, will be assumed to exist in the market.

Prices are determined by supply and demand. Supply summarizes the conditions of scarcity, and demand reflects the conditions of wants. Alfred Marshall, the great English economist, has compared supply and demand to the two blades of scissors. Just as neither blade alone cuts the cloth, so neither supply by itself nor demand by itself can determine price. If a good is scarce but no one wants it, it will have no price and will not be traded on the market. On the other hand, if a good is wanted but is superabundant (such as air to breathe at sea level), it will have a zero price and will not be exchanged. Goods that are wanted because they are useful but that are not scarce are known as "free goods." For a good or service to have a nonzero price, it must be scarce relative to the amount wanted.

MARKET DEMAND

The first point to be emphasized is *effective* demand. Not only must there be a want for a commodity, but this want must be backed up with purchasing power. Hence, by demand we mean the *willingness* and the *ability* to buy. Suppose a genuine Philippine fighting cock sells for $50.

I might want a hundred of them right here and now, but my want counts for nothing in the market unless it is supported by sufficient wherewithal to purchase. My effective demand presupposes some given amount of income and wealth.

Second, effective demand is not just a single quantity. Rather, it is a whole set of possible quantities. This is brought out clearly by the example of the fighting cocks. Assume I have an income of $150 a week and I have no assets I can readily convert into purchasing power. My taste for fighting cocks is such that I want all I can get. But "all I can get" is limited by my budget. If I can get along on $50 a week (for food, shelter, etc.) and if cocks sell for $50, my effective demand is *two*. However, if they sell for $100 my effective demand is *one*, while it is *four* if the price is $25 as long as my income remains unchanged. The essential point to remember is that one cannot say my demand is one, two, three, or four; it all depends upon the price of cocks, my income, and my wealth.

Third, we cannot speak sensibly about demand unless some time unit is specified. Suppose it were said, "At the prevailing market price there are ten million gallons of gasoline demanded by American consumers." Could one tell from this what the demand situation is for gasoline? The statement could mean at the existing price ten million gallons are purchased every minute or every hour or every year. It makes a whale of a difference whether people demand ten million gallons per day or per year. In other words, the quantity demanded cannot be specified without stating it as so much per unit of time—so much per week, per month, or whatever the time period happens to be. This characteristic points up the fact that quantity demanded (like output or income) is a rate of *flow*. The unit of time in which the quantity is measured is largely a matter of convenience; conversion from one time unit to any other is simple. If 70 tons of steel are demanded per week, then it necessarily follows that steel is being demanded at a rate of ten tons per day or about 0.42 tons per hour.

The Demand Schedule

These three properties can be combined to define a demand schedule. *A demand schedule is a relation showing the quantities that would be taken per unit of time on the market at various possible prices.* Consumers' incomes and certain other circumstances besides price that affect the quantity demanded are assumed to remain constant for the purpose of defining a given state of demand.

To construct the demand schedule for some hypothetical commodity, and to gain generality, symbols are very useful. The commodity at hand will be denoted by X. Thus, X can represent bread, shoes, permanent waves, legal advice, or any other particular good or service. For the various quantities or amounts of X, the symbol x will be used. Hence, the

Table 4.1

Demand Schedule for Commodity X

Price of X	Quantity Demanded per Month
$10	50
9	55
8	62
7	70
6	80
5	90
4	105
3	120
2	140

variable x can take on any value from zero amount (per unit of time) to any permissible large value (per unit of time). Finally, the price of X is to be represented by p_x, which may also assume any permissible value.

The relationship between price and quantity demanded can be presented in either tabular or graphic form. Table 4.1 lists prices from $2 to $10 and the corresponding quantities per month that would be taken by consumers at each price. In general, the lower is price the greater is the quantity that would be purchased. We shall want to justify this assumption about consumer behavior. Before doing so, however, let us turn to the alternative method used to express the demand relationship.

A demand curve is a demand schedule plotted on a graph, a geometric

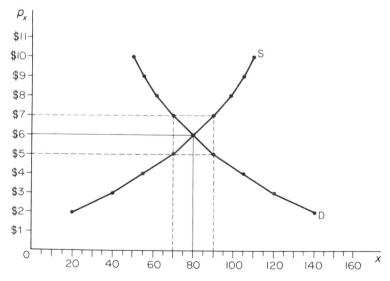

FIG. 4.1.   Demand and Supply Curves for Commodity X

representation of the schedule, and it is helpful to regard it as a picture or photograph of the demand schedule. More exactly, the demand curve is a locus of points showing for each hypothetical price the quantity that would be demanded at that price. The points are plotted on a graph and connected to form an unbroken curve.

Figure 4.1 depicts the demand curve labeled D. On the vertical axis is measured the price of commodity X, where equal vertical distances from zero upward measure equal differences in price. The quantity of X is measured on the horizontal axis, where equal horizontal distances from zero to the right measure equal differences in the quantities of the commodity per unit of time. The point at which the variables on both axes have a zero magnitude (in this case, where both price and quantity are zero) is called the origin.[1]

The postulate that there is an *inverse* relation between price and quantity demanded—that consumers take more at lower prices than at higher prices—means that the demand curve slopes downward toward the right, that it is negatively sloped.[2] The crux of the problem in demand theory is to explain why this behavior is attributed to consumers. Is it sensible to suppose that the demand curve for a product has a negative slope?

For present purposes we can rely on our everyday experience and common-sense reasoning to justify this assumption. One reason for a negatively sloped demand curve is the entrance of new consumers into

[1] Students familiar with analytical geometry will recognize this as the first quadrant of a plane dissected by the Cartesian coordinate system. A plane is divided into four parts by a vertical and a horizontal axis as follows:

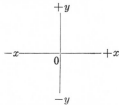

Positive values of the variable y are larger the greater the upward distance from the origin on the vertical axis. The values of y are negative below the origin and are algebraically smaller (larger absolutely with a minus sign) in the downward direction from the origin. The variable x assumes values that are positive and larger as one moves to the right from the origin. Its values are negative to the left of the origin and become algebraically smaller the further one moves to the left. Since we do not work with negative prices or quantities in economics, we use the upper right-hand quadrant of the plane.

[2] The slope of a curve is defined as the ratio:

$$\frac{\text{change in the value of the variable on the vertical axis}}{\text{change in the value of the variable on the horizontal axis}}$$

Briefly, it is the rise or fall in the curve for a given moment to the right or left. The slope will be negative if the variables move in opposite directions; when the numerator is positive (an increase) the denominator is negative (a decrease), and vice versa. If a curve runs from lower left to upper right, the numerator and denominator are both positive or both negative, so the curve is said to be positively sloped.

the market. As the price of a good or service falls, people who were previously unable to buy will enter the market, so the amount demanded increases. Other people will purchase more of the commodity when its price is lower in preference to other commodities that they bought before but that are now relatively more expensive. They will substitute this cheaper commodity for others. Again, when a shop or a department store wishes to move some merchandise rapidly, it has a "sale." Ordinarily the price cuts are sufficient to induce people to buy more than they otherwise would. It is certainly reasonable, therefore, to assume that demand curves are as a rule negatively sloped.

MARKET SUPPLY

The market supply of a commodity is defined as the various amounts of the commodity that sellers would offer on the market at possible alternative prices, assuming other conditions to be the same. It specifies the relation between different possible prices and the corresponding quantities per unit of time that sellers are willing to place on the market. Like the demand schedule, the supply schedule can be presented as a table or a geometric diagram. For commodity X the supply schedule is shown in Table 4.2, indicating that sellers offer larger quantities for sale at higher prices than at lower prices. When the entries in the table are plotted on a graph, they yield the supply curve labeled S in Fig. 4.1.

Table 4.2

Supply Schedule for Commodity X

Price of X	Quantity Supplied per Month
$10	110
9	105
8	98
7	90
6	80
5	70
4	55
3	40
2	20

The supply curve is *positively sloped*. It runs from the lower left-hand corner of the diagram toward the upper right-hand corner. This *direct* relation between price and quantity per unit of time indicates that sellers will offer more at higher prices than at lower prices. A higher price will induce existing sellers to place more of the good or service on the market, and it may induce additional sellers to come into the field.

We must distinguish between commodities whose total quantity is fixed and those whose quantity is variable. Certain goods or services cannot be increased in amount—such rare items as genuine Gutenberg Bibles or paintings by Toulouse-Lautrec are of this kind—although more or less of the existing total can be offered for sale. Generally, we would expect more to be offered for sale at higher prices than at lower prices. When the price is higher, sellers acquire more money. With this greater amount of money they can in turn acquire more of other goods in exchange for the one good they are giving up. The higher is the price of the good they possess, the more attractive its sale will seem. Thus, it is reasonable to suppose that the supply curves of such commodities are positively sloped.

Most commodities are not fixed in quantity. Firms, as the suppliers of commodities, can vary their output. A complete and accurate explanation of the slope of the supply curve must await discussion of the theory of the individual firm. One can present at this point, nevertheless, a rationale for suppliers' behavior that is plausible and that conforms to our common experience. A greater amount of a commodity will be supplied only if its price is higher, because generally the cost per unit of output will increase as output increases. More productive resources must be employed. It is usually necessary to bid these resources away from other uses, so it is likely that they will be more expensive and perhaps less efficient. Since additional costs of production are incurred with increased output, the firms must have additional revenue per unit to cover those costs. Otherwise they could not remain solvent. We are thus led to expect that unless a higher price can be gotten, firms will not incur the additional cost resulting from increased sales. Similarly, if the price in the market were reduced, firms would be motivated to contract output in order to reduce cost. Consequently, ordinary experience supports the proposition that supply curves have positive slopes. Exceptions to this rule will be taken into account in Chapter 13.

MARKET EQUILIBRIUM

Consumers are demanders of commodities and private firms are suppliers in a competitive-exchange economy. The demand schedule or curve represents the relation between various hypothetical prices and the amounts that would be demanded by consumers at each of these prices. Notice the hypothetical nature of the demand relation: *If* the price were A, *then* the quantity demanded would be B; *if* the price were C, *then* the quantity demanded would be D; and so on. The same interpretation is given to the supply relation. These schedules and curves do not tell us that the price *is* so much and the quantity *is* so much. Both the demand and the supply relations are "if, then" types of propositions. How then is the actual price determined in the market? In brief, the quantity demanded depends upon the price, the quantity supplied also depends upon the price, but together the entire demand schedule and the entire supply schedule determine the price.

Figure 4.1 shows how the actual market price is established. At a price of $5, consumers would be willing to take 90 units of X per month; however, at this price we see from the supply curve that sellers would be willing to offer only 70 units per month. A shortage of 20 units per month would exist at a price of $5. Faced with the shortage, consumers would bid against one another for the available quantity offered. This competition would immediately bid the price up, so a price of $5 cannot be the one maintained in the market. It cannot be maintained because forces are set in operation (in this case, consumer bidding) to drive the price upward.

Next, consider the price of $7 per unit of X. At $7, sellers would be willing to offer 90 units per month, while buyers would be willing to take only 70 units per month. A surplus of 20 units per month would result. With a surplus on his hands each seller would try to undercut other sellers in an effort to dispose of his accumulated surplus. An incentive is provided for sellers to reduce price and cut back production. Therefore, neither could $7 be the price maintained in the market, for forces are set in operation to drive the price downward.

The demonstration that price must rise applies to any price below $6 for commodity X. Likewise, the downward push operates on any price above $6. Corresponding to the price movement is an adjustment in the quantities demanded and supplied. As the price moves upward toward $6, the quantity demanded decreases and the quantity supplied increases. Conversely, as the price drops toward $6, the quantity demanded increases and the quantity supplied decreases. These forces continue to operate until the price of $6 and the quantity of 80 units per month are reached. At this price consumers are willing to take the quantity that firms are willing to offer. The market is cleared: there is neither a surplus nor a shortage. Hence, once this price is attained it will be maintained. There exists no force in the market causing sellers or buyers to change their bids or offerings.

An equilibrium in economics is defined as a position that once attained will be maintained. Any position other than the equilibrium is not stable, given that there are no disturbances injected from the outside.[3] In Fig. 4.1 the equilibrium price of X is $6 and the equilibrium quantity of X exchanged on the market is 80 units per month. *This is the point at which the demand curve intersects the supply curve.* The slightest deviation from this price and quantity would automatically set in motion forces that would restore the equilibrium.

The equilibrium values of these variables are the actual or existing

[3] Shifts in the positions of the demand and supply curves will result in a change in the equilibrium point. Attainment of a new equilibrium will be treated in later chapters.

price and quantity predicted by the theory. All other prices and quantities are hypothetical. Remember that the demand and supply relations are interpreted as hypothetical propositions: if the price were such and such, then the quantity demanded or supplied would be such and such. Among all these possible prices and quantities, only one price and one quantity will prevail in the market. The equilibrium price and quantity must be distinguished from other hypothetical prices and quantities, which may satisfy either the conditions of demand or the conditions of supply separately. They do not, however, satisfy both simultaneously.

APPLICATIONS OF DEMAND AND SUPPLY

We have not yet progressed very far in the theory of price. But we are already in a position to see how the concepts of supply and demand can be used to interpret economic phenomena and to make predictions. Two recent incidents in the United States have been selected for analysis. Both illustrate the way in which abstract theoretical concepts can be applied to concrete situations.

Wartime Rationing

The central problem of a wartime economy has been described by the phrase *guns versus butter*. With the economy's resources fully employed it is impossible, without a change in technology or population, to obtain a substantially greater output of all goods and services. A little more of one necessitates a little less of one or more others. When engaged in an all-out war effort, many of the resources of society must be diverted from the production of peacetime goods to implements of war. However, people earn money income from the production of war goods. Consequently, they have more (or at least as much) money to spend on less consumer goods. The result is inflation—rapid rises in prices.

During World War II the American government, and many others, attempted to stop rising prices by imposing legal maximum prices on certain commodities. In the absence of some form of control, commodity prices would have been higher. This can be illustrated with the aid of a diagram. In Fig. 4.2 the demand and supply of a commodity Z are denoted by D and S respectively; the price of Z and quantity per unit of time are represented by p_z and z respectively. The actual numerical scales are not recorded on the axes; instead numerical subscripts on the variables are used to denote particular prices and quantities.

In an uncontrolled market the price will be p_1. At this price the quantity z_1 will be exchanged. Now suppose the government issues a decree that the price of Z shall not be higher than p_0. We see that producers will produce z_0 at a price of p_0, but consumers will wish to purchase z_3 units of Z. The result is a shortage amounting to $(z_3 - z_0)$. Ordinarily

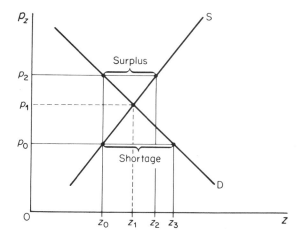

FIG. 4.2. Market for Commodity Z

the price would be bid up to p_1 at which z_1 units would be produced and consumed. Now, however, people are prevented by law from doing so.

Either the commodity Z must be distributed among consumers on a first-come-first-served basis, or it will be sold only to "friends," or some other method of distribution must be found. For reasons of equity the usual method adopted is "rationing." The government issues ration coupons that entitle each consumer to a specified amount. To be successful, enough coupons must be issued to absorb the available quantity supplied and no more. This form of rationing is exactly what happened in many countries during World War II. In the United States gasoline, coffee, tires, butter, and other commodities were price controlled and rationed.

The theory of demand and supply demonstrates why price controls and rationing go hand in hand. If the price ceiling is below the price that would be established in a free market, it is impossible to have such controls without some form of rationing. Even if an equitable system is adopted, the government still has to cope with "black markets," under-the-table deals that violate the price-control law. This, however, is a problem of law enforcement, not economic theory.

Agricultural Price Supports

When the United States government instituted high legal price supports on certain agricultural commodities, economists predicted that large surpluses would result. Price supports were introduced to provide the American farmer with a larger income. It was felt that farmers had been subjected to lower incomes than the nonfarm population. It was felt further that farmers' incomes could be increased by raising the prices of agricultural crops. For specified commodities the government in effect agrees to purchase from farmers all they are willing to sell at a defined support price. If the market price is above the support price, farmers naturally sell on the market. But if the market price is below the support price, farmers sell to the federal government.

Let us see what the demand-supply theory predicts by again making use of Fig. 4.2. Suppose the market price of wheat in the absence of intervention is p_1. Now suppose the support price is set at p_2 by the government. This will force the market price up to p_2 also, for farmers will not offer so much on the market that the price is pushed lower. They have the alternative of selling to the government. At a price of p_2 consumers are willing to purchase the quantity z_0, but farmers are willing to produce the quantity z_2. The surplus not bought on the market amounts to $(z_2 - z_0)$. This surplus, under the conditions of the law, must be bought and stored by the government, using tax receipts as funds to finance the purchase.

This account is not intended to be a complete analysis of price supports. It does not allow for the distribution of income among farmers, changes in population and consumer income, changes in farm technology, the cost of storage to the government, etc. Nevertheless, it is sufficient to illustrate the way in which the economic effects of public policy can be analyzed. It is now a well-known fact that the federal government has, over relatively long periods of time, purchased and stored in warehouses enormous quantities of such goods as wheat, corn, butter, and other farm products. One can clearly see the explanation for surpluses by a relatively simple application of the theory of demand and supply.

A LOOK AHEAD

I stated at the beginning of this chapter that everything else in the chapters on micro theory is an extension of the ideas contained here. We are now in a position to consider more specifically what form that extension will take. A brief summary of the material that lies ahead will provide a perspective of how each part fits into the total picture and an idea of the path we shall follow through the analysis of pricing and resource allocation.

(1) The theory behind the product demand schedule will be investigated. This investigation will take us into the theory of consumer choice, where a more rigorous explanation of consumer demand will be presented.

(2) The characteristics of demand curves will be described, and the forces in the economy that cause changes in the state of demand. In connection with this part of our study we shall examine the interrelations among the markets for different commodities.

(3) The theory behind the product supply schedule and the slope of the product supply curve will be investigated. We shall be led to an analysis of the behavior of individual firms, different industrial structures, and their relation to industry supply.

(4) The characteristics of different supply curves and the causes of shifts in supply will be analyzed.

(5) The preceding four items refer to product markets. We shall also devote attention to resource markets. In these markets firms are demanders and household members are suppliers. We shall study the determination of prices and employment of factors of production and the causes of change in demand and supply in the factor markets.

(6) Finally, we shall consider the ties between product markets and resource markets. And we shall see there are not two different pricing problems but one. Equilibrium in one market implies equilibrium in the other; disturbances in one will produce disturbances in the other. It might be said there is a single set of principles for price determination that applies to either market with appropriate modifications.

PROBLEMS

1. You are given the market demand and supply schedules for a commodity X:

Demand Schedule		Supply Schedule	
Price	Quantity Demanded per Year	Price	Quantity Supplied per Year
$9	40 thousand	$9	85 thousand
8	45 "	8	75 "
7	50 "	7	65 "
6	55 "	6	55 "
5	60 "	5	45 "
4	65 "	4	35 "
3	70 "	3	25 "
2	75 "	2	15 "

(a) Plot the demand curve. Call this Figure 1.

(b) Plot the supply curve. Call this Figure 2.

(c) Plot both the demand and supply curves on the same graph. Call this Figure 3.

(d) Find the equilibrium price and quantity traded on the market.

(e) Give an explanation of the meaning of the equilibrium.

2. You are given the following demand and supply schedules for a commodity Y:

Price	Quantity Demanded per Week	Quantity Supplied per Week
$.10	100	610
.09	200	600
.08	300	575
.07	400	550
.06	500	475
.05	600	450
.04	700	375
.03	800	300
.02	900	200
.01	1,000	0

(a) Consulting only the demand and supply schedules, determine between what two prices the equilibrium price will be. Explain your answer.

(b) Plot the demand and supply curves on the same graph, and read off the approximate equilibrium price and quantity traded.

SUGGESTED READING

B. deJouvenel, "Rent Control: An Example of Price Fixing," Chap. 19 in C. L. Harriss, ed., *Selected Readings in Economics*. Englewood Cliffs, N.J.: Prentice-Hall, Inc., 1958.

D. M. Blank and G. J. Stigler, "Demand-Supply Analysis: Has There Been a Shortage of Engineers?" Chap. 14 in Harriss, ed., *Selected Readings in Economics*.

H. Morrison, "Supply and Demand on Broadway," Chap. 21 in P. A. Samuelson, R. L. Bishop, and J. R. Coleman, *Readings in Economics*, 3rd ed. New York: McGraw-Hill Book Company, Inc., 1958.

Part II

Theory of
Product Demand

5

Theory of Consumer Behavior

Both the prices of products and the prices of factors of production are determined by demand and supply. Since the market demand curve for a product is an aggregate of individual demand curves, and since each individual demand curve originates with an individual consumer, we are led to study consumer behavior and the formal theory of consumer choice.

Some common-sense explanations of consumers' reactions to price changes were discussed in Chapter 4; for three reasons, however, it is desirable to be more exact. First, it is important to avoid the pitfalls of vague explanations, for vagueness permits us to see neither the advantages nor the limitations of theoretical reasoning. Second, a rigorous theory makes clear our assumptions at each step in an argument. Third, as we shall see, the general theory of consumer behavior has implications that are more widespread than reactions solely to prices.

INDIFFERENCE CURVES

The economic theory of consumer choice begins by presenting a description of the tastes and preferences of any single consumer. These are his purely subjective likes and dislikes; they are independent of market prices, his income, or any other objective factors. To simplify the analysis the number of goods or services considered will be limited to two—call them X and Y. So the consumer is limited to choices between these two commodities. Consumption of the commodities X and Y will yield "satisfaction" to the consumer. This satisfaction we call utility.

The amount of utility the consumer enjoys will vary with the amounts of X and Y he consumes. Consumption of one unit of X per unit of time gives the consumer some amount of utility; consumption of 2 units of X per unit of time yields him another amount of utility, different in general from the amount yielded by one unit. Similarly for Y: 7 units of Y will give one amount of utility, and 12 units another amount.

We can consider combinations of the commodities X and Y also. When the individual consumes 4 units of X together with 3 units of Y, he derives a certain total utility. This amount of utility may or may not be the same as the amount he obtains from 2 units of X and 5 units of Y. The problem of describing the consumer's preferences for X and Y can be phrased in the following way: Assuming that the individual is confronted with a range of choices among various possible combinations of X and Y, how can his preferences for the various combinations be described?

Definition

An indifference curve is a locus of points showing the combinations of X and Y that yield equal utility to the consumer. If one combination gives him greater utility than a second combination, the consumer is said to prefer the first combination to the second. Likewise, when the second gives him more utility than the first, he prefers the second to the first. Whenever two combinations of X and Y yield equal utility, the consumer is said to be indifferent between them.

A set of eight different combinations of X and Y is shown in Table 5.1. Let us suppose that each combination yields the same amount of utility as any other. Since the consumer's satisfaction or utility derived from the goods is subjective, we cannot measure it. Consequently, the utility has been designated as U_2, without specifying a numerical value for U_2. For example, 2 units of X and 11 units of Y together yield to the consumer some given amount of utility, labeled U_2. The same amount of utility is obtained from 3 units of X and 8 units of Y, or 4 units of X and 6 units of Y, and so on. Though it is assumed that utility is unchanged by switching from one combination to another, it is not thereby assumed that this utility is observable or measurable in any objective way.

Table 5.1

Combinations of X and Y Among Which the Consumer Is Indifferent

Quantity of Commodity X Consumed, Measured in Dozens per Unit of Time	Quantity of Commodity Y Consumed, Measured in Quarts per Unit of Time	Total Utility Yielded by Each Combination of X and Y
x	y	U
1	16	U_2
2	11	U_2
3	8	U_2
4	6	U_2
5	5	U_2
7	4	U_2
10	3	U_2
14	$2\frac{1}{2}$	U_2

These combinations of X and Y when plotted on a graph are points on an indifference curve. The indifference curve is labeled U_2 in Fig. 5.1. For the moment let us ignore the other curves in the diagram. In the illustration, only the eight combinations are shown as points, but in actuality there would be many more possible combinations to consider. When all combinations that yield equal utility are plotted, they form a continuous curve like the one shown. We now come to a very simple, basic assumption about consumer preferences: *The consumer prefers more of any commodity to less of it, given that the consumption of no other commodity decreases.* Another way of saying this is as follows: If the consumer receives more of any one commodity and no less of any other, his total utility increases.

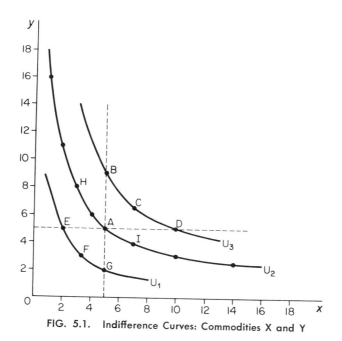

FIG. 5.1.   Indifference Curves: Commodities X and Y

This fundamental assumption is revealed by the three indifference curves drawn in Fig. 5.1. Pick any point on our given indifference curve U_2; it does not matter which one. Suppose we pick point A. Then, A can be compared with any other point *not* on the indifference curve. According to our assumption, points B, C, and D are all preferred by the consumer to point A, for A represents 5 units of X and 5 units of Y. At position B the individual consumes 5 units of X, as before. But he now consumes 9 units of Y—four more than he receives at A. Therefore, by our assumption, B is preferred to A. That is, the combination of X and Y represented by B is regarded by the consumer as superior or preferred to the combination represented by A. Comparisons of A with C and D give the same result. At C the consumer would have more X and more Y; at D he would have more X while having the same amount of Y.

If we next examine points E, F, and G, and compare each of these with A, we see that A is preferred to any one of them. The combination represented by point A includes more of at least one of the goods (more of both as compared to F) and no less of the other. Hence, points B, C, and D are all preferred to A, while A is preferred to E, F, and G.

So far, we have been comparing points off the chosen indifference curve with points on it. Now if we compare different points on the curve U_2, such as A with H or I, we see that no inferiority or superiority results. At A the consumer would have 5 units of X and 5 units of Y. If we were, hypothetically, to take away 2 units of X and give him 3 units of Y, he would be at H. According to his likes and dislikes, however, he would consider himself neither better nor worse off; he is indifferent between the two combinations. The same is true if we move him to I by giving him 2 more units of X and taking away one unit of Y. This amounts to saying that he is indifferent among all combinations of X and Y represented by all points on the same curve, in the sense that all such combinations yield him equal satisfaction. For every consumer there is *some* set of combinations (like A, H, I, etc.) among which he is indifferent. The indifference curve corresponding to this set forms the boundary between those combinations preferred to the given set (like B, C, and D) and those over which the given set is preferred (like E, F, and G).

The indifference curve labeled U_2 tells us that the consumer is indifferent among all combinations represented by points on U_2. But what about combinations not on U_2, like C or E for example? Other combinations regarded as equivalent to C in utility can be found, such as B and D. There will be many others also. The entire set of such equivalent combinations can be plotted to form indifference curve U_3, where any point on U_3 is preferred to any point on U_2. Similarly, all combinations regarded as equivalent to E, among which are F and G, can be found and plotted to form U_1. It follows that any point on U_2 is preferred to any point on U_1.

Figure 5.1 depicts only three of the consumer's indifference curves. But we could consider many more. A consumer's tastes and preferences for X and Y can be described by a whole system of indifference curves, called his indifference map. The indifference map consists of innumerable curves, each one of which depicts combinations that yield the consumer equal utility. It may be useful to imagine these curves as lying "very close" one to the next—or as practically touching but not quite touching. All combinations on a given indifference curve are preferred to all combinations on any lower indifference curve. In moving from a lower to a higher curve the consumer's total utility increases. If he moves to one higher still, his utility increases again. Of course, we cannot read his mind and say *how much* it has increased; we can say only that it has increased. Nevertheless, as we shall see, we need not be able to measure consumers' utilities. If we assume knowledge of the direction of change only, we shall be able to arrive at objective measures of responses to price and income changes.

Starting with the basic assumption that every consumer prefers more goods to less, certain consequences follow. Each indifference curve in the system or indifference map displays three properties. The first two follow necessarily from the basic assumption; the third is an additional reasonable assumption that proves useful for market analysis.

(1) Each indifference curve is negatively sloped over the relevant range.
(2) No indifference curve intersects any other one.
(3) Each curve is convex toward the origin.

Let us consider each of these in turn.

By a negative slope we mean an indifference curve slopes downward to the right. Symbols will again serve to make this notion clear. Let Δx denote a small change in the amount of commodity X, and let Δy denote the corresponding change in the amount of commodity Y. When we have a curve relating x to y (the amounts of X and Y respectively), then the slope of the curve is signified by $\Delta y/\Delta x$.

If this magnitude is negative, it means x increases as y decreases and vice versa. Therefore, a negative slope implies a curve sloping downward to the right with y measured on the vertical axis and x on the horizontal axis. The indifference curves depicted in Fig. 5.1 are clearly negatively sloped at all points. For if we move downward to the right along one of them, we increase x (Δx is positive) and we decrease y (Δy is negative). By moving upward to the left we decrease x (Δx is negative) while we increase y (Δy is positive). Hence, for any move along the curve in either direction the ratio $\Delta y/\Delta x$ must be negative.

But what does this mean in economic terms? The answer can best be given by considering what would result if we allowed any other alternative. There are only three other alternatives: at some or all points the curves are horizontal, they are vertical, or they are positively sloped (run from lower left to upper right). If they were horizontal, the consumer would be indifferent between two combinations, both of which contain the same amount of Y, but one of which contains more X than the other. For example, 6 of X and 6 of Y is equivalent to 7 of X and 6 of Y. Not only does this violate our basic assumption that more is preferred to less; if we allow for it, the consumer must be receiving so much X that he is saturated with it—the additional X in the second combination is worthless to him. Surely, this could happen only if he had a gargantuan amount of X, that is, if he were at some point far out on the x axis. Such an occurrence may be regarded as a rare aberration, so we shall ignore it. The same argument applies to a vertical indifference curve; only the roles of X and Y are reversed. Finally, a positively sloped indifference curve also contradicts the basic assumption. Were this the case, two combinations would be considered equivalent when one contains more of both X and Y. For example, the consumer would be indifferent between a combination of 2 units of X and 2 units of Y and another combination consisting of, say, 10 units of X and 10 units of Y.

The usual situation is one in which the loss of one or more units of one good requires more of the other if the consumer is to maintain a constant amount of utility. This is described geometrically by drawing the indifference curves with a negative slope.

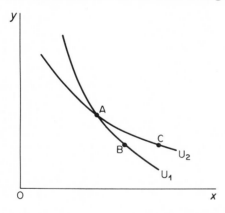

FIG. 5.2.   Intersecting Indifference Curves

The second property of indifference curves states that no one curve intersects any other. That this also follows from the basic assumption can be seen in Fig. 5.2. Here we have two interesting indifference curves. But see what it entails! The consumer is indifferent between the combination represented by point A and the combination represented by point B because these are both on U_1. The consumer is also indifferent between points A and C since these are both on the curve U_2. By our basic assumption all points on U_2 must be preferred to all points on U_1. This means C is preferred to B; however, it is at the same time indifferent to B, for B is indifferent to A and A is indifferent to C. Obviously, C cannot be both preferred to B and indifferent to B at the same time. By drawing intersecting indifference curves we have gotten ourselves into a contradiction.

As a consequence, we require that no two indifference curves intersect. This is not the same as saying they are parallel, or that they are equidistant from each other. They may be spaced farther apart at some points and closer together at others. But within the indifference map they are not allowed to intersect.

The third characteristic of an indifference curve is its convexity toward the origin. In economics the term used to describe this property is *diminishing marginal rate of substitution* of X for Y. It sounds formidable, but it is really rather simple. The marginal rate of substitution of X for Y (denoted symbolically as MRS_{xy}) is defined as the amount of Y the consumer is just willing to give up to get an additional unit of X. Notice, now, that we are defining a property of any single indifference curve. And we know that on any single indifference curve the combinations represented by all points give the same utility. Therefore, diminishing MRS_{xy} means that the more X a consumer receives, the less Y he is willing to give up to get one more unit of X and still preserve the same amount of utility.

Figure 5.3 shows this diagrammatically. At point A the consumer is consuming one unit of X per unit of time and 9 units of Y per unit of time. Starting at this position we can tell how much Y he is willing to give up to get one more unit of X and still maintain the same amount of utility. If the consumer were to receive one more unit of X and maintain the same utility, he would be willing to give up 3 units of Y. That is, he

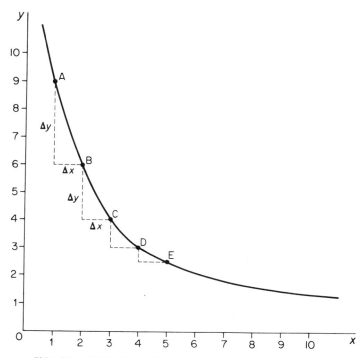

FIG. 5.3. Diminishing Marginal Rate of Substitution of X for Y

would move to position B on the indifference curve, where he receives 2 units of X and 6 units of Y. In order to get another unit of X (3 units instead of 2), he would be willing to give up only 2 units of Y. Notice that the amount of Y he would sacrifice to get additional units of X gets smaller as we move from B to C and then from C to D. At D he has 4 units of X and 3 of Y. Now, again, when he is considering how much Y it would be worth his giving up to get one more X, we find he would give up just ½ unit of Y.

In general, as we move the consumer from point A toward point E he receives more X and less Y. The importance of a unit of Y becomes progressively greater compared to the importance of a unit of X. So the quantity of Y he is willing to give up to get additional units of X and still have the same utility becomes progressively smaller. This is exactly what we mean when we say the MRS_{xy} is decreasing as x increases relative to y.[1] Diminishing MRS_{xy} requires that each indifference curve must be convex toward the origin. Straight lines or curves concave to the origin also have negative slopes, but they do not have diminishing MRS_{xy}. Hence, this assumption is not the same as our first one; it adds an additional property to the curves.

Incidentally, for future reference it is interesting to note the relationship MRS_{xy} bears to the slope of the indifference curve. It can be shown that the marginal rate of substitution of X for Y is equal to *minus* the slope of the indifference curve:

$$MRS_{xy} = -\frac{\Delta y}{\Delta x}$$

The slope is the ratio of the change in y to the change in x, and we saw it is always a negative number. Minus a negative number (multiplying the number by minus one) makes that number positive. The MRS_{xy} is a positive number, the ratio of the amount of Y given up (a positive magnitude) to the amount of X gained (also a positive magnitude). For example, on the indifference curve in Fig. 5.3:

Moving from Points	MRS_{xy}	Slope
A to B	$3/1 = 3$	$-3/1 = -3$
B to C	$2/1 = 2$	$-2/1 = -2$
C to D	$1/1 = 1$	$-1/1 = -1$
D to E	$\frac{1}{2}/1 = \frac{1}{2}$	$-\frac{1}{2}/1 = -\frac{1}{2}$

At any point on the curve, the marginal rate of substitution of X for Y is found by computing the slope and removing the minus sign.

[1] It is easily seen from Fig. 5.3 that MRS_{yx} (the marginal rate of substitution of y for x) decreases as y increases relative to x. That is, the phenomenon works both ways: MRS_{xy} decreases as x increases relative to y, and MRS_{yx} decreases as y increases relative to x.

CONSUMER CHOICE

We have made a fundamental a priori assumption in describing consumers' tastes and preferences, namely, that consumers prefer more goods to less. Using the indifference map of a consumer to express it, we have seen that this simple assumption necessarily implies two others: (1) negative slopes for all indifference curves in the system and (2) nonintersection of the indifference curves. When we add the assumption of diminishing MRS_{xy}, we arrive at a third property, convexity of each curve in the system toward the origin. But description of a consumer's subjective tastes and preferences is not enough to determine his actual choices between goods X and Y in the market. To do this one must impute to the consumer a criterion of action or a goal. Once this has been done, preferences can be translated into a rule of choice.

The Maximization Assumption

Our final assumption refers to consumer behavior rather than to consumer preferences. Preferences must be demonstrated in actual choices, and choices must be directed toward some end. The end of each consumer is assumed to be the maximization of his total utility. That is, the consumer seeks to make his utility or satisfaction the largest possible. In terms of his indifference map, this means he will consume X and Y in such quantities as to get on the highest possible indifference curve.

We must take account, however, of the fact that how high up on his indifference map the consumer can get depends on several constraining factors. Obviously, he may not have enough income to obtain a combination of X and Y on a given indifference curve since the quantities of X and Y he consumes must be purchased in the market. What we have here is an example of the general economic problem defined in Chapter 1. There are alternative uses (combinations of X and Y) among which a scarce quantity (income) must be allocated. If his income is not unlimited, the consumer cannot continue indefinitely moving up from one indifference curve to a higher one.

The Constraints on Maximization

What the consumer would *like* to do has been our concern so far. What he is *able* to do has not been taken into account. Referring again to commodities X and Y, what the consumer is able to do—what combinations of X and Y he can in fact obtain—depends upon the prices of X and Y in the market and upon his income. For purposes of analysis we shall suppose that these are fixed for the time being.

Suppose the consumer's income is $500 per month. For simplicity, let us also suppose he spends all of his income on X and Y. This is merely a convenience that does not hinder the generality of our conclusions. The price of X is $2.50 and the price of Y is $4, let us say. If the consumer were to spend all of his income on good X, i.e., purchase none of Y, he could buy 200 units of X per month. On the other hand, were he to spend all his income on Y, he could buy 125 units of Y per month and no X. Between these two extremes there are many other combinations of X and Y he could purchase.

The straight line in Fig. 5.4 shows the combinations of X and Y that are attainable with the given income of the consumer. The intersection with the horizontal axis indicates he could purchase 200 units of commodity X if he purchases zero units of Y. The intersection with the vertical axis shows he could purchase 125 units of Y if he consumed zero units of X. These intersection points, and all other points on the line, are obtained from the equation

$$(p_x \cdot x) + (p_y \cdot y) = I$$

where p_x denotes the price of X, p_y the price of Y, x the quantity of good X per unit of time, y the quantity of good Y per unit of time, and I the income of the consumer. This equation states that expenditures on X, which equal p_x times x, plus expenditures on Y, p_y times y, exhaust the consumer's income, I. In this case we have $p_x = \$2.50$, $p_y = \$4$, and I = $500. Hence, the equation becomes

$$2.50x + 4.00y = 500$$

Now when y equals zero, the second term on the left of the equality sign is zero, and x equals 500/2.50 or 200 (the intersection with the horizontal axis). Similarly, when x equals zero, then y equals 500/4 or 125, which gives the point of intersection with the vertical axis. There are many other values of x and y that satisfy this equation. For example, if $x = 40$, then $y = 100$; if $x = 80$, then $y = 75$. For every possible value

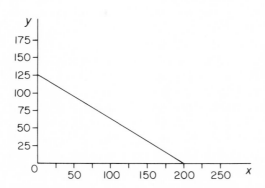

FIG. 5.4.   Budget Line of the Consumer

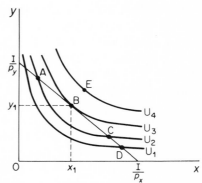

FIG. 5.5.   Consumer Equilibrium

of x from zero to 200 inclusive, the corresponding value of y that satisfies the equation can be found. When these pairs of x and y are plotted, they form the line depicted in Fig. 5.4. A straight line joining the intersection points of the two axes shows all combinations of X and Y that the individual's income will permit him to purchase. It is called the line of attainable combinations or the *budget line* of the consumer.

The slope of the budget line depends upon the price of X and the price of Y. We saw in the previous section that the slope of a line relating x to y is $\Delta y/\Delta x$. In our illustration let us pick as the changes in x and y the changes from the intersection point with one axis to the intersection point with the other.[2] For the change in x we have $\Delta x = 200 - 0$. For the change in y corresponding to this change in x we have $\Delta y = 0 - 125$. Therefore,

$$\frac{\Delta y}{\Delta x} = \frac{0 - 125}{200 - 0} = \frac{-125}{200} = -\frac{2.5}{4}$$

Notice that the slope of the budget line is equal to minus the ratio of the price of X to the price of Y.

This result can be shown to hold in general for any given prices and income. To generalize, as before, let I designate the given income of the consumer, p_x the given price of X, and p_y the given price of Y. We know

$$(p_x \cdot x) + (p_y \cdot y) = I$$

The intersection of the budget line with the x axis (i.e., when $y = 0$) is I/p_x. The intersection with the y axis (i.e., when $x = 0$) is I/p_y. The slope of the budget line is

$$\frac{\Delta y}{\Delta x} = \frac{0 - I/p_y}{I/p_x - 0} = \frac{-I/p_y}{I/p_x} = \frac{-I}{p_y} \cdot \frac{p_x}{I} = -\frac{p_x}{p_y}$$

In general, the slope of the budget line equals minus the ratio of the price of X to the price of Y.

Consumer Equilibrium

In order to determine what the consumer will do, we must bring together what he is *willing* to do with what he *can* do. We must bring together the consumer's indifference map and his budget line. The consumer will be in equilibrium when he has maximized his total utility subject to the constraint given by his budget. He can move back and forth along his budget line, but he cannot move beyond it. His problem, therefore, is to choose the point on his budget line that leaves him with the greatest utility.

The equilibrium of the consumer is shown in Fig. 5.5. Given his in-

[2] Since the budget line is a straight line, the slope will be the same between any two points on the line. We could pick any two points on the line, close together or far apart, in order to measure the slope and come out with the same answer. Use of the intersection points is convenient for our purposes.

come, the consumer can have any combination of X and Y that lies on his budget line. Points A, B, C, and D all lie on the budget line. But the consumer would not choose position A, for the combination of X and Y represented by A yields him a total utility of U_2, whereas the combination represented by B gives him a total utility of U_3; and U_3 is greater than U_2. The same is true of position C. The combination represented by point D yields even less utility—U_1, which is less than U_2. Point B is the equilibrium position of the consumer because it represents the attainable combination of X and Y that puts him on the highest indifference curve. Certainly he would prefer point E, but his budget line does not permit him to attain it, nor does it permit him to obtain any other point on a still higher curve. Point B will give the consumer a greater amount of utility than will any other combination of X and Y attainable with his given income at the given prices of X and Y.

The consumer has maximized utility at the point where the budget line is tangent to an indifference curve.[3] The indifference curve to which the budget line is tangent is the highest one attainable. At the point of tangency the consumer has allocated his income over X and Y in such a way as to maximize the total utility derived from their consumption. Therefore, he will consume x_1 units of commodity X and y_1 units of commodity Y per unit of time.

An equilibrium is a position that once attained will be maintained, and it is easy to see why B must be the equilibrium of the consumer. We have seen earlier in this chapter that the consumer's marginal rate of substitution of X for Y is equal to minus the slope of an indifference curve:

$$\text{MRS}_{xy} = -\frac{\Delta y}{\Delta x} \qquad \text{on indifference curve}$$

We saw also that the ratio of the price of X to the price of Y equals minus the slope of the budget line:

$$\frac{p_x}{p_y} = -\frac{\Delta y}{\Delta x} \qquad \text{on budget line}$$

At the point of tangency, the budget line and the indifference curve have the same slope by definition of tangency. Consequently,

$$\text{MRS}_{xy} = \frac{p_x}{p_y}$$

MRS_{xy} represents the amount of Y the consumer is *willing* to give up to get an additional unit of X and preserve the same amount of utility. The price ratio represents the amount of Y he would *have to* give up to get an additional unit of X. This is so because the only way he can consume more X and less Y is to spend on X the money saved by not purchasing Y. When the marginal rate of substitution equals the price

---

[3] Tangency may be roughly defined as a point at which two curves just touch, neither curve crossing the other.

ratio, the consumer is in a position where he can just do what he is willing to do.

At point A the marginal rate of substitution is greater than the price ratio. The quantity of Y the consumer is willing to give up to get an additional unit of X is greater than the quantity he would have to give up. In this case the consumer can increase his total utility by giving up units of Y to get more X. In our numerical example, it costs him $2.50 to get one more X, which means he has to give up $2.50 worth of Y. But he is willing to give up even more Y than $2.50 worth. Therefore, he will continue to purchase more X and less Y until he is no longer willing to give up more than the market requires. That is, he will move from A along his budget line until he reaches B.

The consumer would not move beyond B to a point like C. At C his MRS_{xy} is less than the price ratio. The amount of Y he is willing to give up to get one more unit of X is less than the amount he would have to give up. Having to pay $2.50 for one more X, he is unwilling to relinquish $2.50 worth of Y. Rather, he would move in the reverse direction, giving up X to get more Y, for each step in this direction increases his total utility. Given his tastes and preferences and given the market conditions, the consumer will settle at point B, where his subjective preferences are in line with the objective possibilities in the market. No movement away from this position in either direction on the budget line can increase his utility.[4]

[4] Sometimes economists use the concept of marginal utility to express this result. The marginal utility of a good X to an individual is defined as the change in his total utility that would result from one more unit of X, when the amount of Y is held constant:

$$MU_x = \frac{\Delta U}{\Delta x} \quad \text{given } y \text{ constant}$$

where ΔU denotes the change in total utility resulting from Δx. The marginal utility of Y to the individual is defined in the same way:

$$MU_y = \frac{\Delta U}{\Delta y} \quad \text{given } x \text{ constant}$$

It can be shown that when total utility is maximized subject to the budget constraint, the ratio of these two marginal utilities is equal to the price ratio:

(1)
$$\frac{MU_x}{MU_y} = \frac{p_x}{p_y}$$

Since MRS_{xy} equals the price ratio it also equals the ratio of marginal utilities:

(2)
$$MRS_{xy} = \frac{p_x}{p_y} = \frac{MU_x}{MU_y}$$

Now we can rewrite equation (1) as

(3)
$$\frac{MU_x}{p_x} = \frac{MU_y}{p_y}$$

This tells us that when the consumer's utility is a maximum, he consumes X and Y in such a combination that the marginal utilities of both goods are proportionate to their prices. A dollar spent on one good will add as much to the consumer's utility as a dollar spent on any other good. When this is the case, there is no reason for him to change his consumption of X and Y; he is in equilibrium.

A clear understanding of the general principle can be facilitated by a practical example. Suppose a young lady has a fixed yearly budget to spend on cosmetics and phonograph records. Imagine that the indifference map in Fig. 5.5 describes her relative preferences for the two commodities. Let x denote amounts of phonograph records consumed per year, and let y denote amounts of cosmetics consumed per year (each commodity being measured in some appropriate units). Suppose, finally, that her utility derived from the consumption of both products is to be made a maximum, given that the price of a defined unit of records is $4 ($p_x$) and that the price of a defined unit of cosmetics is $2 ($p_y$). This means that in order to obtain one more unit of records on the market, she must pay an additional $4. But if she does so, she must sacrifice $4 worth of cosmetics, or 2 units of cosmetics at the given price of $2. The ratio $p_x/p_y = 2/1$.

Now let us examine a point like A on her budget line. Assume at this point her MRS_{xy} is 3. She would be willing to give up 3 units of cosmetics to get one more unit of records; one unit of records will just substitute for 3 units of cosmetics and leave her with the same utility from both combined. If giving up 3 units of cosmetics and getting one more unit of records would leave her utility unchanged, then giving up 2 units of cosmetics and getting one more unit of records would clearly increase her total utility. But the market price ratio is such that she need give up only 2 units of cosmetics in exchange for one more unit of records. Therefore, she will substitute records for cosmetics—move downward to the right along her budget line. And she will continue to do so until she reaches a point of tangency like point B, where MRS_{xy} equals the price ratio of 2/1. At this point she is willing to sacrifice 2 units of cosmetics for one more unit of records leaving her utility unchanged, and she can exchange them on the market at this rate. Therefore, no further gain in utility can be achieved by further substitution.

She will not move beyond the point of tangency to a point like C, for such a movement would decrease her utility. At C she is willing to sacrifice, let us say, $\frac{1}{2}$ unit of cosmetics to get one more unit of records. But at the existing market prices it would still take a sacrifice of 2 cosmetics. If she has to sacrifice 2 while a sacrifice of no more than $\frac{1}{2}$ would leave her utility unchanged, a move from B to C would obviously decrease her utility. Thus, her utility is maximized at the point of tangency.

CHANGES IN CONSUMER EQUILIBRIUM

The point at which the consumer's budget line is tangent to an indifference curve maximizes the consumer's utility. This point of tangency discloses the amounts of the two commodities he will consume given certain conditions, namely, his income and the prices of the two commodities. To complete our analysis of consumer behavior, let us next examine the change in his equilibrium that results from a change in these conditions of choice.

Assuming no variation in prices, an alteration in his income will change the opportunities open to a consumer. A previous illustration took the consumer's income as given at $500 per month. At prices of $2.50 for X and $4.00 for Y his budget equation,

$$2.50x + 4.00y = 500$$

gave rise to the budget line depicted as line I in Fig. 5.6.

Now suppose his income were to rise to $750 per month, while prices remain unchanged. His new budget equation becomes

$$2.50x + 4.00y = 750$$

and his new budget line is labeled II in Fig. 5.6. The effect of the rise in income is to shift the budget line upward to the right. The new intersection point with the horizontal axis is given as $x = 750/2.50 = 300$; while the new intersection point with the vertical axis is given by $y = 750/4.00 = 187.50$. With this change in his conditions of choice, the consumer will move to a new equilibrium point. In order to maximize his utility subject to the budget constraint II, he will consume X and Y

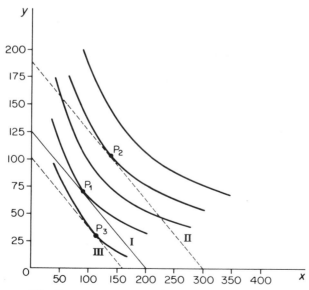

FIG. 5.6. Consumer Equilibria Under Changing Income

in such quantities that the line II is tangent to an indifference curve. That is, he will alter his consumption from the combination represented by point P_1 to that combination represented by point P_2.

Just the reverse situation is represented by line III. Here, beginning with line I, the consumer's income is assumed to drop from $500 to $400. As a consequence, his budget line shifts downward to the left. The new budget equation,

$$2.50x + 4.00y = 400$$

yields the intersection points $x = 400/2.50 = 160$ on the horizontal axis, and $y = 400/4.00 = 100$ on the vertical axis. Again, in order to maximize his utility subject to constraint III, the individual will consume the combination of X and Y represented by point P_3.

In general, when income changes, the consumer will change his consumption pattern. A rise in income shifts the budget line away from the origin, whereas a decline in income shifts it toward the origin. The new budget line in either case is parallel to the old one. Whether he will consume more of both commodities when his income rises, or whether he will consume more of one and less of the other, depends upon the shapes of his indifference curves, which reflect his tastes and preferences. In our example, the rise in income causes the consumer to move from P_1 to P_2, consuming more of both X and Y. The fall in income, however, causes him to move from P_1 to P_3, at which point he consumes less Y but more X. In the final outcome, the new point of tangency depends upon the consumer's relative preferences for X and Y.

Price Changes

Of course, income is not the only condition subject to change. Either of the two prices is variable. To analyze the effects of price changes let us take as our starting point the same initial budget equation

$$2.50x + 4.00y = 500$$

This generates the budget line I in Fig. 5.7, intersecting the horizontal axis at $x = 200$ and the vertical axis at $y = 125$. It is identical with line I in Fig. 5.6, and the consumer is in equilibrium at point P_1.

Now suppose the price of one of the commodities should fall. Let us say the price of X falls from $2.50 to $1.25, while the price of Y and the consumer's income remain unchanged. The new budget equation becomes

$$1.25x + 4.00y = 500$$

As a consequence the x intercept becomes $x = 500/1.25 = 400$. Unlike the case of a change in income, however, the y intercept remains at the same point; it is still $y = 500/4.00 = 125$. The lower price of X causes the budget line to rotate counterclockwise about the point of intersection with the vertical axis. The new budget line is depicted as line IV in Fig. 5.7. To maximize his utility, given the new budget line, the consumer will move to point P_4, at which line IV is tangent to an indifference curve. In this case, a fall in the price of X leads to the consumption of more X and less Y.

Consider next a rise in the price of X from \$2.50 to \$5.00. With the price of Y and his income unchanged the consumer's new budget equation,

$$5.00x + 4.00y = 500$$

is represented by line V. Line V has an x intercept of $x = 500/5.00 = 100$, and the same y intercept as line I, namely, $y = 500/4.00 = 125$. A rise in the price of X produces a clockwise rotation of the budget line about the y intercept. Utility maximization under the constraint V occurs

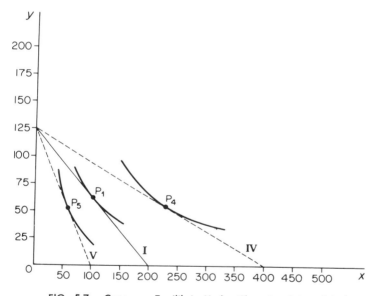

FIG. 5.7. Consumer Equilibria Under Changing Price of X

at the point P_5, where line V is tangent to an indifference curve. At this point the individual consumes less X and less Y as compared to point P_1.

The effects of a change in the price of Y can also be traced. The procedure is the same, except that in this case the budget line rotates about a fixed point on the horizontal axis. The point of intersection of the budget line with the vertical axis does change, but the intersection point with the horizontal axis does not. A fall in the price of Y causes the budget line to rotate clockwise, intersecting the vertical axis higher up.

Naturally, a rise in the price of Y has the reverse effects; the budget line rotates counterclockwise, intersecting the vertical axis farther down.

In general, a change in either price causes the budget line to rotate about a fixed point on the axis that measures amounts of the other commodity. In the final outcome, the new combination of commodities consumed depends upon where the new point of tangency occurs. Given any rotation in the budget line, the location of the new equilibrium point in turn depends upon the shapes of the individual's indifference curves. That is, it depends upon his relative preferences for the two commodities.

PROBLEMS

1. Suppose you are given the following information about a consumer's preferences for two commodities, X and Y.

Combinations Yielding Utility Level U_1		Combinations Yielding Utility Level U_2		Combinations Yielding Utility Level U_3	
X	Y	X	Y	X	Y
1	20	3	22	5	24
2	15	4	17	6	19
3	11	5	13	7	15
4	8	6	10	8	12
5	6	7	8	9	10
6	5	8	7	10	9
8	4	10	6	12	8
11	3	13	5	15	7
15	2	17	4	19	6
20	1	22	3	24	5

(a) Plot on a graph the points corresponding to each entry, and connect the points by a smooth curve to form three indifference curves, one corresponding to each utility level.

(b) Explain why each indifference curve is negatively sloped, why it is convex to the origin, and why the curves do not intersect.

(c) Compute the following marginal rates of substitution of X for Y:

On Curve U_1 When	On Curve U_2 When	On Curve U_3 When
$x = 2$ and $y = 15$	$x = 5$ and $y = 13$	$x = 6$ and $y = 19$
$x = 4$ and $y = 8$	$x = 8$ and $y = 7$	$x = 9$ and $y = 10$

2. For two commodities, X and Y, suppose the price of X is given as $6.00 and the price of Y is $4.00. A consumer is assumed to have an income of $120 per week.

(a) Draw on graph paper the consumer's budget line. Explain its meaning.

(*b*) Draw in the same diagram a set of indifference curves for the consumer, showing that in equilibrium he consumes 10 units of X per week and 15 units of Y per week.

(*c*) Assuming his income rises to $180 per week, draw the consumer's new budget line. Under the assumption that he consumes 15 units of X and 22½ units of Y per week with his higher income, depict his new equilibrium.

3.   Chester, a college student, receives from his father a fixed allowance of $24 per month. His father has stipulated that out of this fixed sum Chester must pay for his laundry, but whatever is left over after paying for his laundry may be used for entertainment. Chester's entertainment is dating. The price of a bundle of laundry is $2. The price of a date is $4; when he dates, Chester always takes the girl to the local movie, for an ice cream soda, and then straight to her dormitory—all of which costs $4. Since Chester is a charming fellow, he can get any quantity of dates by paying $4 per date.

(*a*) Draw a diagram showing Chester's budget line.

(*b*) On the same diagram superimpose Chester's indifference curves. Assuming he maximizes his utility from dates and laundry, depict his equilibrium if he consumes 4 dates and 4 bundles of laundry per month.

(*c*) When Chester is in equilibrium, what is his marginal rate of substitution of dates for laundry? How did you obtain this answer?

(*d*) Now suppose the coeds get together and decide Chester shall have no dates unless he spends $6 per date, but he may have any quantity he wants at this price. Depict his new equilibrium. Will he consume more or less dates?

SUGGESTED READING

R. H. Leftwich, *The Price System and Resource Allocation*, 3rd ed., Chaps. 4, 5. New York: Holt, Rinehart & Winston, Inc., 1960.

W. S. Vickrey, *Microstatics*, pp. 15-56. New York: Harcourt, Brace & World, Inc., 1964.

6

Derivation of Demand

The theory of consumer behavior sets the foundations for analysis of product demand. In this chapter the demand curve of a single consumer will be derived and the market demand curve on the part of all consumers as a group obtained by aggregation. Then the attributes of this market curve will be examined.

UTILITY AND THE DEMAND CURVE

By extending the indifference analysis of choice an individual's demand curve "falls out" of the theory. Suppose the commodity in question is X. There are several determinants of the quantity demanded: the price of the commodity, prices of other commodities, the consumer's income, and so forth. We can write this symbolically in the following way:

$$x_d = d(p_x;\ p_y,\ p_z,\ \cdots;\ \mathrm{I};\ \mathrm{T})$$

where the symbol x_d denotes the quantity of X demanded by the consumer per unit of time; p_x denotes the price of X; p_y, p_z, etc. denote the prices of Y, Z, and all other commodities; I denotes the consumer's income per unit of time and T his tastes and preferences. The equality sign and the letter d may be taken to mean "is a function of." That is, the entire expression says the quantity of X demanded by the consumer on the market, x_d, is a function of—or depends upon—everything inside the parentheses.

This is a quite general statement. Anything we can think of as affecting the quantity of a commodity demanded by a consumer can be summarized under one or another of these variables. At the moment, however, our interest is centered on the demand curve, which relates the quantity of X demanded to the price of X only. In order to do this we shall conceptually hold everything else inside the parentheses constant:

$$x_d = d(p_x;\ \bar{p}_y,\ \bar{p}_z,\ \cdots;\ \bar{\mathrm{I}};\ \bar{\mathrm{T}})$$

The "bars" over the variables signify that we are holding them constant—removing their influence on changes in the quantity demanded. These other variables will be considered in the next chapter. For the present we are left with a relationship between x_d and p_x, and we want to inquire into the nature of this relationship.

A demand curve for a consumer shows the different quantities he would purchase at various possible prices. The theory of consumer equilibrium will permit us to derive this curve under the assumed constancy of the other determinants of demand. Again, for simplicity, consider only two goods, X and Y. The consumer's income, the price of Y, and his tastes and preferences (his indifference curves) are held constant. Then by varying the price of X, we can observe what happens to the quantity of X taken.

Suppose the consumer is initially in equilibrium at point A in Fig. 6.1.

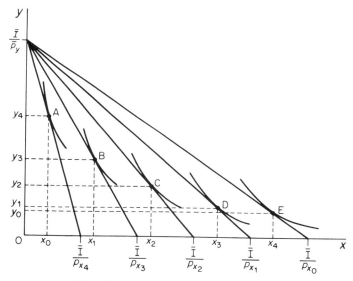

FIG. 6.1.   Price-Quantity Relationship for X

His income is fixed at $\bar{I}$, and the price of Y is fixed at $\bar{p}_y$. Let the price of X be given to him as p_{x_4}. Now let the price of X fall to p_{x_3}. The budget line will swing toward the right with a "hinge" at the intersection with the vertical axis. Since I and p_y do not change, then I/p_y does not change, and the point of vertical intersection does not change (the consumer could still purchase the same quantity of Y if he were to spend all his income on it). However, as we saw in the preceding chapter, the intersection with the horizontal axis moves to the right. With I constant and p_x reduced from p_{x_4} to p_{x_3}, the ratio I/p_x is increased. This amounts to saying that if the consumer were to spend all his income on X, he could now purchase more of it.

Since the consumer maximizes his utility, he will move to that point on the new budget line at which the budget line is tangent to an indifference curve. In this case he moves from equilibrium point A to equilibrium point B. The new budget line is necessarily tangent to a higher indifference curve. If we let the price of X fall again, this time to p_{x_2}, which is smaller than p_{x_3}, the consumer would move to point C on a still higher indifference curve by the same reasoning. By considering the price p_{x_1}, lower than p_{x_2}, and then the price p_{x_0}, lower than p_{x_1}, the consumer moves to D and then to E. These reactions to different prices of X follow from the assumption that the consumer maximizes his total utility.

Initially, at A, the consumer consumed x_0 units of X and y_4 units of Y; at B he consumes x_1 of X and y_3 of Y; then, at C he consumes x_2 of X and y_2 of Y, and so on. We are interested only in the commodity X, so for the present we shall ignore the effects on Y. Notice that x_4 is greater than x_3, which in turn is greater than x_2. A general conclusion emerges: the lower is the price of X, other things constant, the greater is the amount of X taken. Naturally, if we started with a low price of X and considered consecutively higher ones, we would get the same result. The consumer would move from E to D to C to B to A as higher prices were considered.

All the information required for constructing the consumer's demand curve is now available. The demand schedule is presented in Table 6.1, and the demand curve is drawn in Fig. 6.2. The table includes only the five alternative prices discussed, but the demand curve is drawn to show many other prices and the corresponding quantities that would be taken. Each point of equilibrium on the consumer's indifference map, like A, B, and C, gives rise to one point on his demand curve. Therefore, at each point on the de-

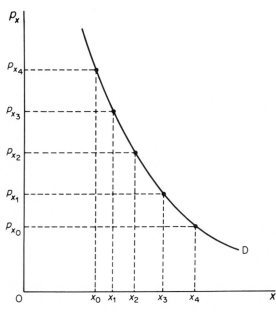

Table 6.1

Consumer's Demand
Schedule for X

Price of X	Quantity of X Demanded per Unit of Time
p_x	x
p_{x_4}	x_0
p_{x_3}	x_1
p_{x_2}	x_2
p_{x_1}	x_3
p_{x_0}	x_4

$$p_{x_4} > p_{x_3} > p_{x_2} > p_{x_1} > p_{x_0}$$
$$x_4 > x_3 > x_2 > x_1 > x_0$$

FIG. 6.2. Consumer's Demand Curve for X

mand curve the consumer is in equilibrium in the sense that he is maximizing his utility.

Notice that the consumer's demand curve has the negative slope ordinarily assumed by economists. The market demand curve, the total demand by all consumers, is obtained by simple aggregation. At a price such as p_{x_3} the individual in question is willing to purchase x_1 units of X. To this quantity is added the amounts that would be taken by all other consumers in order to arrive at the total quantity that would be taken on the market at a price of p_{x_3}. Similarly, at each other alternative price the quantities demanded by different consumers are summed. When the summed quantities at all possible prices have been recorded and plotted on a graph, the result is the market demand curve for X. Geometrically speaking, the market demand curve is the horizontal summation of all individual demand curves. Given that each individual curve is negatively sloped, the market curve must also be negatively sloped.

The indifference theory of consumer choice has permitted us to proceed from the area of subjective tastes and preferences to the area of objectively measurable magnitudes. Though individual utilities cannot be observed and measured, the relationship between quantities and prices on the market can be. Although it is still an abstract economic theory, analysis of consumer choice yields a prediction that is in principle testable against empirical evidence.

PRICE ELASTICITY OF DEMAND

Granted that, in general, market demand curves are negatively sloped, they need not all have equal slopes. When the price of a product X, denoted by p_x, is measured on the vertical axis and the quantity of the product X per unit of time, denoted by x, is measured on the horizontal axis, the slope of the demand curve is $\Delta p_x/\Delta x$, where Δ again signifies "a small change in."

Generally, this will be a negative number for any product. But it need not be the same negative number for all products. For instance, suppose the price of eggs falls by 10 cents and the quantity demanded increases by 50 dozens per day. Over this range the slope of the demand curve for eggs is $-10/50$ or $-1/5$. Suppose the price of cheese falls by 10 cents and the quantity demanded increases by 20 pounds per day. The slope of the demand curve for cheese over this segment of the curve is $-10/20$ or $-1/2$. The slopes of both demand curves are negative, but they differ in numerical value.

The Concept of Price Elasticity

It appears that the slope of a demand curve is an adequate indicator of the responsiveness of quantity demanded to price changes; a moment's reflection, however, will show that this is not the case. A mere alteration in the units in which price or quantity is expressed will change the slope of the demand curve, even though there has been no real alteration in demand itself. If the price of eggs falls by 10 cents, the quantity demanded increases by 50 dozens; the slope thus measured is $-1/5$. Now let the price of eggs be quoted in dollars rather than cents; the demand curve is redrawn, measuring price on the vertical axis in dollars. The same price change is now $-1/10$ instead of -10, i.e., a 10-cent change is a change of $1/10$ dollars. The slope of the curve becomes $-\frac{1}{10}/50$ or $-1/500$. The actual response of quantity demanded to the price change has not really altered, but the expression of price in dollars rather than in cents yields a different slope to the curve.

The same holds true if one redefines the units in which quantity is expressed. Twenty pounds of cheese is the same as $1/100$ of a short ton. By expressing cheese in short tons rather than pounds, the slope of the demand curve becomes $-10/\frac{1}{100}$ or -1000. Measurement of cheese in pounds yielded a slope of $-1/2$. Unfortunately, then, the slope is an ambiguous measure of the responsiveness of quantity taken to changes in the price.

Furthermore, comparison of the slopes of two different demand curves is not a reliable basis for comparing the price-responsiveness of two different commodities. A price decrease of 2 dollars for men's shoes may increase the quantity demanded by 10,000 pairs per year. A price decrease of 2 dollars for refrigerators may increase the quantity demanded by 50 refrigerators per year. But comparison of the slopes of the two demand curves ($-2/10,000$ versus $-2/50$) tells us nothing about their comparative degrees of response to price change. For a 2-dollar price change is substantial in the case of shoes while it is negligible in the case of refrigerators.

These difficulties are overcome by measuring not absolute changes in price and quantity but rather *percentage* changes. The price elasticity of demand, an unambiguous measure of the responsiveness of quantity demanded to price changes, is defined as *the percentage change in the quantity of a commodity demanded in response to a percentage change in the price of that commodity, when the price change is small.* For the commodity X, the price elasticity of demand is written symbolically as

$$e_{p_x} = \frac{\dfrac{\Delta x}{x}}{\dfrac{\Delta p_x}{p_x}}$$

The numerator in this expression is the percentage change in the quantity of X demanded, the numerical change in x measured relative to the base amount. The denominator is the percentage change in the price of X that gave rise to the change in quantity taken.

The price elasticity of demand is a pure number obtained by dividing one percentage by another. As such, it is independent of the units in which price and quantity are expressed. The elasticity will be the same regardless of whether the price is quoted in dollars, cents, hundreds of dollars, or any other monetary unit. The quantity may be measured in single units, pounds, tons; or in bushels or pecks. This pure number escapes the difficulties inherent in measurement by absolute changes, and it permits one to compare the responsiveness to price on different demand curves.

For instance, suppose the price elasticity of demand for wool carpets in the United States is computed as -2.7, while the price elasticity of demand for pipe tobacco is computed as -0.8. The demand curves for the two commodities can be directly compared. For a one per cent change in the price of wool carpets, the quantity demanded will change in the opposite direction by 2.7 per cent. A one per cent change in the price of pipe tobacco will result in a change in the quantity demanded of 8/10 of one per cent, the change being in the opposite direction to the price change. Therefore, the demand for wool carpets is more price elastic than the demand for pipe tobacco, so the quantity demanded is more responsive to price changes.

The Computation of Elasticity

Except in one isolated case (to be discussed in the next section) the price elasticity is a negative number. This is made clear by rearranging the definition of elasticity with the aid of a little algebra:

$$e_{p_x} = \frac{\dfrac{\Delta x}{x}}{\dfrac{\Delta p_x}{p_x}} = \frac{\Delta x}{x} \cdot \frac{p_x}{\Delta p_x} = \frac{\Delta x}{\Delta p_x} \cdot \frac{p_x}{x}$$

Consider the formula in its final form on the extreme right. We know that p_x and x must, in general, be positive magnitudes, so p_x/x is positive. But $\Delta x/\Delta p_x$ is a negative number because the slope of the demand curve is negative. Consequently, the elasticity must be a negative number. Though always negative, on any given demand curve it is not necessary that the elasticity be the same at all points on the curve. In fact, a curve with the same elasticity at all points is the exception rather than the rule.

Point Elasticity. Since elasticity will vary from one point to another on the demand curve, being a different negative number at different points, it is desirable to have a means of computing its numerical value. A simple geometric method is available. Suppose we consider first the straight-line demand curve presented in Fig. 6.3. At the point P, or any other point, $\Delta p_x/\Delta x$ is the slope of the line. For a straight line the slope will be the same whether we choose an infinitesimal movement away from P or a very large one. We can start at P and consider a Δp_x of any size and its corresponding Δx. Choosing a drop in price from P to zero, $\Delta p_x = -PC$. Since we are considering a fall in price, the change in price is negative and equal to the distance PC. The resulting increase in quantity demanded is geometrically equal to CB. Whether we measure the slope over this range or any other,

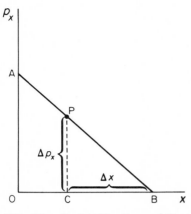

FIG. 6.3. Straight-Line Demand Curve
for Commodity X

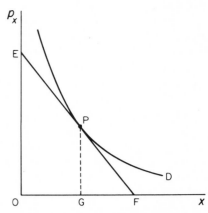

FIG. 6.4. Curved Demand Curve
for Commodity X

it will be the same on a straight-line demand curve. Hence, we can say that
in the case of this straight-line demand curve the slope is

$$\frac{\Delta p_x}{\Delta x} = \frac{-PC}{CB}$$

at all points on the curve—including, of course, point P. To fit this into the
elasticity formula we shall invert the fraction:

$$\frac{\Delta x}{\Delta p_x} = \frac{CB}{-PC}$$

The price at point P is equal to the distance PC, and the quantity demanded
is equal to the distance 0C. Thus, at a point designated by P the elasticity
is given by

$$e_{p_x} = \frac{CB}{-PC} \cdot \frac{PC}{0C} = -\frac{CB}{0C}$$

Notice that the distance CB is equal to the distance from the quantity of
X at which elasticity is being computed to the quantity of X at which the
curve intersects the horizontal axis. The distance 0C is the distance from the
origin to the quantity of X at which elasticity is being computed. The greater
is the former distance relative to the latter, the more elastic will be the demand curve.

This geometric technique can be extended to demand curves that are not
straight lines, as the demand curve labeled D in Fig. 6.4. When the point P
at which elasticity is to be measured has been chosen, a tangent to the demand curve at that point is drawn. Then at P the slope of the demand curve
and the slope of the tangent are identical. Hence, their elasticities must be

identical at that point—but only at that point. As a result of this identity, one can proceed as in the case of a straight-line demand curve, measuring the elasticity of the tangent at P, which gives the elasticity of the curve D at that point. Thus, in our example:

$$e_{p_x} = \frac{GF}{-PG} \cdot \frac{PG}{0G} = -\frac{GF}{0G}$$

The concept of elasticity at a point on the demand curve is the precise meaning of elasticity. However, the geometric method of computing point elasticity at times becomes awkward. Often one is given the demand schedule in the form of a table but not the curve. Then, the curve has to be drawn before one can proceed to compute elasticity. Of somewhat less importance is the fact that the geometric method is subject to visual limitations. Errors may be committed in plotting the curve and judging distances. Therefore, it is desirable to have a method that is at once more exact and quicker. It is worth noting that such a mathematical method is available. It involves the differential calculus and is beyond the scope of this book. Nevertheless, there is a short-cut approximation to this method called arc elasticity.

Arc Elasticity. Instead of measuring elasticity at a single point, arc elasticity measures the elasticity between two points on the demand curve that lie close together. Before proceeding to the computation we must note a certain difficulty that arises when we attempt to use this method. Assume we are given the following demand schedule for a commodity X.

Price of X in Cents	Quantity of X per Unit of Time in Pounds	Point on the Demand Curve
p_x	x	
$p_0 = 20$	$x_0 = 50$	A
$p_1 = 15$	$x_1 = 100$	B
$p_2 = 10$	$x_2 = 200$	C
$p_3 = 5$	$x_3 = 400$	D

Suppose we wish to measure elasticity between what would be points B and C on the demand curve if we were to draw it. We see immediately that $\Delta p_x = p_2 - p_1 = 10 - 15 = -5$; and $\Delta x = x_2 - x_1 = 200 - 100 = 100$. So far so good! But a question arises. What values are we to substitute in the formula for x and p_x? If we choose x_1 and p_1 as the bases for measuring the percentage change, we have

$$e_{p_x} = \frac{\dfrac{100}{100}}{\dfrac{-5}{15}} = \frac{100}{100} \cdot \frac{15}{-5} = \frac{1,500}{-500} = -3$$

However, we might just as well have chosen x_2 and p_2 as the bases. Then, we would get

$$e_{px} = \frac{\dfrac{100}{200}}{\dfrac{-5}{10}} = \frac{100}{200} \cdot \frac{10}{-5} = \frac{1,000}{-1,000} = -1$$

What we end up with is two different measures of elasticity, depending upon whether we choose one or the other base for determining the percentage change. To emphasize this fact and to make the meaning of arc elasticity clear the demand curve for X has been drawn without numerical scales in Fig. 6.5. When elasticity is to be measured between points B and C, the changes in price and quantity are uniquely determined. But the figure

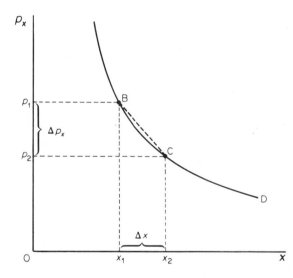

FIG. 6.5.   Arc Elasticity on Demand Curve for Commodity X

we obtain for elasticity depends on whether we choose B or C as the starting point. If we move from B to C, the elasticity turns out to be −3; whereas if we move from C to B, the elasticity is −1. And there is no good reason for moving in one direction rather than the other.

To overcome these discrepancies, several arc formulas have been devised. They amount to taking an average between the value arrived at by moving from B to C and the value arrived at by moving in the reverse direction. One such arc elasticity formula is

$$e_{px} = \frac{\dfrac{x_2 - x_1}{x_2 + x_1}}{\dfrac{p_2 - p_1}{p_2 + p_1}} = \frac{\dfrac{\Delta x}{x_2 + x_1}}{\dfrac{\Delta p_x}{p_2 + p_1}}$$

where x_2 and x_1 are the quantities at the two points and p_2 and p_1 are the prices, with p_2 corresponding to x_2 and p_1 corresponding to x_1. Between the points B and C on the given demand curve the arc elasticity of demand is

$$e_{p_x} = \frac{\dfrac{200 - 100}{200 + 100}}{\dfrac{10 - 15}{10 + 15}} = \frac{100}{300} \cdot \frac{25}{-5} = \frac{2,500}{-1,500} = -1\tfrac{2}{3}$$

It is seen that this measure lies between the two other measures, namely between -3 and -1.

There are both advantages and limitations of the arc formula. Its primary advantage is that it enables us to compute the elasticity between points on the demand curve without having actually to draw the curve with precision on graph paper. For the given demand schedule we have computed the arc elasticity between B and C. We can quickly compute the elasticity between A and B and also between C and D. Between A and B we have

$$e_{p_x} = \frac{\dfrac{x_1 - x_0}{x_1 + x_0}}{\dfrac{p_1 - p_0}{p_1 + p_0}} = \frac{\dfrac{100 - 50}{100 + 50}}{\dfrac{15 - 20}{15 + 20}} = \frac{50}{150} \cdot \frac{35}{-5} = \frac{1,750}{-750} = -2\tfrac{1}{3}$$

Between C and D,

$$e_{p_x} = \frac{\dfrac{x_3 - x_2}{x_3 + x_2}}{\dfrac{p_3 - p_2}{p_3 + p_2}} = \frac{\dfrac{400 - 200}{400 + 200}}{\dfrac{5 - 10}{5 + 10}} = \frac{200}{600} \cdot \frac{15}{-5} = \frac{3,000}{-3,000} = -1$$

The arc formula, however, has certain limitations that require caution in its use. It is but an approximation to the more exact concept of point elasticity. It will be a close approximation if the points between which elasticity is measured lie close together; but it will be a very poor approximation if the points are too widely separated. The formula measures the elasticity of an arc joining the two points, like the arc joining B and C in Fig. 6.5. The farther apart are the two points, the greater will be the divergence between the arc and the curve. And consequently, the greater will be the discrepancy between elasticity on the curve and elasticity on the arc. As we let points such as B and C move closer together, the arc moves closer to the curve. In the limit as B becomes almost identical with C, the arc becomes almost identical with the curve, and the arc measurement becomes almost identical with the measurement at a point on the curve. This is why it is said that the arc elasticity is a computational approximation to the more exact concept of point elasticity. As Δp_x is allowed to approach zero, the arc approaches a tangent to the demand curve at a point.

Classifications of Elasticity

More often than not the price elasticity of demand varies from one point to another on the demand curve. Let us consider the straight-line demand curve drawn in Fig. 6.6. Three different points on the curve are indicated: P_0, P_1, and P_2. For the moment we shall concentrate on P_0. This point was deliberately chosen such that the distance $0C_0$ on the horizontal axis equals

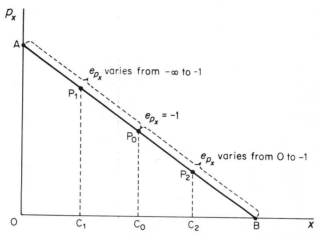

FIG. 6.6.   Varying Price Elasticity on a Straight-Line Demand Curve

the distance C_0B, i.e., the point C_0 is midway between 0 and B. Employing the geometric method for measuring elasticity at this point we have

$$e_{px} = \frac{C_0B}{-P_0C_0} \cdot \frac{P_0C_0}{0C_0} = -\frac{C_0B}{0C_0}$$

But we have just said that $0C_0$ equals C_0B. Therefore, the price elasticity at point P_0 must equal minus one.

Let us turn next to point P_1. The elasticity at this point is

$$e_{px} = \frac{C_1B}{-P_1C_1} \cdot \frac{P_1C_1}{0C_1} = -\frac{C_1B}{0C_1}$$

Comparing this with elasticity at P_0, a glance at the figure reveals that C_1B is greater than C_0B, and $0C_1$ is less than $0C_0$. Therefore, the numerical value $C_1B/0C_1$ must be larger than $C_0B/0C_0$ (which we have seen equals one). But there is a minus sign attached. It follows that $C_1B/0C_1$ is less than one algebraically, which means it is greater than one in absolute magnitude with a minus sign. For example, it might be -1.5 or -7 or -1000.

Finally, let us compare point P_2 with point P_0. The price elasticity at point P_2 is

$$e_{p_x} = \frac{C_2B}{-P_2C_2} \cdot \frac{P_2C_2}{0C_2} = -\frac{C_2B}{0C_2}$$

In this case the distance C_2B is less than C_0B, and $0C_2$, is larger than $0C_0$. The ratio $C_2B/0C_2$ must be smaller than the ratio $C_0B/0C_0$. Taking account of the minus sign, we know the price elasticity at P_2 must be greater than minus one algebraically—less than one in absolute magnitude with a minus sign. Its value might be -0.999 or $-1/2$ or -0.00003.

A general conclusion can be inferred from this illustration. For the straight-line demand curve, the price elasticity equals minus one at the point whose value on the horizontal axis is midway between the origin and the intersection of the demand curve with the horizontal axis. To the left of this point elasticity ranges from minus one (but not including minus one) to minus infinity; it varies from minus one (not including minus one) to zero to the right of the point. More generally, from the definition of elasticity and the knowledge that the slope of a straight-line demand curve is constant, it is seen that $\Delta x/\Delta p_x$ is the same value at any point on the curve. Moreover, it is a negative number because the demand curve is negatively sloped. It follows that the price elasticity must be a negative number since p_x/x is a positive number. Now as we move upward to the left along the curve, p_x becomes larger and x becomes smaller. With $\Delta x/\Delta p_x$ a constant negative number and p_x becoming larger relative to x, the elasticity must move in the direction from zero at one extreme toward minus infinity at the other.

This argument holds strictly for a straight-line demand curve. Nevertheless, in the case of a curved demand curve, there is a *tendency* (but only a tendency) for the same pattern to occur. Of course, $\Delta x/\Delta p_x$ is negative at all points on the curve just as it is on the straight-line demand curve. As one moves upward to the left, p_x increases relative to x and this component of the elasticity formula, p_x/x, increases. When it does, the elasticity tends to become larger negative. However, in this case the slope of the demand curve is not constant. It may increase or decrease, so $\Delta x/\Delta p_x$ increases or decreases, as we move in one or the other direction along the curve. That is why we say there is only a tendency for elasticity to move in the direction from zero toward minus infinity as we move upward to the left. The change in slope may enforce the increase in p_x/x or counteract it. In the final analysis, the most advisable procedure is to measure elasticity by the arc formula for different *small* segments of the demand curve. Then one can tell precisely how elasticity changes from one part of the curve to another. The important point to remember is that in the usual case one cannot assume a priori that a given demand curve has a given elasticity, nor that the elasticity is invariant with respect to movements over the entire range of the curve.

With regard to its numerical value economists have distinguished five categories of price elasticity:

(1) Zero elasticity of demand in which e_{p_x} equals zero.
(2) Relatively inelastic demand in which e_{p_x} is between zero and minus one.
(3) Unit elasticity of demand in which e_{p_x} equals minus one.
(4) Relatively elastic demand in which e_{p_x} is between minus one and minus infinity.
(5) Infinitely elastic demand in which e_{p_x} equals minus infinity.

Categories (1) and (5) are special cases in which the elasticity can be determined simply by looking at the demand curve. Fig. 6.7 shows a demand curve, labeled D, that has zero elasticity at all points on the curve. Such a demand curve constitutes a straight vertical line. In this event for any change in price, Δp_x, the change in quantity demanded, Δx, is zero. Therefore, the formula for elasticity will yield the numerical value of zero at any point on the curve. Such a demand curve is sometimes called *infinitely inelastic* be-

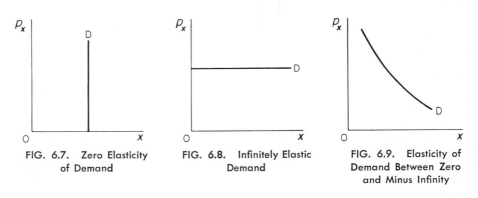

FIG. 6.7. Zero Elasticity of Demand

FIG. 6.8. Infinitely Elastic Demand

FIG. 6.9. Elasticity of Demand Between Zero and Minus Infinity

cause consumers show no response whatsoever to price changes; they will purchase just as much at any one price as they will at any other. At the opposite extreme is the infinitely elastic demand curve depicted in Fig. 6.8. Here the demand curve is drawn as a straight horizontal line, indicating that the elasticity formula yields a value of minus infinity at any point on the curve. We may interpret this as follows. For any change in price, even a very minute one, the change in quantity demanded is infinitely large. Given any Δp_x, the magnitude Δx is infinite, so e_{p_x} equals minus infinity. In more common-sense terms it means that consumers will purchase any quantity at the given price, but will purchase none at any higher price.

Needless to say, categories (1) and (5) are extremes. One very seldom encounters them in practice. Still the curve may be vertical or horizontal over some small segment. Within some restricted (usually quite small) price range there may be no reaction to price change or there may be an infinite reaction. Much more likely than either of the extreme cases is the case depicted in Fig. 6.9, where the price elasticity is between zero and minus infinity. Notice that we cannot tell merely by looking at the curve what its numerical magnitude will be. To determine whether this curve is relatively elastic, relatively inelastic, or of unit elasticity over any segment it would be necessary to compute the numerical value of elasticity. And for this purpose the arc formula will prove to be most convenient.

There is one more point on terminology that must be made clear. Though the price elasticity is a negative number, when economists speak of elasticity we often ignore the minus sign for the sake of ease in expression. Thus, we speak of elasticities of one, more than one, or less than one. The five categories can be reduced to three by the following delineation, where the minus sign of the elasticity coefficient is ignored:

(1) Inelastic demand: elasticity coefficient of less than one.
(2) Unit elasticity: elasticity coefficient equal to one.
(3) Elastic demand: elasticity coefficient greater than one.

Zero elasticity of demand may be regarded as a special case of (1), and infinitely elastic demand can be treated as a special case of (3). Because it is a more convenient language I shall follow this verbal convention. Therefore, when I refer to elastic demand, I mean one whose numerical value, disregarding the sign, is greater than one; and likewise for the other two categories. In using this terminology one should keep in the back of his mind, however, that the minus sign should be appended whenever any actual calculation is made.

Elasticity and Total Expenditures

Total expenditures on a commodity by consumers are the total sales receipts of firms that sell the commodity. Both are equal to the price per unit of the commodity multiplied by the quantity sold or bought, since the quantity sold must equal the quantity bought. There exists a relationship between the price elasticity of demand and these total expenditures, a relationship that is of foremost interest to the sellers.

Suppose we consider the effect on total expenditures of a small decrease in the price of the commodity in question. One might be tempted to conclude that since the price is to be lower, the total money outlay of consumers—hence, the total receipts by sellers—would also be less. However, the effect on total expenditures depends upon what happens to the quantity purchased, and this in turn depends upon the elasticity of demand. If the demand curve for the product is inelastic (zero elasticity or relatively inelastic) the fall in price is proportionately greater than the increase in quantity taken. In this event total expenditures will indeed decrease. On the other hand, if the demand curve is elastic over the relevant segment, the fall in price is more than compensated for by the increase in quantity taken; so total expenditures on the commodity will actually increase. Finally, the elasticity may be exactly one. Then, the proportionate fall in price is exactly equal to the proportionate increase in quantity demanded. The price decrease is exactly offset by the quantity increase so that total expenditures remain unchanged.

The effects of price changes on total expenditures can be shown diagrammatically. In Fig. 6.5, the demand curve for commodity X is drawn. Suppose the initial situation is given by point B at which the price of X is p_1 and the quantity purchased and sold is x_1. What would happen to total expenditures on X if its price were reduced to p_2? First, note that the initial total expenditures on X are given by p_1 times x_1, which is equal to the area of the rectangle formed by $0p_1Bx_1$. When the price is reduced to p_2, the quantity taken by consumers increases to x_2. The new total expenditures are measured by the area of the rectangle $0p_2Cx_2$. If the second rectangle is larger than the first, total expenditures have increased; if it is smaller, they have decreased; and if it is the same size as the first, total expenditures have remained unchanged. Now the size of the second rectangle compared to the first depends upon the price elasticity of demand for X between B and C. On an elastic segment of the curve, the area of the second rectangle will exceed the area of the first. On an inelastic segment, the area of the second rectangle will be smaller than the area of the first. If the elasticity is unity between B and C, the areas of the two rectangles will be equal.

The effects of different elasticities on total expenditures can be summarized in the following scheme.

Between Any Two Points on a Demand Curve

If	*Then*
Demand is price inelastic	Total expenditures move in the same direction as price.
Demand is price elastic	Total expenditures move in the same direction as quantity taken.
Demand has unit price elasticity	Total expenditures do not change when price changes.

An entrepreneur contemplating changes in the price of his product is directly concerned with the consequent changes in total consumer expenditures; for, as we have seen, these are his total sales receipts. If the demand for his product is relatively inelastic, for example, a price increase would increase total receipts at the same time that it decreased the quantity sold. But a decrease in the quantity produced and sold would reduce his total cost of operation, so the net effect would be to increase his total profit. However a price decrease would not be advisable because it would reduce total receipts when the quantity sold increased. The expanded production and sales would entail higher total cost. Hence, profit would decline as a result of such action.

How elastic a demand curve is depends upon the nature of the commodity under consideration and upon consumers' attitudes toward it. The main factors influencing elasticity are (1) the availability of close substitutes for the commodity, (2) the relative importance of the commodity in the budgets of consumers, and (3) the variety of uses to which the commodity can be put.

The availability of close substitutes in consumption is the most important determinant of price elasticity. Rice is a substitute for potatoes in consumption because they are both starches; public transportation is a substitute for private automobile travel. The greater the number of substitutes and the greater their degree of substitutability, the more elastic the demand for a given commodity will tend to be. If the price of the given commodity rises while the prices of others are unchanged, and if there are no other goods regarded by consumers as similar to the one whose price has risen, it is unlikely that the quantity demanded will decline very much. If, on the other hand, there are close substitutes, then the quantity demanded tends to decline significantly as consumers shift from the higher priced to the lower priced goods. For example, if the price of swordfish rises and the prices of other fish remain the same, consumers will be moved to substitute halibut, whitefish, or other fish for swordfish in their diets. Conversely, if its price falls, they will be inclined to shift from other fish to swordfish.

The price of a commodity relative to the size of consumers' incomes is a second factor influencing elasticity. Consumers are not likely to be very responsive to changes in the prices of such items as shoe polish, chewing gum, spices, or other goods whose prices are small relative to income size. Increased expenditure on them puts no significant strain on the family budget, and decreased expenditure on them puts little additional cash in the pockets of the householders. But goods that require large outlays, such as refrigerators or furniture, are likely to vary considerably in response to price changes. Consumers are more price conscious and more willing to consider substitutes. Also, such goods usually are durables, so that purchases can be deferred (until they are "on sale," for example).

The third main determinant of elasticity is the variety of uses to which a commodity can be put. The greater the number of uses in consumption, the more price elastic the demand for the commodity is likely to be. For a highly specialized product like grass seed, it is to be expected that alterations in its price will not result in large changes in the quantity demanded. It cannot be used for much besides sowing grass, so there is little room for variation in the quantity taken. In comparison, a product like pine lumber has many different uses. A fall in its price may make it economically desirable for a use that would not be considered at the higher price, and a rise in its price may prohibit its use altogether. These supplementary uses tend to make the demand more elastic.

It should be emphasized that all three criteria, and possibly some minor ones such as habit and prestige factors, need to be considered. Each criterion is but the expression of a tendency, and one may operate to offset the effect of another. The elasticity of demand is the combined effect produced by complementary and opposing forces, in which the final result depends upon their relative strengths.

PROBLEMS

1. The following market demand schedule for a commodity X is given.

Price of X	Quantity of X Demanded per Year
$10	100
9	200
8	300
7	400
6	500
5	600
4	700
3	800
2	900
1	1,000

(a) Compute by the arc formula the price elasticity of demand between the prices of $9 and $8. According to the computed elasticity, would expenditures on X increase or decrease if the price fell from $9 to $8? Why? Prove this by computing total expenditures at $9 and again at $8, noting the difference.

(b) Compute the price elasticity between $4 and $3. According to the elasticity, would expenditures on X increase or decrease if the price rose from $3 to $4? Why? Prove this by computing expenditures at each price and noting the difference.

SUGGESTED READING

A. Marshall, *Principles of Economics*, 8th ed., Book III, Chap. IV, and Book V, Chaps. I–III. London: Macmillan & Co., Ltd., 1920.

7

Causes of Shifts in Demand

So far I have been discussing the characteristics of a given stationary demand curve—drawn under the assumption that prices of other products, consumers' incomes, and consumers' tastes are all constant. It is plausible to continue to assume that consumers' tastes do not change; we do not find in practice that they are highly fluctuating. Instead, tastes appear to be relatively stable and change only slowly over long periods of time. Consumers' incomes and prices of other commodities do not show the same degree of stability, however. These determinants of demand are susceptible to short-run, sometimes violent, fluctuations.

EFFECTS OF CHANGES IN INCOME

It will help to keep our ideas in order if we first concentrate on income while continuing to hold other prices constant. In addition, to isolate the effects of income changes upon the quantity demanded, let us assume that the price of the commodity in question is also constant. Of all the determining variables included within the parenthesis of the symbolic expression of the demand function only income is allowed to vary.

Indifference Curves and Engel Curves

Just as consumers' reactions to price changes are founded upon utility theory, so too reactions to changes in income are based upon the same analytical structure. Figure 7.1 depicts several equilibria for a single consumer, each one corresponding to a different income when the prices of both commodities X and Y are held constant. As a starting point let the price of X be p_{x_1}, let the price of Y be p_{y_1}, and let income equal I_1. The individual maximizes his utility at point A, consuming x_1 units of X and y_1 units of Y.

Now suppose the consumer's income rises to I_2 so that his budget line shifts upward and to the right, parallel to the initial budget line. Given a greater income, the new budget line is tangent to a higher indifference curve, and at the point of tangency (point B) the individual consumes x_2 units of

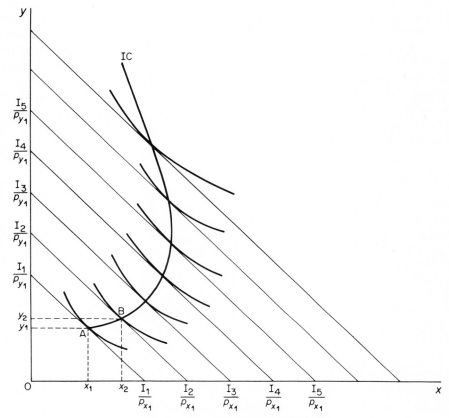

FIG. 7.1. **Income-Consumption Relationship**

X and y_2 units of Y. Consumption of both goods increases in response to the rise in income.

More generally, instead of just two different incomes, a whole range of alternative incomes can be considered. Then it is possible to describe the amounts of both commodities that would be consumed at all possible income levels. Allowing income to expand to I_3, then to I_4, and so on, Fig. 7.1 traces the individual's *income-consumption curve*, labeled IC in the diagram.

From this indifference curve analysis, a relationship between consumption of a particular good and income emerges. The quantity of X that would be consumed at each possible income is determined, and the same holds true for Y. A geometric curve relating consumption of a good to income is called an Engel curve after its originator, Ernst Engel, a German statistician of the late nineteenth century. The curve IC in Fig. 7.1 generates the two Engel curves drawn in Figs. 7.2 and 7.3, where income per unit of time is measured on the horizontal axes and quantity demanded per unit of time is measured on the vertical axes.

Applying information from Fig. 7.1 to commodity X in Fig. 7.2, we see that an income equal to I_1 yields x_1 units of X demanded by the consumer. If income were to be I_2, consumption of X would be x_2 units. Up to an income of I_5 the individual's Engel curve for commodity X is positively sloped, indicating that as income rises his consumption of X also rises. Notice, however, that the increments of x (Δx) get smaller and smaller as I is allowed to increase by equal increments (ΔI). After a point, namely, an income of I_5, the Engel curve turns downward, signifying that the quantity of X consumed would actually decrease if income were to continue to increase. That is, Δx becomes negative for ΔI positive.

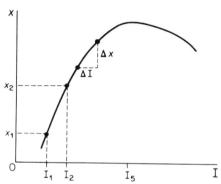

FIG. 7.2.   Engel Curve, Commodity X

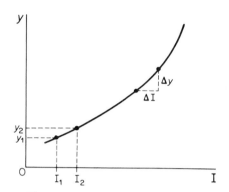

FIG. 7.3.   Engel Curve, Commodity Y

In general, a positively sloped segment of an Engel curve denotes a direct relationship between income and consumption of the commodity in question over that income range, while a negatively sloped segment denotes an inverse relationship. An Engel curve such as that shown in Fig. 7.2 might pertain to certain food items. Starting at a very low income, more is demanded as income rises. Eventually, however, other foods replace this one in the consumer's diet when he regards himself as affluent enough to switch over to better quality.

Consumption of commodity Y in Fig. 7.3 shows a different behavior. The rise in income from I_1 to I_2 produces a relatively small rise in the consumption of Y, from y_1 to y_2. But unlike the Engel curve of commodity X that of commodity Y remains positively sloped over the entire income range being considered. Moreover, as income expands by equal increments (ΔI) the increments of y (Δy) become larger and larger. Certain types of recreation might well be characterized by this form of an Engel curve. At low incomes a rise in income permits a relatively small increase in the consumption of recreation, because it is felt that "necessities" have a prior claim on the added income. As income continues to expand, and "necessities" are met, it becomes possible to spend more on recreation.

Income Elasticity of Demand

Since a given market demand curve conceptually holds constant the incomes of consumers, it follows that a change in income will shift the position of the demand curve. In what direction the market demand curve shifts depends in turn upon the slopes of consumers' Engel curves. Indeed a single Engel curve for all consumers can be constructed. This curve then shows the net reaction to income changes on the part of all consumers taken as a group. For the commodity in question if the Engel curve is positively sloped, expansions of total income will increase market demand and contractions will decrease demand.

To illustrate, Fig. 7.4 depicts the market demand curve for commodity X in three different positions. Let D_1 denote the curve in its initial position,

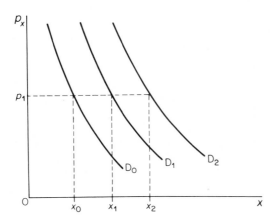

FIG. 7.4. Shifts in Market Demand for Commodity X

for which the price of Y and total consumer income are both constant. Assume the Engel curve drawn for all consumers as a group is positively sloped at the given level of income. Holding the price of Y fixed, suppose income rises. At a price of p_1 the quantity of X demanded on the market increases from x_1 to x_2 units. And the same would hold true for any other price of X we might have chosen. Had the price been higher or lower initially, it still follows that consumers would purchase more at that price when income rises. The demand curve moves from position D_1 to D_2, which is drawn for another constant income higher than the income for which D_1 was drawn. Conversely, a fall in income would shift the demand curve to the left, to a position like D_0.

The demand curves for most goods respond to income changes in the way described. They are called *superior* goods—sometimes referred to as "normal" goods because they are the usual ones. Since the Engel curve for all consumers as a group is positively sloped, demand changes in the same direction as income.

There is a small class of goods, however, that does not respond in this way. A rise in income produces a decrease in demand, the market demand curve shifts to the left; and a drop in income causes an expansion of demand, a shift to the right of the market demand curve. When this happens, the good is called an *inferior* good. Hamburger is a classic example. As income increases, consumers substitute better cuts of meat for hamburger, such as sirloin steaks. Other examples of inferior goods might be the cheaper lines of cosmetics or clothing. Because changes in income permit consumers to upgrade or downgrade the quality of goods they consume, a demand curve like D_0 in Fig. 7.4 would correspond to a relatively high income and D_2 to a relatively low income if X is an inferior good.

An inferior good has an Engel curve for consumers as a group that is negatively sloped, reflecting a decline in total consumption when income rises. One would seldom encounter an Engel curve that slopes downward over the entire range of the curve. Nevertheless, a good might be inferior over some income range and superior over another, with the result that the Engel curve is negatively sloped over some segments and positively sloped over others. Even when the slopes of Engel curves for two or more commodities have the same sign, except by accident they will not be identical curves. Just as several types of negatively sloped demand curves are possible, so several varieties of positively sloped Engel curves are possible for different commodities, some rising faster than others and each one having a different positive slope at different points on the curve.

A numerical measure of the degree of responsiveness of quantity demanded to income change is given by the income elasticity of that good. It is defined in the same way as price elasticity. In symbolic notation for the commodity X:

$$e_\mathrm{I} = \frac{\dfrac{\Delta x}{x}}{\dfrac{\Delta \mathrm{I}}{\mathrm{I}}}$$

where the numerator is the percentage change in the quantity of X demanded in response to the percentage change in income shown in the denominator.

Superior goods always have positive income elasticities, while inferior goods have negative ones. If the income elasticity for any commodity is zero, then the demand for that commodity shows no response whatever to a change in income. Given that X is a superior good, the positive value of e_I tells how responsive the demand for X is to income; the larger the value of e_I, the more responsive is demand to an income change. Similarly, for X as an inferior good, the larger is the value of e_I with a minus sign, the more does the demand for X decrease as income increases. Although most commodities have positive income elasticities, of course, the numerical value of elasticity need not be the same for all levels of income. As a matter of fact, it is conceivable that for any given commodity, its income elasticity may be zero or negative at some income levels, even though it is positive at most income levels.

It can be seen that income elasticity provides valuable information for economic science and for public policy. At the same income level, commodities such as recreation or fur coats have quite different income elasticities from those of food or housing. An arc formula analogous to the arc formula for price elasticity can be constructed, and the income elasticities of different commodities at various income levels can be compared.

EFFECTS OF CHANGES IN OTHER PRICES

We shall next take the prices of other goods out of the category of things held constant. To concentrate on their effects, income is put back into this category, along with the price of the commodity in question, and the influence of changes in other prices is examined in conceptual isolation.

Indifference Curves and Commodity Substitution

Continuing the case of two products, X and Y, Fig. 7.5 presents the impact of a change in the price of Y upon the demand for X by an individual consumer. With an income of I_1 and given prices p_{x_1} and p_{y_1}, the consumer is

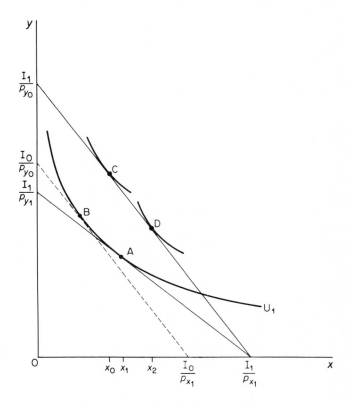

FIG. 7.5.   Income and Substitution Effects

initially in equilibrium at point A. Now suppose the price of Y falls from p_{y_1} to p_{y_0}, and other things remain the same. The consumer's budget line rotates clockwise about a fixed point on the horizontal axis. Since income and the price of X are constant, the horizontal intercept is unchanged. But with a lower price of Y the vertical intercept I_1/p_{y_0} is larger.

When the consumer adjusts to his budget alteration, he moves either to point C or to point D, depending upon his tastes and preferences. The indifference curves associated with points C and D are to be interpreted as alternative possibilities, not as curves that coexist simultaneously. We are primarily interested in what happens to his demand for commodity X. And it is seen that at C he would consume less (x_0 as compared to x_1 units) while at D he would consume more (x_2 units) in response to a drop in the price of the other commodity.

This movement from A to either C or D, called the total effect of the price change, can be broken down into two components: (1) a pure substitution of the lower-priced good for the higher-priced one, and (2) an income effect due to an alteration in real income created by the price change. Notice first that a fall in the price of Y has actually increased the consumer's *real* income, his purchasing power. With the same money income he could buy the same amounts of X and Y that he did before the price of Y fell, and still have something left over. This money income "left over" acts just like a pure rise in money income. He can use it to purchase more of X, more of Y, or more of both. To illustrate, suppose the prices of X and Y are each $1. Given a money income of $100, assume an individual purchases 50 units of each. Now let the price of Y drop to 50 cents. He can consume 50 units of each by spending $75, leaving him with $25 additional purchasing power. This rise in real income due to the price drop is logically and conceptually no different than a $25 increase in money income.

Since a lower price of Y, with constant money income and a constant price of X, is equivalent to a rise in money income, the price decline has an "income effect." To isolate the substitution effect of the change in price we shall conceptually take away from the consumer the amount "left over." That is, we shall compensate for the income change by temporarily removing its influence. This is done by shifting the budget line toward the origin. How far toward the origin? Far enough to restore the consumer's original utility level. By reducing his money income from I_1 to I_0 we make the consumer no better off than he was before the price change—in the sense that his equilibrium point lies on the same indifference curve. With a money income of I_0, and given that the prices of X and Y are p_{x_1} and p_{y_0} respectively, the broken-line budget constraint is tangent to indifference curve U_1. Thus, we isolate the substitution effect of Y for X. When Y is cheaper than X, the consumer moves from point A to point B along the indifference curve U_1.

We know, however, that his real income has risen in actuality. Therefore, let us next restore to him the money income we initially took away. We conceptually return the difference between I_0 and I_1, shifting the budget line upward to the right. The consumer moves from point B to, say, point C.

At point C as compared to point B he consumes more of both X and Y. This is the income effect of a change in the price of Y.

Granted that X and Y are both superior goods, the income effect operates to increase the quantity demanded of both. If the substitution effect is stronger than the income effect, the net effect is to increase the quantity demanded of Y and to decrease the quantity demanded of X, whose price has not changed. Thus in Fig. 7.5 at point C as compared to the original point A the consumption of Y is greater and the consumption of X is smaller because the substitution effect dominates.

It is not necessary, though, that the substitution effect dominate in all cases. Point D presents an example in which the income effect outweighs the substitution effect. In response to a drop in the price of Y from p_{y_1} to p_{y_0}, the consumer moves from point A to point B, given the compensating variation in income. This is the substitution effect, and as before less X is consumed. Replacing the income taken away will result in the income effect, a movement from B to D. Moreover, the income effect on commodity X is stronger than the substitution effect. Notice that the net effect of a decrease in the price of Y is to increase the consumption of Y *and also to increase the consumption of* X. Point D entails more of both X and Y as compared to point A.

Cross Elasticity of Demand

The foregoing utility analysis shows that a given change in the price of commodity Y may either increase or decrease an individual's demand for commodity X. If the majority of consumers move from points like A to points like C, the aggregate market demand for X will decrease. On the other hand, if most move to points like D, the market demand for X will increase in response to a fall in the price of Y.

Among interrelated goods an important distinction is that drawn between goods that are substitutes in consumption and those that are complements in consumption. If X and Y are *substitutes* in consumption, a fall in the price of Y decreases the demand for X, and a rise in its price increases the demand for X. If X and Y are *complements* in consumption, a fall in the price of Y increases the demand for X, and a rise in its price decreases the demand for X.

Figure 7.4 serves to illustrate the effects of substitution and complementarity. Let D_1 once more denote the curve in its initial position, for which the price of Y is a given constant. To begin, let us suppose that X and Y are substitutes for each other. They are like butter and oleomargarine, or pork and lamb. We first wish to know what will happen to the demand for X if the price of Y *rises*. Since Y becomes more expensive relative to X, consumers will shift from Y to X. They replace Y by X in their consumption pattern. Consequently, for any given price of X more will be taken, a phenomenon represented geometrically as a shift to the right in the demand curve for X. For any price of X we might pick, such as p_1, the quantity taken is x_2, which is greater than x_1. And the same holds for any other price of X we might choose. The demand curve moves from a position like D_1 to D_2, which is drawn for another constant price of Y higher than the price for which D_1 was drawn. Conversely, if the price of Y *falls* by a certain amount, consumers substitute Y for X because Y is now relatively less expensive. Then for any price of X, such as p_1, less of X is consumed, e.g., x_0, which is less than x_1. The curve shifts to the left to a position like D_0. To illustrate, if the price of pork rises, consumers will substitute lamb for pork, demanding a larger quantity of lamb at any given price of lamb. Just the reverse reaction follows upon a fall in the price of pork.

Next let us suppose that X and Y are complementary to each other in consumption. Shirts and neckties or automobiles and gasoline are illustrations of complementary goods. In the case of complements, price changes in Y have effects on the demand for X just the opposite of substitutes. A *rise* in the price of Y means that less of Y will be demanded (consumers move upward to the left along their demand curve for that product). Since less of Y is consumed and since X complements Y, less of X will be consumed for any price of X. If automobiles rise in price and consumers purchase fewer automobiles, then the consumption of gasoline will decline even though its price is unchanged. At p_1, for example, consumers demand x_0 of X, which is less than x_1, and the same is true for any other price of X. The demand curve for X shifts to the left to a position like D_0. Just the reverse holds for a *fall* in the price of Y. More Y is consumed, entailing a greater consumption of X, so the demand curve for X shifts to the right to a position like D_2. A lower price and greater consumption of shirts will stimulate the demand for neckties.

If D_1 is treated as the demand curve for X in its initial position, then increases in the demand for X (shifts to the right in the curve) are produced by reductions in the prices of complements, or by rises in the prices of substitutes, or by both operating together. Decreases in the demand for X (shifts to the left in the curve) result from rises in the prices of complements, or reductions in the prices of substitutes, or by both operating together.

The cross elasticity of demand is a quantitative measure of the extent to which commodities are related to each other. The cross elasticity of demand for X with respect to the price of Y is defined as the percentage change in the quantity of X demanded that results from a percentage change in the price of Y, when the price change is small. The cross elasticity of the demand for X with respect to the price of Y is written symbolically as

$$e_{p_y} = \frac{\dfrac{\Delta x}{x}}{\dfrac{\Delta p_y}{p_y}}$$

Like the income elasticity concept, observe that the cross elasticity concept differs from the price elasticity concept only in that p_y is substituted for

p_x in the price elasticity definition. The numerator in the above expression is the percentage change in the quantity of X demanded that results from the percentage change in the price of Y, shown as the denominator. It is a measure of the responsiveness of the quantity of X taken to changes in another price rather than in its own price.

If this magnitude is zero, then the quantity of X demanded does not change when the price of Y changes. The demand for X is completely independent of the price of Y. One would expect to find its value as approximately zero for commodities that have very little or no connection with each other, such as the effect of the price of seashells on the demand for shoelaces. The larger is its value, either positive or negative, the more closely are the two commodities interrelated.

The cross elasticity of demand has a significant bearing on the relationships between substitute and complementary commodities. *When two commodities are substitutes for each other, the cross elasticity is positive.* Granted that X and Y are substitutes in consumption, we have seen that a fall in the price of Y reduces the demand for X, and a rise in the price of Y increases the demand for X. It follows that Δx will be positive whenever Δp_y is positive, and negative whenever Δp_y is negative. Hence, e_{p_y} will be positive. For X and Y as complements, just the opposite holds. *Complementary goods show a negative cross elasticity.* Whenever Δp_y is positive, Δx is negative, and Δx is positive when Δp_y is negative. Therefore, e_{p_y} will be negative. Given that two goods are substitutes, the larger is e_{p_y} with a plus sign, the greater is the degree of substitutability between X and Y. Given that the two goods are complements, the larger is e_{p_y} with a minus sign, the closer is the degree of complementarity between X and Y.

Take note that these propositions state: *if* the goods are known to be substitutes or complements, *then* it follows that the cross elasticity will have a particular sign. But it does not work both ways. We cannot say, for example, that if cross elasticity is negative, then the goods are complements. The explanation for this lack of symmetry lies in the income and substitution effects of price changes.

Complementary goods show a negative cross elasticity. Nevertheless, even though two goods are substitutes in consumption—in the sense that the substitution effect alone operates in the appropriate way—a fall in the price of Y can have the result of increasing the demand for X. A positive income effect on X may outweigh the substitution effect, so the cross elasticity is negative in this case as well. If substitutes are defined as goods for which the substitution effect outweighs any positive income effect, we can then say that substitutes show a positive cross elasticity *and* that a positive cross elasticity signifies substitutes in consumption. A negative cross elasticity, on the other hand, implies either complements in consumption or a stronger positive income effect on X.

Actual instances of a dominating income effect are likely to be rare. The income effect is spread over a multitude of different commodities, so its impact on any one is probably quite small. But the substitution effect (or the complementarity effect) is likely to be very strong between any two particular goods. Keeping in mind the reservation mentioned above, therefore, for most practical purposes we may take a positive cross elasticity to be indicative of substitute goods and a negative cross elasticity to be indicative of complementary goods.

SUMMARY OF CONSUMER DEMAND THEORY

The demand by consumers for any commodity can be expressed in terms of a relationship between the quantity demanded of that commodity and all the variables that determine it. For any commodity X the demand relationship is written in symbolic notation as

$$x_d = d(p_x; \; p_y, \; p_z, \; \cdots; \; I; \; T)$$

where x_d denotes the quantity demanded of commodity X by consumers per unit of time; p_x denotes the price of X; p_y, p_z, etc., denote the prices of other goods Y, Z, etc., that influence the quantity demanded of X; I denotes consumers' income per unit of time; and T denotes consumers' tastes. The equality sign and the symbol d mean that x_d is a function of, or depends upon, all the variables inside the parentheses. From the utility theory of consumer behavior, employing the axiom that each consumer maximizes his utility, it is possible to specify the way in which each of these determining variables influences the quantity demanded.

Geometrical diagrams are used as tools to represent the way in which each variable taken separately exercises its influence on the quantity demanded, under the assumption that all other variables are conceptually held constant. Tastes are assumed to be stable, but all other variables in the parentheses are allowed to vary. And a curve describes the way in which the quantity demanded is related to each of these. For example, one can construct an Engel curve relating the quantity demanded to income for constant prices and tastes. Reactions of the quantity demanded to income are then described by movements along this curve. And changes in the price of this commodity or changes in the prices of other commodities cause the entire Engel curve to shift position. One might also construct a curve relating the quantity demanded of X to, say, the price of Y. Then responses in the quantity of X demanded to changes in any other price, including its own, or to changes in income, can be represented by shifts in the position of this curve. Economists have found it more convenient and useful, however, to relate the quantity demanded to its own price, and to denote responses to its own price by movements along the curve. This is the familiar demand curve drawn for constant prices of other commodities, income, and tastes. Variations in these other variables result in shifts in the entire demand curve. Consequently, when a demand schedule and its corresponding curve are constructed, one does not in effect state that these other variables are *in fact* fixed; it is assumed only that they are provisionally or conceptually held constant for the purpose of investigating the effects of the price of X on the quantity of X demanded. Account is taken of these other determinants of demand in that they fix the position of the demand curve, causing it to shift position when they fluctuate.

Quantitative measurements have been devised to determine the degree of influence exerted by the determining variables on the quantity demanded. Price elasticity of demand measures the responsiveness of the quantity demanded to changes in the price of the commodity. Cross elasticity of demand measures the degree of influence exerted by the prices of other commodities, especially the prices of substitutes and complements. Finally, the income elasticity of demand enables one to distinguish between superior and inferior goods and to measure the responsiveness of quantity demanded to income changes.

Since in demand theory one must deal (1) with movements along a given demand curve and (2) with shifts in the position of the curve, it is necessary that certain distinctions in terminology be made clear. When I speak of a *change in demand* I shall mean a shift in the demand curve, not a movement along a given demand curve. For a movement along the curve in response to a price change I shall speak of a *change in the quantity demanded*. Thus, apparently contradictory statements can be reconciled. One often hears such statements as "The demand went up and therefore price went up" and "Price went up and therefore demand went down." The first entails a correct conclusion if by *demand went up* one means demand increased. That is, the demand curve shifted to the right, so it intersects the supply curve at a higher price. The second statement entails a correct conclusion if by *demand went down* one means the quantity demanded, as distinct from demand, decreased. This is a movement upward and to the left along the stationary demand curve. To avoid such ambiguities it is common practice to restrict the phrase *change in demand* to a shift in the demand curve. Movements along the stationary demand curve are referred to as changes in the quantity demanded. This distinction in terminology underscores the precise meaning of demand as a relationship between quantity demanded and price.

PROBLEMS

1. Suppose it is known that commodities Y and Z are both substitutes in consumption for commodity X. Initially the price of X is $5 and the quantity demanded is 150 units per week. At the same time the price of Y is $8 and the price of Z is $2.

(*a*) Assume the price of Y falls to $7 while the price of Z is unchanged. All other product prices and consumer income are also constant. When the price of Y falls, it is observed that the quantity of X demanded at $5 declines from 150 to 100 units. Using the arc formula

$$e_{p_y} = \frac{\dfrac{x_2 - x_1}{x_2 + x_1}}{\dfrac{p_{y2} - p_{y1}}{p_{y2} + p_{y1}}}$$

compute the cross elasticity of demand for X with respect to the price of Y.

(b) Assume the price of Z falls from \$2 to \$1 while the price of Y remains at its initial value of \$8. All other product prices and income are also constant. When the price of Z drops, it is observed that the quantity demanded of X at \$5 declines from 150 to 50 units per week. Using the arc formula

$$e_{p_z} = \frac{\dfrac{x_2 - x_1}{x_2 + x_1}}{\dfrac{p_{z2} - p_{z1}}{p_{z2} + p_{z1}}}$$

compute the cross elasticity of demand for X with respect to the price of Z.

(c) Over the range of price changes given, is commodity Y or commodity Z the closer substitute for commodity X? Explain.

2. At a price of \$5, suppose the quantity demanded of commodity X is 500 units per month. At a price of \$5 the quantity demanded of commodity Y is 1000 units per month. Both of these conditions hold when total consumer income is \$10 billion per month. Now assume that consumer income rises to \$12 billion per month while all product prices are constant. As a consequence the quantity of X demanded at a price of \$5 changes to 550 units per month; the quantity of Y demanded at \$5 changes to 900 units per month.

(a) Using the arc formula

$$e_I = \frac{\dfrac{x_2 - x_1}{x_2 + x_1}}{\dfrac{I_2 - I_1}{I_2 + I_1}}$$

compute the income elasticity of demand for X.

(b) Using the arc formula

$$e_I = \frac{\dfrac{y_2 - y_1}{y_2 + y_1}}{\dfrac{I_2 - I_1}{I_2 + I_1}}$$

compute the income elasticity of demand for Y.

(c) Over the given income range, which commodity is the inferior good? Explain.

SUGGESTED READING

G. J. Stigler, *The Theory of Price*, rev. ed., Chap. 4. New York: The Macmillan Company, 1952.

J. S. Duesenberry and L. E. Preston, *Cases and Problems in Economics*, Chap. 3. Englewood Cliffs, N. J.: Prentice-Hall, Inc., 1960.

8

Applications of
Demand Analysis

In a competitive market the equilibrium price of a commodity, the price prevailing in the market, is determined by both demand and supply. In this chapter our interest will be centered on the analysis of factors influencing demand, and on their consequences for price, expenditures, and production. We shall allow for changes in both demand and supply, but the causes of changes in supply will not be treated in detail. A full description of the determinants of market supply under competition must await the analysis of cost and production that follows in Chapters 9–14. Having studied the theory of consumer behavior and the characteristics of demand, however, we are in a position to examine the demand side of the market in considerable detail.

THEORETICAL APPLICATIONS

Substitute Commodities

One of the most intricate problems in demand theory is the interrelationship of two or more commodities. Suppose we are interested in two substitutable goods, butter and oleomargarine. To analyze the effects of change, it is necessary to have some starting point from which change can be measured, so we begin with initial equilibrium in the markets for both commodities. The hypothetical market conditions for butter and oleomargarine are depicted in Fig. 8.1 and 8.2 respectively. The price of butter is denoted by p_b and is measured on the vertical axis of Fig. 8.1; the quantity of butter per unit of time, represented by b, is measured on the horizontal axis. Similarly, for oleomargarine, p_m on the vertical axis of Fig. 8.2 signifies its price and m on the horizontal axis its quantity per unit of time.

For the moment we shall ignore the broken demand and supply curves and concentrate on the solid curves in both diagrams. D_b is the demand curve, and S_b the supply curve, for butter. Likewise, D_m and S_m represent the demand and supply curves respectively for oleomargarine. It is seen from Fig. 8.1 that p_{b_1} is the initial price of butter, and b_1 is the initial quantity

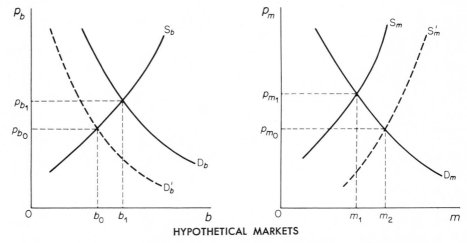

HYPOTHETICAL MARKETS

FIG. 8.1.   For Butter   FIG. 8.2.   For Oleomargarine

bought and sold. Figure 8.2 shows that p_{m_1} is the price of oleomargarine at which m_1 is the quantity exchanged on the market. Equilibrium exists in each market.

We postulate that the supply of oleomargarine increases. This might result from some technological improvement or a reduction in the prices of resources used in its manufacture. Whatever the cause, we wish to know what effects the increase in supply will have upon (1) the price and quantity traded of oleomargarine, and (2) the price and quantity traded of butter. To isolate these effects we assume nothing happens at the same time to the supply curve for butter or to the demand curve for oleomargarine. If we know that in fact they too have changed, we can take this into account later, after we have examined the effect of the change in the supply of oleomargarine.

The increase in supply of oleomargarine is shown in Fig. 8.2. The supply curve shifts to the right and in its new position is denoted by S'_m. Since the demand for oleomargarine has not changed, the price of oleomargarine falls to p_{m_0} and the quantity traded on the market increases to m_2. A new equilibrium is determined in that market.

The reason consumers move downward and to the right along their demand curve for oleomargarine is that oleomargarine becomes cheaper relative to butter when the supply of oleomargarine increases. Consumers substitute oleomargarine for butter in consumption. When the prices of butter and oleomargarine were p_{b_1} and p_{m_1} respectively, consumers were in equilibrium. With the increased supply of oleomargarine, however, the price of oleomargarine drops, and consumers begin substituting; they begin replacing butter by oleomargarine for various uses in their consumption pattern. Hence, at the price p_{b_1} consumers would take less butter, and likewise for any other price of butter that might have prevailed at the former equilibrium. This is equivalent to saying that the demand curve for butter shifts to the left.

The decrease in demand for butter continues until consumers no longer wish to make further substitutions, when the price of butter has been reduced to a level at which consumers regard the price spread between the two goods as one at which they are again in equilibrium. The new equilibrium price of butter is shown as p_{b_0} in Fig. 8.1. The effect on butter of an increase in supply of oleomargarine is to decrease the demand for butter to D_b'—with the result that the price of butter falls to p_{b_0} and the quantity exchanged is reduced to b_0.

Note that both prices have fallen; but the quantity demanded and supplied of oleomargarine has increased while the quantity of butter has decreased. Of course, the roles played by butter and oleomargarine in this illustration can be reversed. The results are equally valid if one substitutes the word *oleomargarine* everywhere the word *butter* appears, and vice versa. Also, the analysis extends to a decrease in the supply of one good rather than an increase. Then the supply curve for the good in question shifts to the left, raising the price of that good and decreasing its quantity as consumers substitute the other good for it. This substitution is reflected in an increased demand for the other good, with a consequent rise in its price and an increase in the quantity exchanged.

There is a related question that bears on this problem. Clearly in our illustration the total expenditures on butter have declined, for both its price and quantity exchanged have declined. But what about the total expenditures on oleomargarine? One might be tempted to conclude that since less is spent on butter, more must now be spent on oleomargarine. Not necessarily! This would be true if the price elasticity of demand for oleomargarine were greater than one. If, on the other hand, the demand for oleomargarine is price inelastic, total expenditures on the commodity decrease when its price falls. And then less is spent on both commodities. The possibility of this result is not surprising if one remembers that there are other complementary and substitute goods for both oleomargarine and butter on which more or less can be spent. The money not now spent on either of these can be spent elsewhere.

There is another interesting question here that will be left unanswered. What if the two goods in question are complements in consumption rather than substitutes? Then what would be the effect of an increase (or decrease) in the supply of one on the prices and quantities exchanged of each? The solution to this problem is left as an exercise.

Incidence of Taxation

A second area in which demand theory provides valuable information is that of taxation. Suppose the government imposes a tax on a given commodity; call it commodity X. This tax is assumed to be a fixed amount per unit of the commodity sold. Furthermore, it is collected by the government from the sellers, the usual procedure followed by the government in such cases to facilitate enforcement. Two questions are posed: (1) What will happen to the price of the commodity and the quantity exchanged? (2) Who will pay the tax? The latter question needs some amplification. By "Who pays the tax?" is meant "Do sellers pay all of it?" or "Do buyers pay all of it?" or "Do they share it? and, if so, who pays the greater part?" The final resting place of the tax, the extent to which it is passed on from sellers to buyers in this case, is called the incidence of taxation.

Figure 8.3 represents the market for commodity X. The initial market demand for the commodity is given as curve D, and the supply as S. A price of p_1 prevails and an amount x_1 of the commodity is exchanged on the market.

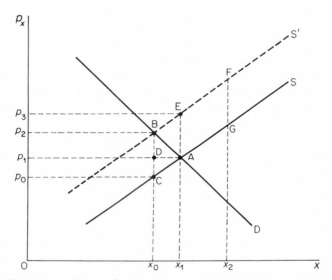

FIG. 8.3.   Incidence of a Fixed Tax per Unit of the Commodity Sold

Given these initial conditions, let a tax of a given amount per unit sold be imposed. To isolate the effects of the tax alone, assume no change in demand occurs concurrently and nothing else happens to alter the supply curve. The consequence of the tax is to shift the supply curve to the left. A moment's reflection on the reactions of sellers will show why this is so. The supply curve tells us the minimum prices at which alternative quantities of the product would be offered on the market. When the tax is collected from sellers, they attempt to raise their prices by the amount of the tax in an effort to pass the tax on to the buyers. Pick any quantity, such as x_0 in the diagram. If before the tax sellers must have a price of at least p_0 by definition of the supply curve, then they will charge a price of p_2 for that quantity, where the amount of the tax is p_2 minus p_0 per unit sold. That is, sellers must still receive the same *net* price (market price minus the tax per unit) that they did before the tax. This is true for x_0 and for any other quantity.

For the quantities x_1 and x_2 the price charged to buyers inclusive of the tax will exceed the old price by the amount of the tax.

This reaction on the part of sellers can be described by raising the supply curve by the amount of the tax per unit of the commodity. Such a shift in the position of the supply curve is equivalent to saying that for every possible quantity offered, the price sellers will charge is higher by the amount of the tax per unit. The market supply curve in its new position will lie above the former supply curve by a distance equal to the amount of the tax per unit; S' is parallel to S and the distance between them for any value on the horizontal axis equals the amount of the tax. Hence, in Fig. 8.3 the tax per unit equals the vertical distance from C to B, which in turn equals the distance from A to E and also the distance from G to F. But raising the supply curve in this way is tantamount to shifting it to the left by a fixed distance at each point; for each possible price less will be offered on the market. There is a decrease in supply.

The consequence on price and quantity exchanged are seen immediately. Since the demand curve does not shift, it intersects the supply curve at the point B, at which the price is p_2 and the quantity traded is x_0. The effect of the tax is to raise the price of the product and reduce the quantity exchanged.

We saw that producers attempt to pass the tax on to consumers. But are they completely successful? In the final outcome consumers who purchase the commodity pay a price of p_2. Since the tax collected from sellers by the government is p_2 minus p_0, however, the net price received by sellers after the tax is p_0. Before the tax any buyer purchasing the product paid p_1. Now he pays p_2. It follows that the part of the tax he pays is p_2 minus p_1. Before the tax sellers received p_1, whereas after charging p_2 and paying the tax to the government, they receive p_0. They still pay a part of the tax, namely p_1 minus p_0. The total amount of the tax per unit is indicated in Fig. 8.3 by the vertical distance from point C to point B. The portion paid by consumers equals the distance from D to B; that paid by producers equals the distance from C to D.

The common-sense explanation of this theoretical analysis is clear. Starting with a price of p_1, sellers contemplate raising the actual price to p_3, where $(p_3 - p_1)$ equals $(p_2 - p_0)$ in the diagram. But there is no equilibrium at point E. Consumers would not be on their demand curve, indicating that they are unwilling to pay p_3 for a quantity of x_1. Finding that they cannot sell x_1 at a price of p_3 sellers are forced to charge a lower price. Given the new supply conditions, point B is the only price-quantity combination that satisfies both the demand and supply relationships. Sellers find the demand to be such that they can charge at most p_2, at which price they are compelled to pay part of the tax.

There are conceivable situations under which one or the other party would bear the full burden of the tax. If demand for the product has zero price elasticity, a tax of p_3 minus p_1 is borne entirely by consumers. They will take x_1 at a price of p_1; but they will also take x_1 at a price of p_3. Therefore, sellers can raise the price by the full amount of the tax per unit and suffer no cutback in sales. At the opposite extreme the demand for X is infinitely price elastic, which means consumers would pay p_1 for any quantity but no higher price. The price cannot rise when supply decreases, so the full impact of the tax is felt in a decline of the quantity sold. The demand curve is horizontal and intersects S′ at a price of p_1. Since a tax of $(p_3 - p_1)$ is collected by the government from sellers and since the price charged by sellers does not rise, the full burden of the tax falls on the sellers.

These two extreme cases, zero elasticity under which buyers pay the full tax and infinite elasticity under which sellers pay the full tax, illustrate the importance of price elasticity of demand for the incidence of taxation. The proportionate shares of the tax borne by the two groups in all intermediate cases depend upon the elasticity of demand over the relevant segment of the demand curve. The more price elastic is the demand for the product over that range, the smaller will be the share paid by consumers. Obviously, measurements of price elasticity of demand are very useful in deciding which commodities the government shall tax in pursuing an enlightened tax policy. If a sales tax is one designed to affect consumers primarily, then it should be imposed on commodities with very inelastic demands. If, on the other hand, the tax is intended to rest lightly on consumers but to bear strongly on producers, commodities with more elastic demands should be chosen.

Production and Price Effects of Income Changes

Sometimes economists, businessmen, or public officials wish to know what effects an increase in national income will have upon the outputs of various commodities. When households receive an addition to their disposable or spendable income (resulting perhaps from a reduction in the income tax) questions may arise as to the direction and extent to which the prices and production of various commodities will be altered. For any given commodity the consequences of a change in income on its price and output depend upon two things: (1) the income elasticity of demand for that commodity and (2) its price elasticity of supply.

The price elasticity of supply is defined formally in the same way as the price elasticity of demand, and the same methods of computation are employed. It is the percentage change in the quantity supplied in response to a percentage change in the price of the commodity, where the price change is small. The difference between the price elasticities of demand and supply lies in their signs. In general the price elasticity of supply is a positive number rather than a negative number because the supply curve is positively sloped. And it may vary from zero (corresponding to a vertical line) to infinity (corresponding to a horizontal line). The greater is its positive value, the greater is the elasticity of supply. Changes in total expenditures—or sales receipts—as one moves along a supply curve always move in the same direction as price changes, because price and quantity increase and decrease together. There is no question about whether a given price change increases or decreases total expenditures. Hence, there is no need to delineate supply elasticities into categories of unity, more than unity, or less than unity. Comparisons among different numerical values of elasticity at various points on a given supply curve and comparisons among different supply curves are still useful, however, as we shall see.

Suppose that households receive an increase in income. We wish to compare the effects of this on two commodities, X and Y. For convenience, we shall assume that their quantities and prices are measured in the same units. The markets for X and Y are depicted in Fig. 8.4 and 8.5 respectively. Ignore the broken-line supply curve in Fig. 8.5 for the moment, and assume that

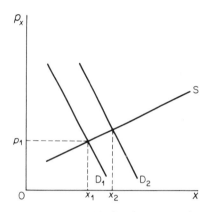

FIG. 8.4. Market for Commodity X

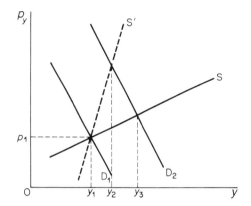

FIG. 8.5. Market for Commodity Y

the solid curve labeled S represents actual supply. The curves labeled D_1 in both diagrams are the initial demand curves. Further assume that the supply curves S for the two commodities are identical and stationary, and also that the initial equilibrium prices are the same for both commodities, namely p_1.

Now suppose that a given fixed increase in consumer income occurs. Both commodities are assumed to be superior goods, so the demand for each increases when income rises. Nevertheless, they have quite different (positive) income elasticities of demand; the income elasticity for X is very small relative to the income elasticity for Y. This means that for a given increase in income the demand curve for Y will shift to the right by a greater distance than will the demand curve for X. D_2 in both diagrams represents the demand curves in their new positions. Then the effect of the increase in income is to increase the quantity traded of Y much more than it increases the quantity traded of X. The expansion from y_1 to y_3 is almost double the expansion from x_1 to x_2. And, incidentally, the price of Y rises more than does the price of X. For two commodities with identical price elasticities of supply, the one with the greater income elasticity of demand experiences the greater responsiveness in output—and its final price rise will be somewhat more.

Suppose, however, that instead of S the supply curve for Y were S' in Fig. 8.5. This supply curve is much less price elastic than is S. Were this the case, the greater income elasticity of demand possessed by Y would not result in a final increase in the output of Y which exceeds the increase in the output of X. The horizontal distance between y_1 and y_2 is smaller than the distance between x_1 and x_2. A very small price elasticity of supply has counteracted the greater income elasticity of demand. In the case of commodity Y the increase in income is felt almost entirely in an upward movement in its price.

It follows that the effects of an increase in income on the prices and outputs of two or more commodities depend upon their comparative income elasticities of demand and price elasticities of supply. For identical price elasticities of supply, the commodities with the greater income elasticities of demand experience proportionately greater expansions in output. And for the same income elasticities of demand, the commodities with the greater price elasticities of supply experience proportionately greater expansions in output. Given sufficient differences in these two elasticities, the results of an increase in income will hinge on their relative strengths. For together they determine whether the rise in income will find its effect primarily in greater production or primarily in price increases. Again it can be seen that abstract theoretical concepts such as elasticities have widespread applications in concrete situations.

Less Obvious Examples

There is a temptation to assume that the theory of demand applies only to certain privately produced goods and services, such as food, automobiles, wigs, or babysitting services. Substitution of one good for another in response to price changes and variations of consumption in response to income changes are apparent. But some other consumable products—especially those supplied by nonprofit institutions or the public sector of the economy —may be viewed in terms of socially determined needs or fixed quantities established by custom. More careful examination reveals, however, that the theory of demand is no less applicable to these "commodities."

The demand for hospitalization is one example. It would appear on the surface that the decision to be hospitalized and the duration of stay are based solely upon a physician's prescription rather than the price of hospitalization. On the contrary, the quantity of hospital care consumed per unit of time can be varied by a patient. Except in emergency cases, if hospitalization costs are extremely high, people will remain at home with family care, or leave the hospital after only a short stay and complete their recuperation at home. If the cost (price) of hospital care declines, people will enter for less serious illnesses and remain longer. The experience with socialized medicine in Europe has revealed this pattern of behavior. The same applies to the purchase of drugs and medical advice. If prices are high, consumers substitute home remedies for manufactured drugs, or they simply bear with a virus rather than consult a physician; warts are not removed; physical checkups are foregone. At lower prices, comfort and faster recovery are substituted, so the quantity consumed is inversely related to price.

The demand for vacations is another example. It would seem that the theory of demand has no relevance. After all, an individual employed by a business firm is normally allowed one vacation of a specified duration each year. How can more or fewer vacations be taken in response to changes in price or income? One must ask, in turn, what constitutes a flow of vacation services per unit of time. A fixed amount of time off the job with pay can be spent repairing the house, working at another temporary job, going to ball games, visiting national parks, traveling in Europe, etc. A consumer can purchase more vacation in the sense that he can spend more of the time released from regular employment in leisure activities or in consuming more services offered by hotels, parks, and other sources of recreation. If the prices of such services decline, families will purchase a larger quantity per fixed period of time. Furthermore, as the family income rises, it is possible for the head of the household to request additional unpaid time without sacrificing as many other goods and services purchased out of income. Extended vacation time is probably a major superior good in the American economy.

Goods and services supplied in whole or in part by the public sector are often referred to as needs, in contrast to variable quantities demanded by the population. Consider the demand for water. People cannot live without water. However, we can and do live with more or less, depending upon the price of water. In arid regions, people conserve water because it is very costly to pump the water from great depths or to pipe it in from distant regions, and therefore the price is relatively high. Residential areas have smaller lawns, sidewalks are swept rather than washed, automobiles are washed less often. Where water is plentiful, it is cheaper, and as a consequence, is used in larger volume. Thus, the quantity demanded in the entire economy varies inversely with price because of different prices and quantities demanded in the various regions of the economy.

The theory of demand applies also to education, police protection, municipal parking areas, antiballistic missiles, mental health services, and a host of other goods and services that are not normally construed as commodities exchangeable in the market place. Each such good or service requires the use of resources if it is to be provided. Consequently, it must be paid for, whether the payment is made explicitly in the form of a quoted market price or implicitly through charitable contributions or tax payments to the public authority. The essential point is that the quantity wanted by consumers depends upon the price that has to be paid and upon their ability to pay (income). The theory of demand is an analysis of choices among alternatives. A *need* may be defined as something for which there are no substitutable alternatives. Anything that is not free and has substitutable alternatives will be wanted in variable amounts that depend upon the income of the users and the price of that thing relative to the price of its substitutes, whatever they may be. The theory of demand is an analytical framework, which, with proper adaptation to each particular institution or custom, helps to explain the quantities of all nonfree goods or services produced and consumed in society.

STATISTICAL MEASUREMENT OF DEMAND

Applications of demand theory to hypothetical problems enables us to see how the concepts of analysis can be used to interpret and to explain market phenomena. Given fluctuations in the market for any commodity, or certain disturbances imposed from the outside, the consequences on price and quantity traded can be traced. These fluctuations or disturbances are expressed by means of changes in demand and/or supply. Concepts such as price, cross, and income elasticities are brought to bear on the problem in order to determine the effects on total expenditures, on production or consumption.

Notice that in hypothetical problems it is assumed that the demand and supply curves are known (their positions and slopes are known). It is also assumed for either curve that both the direction and the magnitude of any shift are known. Since the commodity is hypothetical and since we are interested in the methods of analyzing the effects of change, this is a valid and useful procedure. Given the principles of economic theory, we can tell in what *direction* price and quantity traded will change in response to given changes in income, taxes, other prices, and so forth. Whether price will rise or fall or remain unchanged, for example, can be predicted from knowledge of the theory. Not only the direction but also the *magnitude* of price-quantity changes can be determined precisely, because we have already assumed that we know the extent as well as the direction of shifts in the curves.

For an actual commodity in which we might be interested, economic theory will again enable us to predict the *direction* of price-quantity changes in response to alterations in income or other prices considered in isolation. But *how much* they will change is another matter. Unless we do in fact know the demand and supply conditions for the actual good, we cannot answer the question of how much price and quantity exchanged will be altered by any shift in demand or supply.

The significance of this distinction can be seen by asking the following questions: Can we tell, merely by thinking about it, what the demand is for flowers in the United States today? Can we tell what it was two years ago? Can we tell what the demand is for automobiles? for education? for medical services? Obviously we cannot. And unless we can answer that, by some means, we do know what these demand conditions are in fact, we are unable to answer quantitative questions about changes in their prices and quantities. Knowledge of theory will tell us whether a change in their respective supplies would raise or lower prices, if their demands do not change. But we cannot say by how much prices would change. Similarly, we can tell that a rise in income—if other prices and tastes remain constant—would increase their demands, with a consequent rise in prices and an expansion in quantities traded, if their supplies do not change. Determining how much prices would rise or fall, however, requires something in addition to theoretical reasoning: factual quantitative knowledge of demand and supply.

Theory and Measurement

This book is a text on economic theory. If theory is to be perceived in its proper perspective, it should be viewed in terms of its role in a complete economic investigation. Just like theory in any other discipline, economic theory is intended to predict behavior—the behavior of such economic variables as prices, quantities produced and consumed, or income. The abstract theory of indifference curves, demand curves, and supply curves may seem at first glance to be far removed from everyday experience. How do we know there are such things as demand curves? If they are more than pure abstractions, how do we identify them? The answer to the question of whether such abstractions are worthwhile depends upon whether their counterparts can be identified in the real world. To apply it in concrete cases, the skeleton of formal theory must be fitted with the flesh of observable data.

This is where statistics comes in. They provide the knowledge required to make specific quantitative predictions; they are the necessary "something" supplementing theory in economic inquiry. Just as the observation of facts in itself provides no explanation of their behavior, so theory in itself is not the complete economic inquiry. Statistical methods permit measurements of demand and supply and tests of the reliability of demand and supply theory.

The general procedure followed by economists is that of fitting demand and supply curves to empirical data by means of statistical methods. Once we know what the demand for shoes is in New York City, for instance, and we know what the supply is, we can predict the price of shoes in New York. Further, once we know the direction and amount by which either curve changes, we can tell how much the price and quantity traded will change. We can compute the price, cross, and income elasticities of demand for shoes in New York City if such measurements are wanted. To arrive at these quantitative measurements the theory must be applied to data on the variables entering into the theory.

The Estimation of Demand

Although a demand curve cannot be observed directly, the price and quantity of the commodity exchanged can be observed. For any commodity the price observed at any point in time and at any one place is interpreted as an equilibrium price. Thus, if on July 1, 1963, the price of wheat on the Chicago Commodity Exchange was two dollars per bushel, this is viewed as the equilibrium price of wheat in that market. Similarly, if the average price of automobiles in the United States during the year 1964 was three thousand dollars, this is treated as the equilibrium price during the one-year interval. The observed quantities demanded and supplied are interpreted in the same way. Consequently, if an observed price-quantity combination is plotted on a pair of axes, the point so obtained is regarded as the point at which the demand and supply curves intersect.

More than one observation of price and quantity is necessary, however, to estimate an empirical demand curve. One price and its corresponding quantity yield a single equilibrium point. Of course, this point lies on the demand curve, but the demand curve cannot be observed merely by observing one point on it. The procedure followed is to collect a sample of many prices and their corresponding quantities, i.e., a set of several equilibria where each observation comprises one equilibrium point, and then to estimate the demand curve from this sample.

Published data are available to the economist. Government agencies and private institutions regularly publish series on the prices and quantities traded of many commodities. To make up his sample there are two kinds of data that an economist may consult. One is called time series data. These data are a set of observations of prices and quantities that occurred in the same place at different times. For example, the data presented in Table 8.1 consist of two time series, one on price and the other on quantity traded. Each price-quantity combination comprises one observation. The observations occurred in one place (the United States) at various times—in this case in ten different years. Table 8.2 shows an imaginary cross-section sample.

	Table 8.1 Hypothetical Time Series Sample for Commodity X, the United States			Table 8.2 Hypothetical Cross-Section Sample for Commodity X, Year 1959	
	Average Price of X	*Average Quantity of* X *Traded*		*Average Price of* X	*Average Quantity of* X *Traded*
1950	$1.30	37,500	New York	$1.15	177,000
1951	1.00	52,500	Boston	1.20	146,000
1952	1.05	42,410	Chicago	1.10	210,000
1953	.90	40,010	Detroit	1.07	180,000
1954	1.15	41,250	Kansas City	1.15	97,000
1955	1.30	34,950	New Orleans	1.02	200,000
1956	1.55	15,000	Denver	1.25	100,000
1957	1.70	17,500	Seattle	1.33	100,000
1958	1.40	21,250	San Francisco	1.41	85,000
1959	1.20	25,000	Los Angeles	1.45	80,000

Here the prices and quantities are average prices that occurred in the same year but in different places—in ten different large cities. Use of time series or cross-section data depends on the kind of information desired. To estimate the demand curve in one year, cross-section data are appropriate. To estimate demand over a period of years, time series are necessary. Regardless of which type is used, the sample yields a set of observations on the price and quantity exchanged of the commodity under consideration.

In terms of a geometric diagram each observation determines a single point. In Table 8.1, the price and quantity in 1950 yield one point, the price and quantity in 1951 yield a second point, and so on. For the complete sample a so-called *scatter diagram* of ten points would be obtained. Similarly, in Table 8.2, the price-quantity combination in New York is plotted as one point, the price-quantity combination in Boston as a second, and so on until a scatter of ten points results. In either type of sample the observations can be plotted on a pair of axes to provide a set of ten points. More generally, for a sample of any given size there is a point corresponding to each observation in the sample. The larger is the sample, the greater will be the number of points.

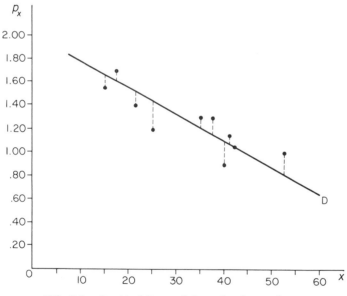

FIG. 8.6.   Empirical Demand Curve for Commodity X

Figure 8.6 depicts the scatter diagram of ten points corresponding to the ten sample observations shown in Table 8.1. For the moment ignore the curve labeled D and the broken vertical lines joining the points to the curve, and concentrate solely on the points. The price of X is scaled on the vertical axis and the quantity of X per unit of time on the horizontal axis. Each observation on p_x and x permits us to plot one point, and the total of ten observations yields the scatter of ten points. It is seen that the scatter roughly follows the shape of a demand curve.

The usual procedure for fitting a demand curve to a scatter of points is to draw that curve which most closely fits the scatter of points. That is, the curve is drawn so that the sum of the squared values of the deviations between the curve and the points is a minimum. The curve labeled D in Fig. 8.6, for example, is intended to represent the curve that best fits the scatter of points. The deviations between the observed points and the statistical demand curve are shown by the vertical broken lines extending from the points to the curve. The distances between the points and the curve show the amounts of error that would be committed in estimating prices from the curve so obtained. That is, the points show actual prices; the curve shows the prices that would be predicted for various quantities. The difference is the error in prediction. The curve is fitted in such a way that these errors are made the least possible. The reader familiar with statistics will recognize this as an application of simple regression analysis to economics.[1]

The empirical demand curve obtained by generating the best fit to a scatter of points is an estimate of the "true" demand curve for the commodity. It is assumed that a "true" demand curve exists and that the sample data may be used to arrive at an estimate of it. This is not to say that the estimate is necessarily a good one. Any given estimate may be "way off." But there are ways of judging this. The demand curve computed from the sample will be a true and reliable estimate of the actual market demand curve if certain statistical conditions are satisfied. These conditions are set up by the statistical theory of sampling, which is founded upon probability theory.

Generally, the sample used to estimate the demand curve is chosen at random. Errors of sampling prohibit one from making statements about the true demand curve with certainty. From knowledge of the sample, inferences can be made with a specified degree of probability. Given that certain conditions are met, after the demand curve is fitted to the sample data it is inferred that the statistical curve is an estimate of the demand curve for X. This statement is only probable, not certain, but its degree of probability, that is, its probability of being correct, can be specified. This means that if one were to apply the computed demand curve to predict prices and quantities traded, one could expect to make correct predictions (within certain limits) in a predetermined percentage of cases in the long run. Another way of saying this is as follows: Regard the computed demand curve as a hypothesis. The hypothesis in effect states that this computed demand curve is the true or actual demand curve in the market. We can accept or reject this hypothesis on the basis of factual evidence. If our estimate is a good one, we accept the hypothesis as probably true. Furthermore, by probably

---

[1] Those who wish to pursue in further detail the application of statistics to economics may wish to consult M. J. Brennan, *Preface to Econometrics* (Cincinnati: South-Western Publishing Co., 1960), Chaps. 19, 20, 23, and 24.

true we mean the probability of our making a mistake in accepting it is less than some (small) amount.

In Fig. 8.6 the points are very conveniently scattered to form a pattern that resembles roughly the shape of a demand curve. The economist working with actual data, however, may not encounter such a fortunate distribution of points. Three basic sample outcomes can be distinguished, and usually he will find some variation of one of the three. For a commodity called X these three scatters are shown in Figs. 8.7, 8.8, and 8.9.

Figure 8.7 reveals a scatter similar to the scatter shown in Fig. 8.6. It corresponds to the shape of a demand curve and each point represents a theoretical equilibrium. Therefore, the scatter indicates that the supply curve has been shifting substantially and that the demand curve is relatively stable. The variables that cause changes in demand (income, other prices, population, tastes) have a relatively small net impact. But variables that cause changes in supply (factor prices, technology) are fluctuating. If the demand curve is highly stable relative to the supply curve, then changes in price and quantity traded are due mostly to shifts in supply. As a result, the data identify the demand curve. In this situation the demand curve can be estimated by the simple regression analysis already described. The supply curve, however, cannot be estimated at the same time.

Figure 8.8 represents a different empirical outcome. If the determinants of changes in demand have been fluctuating and the supply curve has been relatively stable, the scatter traces an approximation to the supply curve. In this case simple regression analysis based on the sample of observations will reveal the supply curve. Then the supply curve for X can be estimated by these methods but the demand curve cannot.

Finally, there may arise the situation shown in Fig. 8.9, in which both curves have fluctuated. The points group themselves around neither a demand curve nor a supply curve. A simple regression of quantity traded on price will reveal neither one curve nor the other, but rather some mixture of

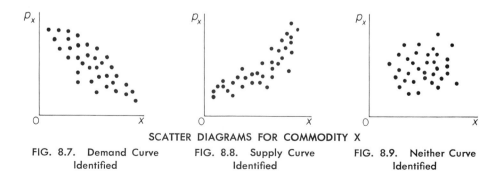

SCATTER DIAGRAMS FOR COMMODITY X

FIG. 8.7. Demand Curve
Identified

FIG. 8.8. Supply Curve
Identified

FIG. 8.9. Neither Curve
Identified

both. The curve estimated from the sample cannot be identified as either one or the other.

This case is by no means hopeless, however. Even though the third situation is encountered, advanced statistical methods permit one to estimate both the demand and supply curves under appropriate conditions. So-called multiple regression analysis provides a technique for isolating the variables that produce shifts in demand and holding them constant. The variables that cause shifts in supply can be treated in the same way. Then after removing their influences from the original data, the adjusted data may reveal both curves. Other advanced statistical methods can be used to achieve the same result. One should bear in mind, though, that these methods may not always be successful. Part of the research carried on by economists is that of developing new and better techniques for coping with identification problems such as these.

Examples of Empirical Research

Many theoretical relationships have been measured and economic theories tested by reference to empirical data. Only measurements of demand will be discussed here; studies of supply and cost will be considered in Chapter 14. The practical significance of empirical demand studies—both for economic analysis itself and for public policy—can be illustrated by reviewing briefly some examples of quantitative measurements made in the field of economics.

One of the earliest statistical studies of market demand was made by Professor Henry Schultz of the University of Chicago,[2] whose pioneering work set the stage for much subsequent research. He estimated the demands for wheat, sugar, corn, meats, and several other agricultural commodities in the United States. The estimate for wheat was made from a time series sample covering the period from 1921 to 1934 inclusive. He found that the demand curve did not shift significantly. After estimating demand he computed the price elasticity of demand for wheat as approximately −.21 for the period covered, the fitted demand curve being such that it had the same elasticity at all points. For each one per cent change in the price of wheat the quantity demanded changed in the opposite direction by about 2/10 of one per cent on the average. The implications of a relatively inelastic demand for total expenditures on wheat, and for other purposes, can be readily inferred.

J. R. N. Stone has measured the demand for several commodities in the United States and the United Kingdom.[3] From time series data covering the period 1929 through 1941 he has estimated the quantity demanded of tobacco per year in the United States as a function of the annual average

---

[2] H. Schultz, *The Theory and Measurement of Demand* (Chicago: University of Chicago Press, 1938).

[3] R. Stone, "The Analysis of Market Demand," *Journal of the Royal Statistical Society*, CVIII (Parts III–IV, 1945).

price of tobacco, consumers' income per year, and the annual average price of all other commodities taken as a group. From his computations he derived a price elasticity of demand for tobacco of −.266 for the period studied. The income elasticity he estimated to be .325; and the cross elasticity of demand with respect to the price of all other commodities as a whole he found to be .59.

James Tobin conducted a study of the demand for all foods combined in the United States.[4] Using time series from 1912 through 1948, he found that the price elasticity of demand for all food products was about −.53 and he estimated the income elasticity of demand to be approximately .45.

The demand for automobiles in the United States has been measured by several economists. One such measurement was made by D. B. Suits.[5] His data consist of time series covering the period 1929 through 1956. From his measurement of demand for new automobiles he computed the price elasticity of demand as −.58, where price was defined as the monthly payment on installment purchases. The income elasticity of demand for automobiles was estimated to be 4.16. For purposes of comparison it may be noted that the income elasticity of demand for the stock of refrigerators has been found to range from .57 to .83, depending upon the period utilized in a cross-section study.[6]

These are but a few examples chosen from a vast number of empirical investigations that have been undertaken in the past and that are in progress today. In these studies the general theory of demand is applied to specific commodities. Statistical analysis is used to test the predictions of demand theory and to estimate its quantitative characteristics from observations on prices, quantities traded, income, and other variables. In repeated tests, measurements, and revisions of the theory, both the advantages and the limitations of the theory are exposed. Not all of the results are satisfactory. And much remains to be done. Yet the outcome to date has been a verification of the general principles underlying the theory of demand.

CONCLUSION

The few theoretical applications of demand theory discussed in this chapter show the way in which abstract concepts can be used to solve practical problems. These illustrations by no means exhaust the possibilities for application; they are merely suggestive. As tools of analysis, theoretical systems can be adapted to a variety of uses to explain the directional effects of certain changes in the economy. Quantitative knowledge of these effects requires that the theory be supplemented with statistical investigations. Modern

[4] J. Tobin, "A Statistical Demand Function for Food in the United States," *Journal of the Royal Statistical Society*, CXIII (Part II, 1950).

[5] D. B. Suits, "The Demand for New Automobiles in the United States 1929–56," *Review of Economics and Statistics*, XL (August 1958), 273–80.

[6] H. L. Miller Jr., "The Demand for Refrigerators: A Statistical Study," *Review of Economics and Statistics*, XLII (May 1960), 197–202.

statistical inference is a method employed to test the probable validity of theoretical predictions and to estimate the quantitative properties of economic relationships.

The implications for public policy are clear. Applied to sales taxes, income taxes, welfare expenditures, support of agricultural prices, or subsidies for labor migration out of depressed economic areas, the information provided by theoretical and empirical economic studies can act as a guide for sound government policy.

PROBLEMS

1.   Suppose the government pays butter producers a subsidy of a fixed amount per pound of butter sold. Given that butter and oleomargarine are substitutes in consumption and assuming no other shifts in demand or supply from any other source:

(*a*) Trace the effects of the subsidy on the price of butter and the quantity consumed.

(*b*) Trace its effects on the price of oleomargarine and the quantity consumed.

2.   Suppose the income elasticity of demand for a particular commodity is positive and quite large. Consumer income rises but the quantity of the commodity consumed declines. How do you explain this?

SUGGESTED READING

K. E. Boulding, *Economic Analysis*, 3rd ed., Chap. 8 and Appendix to Chap. 8. New York: Harper and Bros., 1955.

O. H. Brownlee and E. D. Allen, *Economics of Public Finance*, 2nd ed., Chap. 16. Englewood Cliffs, N. J.: Prentice-Hall, Inc., 1954.

M. J. Brennan, *Preface to Econometrics*, Chaps. 19, 20, 23, 24. Cincinnati: South-Western Publishing Co., 1960.

G. Shepherd, *Agricultural Price Analysis*, 4th ed., Chaps. 4, 6, 7. Ames: Iowa State College Press, 1957.

E. Working, "What Do Statistical Demand Curves Show?" in G. J. Stigler and K. E. Boulding, eds., *Readings in Price Theory*. Chicago: Richard D. Irwin, Inc., 1952.

G. J. Stigler, "The Limitations of Statistical Demand Curves," *Journal of the American Statistical Association*, XXXIV (September 1939), 469–81.

Part III

Theory of
Production and Cost

9

Production Functions

The theory of demand begins with an analysis of the individual consumer. Since market supply originates with producing firms, the theory of supply naturally begins with the study of the individual firm. Analyses of the consumer and the firm set the foundations for market demand and supply respectively, which together determine the price and quantity traded on the market.

Although the basic theoretical principles are analogous, determining the conditions of supply is somewhat more complicated than determining the conditions of demand. The type of industry that produces the commodity in question is a basic, and sometimes complex, factor in studies of supply, for different industries are characterized by varying degrees of competition that influence the conditions of supply. Chapters 12–14 will discuss the purely competitive industry, and Chapters 15–19 will be devoted to monopoly and the forms of nonpure competition. For the present, the form of industrial organization can be ignored. We shall be concerned with the principles of production and cost as they apply to a single firm. These principles are not influenced by the number of firms in the industry, nor are they affected by the degree of competition among firms in the sale of the product. The theory of production presented in this chapter provides the basis for the development of a firm's cost of production. In this sense the analysis of cost in the next two chapters builds upon the topics discussed here.

THE CONCEPT OF A PRODUCTION FUNCTION

Not only manufacturing establishments but retail stores, banks, amusement parks, and other types of firms purchase resources for use in producing some good or service. A particular combination of human and nonhuman resources results in a given output. Some firms utilize more of one resource than do others; some use resources that others do not. Yet, basically, all firms employ various resource inputs to generate their product output. *Production function* is the term used to describe the relationship in a firm between alternative quantities of physical inputs and the physical output that results from each quantity. The production function does not itself have any monetary characteristics. This input-output relationship is totally independent of the product price or the prices of resources used. Though these prices will ultimately affect the firm's decision of what and how much to produce, they do not enter into the production function.

A firm's production function can be expressed symbolically, just as the demand function was expressed symbolically on page 91. Suppose a firm produces a good or service called X. Let x denote the quantity of this product per unit of time. Suppose, further, that it utilizes four factors of production to produce X. Call them A, B, C, and D, where their quantities per unit of time are denoted by a, b, c, and d respectively. Then the expression

$$x = f(a, b, c, d)$$

states that the quantity of X produced per unit of time is a function of (or depends upon) the quantities of A, B, C, and D used by the firm per unit of time. The firm can increase or decrease output by increasing or decreasing the quantities of one or more inputs.

The specific form taken on by this function depends upon the prevailing state of technology. That is, output is determined partly by the quantities of resources used and partly by the production techniques adopted by the firm. For illustration, consider the following example.

Production Technique	Resource Inputs	Product Output
Technique I	10 units of each	1,000 units
	20 units of each	2,000 units
	30 units of each	3,000 units
Technique II	10 units of each	1,500 units
	20 units of each	2,500 units
	30 units of each	3,500 units

By adopting Technique I the firm is able to produce 1,000 units of X with 10 units each of A, B, C, and D. Employment of 20 units of each resource yields 2,000 units of X, and 30 units of each give 3,000 units of X. The entire relationship between inputs and outputs is different under Technique II, which generates more output for each combination of inputs and which is more efficient than Technique I. The firm can vary its output by varying its inputs with a given production technique, by switching from one technique to another, or by taking both actions simultaneously. The efficiency of different techniques will determine what output can be obtained from each combination of inputs. The prevailing state of technology sets a limit to efficiency, however, and determines the most efficient technique available to the firm.

In order to define a firm's production function it is assumed that the firm utilizes the most efficient technique available, and that this technique does not change. Thus, if the state of technology makes Technique II the most efficient technique possible, then the relationship between various combinations of inputs and the resulting outputs under Technique II *is defined* as the firm's production function. In other words, for any given production function a constant state of technology is assumed to exist, such that *the output obtained from each alternative quantity of inputs is the maximum output for that quantity of inputs*. In symbolic terms, each numerical value of x corresponding to specified numerical values of a, b, c, and d is interpreted as the largest possible value of x corresponding to those specified values of a, b, c, and d.

Most of this chapter will be centered upon the form of a firm's production function. We shall investigate the way in which output varies as inputs are varied under conditions of a constant state of technology. This does not mean that changes in the state of technology cannot be taken into account. As should now be apparent, and as we shall see in detail later, a change in the state of technology alters the entire production function, so that more or less (maximum) output is produced for each combination of inputs.

Isoquants

By restricting the analysis to two resource inputs, production theory utilizes a method similar to the indifference curves of consumer theory. As a matter of fact, the same *formal* apparatus applies to the production possibilities of a single firm as well as to the utility possibilities of a single consumer. An isoquant is a geometric curve that looks like a consumer's indifference curve, which is drawn on a set of axes measuring the amounts of two different commodities. Each point on the curve shows the utility derived from a combination of the two commodities consumed, and the entire curve traces all combinations of the two products that yield equal utility. An isoquant is drawn for a single firm rather than a single consumer. Along the two axes are measured the amounts of two resource inputs. A point on the isoquant shows the output produced by a combination of two inputs; and the entire curve traces all input combinations that yield the same output.

In Fig. 9.1 two resources, A and B, are assumed to be used in the production of a commodity X. The amounts of A and B per unit of time, denoted by a and b, are measured along the horizontal and vertical axes respectively. Only five of the firm's isoquants are drawn. Of course, the production function is described by a system of innumerable isoquants, one for each level of output, just as the consumer's utility function is described by a system of innumerable indifference curves.

The isoquant labeled x_1 shows all combinations of A and B that can be used to produce x_1 units of commodity X. The isoquant labeled x_2 shows all combinations of A and B that can be used to produce x_2 units of X, where x_2 is greater than x_1, and so on. Thus, the firm can obtain x_4 units of product by using a_3 units of A with b_2 units of B; it can also obtain x_4 units of product

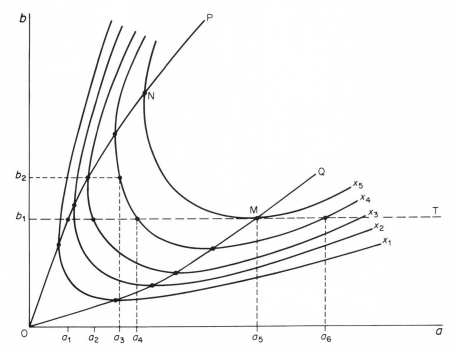

FIG. 9.1. Production Function Expressed by Isoquants: Product X Produced with A and B

by using a_4 units of A combined with b_1 units of B, or any other combination of A and B corresponding to that isoquant. Greater amounts of output are represented by higher isoquants.

Properties of Isoquants

Consumer indifference curves were shown to have three properties: negative slopes, nonintersection with any other indifference curve, and convexity toward the origin. Subject to some exceptions to be indicated below, isoquants possess the same three properties.

Except for the segments of the isoquants lying outside the boundaries designated by the lines 0P and 0Q in Fig. 9.1, the isoquants slope downward from left to right. The segments outside these boundaries we may ignore for the moment. Over the relevant range the negative slope of an isoquant is determined by the technical substitutability of A for B in the production of X. Just as two commodities may be substitutes in consumption, so two resources may be substitutes in production. Generally, the combination of resources necessary to produce a given output can be varied by substituting quantities of one for quantities of the other. If less of one is used, more of the other must be used to compensate for its loss—if output is to remain constant. Since the slope of an isoquant is given by

$$\frac{\Delta b}{\Delta a}$$

this magnitude must be a negative number. A decrease of b requires an increase of a and vice versa for any movement along the isoquant, that is, for a constant total physical product.

The rationale for nonintersecting isoquants is formally the same as that used to explain nonintersecting indifference curves. If two isoquants were to intersect, it would mean that one combination of resources could at the same time produce two different amounts of product. For instance, 10 units of A and 5 units of B could produce at the same time 100 units of X and 200 units of X. This is inconsistent with our basic assumption that the firm uses but one system of technology. If the firm uses the most efficient productive technique and no other, only one level of output can result from any given combination of resources.

Finally, each isoquant is convex toward the origin. Convex indifference curves resulted from the assumption of diminishing marginal rate of substitution of one good for another in consumption (see Chapter 5). Similarly, convex isoquants stem from the assumption of diminishing marginal rate of substitution of one resource for another in production. The rate at which A may be technically substituted for B declines as more A is used relative to B with output constant. As A is substituted for B by equal increments, additional units of A will compensate for smaller and smaller units of B. Suppose labor and tools are combined to build 50 wooden benches of a given size in a week. If one continues to use more labor and less tools, a unit of tools becomes more valuable relative to a unit of labor—in the sense that it takes more and more units of labor to compensate for the lost productive power of a unit of tools. It becomes more difficult to substitute labor for tools and still maintain the same output of benches.

The marginal rate of technical substitution of A for B is a positive magnitude, equal to minus the slope of the isoquant at any given point. Using the symbol MRTS_{ab} to denote this concept, we have

$$\mathrm{MRTS}_{ab} = -\frac{\Delta b}{\Delta a}$$

Ridge Lines

The lines labeled 0P and 0Q in Fig.9.1 form the boundaries between the area in which the isoquants are negatively sloped (within the lines) and the areas in which they are positively sloped (outside the lines). Isoquants differ from indifference curves in this respect, that they are positively sloped over some segments.

Consider one isoquant in Fig. 9.1, say that corresponding to an output of x_5 units. There is some minimum quantity of B necessary for its production. This is the amount b_1. For any amount of B less than b_1 the quantity x_5 cannot be produced, indicated by the fact that the isoquant does not extend below the vertical distance $0b_1$ (or a_5M, which equals $0b_1$). The point M is the point at which A has been substituted for B to the extent possible without reducing x. If a is increased without also increasing b—if the firm moves horizontally to the right or downward to the right—total output will decrease. The marginal rate of substitution of A for B has declined to zero at point M. Further applications of A require that inputs of B also be expanded if output is to be prevented from falling.

On the same isoquant the point N corresponds to the minimum amount of A necessary to produce x_5 units. In moving from M toward N the marginal rate of substitution of B for A declines until it reaches zero at point N. To maintain output, further additions of b must be accompanied by increases of a as well; otherwise total output would decrease.

Identical properties apply to the other isoquants in the system. Each has a point like M at which the curve is horizontal and one like N at which it is vertical. The lines 0P and 0Q in the diagram are called ridge lines. 0Q traces all the points at which $MRTS_{ab} = 0$, while 0P traces the points at which $MRTS_{ba} = 0$. Both marginal rates of substitution are positive only within the area bounded by the ridge lines. We shall return to Fig. 9.1 and make use of these concepts in deriving the so-called product curves of a firm.

THE LAW OF DIMINISHING RETURNS

It is desirable to distinguish two types of change in output resulting from variations in resource inputs: (1) changes caused by varying *all* inputs simultaneously, and (2) changes caused by varying some inputs while holding others constant. These two types of change correspond respectively to what economists call the long run and the short run.

In many practical situations a firm cannot alter some of its resource inputs. Within some time period, the amount of land available, the size of physical plant, or the amount of skilled labor may be fixed in fact. In such situations the second type of change, the short run, must apply. The long run, on the other hand, entails a practical situation in which all resource inputs are variable. We shall first examine the way in which output varies with respect to variations in any one input with others held constant, giving rise to what has been termed the law of diminishing returns. Later, we shall drop the assumption of fixed inputs and allow all to be variable. Varying all inputs simultaneously is called varying the firm's "scale of plant," and gives rise to the law of diminishing returns to scale.

The law of diminishing returns is a general statement about the form a production function will take. More specifically, the law describes a relationship between variations in product output and variations in one resource input, the amounts of all other resources being held constant. If the input of any one resource is increased by equal amounts per unit of time while the inputs of all other resources are conceptually held constant, the total output of product per unit of time will increase by successively smaller increments. As the variable resource is increased, total product increases, but after some point its rate of increase slows down. And if the equal additions of the variable input are carried far enough, total product will reach a maximum and then decline.

There are several aspects of this definition that must be carefully noted. First, the point at which diminishing returns set in may be at a very small or a very large quantity of the resource being varied. The law does not state that diminishing returns become operative at relatively small quantities of the variable resource—only that at *some point* the increments in output become smaller. Furthermore, the amount of the variable factor of production at which diminishing returns appear is likely to be different for different products and for different firms producing the same product.

Second, the relationship between output and the variable input is of the "if, then" type. For example, if a equals one, x equals 10; if a equals 2, x equals 15; and so on. It does not state a *is* equal to one and therefore x *is* equal to 10, etc. The different inputs of the variable factor of production refer to alternative quantities used. They do not refer to chronologically successive applications of additional units, such as one unit today and one unit tomorrow to make two units tomorrow.

Third, the word *maximum* has been used in two connections. In the discussion of technology it was said that each numerical magnitude of x is a maximum—a maximum for one particular combination of inputs. Thus, suppose b, c, and d are all fixed at 2 units. Then, let x be 10 if a equals one, let x be 15 if a equals 2, let x be 18 if a equals 3. Now for a equal to one and b, c, and d each equal to 2, we say 10 is the maximum x *for this combination of inputs*. Likewise, for a equal to 2 with other inputs each equal to 2, we say 15 is the largest x that can be gotten from 2 units of A and 2 units each of B, C, and D. Were 3 units of A combined with the same amounts of other resources, the largest x attainable would be 18. Different amounts of the product X result from different combinations of resource inputs using the most efficient production technique. But now one of these *efficient* values of x is larger than any of the others. In this example 18 is the largest value of x. It is this maximum that is referred to in the law of diminishing returns. When we say that x will increase by smaller and smaller increments, may eventually reach a maximum, and then decline, we refer to the maximum among all the values of x achieved by varying a.

Illustration of Diminishing Returns

The law of diminishing returns is consistent with what has been observed in actual experiments—and with what might be expected even in the absence of empirical observations. Agricultural production is a good example. It stands to reason that as more and more labor is combined with fixed quantities of land, fertilizer, seed, and machinery, the total product will increase. But eventually the rate of increase in total output will slow down. After a point the fertilizer, seed, and machinery must be used less and less effectively because of the growing number of laborers. The same applies to any one of the other inputs. Heavier applications of fertilizer with a constant amount of other inputs show diminishing returns very quickly.

Table 9.1

1	2	3	4	5	
Capital	Labor	Total Physical Product	Marginal Physical Product of Labor	Average Physical Product of Labor	
100	0	0	0	0	⎫
100	1	10	10	10	⎪
100	2	30	20	15	⎬ Stage I
100	3	60	30	20	⎪
100	4	100	40	25	⎭
100	5	125	25	25	⎫
100	6	138	13	23	⎪
100	7	147	9	21	⎬ Stage II
100	8	152	5	19	⎪
100	9	153	1	17	⎭
100	10	153	0	15 3/10	⎫
100	11	151	−2	13 8/11	⎬ Stage III
100	12	144	−7	12	⎭

To simplify matters let us suppose a commodity is produced by two factors of production, labor and capital. Assume the quantity of capital is fixed. Table 9.1 shows the results of a hypothetical experiment in which alternative quantities of labor are combined with a fixed amount of capital.

Column 2 lists the alternative quantities of labor combined with 100 units of capital, and column 3 shows the total product resulting from each combination. When no labor is combined with capital, total product is zero, for we assume any production requires both resources.[1] The third column

---

[1] This does not necessarily apply to every productive operation. There are some commodities in the production of which not all resources are essential, so some positive amount can be produced in the absence of one or more inputs. There are others for which more than one unit of the variable resource is required before output exceeds zero. However, these considerations do not alter the general conclusions with respect to diminishing returns.

indicates that increasing returns occur with applications of the first four units of labor. Each successive one-unit increment of labor adds more to total output than does the preceding one. Strictly speaking, this is not absolutely necessary. Diminishing returns could set in at the outset, but more generally a firm will experience increasing returns at first. Diminishing returns become operative after the fourth unit of labor. In moving from the fourth to the fifth, then from the fifth to the sixth, and so on, each successive unit increment of labor adds less to the total product than does the preceding one. This illustration has been carried to the point—at 10 units of labor—where additional units of labor result in decreases in total product.

The operation of diminishing returns is seen more clearly by reference to the fourth and fifth columns. Column 4 shows the marginal physical product of labor. The marginal physical product of a resource is defined as the change in total product that results from a small change in the quantity of the resource used. It is computed by dividing the change in output by the change in the variable input that gives rise to the change in output. When dealing with one-unit changes in the variable resource, as we have done with labor in this example, the change in the variable input is equal to one. Thus, in increasing labor from zero to one unit the change in labor is equal to one. Total product increases by 10 units. Hence, the marginal physical product of labor is 10/1 or 10. When labor increases from one to two units, total product increases from 10 to 30, so the marginal physical product of labor is 20/1 or 20.

It can be seen that the marginal physical product of labor rises in Stage I, reaches a maximum, and then declines throughout Stage II. Finally, in Stage III it is zero and then negative, while still declining. The law of diminishing returns can be stated more succinctly by saying that after some point the marginal physical product of the variable resource diminishes. For "successive increments of the product obtained by successive increments of the resource" is merely a more awkward way of saying "the marginal physical product of the resource."

The average physical product of labor is shown in column 5. The average physical product of a resource is defined as the amount of output per unit of the resource employed. It is computed by dividing total physical product by the quantity of the resource used to produce it. For example, when total product is 60, three units of labor are used, so the average physical product of labor is 60/3 or 20. Considering all entries in Table 9.1 the average physical product of labor is seen to rise in Stage I, reach a maximum, and decline throughout Stages II and III. Therefore, in Stage II both the marginal and the average products are declining. Unlike the marginal product, the average product never becomes negative. Since neither total physical product nor the amount of labor used are ever negative, division of one into the other will never yield a negative number.

Derivation of the Product Curves

Table 9.1 illustrates the product schedules for a firm. When the entries in such a table are plotted on a graph and the points connected, they yield the corresponding product curves. Rather than following this procedure, however, derivation of the product curves from the firm's isoquants will contribute more to an understanding of the production function itself. Returning to Fig. 9.1, let A be the variable resource and B the fixed one. The first step is to choose the level at which the input of B is to be held constant. Suppose it is b_1 units per unit of time. By allowing a to vary with b fixed at b_1, we move along the horizontal line b_1T, and the variations in output are found from the isoquants.

For larger inputs of A different isoquants are encountered. Given that $b = b_1$, when $a = a_2$, the firm is on the isoquant labeled x_3. For $a = a_4$, $x = x_4$; and for $a = a_5$, $x = x_5$. Total output is expanding and reaches a maximum when a_5 units of A are employed with the fixed amount of B. The line b_1T intersects lower and lower isoquants as further movements to the right are considered. Expansion from a_5 to a_6 units reduces total output from x_5 to x_4 units.

As an alternative the input of A could be held constant conceptually and b allowed to vary. Then movements along a *vertical* line would generate a relationship between variations in x and b for fixed a. And variations in output would display the same behavior with respect to variations in b as those found in the case of a. In order to trace the argument along a single thread, however, we shall continue with the case of variable a.

If Fig. 9.1 contained all isoquants of the production function, and if all possible amounts of A and the corresponding quantities of product were plotted, a continuous curve would emerge. This relationship between x and a is depicted in the upper panel of Fig. 9.2, where units of the variable input are measured on the horizontal axis and total product is measured on the vertical axis. The behavior of total product leads to the corresponding curves shown in the lower panel. Here again the horizontal axis measures alternative units of A. But the vertical axis measures output per unit of the variable input. The production curves in both panels are labeled with the following shorthand notations:

Total Physical Product: $\qquad\qquad$ TPP $= x$

Marginal Physical Product of A: $\qquad$ $\text{MPP}_a = \dfrac{\Delta x}{\Delta a}$

Average Physical Product of A: $\qquad$ $\text{APP}_a = \dfrac{x}{a}$

In the second definition the Δ again means "a finite change in," and Δa may be taken as equal to one.

All three curves are assumed to emerge from the origin. The total physical product curve is concave upward from zero to a_0 units of A, and concave downward thereafter. The upward concavity of the TPP curve indicates increasing marginal returns: equal increments of A increase the total output of X by successively larger amounts. The downward concavity of the TPP

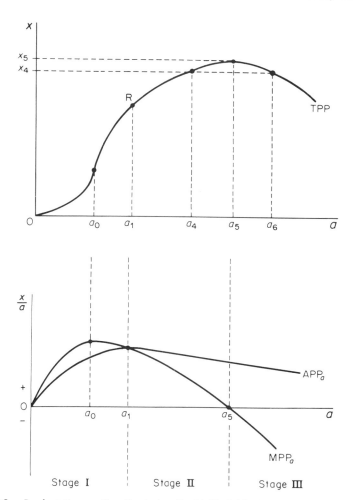

FIG. 9.2.   Product Curves: Firm Producing X with Variable Input A and Fixed Input B

curve between a_0 and a_5 units of A signifies diminishing marginal returns. Successive equal increments of A produce smaller and smaller increments of output. Over this segment the TPP curve is still rising, however. It is only when more than a_5 units of A are applied that total output falls, signifying decreasing returns.

There is a close relation between the total physical product and the marginal physical product of A. Geometrically speaking, the slope of the TPP curve for any given value of a equals the MPP_a for that value of a. The height of the MPP_a curve above the horizontal axis equals the slope of the TPP curve at any particular value of a. The MPP_a curve rises from zero to a_0 units of resource A, which entails a TPP curve with upward concavity. The amount of A is being continually increased by one-unit increments, so Δa is always equal to one. Since

$$\text{MPP}_a = \frac{\Delta x}{\Delta a}$$

by definition, when MPP_a is rising each successive Δx must be larger than the preceding one. The MPP_a curve reaches a maximum at a_0 units of resource A and declines thereafter, also signifying that diminishing returns have set in. For as MPP_a gets smaller, each successive Δx must be smaller than the preceding one. At a_5 units of resource A the marginal physical product of A is zero. It is at this quantity of resource A that total physical product is a maximum. After a_5 units of A the diminishing MPP_a becomes negative. The Δx corresponding to each (positive) Δa is negative. When MPP_a is negative, it follows that TPP must be decreasing—the TPP curve has a negative slope.

The average physical product of resource A rises to a maximum at a_1 units. It declines for all successive additions of A beyond a_1 units; though, as we have seen, it does not fall below the horizontal axis because x/a cannot be negative. The APP_a curve can also be obtained from the TPP curve by a geometrical device.[2] Suppose we wish to know the average physical product of A when a_1 units of resource A are used. The total physical product is given by the vertical distance $a_1\text{R}$. The number of units of resource A used is given by the horizontal distance $0a_1$. Since average physical product is defined as total physical product divided by the amount of the resource used, the APP_a equals $a_1\text{R}/0a_1$. This computation locates one point on the APP_a curve, that corresponding to a_1. For each alternative unit of resource A, such as a_0 or a_4, the computation is repeated, and the set of all such points traces the APP_a curve.

Granted these relationships of the marginal and average products to the total product, there is also an important connection between the marginal and average products themselves. First, consider the values of a to the left of a_1. Notice that the MPP_a curve lies above the APP_a curve and that the APP_a is rising. Next, consider the values of a to the right of a_1. The MPP_a curve lies below the APP_a curve and the APP_a is falling. At a_1 the APP_a is a maximum and equal to the MPP_a. Moreover, a general statement can be made about the relationship between the marginal and average physical products. Whenever the MPP_a is greater than the APP_a, the APP_a must

[2] See the section on geometry in the Mathematical Appendix.

rise; whenever the MPP_a is less than the APP_a, the APP_a must fall; whenever they are equal, the APP_a neither rises nor falls—in this case it is a maximum.[3]

THE THREE STAGES OF PRODUCTION

In the production curves depicted in Fig. 9.2 three stages of production have been demarcated. Upon the economic meaning of these three stages hinges the value of the production curves to the firm.

Characteristics of the Three Stages

Stage I occurs from zero to a_1 units of resource A in Fig. 9.2. It is characterized by (1) increasing total physical product, (2) increasing average physical product, and (3) increasing and then decreasing marginal physical product. Stage I is called the stage of *increasing returns* because either the marginal or the average physical product of resource A is rising for any value of a. For some values of a (i.e., up to a_0) both are rising.[4]

Stage II, between a_1 and a_5 units of A, is called the stage of *diminishing returns*. It is characterized by (1) increasing total physical product, (2) diminishing average physical product, and (3) diminishing but positive marginal physical product. Both APP_a and MPP_a are declining, but since the MPP_a is still positive, TPP continues to increase. Stage II continues up to a_5 units of resource A, at which the total product is a maximum and the marginal physical product of A is zero.

In Stage III a change in the direction of the TPP curve is experienced for the first time. In this stage (1) total physical product is decreasing, (2) average physical product continues to diminish, and (3) marginal physical product continues to diminish but is negative. What distinguishes Stage III from both I and II is the negative MPP_a. Hence, Stage III is called the stage of *decreasing returns*.

[3] This is a general relationship between any marginal and average concepts, whether they be marginal and average heights, weights, products, costs, temperatures, or what not. To illustrate, suppose 10 wooden blocks are on a scale and the total weight is 100 pounds. Then the average weight is 100/10 or 10 pounds per block. Now consider adding a block greater in weight than the average, say 21 pounds. The marginal weight is 21 pounds. What happens to the average? It rises to 121/11 or 11 pounds. Since the marginal is greater than the average, the average rises, but it is still smaller than the marginal. Suppose, on the other hand, that the weight of the additional block were less than the average, say 5 pounds. The marginal weight is 5, and the average becomes 105/11 or about 9.55 pounds. The average *falls* but it is still greater than the marginal. Finally, suppose the weight of the additional block were 10 pounds, equal in weight to the average. The average becomes 110/11 or 10 pounds. Since the marginal equals the average, the average does not change.

[4] The APP_a is increasing throughout this stage. Consequently, some writers have defined the law of diminishing returns in terms of the average rather than the marginal product of the variable input. Actually, it makes little difference which definition is adopted. If MPP_a eventually declines, APP_a must likewise decline. The essential point remains regardless of which expression of the law is used, namely, that the designation of Stage II is that in which both the marginal and average products are positive but diminishing.

It appears intuitively obvious that the firm will want to avoid Stage III. To expand the applications of resource A to the point where reductions in output result is anything but efficient. One might suspect that the firm would wish to avoid Stage II also; for only in Stage I can it achieve increasing returns. The crux of the apparent desirability of Stage I springs from our failure to take into account what is happening to the marginal and average physical products of B in that stage. The curves drawn in Fig. 9.2 tell us what happens to the marginal and average products of A as the amount of A is increased relative to the amount of B. But they tell us nothing about what happens to the marginal and average products of B.

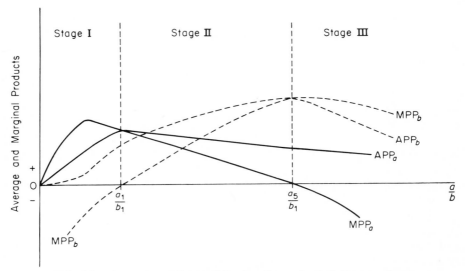

FIG. 9.3. Average and Marginal Product Curves for Both Resource Inputs

If we make a convenient methodological assumption, we can draw the marginal and average physical product curves of both resources in the same diagram.[5] The curves for both resources can be plotted against the ratio of A to B. In Fig. 9.2 the ratio, amount of A to amount of B, is denoted by a/b and measured on the horizontal axis. The vertical axis is used to measure the marginal and average physical products of either resource.

To begin, assume the quantity of resource B is a fixed amount; call it b_1 units of B per unit of time. A movement to the right on the horizontal axis increases the ratio of a to b; a_5/b_1 is larger than a_1/b_1, for example. A move-

[5] The assumption required is that equal proportional increases (decreases) in both resources will increase (decrease) total output in the same proportion. For example, if both A and B are doubled, output will double; or if both A and B are reduced by two-thirds, output will decrease by two-thirds. The assumption is introduced merely to make the analysis manageable. It permits us to plot the curves for both resources in the same diagram, but it does not alter the general principles of production already discussed.

ment to the left decreases the ratio of a to b. Hence, with b fixed the ratio changes in the same direction as changes in a. It is not necessary to assume b is fixed to make use of the diagram. We could let A be the fixed input and B the variable one. If the quantity of A is fixed, increased applications of B mean movements to the left on the horizontal axis; for the ratio a/b thereby becomes smaller. Reductions in the amount of resource B increase a/b and result in movements to the right. One could even let both resources be variable, so that any change in either a or b or both will alter the ratio a/b. However, let us return for the moment to the simpler case in which only A is variable. Since under our assumption the average and marginal products depend solely upon the ratio in which the resources are combined, holding B fixed is merely a special way of altering the ratio a/b.

Even if the resource A were free, it would not be worthwhile to use any quantity in excess of a_5 units, for a negative MPP_a means a reduction in total output. The firm is even less inclined to move into this region when resource A is not free, which is practically always the case. Why employ additional units of a resource that reduce total output when these units have to be paid for?

But notice what happens to the marginal physical product of resource B in Stage I. The MPP_b curve is below the horizontal axis, representing a negative marginal product for resource B. Just as the ratio of a to b is too large in Stage III, so it is too small in Stage I. The amount of A joined with the fixed amount of B is so small that B is inefficient. For example, it might be a case of too few laborers (resource A) tending a blast furnace (resource B), so that the blast furnace cannot be operated effectively. Since labor is being used too sparsely, expansion of labor inputs will permit specialization of tasks and more effective use of the blast furnace to bring about successively greater additions to output. Too many cooks combined with a stove can reduce the output of stew, but so can too few cooks.

If possible, the firm will avoid both Stage I and Stage III because negative marginal returns exist for one or the other resource in these stages. Instead, the firm will actively seek diminishing returns for both resources. In the stage of diminishing returns the average and the marginal physical products of both resources are diminishing, but the marginal physical products of both are positive. With B fixed, an additional input of A increases total product; had A been fixed and B variable, an additional input of B would likewise increase total product.[6]

---

[6] It can be shown (see Mathematical Appendix) that the marginal rates of substitution are equal to the ratios of marginal products:

$$MRTS_{ab} = MPP_a/MPP_b \qquad MRTS_{ba} = MPP_b/MPP_a$$

Therefore, since $MRTS_{ab} = 0$ on the ridge line 0Q and is negative to the right of 0Q in Fig. 9.1, the MPP_a is also zero and negative respectively. Similarly, with $MRTS_{ba} = 0$ on 0P and negative to the left of 0P, MPP_b is zero and negative respectively. The area bounded by the ridge lines is a more general representation of Stage II, with Stage I to the left and Stage III to the right when both inputs are variable.

Underlying Determinants of the Three Stages

We have assumed that a firm will attempt to be economically efficient. In terms of its production function the firm would attempt to operate somewhere in Stage II. Too much labor per unit of capital, for example, has the same result as too much capital per unit of labor. Whenever any one resource is being used so sparingly that its average physical product rises as more of it is used, some other resource is being used so heavily that its marginal physical product is negative.

We say the firm will *attempt* to achieve Stage II. This does not necessarily mean that the firm will therefore be able to do so. There are two reasons why it may not be able to operate in the stage of diminishing returns for all resources. First, there may be limitations on the availability of some resources. Second, there may be indivisibilities in some resources.

Suppose the firm whose production function is depicted in Fig. 9.3 is in Stage I. It can move into Stage II by increasing the employment of resource A, given that the amount of resource B is fixed. But suppose the firm cannot obtain more A. Resource A is still a variable resource. There is a limit, however, to its variability—in this case it is variable from zero to a_1 units, but not beyond. Then, the firm is prevented from obtaining diminishing average and marginal returns for A, and it must tolerate negative marginal returns for B. Resource A might be some special kind of skilled labor, such as managerial ability of a specified quality for example.

We can also let B be the variable resource combined with a fixed amount of A. In Fig. 9.3, increasing the quantity of B with a fixed amount of A is a movement to the left along the horizontal axis. Now suppose the firm is in Stage III. Then, the ratio a/b is too large. The firm can move into Stage II, and so avoid negative marginal returns to resource A, by increasing b. If resource B is variable only up to a point, it may not be possible for the firm to move as far as Stage II. Resource B might represent capital, and the firm's credit rating may not be adequate to attract more capital. Some inefficient small farms and retail stores might be in this position.

There may also be a lower limit to the variability of a resource. Suppose the firm is in Stage I and a_1 is the maximum available amount of resource A. If B can be reduced to an amount less than b_1, Stage II can still be achieved. If the smallest unit of resource B is larger than b_1, however, this cannot be done. Resource B may not be divisible into any unit smaller in size than b_1. For example, the firm might be a manufacturing establishment in which A represents labor and B the physical plant. Suppose labor has been increased to the available limit and the firm is still in Stage I. Then, it will reduce the amount of physical plant used. Space will be left unused and machines idle. Given the size of the machines, one machine may still be too much capital equipment for the amount of labor used. If it does not use the one machine, the firm must produce zero output; and if it does use the machine (or more than the one) it operates in Stage I. A smaller machine would be appropriate, but if no smaller machine exists, the firm will have to operate in the region of negative marginal returns for the one it does use. Notice that using the machine for a shorter number of hours will not solve the problem. For the negative marginal returns arise from indivisibility in the size of the machine and not the number of hours it is used.

Another example is the case of a farm using a tractor of a given size. The smallest tractor may be too large; it crushes some of the crop when used (negative marginal returns). Yet using the tractor half time is not the same as using a half-sized tractor. During the hours when it is used the tractor still crushes some of the crop. Negative marginal returns are due to the indivisibility of a unit of tractor, not to hours of use.

Indivisibility of resource B may force the firm into Stage I. Likewise, indivisibility of resource A can force the firm into Stage III. If in Fig. 9.3 the amount of B has been expanded to its limit of b_1 units, a reduction in A to less than a_5 units will permit the firm to move from Stage III to Stage II. If resource A cannot be divided into a unit smaller than a_5, the firm must operate with negative marginal returns for A.

THE LAW OF DIMINISHING RETURNS TO SCALE

To establish our bearings let us summarize the discussion up to this point. The law of diminishing returns applies to each of the resources taken separately. There will be diminishing returns to A if B is fixed, and there will be diminishing returns to B if A is fixed. Indeed, the law has even broader generality. As previous discussion has implied, diminishing returns will become operative as one resource is increased relative to the other. When A and B are both variable but A is increased in greater proportion than B, diminishing returns to A will eventually set in. Likewise, if B is increased in greater proportion than A, diminishing returns to B will occur.

Let us now turn to another question, the question of returns *to scale* mentioned earlier in the chapter. To isolate the aspect of scale in a firm's production function we shall assume there is no alteration in the proportions in which resources are combined. What happens to output as both resources are expanded in the same proportion turns upon the question of how far apart the isoquants lie in Fig. 9.1.

Illustration of Returns to Scale

The law of diminishing returns to scale states that successive proportionate increments in *all* inputs simultaneously will eventually lead to less than proportionate increments in output. Table 9.2 shows inputs of capital and labor in columns 1 and 2 respectively. The resulting product output is recorded in column 3. In order to isolate the effects of scale it is assumed that the inputs are increased in the same proportion. More exactly, the ratio of capital to labor remains equal to one as both are increased.

Variations in output in response to changes in all inputs may also be divided into three stages. The first is that of increasing returns to scale. This stage is shown in Table 9.2 from zero to 4 units of each input. Successive one-unit increments in both inputs lead to successively larger increments in total output. Thus, increasing both inputs from zero to one increases output by 5; increasing both inputs from one to 2 increases output by 7; and so on. The firm may then enter a second stage called the stage of constant returns to scale. For each successive one-unit increase in each input, total output increases by equal increments. For instance, increasing both capital and labor from 5 to 6 units raises output by 10; increasing both inputs from 6 to 7 again raises output by 10. Moreover, the percentage increases in output

Table 9.2

1	2	3	
Capital	*Labor*	*Total Physical Product*	
0	0	0	Stage of
1	1	5	Increasing
2	2	12	Returns to
3	3	25	Scale
4	4	40	
5	5	50	Stage of Constant
6	6	60	Returns to
7	7	70	Scale
8	8	78	Stage of
9	9	85	Diminishing
10	10	90	Returns to
11	11	92	Scale
12	12	93	

equal the percentage increases in inputs. Eventually, however, the firm will enter into a third stage, that of diminishing returns to scale. One-unit increases in all inputs yield successively smaller additions to output. Increasing capital and labor from 8 to 9 expands output by 7; a further one-unit increase, from 9 to 10, raises output by 5; and so on.

Isoquants

Returns to scale are built into the description of the production function by the distance separating isoquants. Figure 9.4 portrays a segment of an entire production function. For illustrative simplicity the resource input measured on the horizontal axis is designated as a; to establish correspondence with Table 9.2, this input can be considered labor services. On the horizontal axis is measured the input quantity b—or capital services for correspondence with Table 9.2. Of course, a third axis is implied, on which the flow of output is measured. This axis may be considered as extending outward from the printed page. Thus, the isoquants with larger numbers assigned to them represent distances that are farther from the printed page.

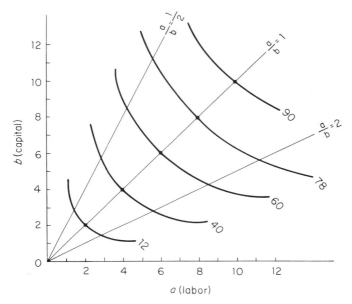

FIG. 9.4. Returns to Scale Expressed by Isoquants

Three rays have been drawn out of the origin. Each ray represents a fixed ratio of a to b as both inputs are allowed to vary. The ray labeled $a/b = 1$ can be compared directly with Table 9.2. When 2 units of a (labor) are combined with 2 units of b (capital), output is 12 and the firm is in the stage of increasing returns to scale. The firm would remain in this stage up to a combination of 4 units of a and 4 units of b, at which output equals 40 units.

At a combination of 6 units of each input, output is 60 and the firm is in the stage of constant returns to scale. The equal inputs of 8, 10, and 12 generate outputs of 60, 78, and 90 respectively. Therefore, the firm is in the stage of diminishing returns to scale.

Proportionate increments in all inputs do not mean that the inputs must be combined in equal amounts. The ray labeled $a/b = 2$ also illustrates returns to scale for a different, though fixed, ratio of resource inputs. Movements upward to the right along the ray entail proportionate increments in both inputs. For this particular ratio, the transition from one stage of returns to another occurs as well. However, as compared to the ratio $a/b = 1$, the transition occurs at a different combination of inputs and a different output. The same interpretation applies to the ratio $a/b = 1/2$.

Any fixed ratio of inputs determines a ray; there is one ray for each ratio. In order to display the assumption of varying returns to scale, the production surface in three dimensions is drawn in such a way that any one of the many rays will generate the result that diminishing returns to scale set in at some quantities of a and b that satisfy the particular fixed ratio.

Returns to Scale and Product Curves

From the three-dimensional production surface, the relationship among different two-dimensional total product curves can easily be derived. The total product curve depicted in Fig. 9.2 was drawn for a specified constant amount of resource B, b_1 units. Had we held the quantity of B constant at some other level, say b_2 units, a different product curve would have been obtained—but similar in shape to the TPP curve drawn in the diagram. When plotting output against alternative amounts of A, the TPP curve so obtained depends upon the level at which we choose to hold resource B constant. Therefore, there is an entire family of such TPP curves, one for each value to which b is set equal. For four illustrative values of b the corresponding TPP curves are depicted as the broken curves in Fig. 9.5. With $b = 1$ and held constant, output varies along the TPP curve so labeled as inputs of A are varied. For $b = 4$, *and held constant*, output varies along another TPP curve with respect to variations in a, and so on for every possible value of b.

By varying both inputs simultaneously the firm moves from one broken curve to another. The unbroken (solid) curve in the diagram traces the way in which output varies as both inputs are increased in the same proportion. Hence, employment of one unit of A and one unit of B places the firm at point P_1. Expansion of both inputs to 4 of A and 4 of B yields an output corresponding to point P_2. Point P_3 results from $a = 7$, and $b = 7$, while P_4 is obtained from $a = 10$ and $b = 10$.

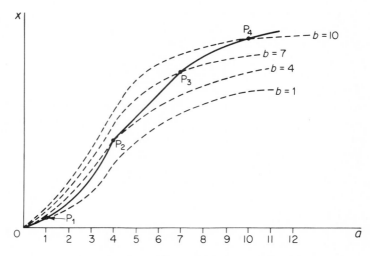

FIG. 9.5.   Returns to Scale in the Production Function

Returns to scale are represented by the shape of the solid curve. From zero units of each resource to 4 units the curve is concave upward, indicating increasing returns to scale. From 4 to 7 units of each resource the solid curve is a straight line, representing constant returns to scale. Finally, beyond 7 units of each resource the curve is concave downward, expressing diminishing returns to scale.

Underlying Determinants

On the face of it constant returns to scale might appear to be the universal rule. After all, if one man with one spade can dig a pit of a given size in a day, then two men with two spades should be able to dig two such pits. Or if an automobile plant can produce 100 cars per day, then addition of another identical plant should raise output to 200 cars per day. Is this not the way verbal algebra problems are set up in elementary school? Indeed, constant returns to scale are operative over quite broad ranges of output in some productive operations. If all resource inputs were indefinitely divisible and available in infinite quantities, constant returns to scale would characterize the entire production function. The solid curve in Fig. 9.5 would be a straight line out of the origin. Absence of constant returns to scale over some spans of output springs essentially from the same forces that influence the shapes of product curves under the condition that some inputs are fixed.

For relatively small outputs technological indivisibilities in A or B impart upward concavity to the solid curve in Fig. 9.5. If a resource is indivisible, such that the smallest practical size is "too much" when combined with relatively small amounts of others, that resource will not be used to best advantage at small outputs. A case in point is a motor-driven conveyor used to raise materials in building construction. When too few laborers and materials are combined with it, the conveyor has to stand idle for some periods—performing no productive operation while men distribute the materials raised or supplies are awaited because too few delivery trucks are used relative to conveyor capacity. Then, the conveyor must run for some periods with no load, or it must be turned on and off, thus consuming more motor fuel per raised load. With expansion in all other inputs—trucks, materials, and laborers—its use is also expanded as additional laborers speed the distribution of more raised materials. The reduction in idle time will result in additions to output (constructed building parts) greater in proportion than equal proportionate increases in all inputs, which means increasing returns to scale. Very often indivisibilities such as these can be circumvented. The conveyor might be used on alternate days—one day on this job and the next on another—so that delivery and distribution of materials could be performed on the off-day. Perhaps a smaller conveyor would lead to a more steady flow of raised materials. However, a smaller conveyor may not exist, and movement from one project to another on alternate days may not be feasible. Opportunities to achieve divisibility in usage may run into practical obstacles. If so, the firm will experience increasing returns to scale as the indivisible inputs are used more effectively.

More important than indivisibilities is the limitation on available resources that lies at the heart of diminishing returns to scale. As the size of the firm grows, scarcity in resources *of a given quality* becomes significant. In effect, all resources cannot be increased in the same proportion because changes in quality occur. Diminishing returns become operative because in reality some inputs are increased relative to others. This is most likely to find expression in human resources. When personnel of less skill must be employed, expansions in the number employed actually increases faster than additions of manpower. Though it is adding men in the same proportion as other inputs, in reality the firm is not increasing labor *power* or *services* in the same proportion. Ultimately this will reduce to variations in managerial ability, especially at the top level. With growing size greater complexities emerge. Administrative officers have less direct contact with the daily operations of the firm, and decisions must be left to subordinates (or secretaries). If management of the same quality could be increased indefinitely at every level in the hierarchy, diminishing returns to scale could be avoided. Eventually, however, at some size, rigidities and lack of communication will set in, leading to the well-known concept of "red tape."

SHIFTS IN THE PRODUCTION FUNCTION

A firm's production function describes the relationship between all possible combinations of inputs and the (maximum) output corresponding to each combination. It was seen earlier that this entire relationship is determined by the state of technology. Consequently a technological change will alter the entire function. The locomotive, the internal combustion engine, nitrogen fertilizer, and nuclear energy are examples of discoveries that have led to changes in the state of technology. The state of technology improves when some invention or other type of innovation permits the adoption of more efficient production techniques. The innovation need not apply only to material, nonhuman resources. A change in the quality of human resources due to the introduction of mass education, for example, has altered the state of technology in the Western world.

In this connection a careful distinction must be made between (1) a change in the production function and (2) a shift in the product curves. Whether they amount to the same thing depends upon which product curves one has in mind. Consider the product curves drawn in Fig. 9.2, for example. We have seen that the curves will shift position if the amount of B is changed. And this holds true with a constant state of technology. This is shown in Fig. 9.5. However, the solid curve in Fig. 9.5 allows for variations in both resource inputs. Consequently, given the state of technology, the solid curve cannot shift position.

A technological change will shift all curves in Fig. 9.5. Since it involves a different production technique, technological improvement changes the output obtainable by varying one input with the other fixed (indeed it does shift the position of the curves in Fig. 9.2). Furthermore, it alters the output obtainable from variations in all resources. Technological change shifts the solid curve and all the broken curves *because it shifts the entire system of isoquants*. A technological improvement shifts all curves upward, a technological deterioration (due to a war perhaps) shifts all of them downward.

PROBLEMS

1.   Assume a firm produces a product using two factors of production, which are denoted by A and B. The amount of B is fixed at 10 units per unit of time. The following table shows how total output varies as the amount of A is varied.

Amount of B	Amount of A	Total Product	Amount of B	Amount of A	Total Product
10	0	0	10	110	390
10	10	5	10	120	410
10	20	20	10	130	425
10	30	40	10	140	435
10	40	80	10	150	440
10	50	150	10	160	442
10	60	210	10	170	443
10	70	260	10	180	440
10	80	300	10	190	430
10	90	335	10	200	400
10	100	365			

(*a*) Compute the average and marginal physical products of A corresponding to each alternative amount of A.

(*b*) Plot the total physical product curve on graph paper as Figure 1.

(*c*) Plot the average physical product curve and the marginal physical product curves in the same diagram as Figure 2.

(*d*) Distinguish the three stages of production, describe their characteristics, and explain their meaning.

(*e*) Suppose the resource A is free; the firm can have any quantity it wishes without having to pay anything for it. Approximately how much of A would the firm use? Why would it not use more? Why not less?

2.   For the same firm, let us now assume the amount of B is altered. The effects on total product are shown in the following table.

Amount of B	Total Product for Each Amount of A
10	Given in Problem 1
20	40 units greater than in Problem 1
30	20 units greater than in Problem 1

(a) The TPP curve for 10 units of B was drawn in Figure 1 of the preceding problem. Redraw the curve and label the diagram Figure 3. Also plot in Figure 3 the TPP curve when B equals 20 units and the TPP curve when B equals 30 units.

(b) When B is increased from 10 to 20 units (and A is varied from 10 to 20 units), is the firm in a state of increasing, constant, or diminishing returns to scale? Explain.

(c) When B is increased from 20 to 30 units (and A is varied from 20 to 30 units), is the firm in a stage of increasing, constant, or diminishing returns to scale? Explain.

(d) Suppose an invention improves the state of technology so that the firm can adopt a more efficient production technique. How would you express its effects upon production in terms of the curves drawn in Figure 3? Explain.

SUGGESTED READING

J. M. Cassels, "On the Law of Variable Proportions," in *Explorations in Economics*. New York: McGraw-Hill Book Company, Inc., 1936. (Reprinted in *Readings in the Theory of Income Distribution*, pp. 103–18. Philadelphia: The Blakiston Co., 1946.)

F. Machlup, "On the Meaning of the Marginal Product," in *Explorations in Economics*. (Reprinted in *Readings in the Theory of Income Distribution*, pp. 158–374.)

F. L. Patton, *Diminishing Returns in Agriculture*, pp. 1–35. New York: Columbia University Press, 1926.

10

Short-Run Costs
of Production

In the absence of serious indivisibilities and stringent limitations on resource availability, a firm will operate in the stage of diminishing returns
to all inputs. But the theory of production does not specify which one of
the outputs encompassed by this stage the firm will produce. The final output
decision depends upon both revenue and costs, monetary considerations
that are not accounted for in the production function. Nevertheless, the
behavior of cost—and to the extent that cost affects output, the firm's
ultimate output decision—rests upon the nature of the production function.

THE ECONOMIC CONCEPT OF COST

Opportunity Cost

Resources employed in one use generate a certain amount of product. From
an economic perspective the "real" cost of this product is what these resources could have produced in another employment, the output that has
been sacrificed by their present employment. More exactly, the real cost is
the *maximum* quantity the resources could have produced in any other employment. Economic cost is described as "opportunity cost" because the
cost arises from the foregone opportunities of the resources in question.
When economic cost is measured in money rather than in physical magnitudes, it is the maximum value of other products that determines the cost
of producing this one. Therefore, opportunity cost expressed in money depends upon the market value or price of alternative commodities as well as
upon the physical productivity of the resources in different uses.

The common sense behind the opportunity-cost principle is rather simple.
Social costs are in actuality opportunity costs. Given that resources are
fully employed, society can procure more of one good only by sacrificing
some of another. Resources must be transferred from one employment to
another, relinquishing what they could produce elsewhere in order to gain
more of the one toward whose production they are directed. From the viewpoint of an individual also, the economic cost of accepting employment in

one firm is foregone income—the maximum income that person could earn by having instead taken a job elsewhere. Moreover, if markets are perfect,[1] the money expended on resources by a firm will equal the opportunity costs of the resource owners. Unless a firm does pay resource owners at least what they could earn by selling their resource services elsewhere, those resources will be transferred to some other firm. In general, a firm must pay enough to hold on to its resources or to attract the desired quantities away from alternative employments.

In their accounting procedures many firms do not use the economic definition of cost. What the firm records as its expenses of operation are frequently not the same as the economic costs of production. A brief example will make this clear. Let the firm under consideration be a grocery store. Assume an entrepreneur rents store space and provides capital equipment such as counters, shelves, etc. He hires one clerk and also works in the store himself. It is common practice for such a person to count as the firm's profit all income accruing to him after the expenses of operation have been met. The firm's income statement at the close of a year might appear as follows:

Revenue from Sales		$50,000
Less Costs:		
Payments for merchandise	$40,000	
Rent for store space	2,000	
Clerk's wages	3,000	
Total Costs		45,000
Total Profit		$5,000

The entrepreneur may view the firm's profit as $5,000, but the economist does not treat the $5,000 as profit—or he does not necessarily regard all of it as profit because the economic definition of cost differs from that shown in the income statement. Since the entrepreneur works in the store, he has contributed labor services. Some of his $5,000 income ought to be considered as wages rather than profit. Also, the entrepreneur has contributed capital equipment, the return on which is regarded as interest on his investment. These two items, the entrepreneur's own wages and his interest return for a capital input, are costs to the firm considered as an entity in itself.[2]

A question arises as to how much should be allowed for the entrepreneur's wages and interest. The answer is provided by the opportunity-cost principle. In deducting wages and interest from total revenue to arrive at the firm's profit, their dollar amounts are set equal to the maximum amounts the entrepreneur could earn by using these resources in alternative employments. Suppose the maximum labor return he could earn in similar employments is

[1] For our present purposes markets may be said to be perfect if no one trader can exercise control over the price and if all resources are perfectly mobile among employments.

[2] See the definition of a firm discussed in Chapter 2.

$3,000 per year, and the maximum return on the same dollar investment employed in any other productive endeavor is $1,500. When these two items are included as costs to the firm, total cost becomes $45,000 plus $4,500, or $49,500; and the firm's pure profit becomes $500. On the other hand, had the maximum alternative wages and interest added up to $6,000, the firm would incur a net loss of $1,000.

Explicit costs are those arising from contracts between the entrepreneur and other persons. They are what one usually thinks of as the firm's expenses of operation. Overhead, labor payroll, and payments for raw materials are ordinarily included as long as they result in a transfer of funds from the entrepreneur to other persons. In our example of the grocery store, the expenditures for inventories, the rent, and the clerk's salary are explicit costs.

Implicit costs of production may be thought of as those costs arising from a contract between the entrepreneur and himself, i.e., between the entrepreneur in his role as entrepreneur and the entrepreneur in his role as resource owner. They are the costs of self-owned or self-employed resources that are frequently omitted as costs in the accounting procedures followed by firms. In our example, the entrepreneur's own wages (arising from a labor contract we *impute* to the entrepreneur) and an interest return (arising from an *imputed* interest contract) are implicit costs of production to the firm.

Insofar as any payment to the owner of a resource is contractual, it is counted as an economic cost. The contract need not be conceived of as a written legal document, or even an explicit verbal statement. The criterion for judging whether an item is to be counted as a cost in the economic sense depends upon whether it can be interpreted as an agreed-upon remuneration for services rendered by resources. It is required only that it be a fixed payment for each unit of the resource service used per unit of time, such as a wage rate per hour or an interest rate per year. Then it assumes the nature of a contract. Whether there will be an imputed contract (creating an implicit cost) depends upon whether the entrepreneur supplies resource services to the firm like any other resource owner. Thus, payments by the entrepreneur to himself in his capacity as resource owner are set equal to the maximum earnings he could obtain from this resources in alternative employments. If our grocer could sell his labor services to another grocery firm and invest his capital elsewhere, he might be able to increase his income by doing so. In order to determine the profitability of his grocery firm, the firm's costs should include its implicit costs. Otherwise the entrepreneur cannot tell whether the firm is making a pure profit over and above the earnings he could obtain by merely selling his labor and capital services to some other firm.

The example of a grocery store may prove to be misleading unless it can be shown that similar applications of explicit and implicit costs can be made to larger and more complex firms. In a large corporation the stockholders are the owners of the firm's factory buildings, equipment, inventories, and other assets. We regard the stockholders as entrepreneurs, and the corporation executives are owners of a particular kind of labor service, namely managerial ability. The executives are paid a salary by the firm—a contractual payment in exchange for their labor, which is an explicit cost. The executives may also be stockholders, but for that matter so may the firm's secretaries, truck drivers, or other employees. Whoever the stockholders are, whether they do or do not receive wages or salaries from this firm, they do receive dividends. Economically speaking, some portion of a dividend (or perhaps all of it) is an implicit cost to the firm, not profit. A dividend payment equal to what the stockholders could earn had they invested elsewhere is an implicit cost. It is similar to the grocer's return on his investment. If for each $100 invested a dividend of $5 is paid, and if $4 is the maximum that could be earned elsewhere, then $4 is counted as cost and $1 as profit. The cost of the resources obtained by the firm with the stockholders' money is the value of the alternative products foregone by holding the money where it is. To hold the money where it is, the corporation must pay a return to the stockholders at least equal to the return they could earn if they put their money at the disposal of any other firm. Therefore, regardless of the size or structure of a firm, whether it be a small single proprietorship or a gigantic corporation, its economic costs of production are related to opportunity costs. And opportunity costs expressed in money include both explicit and implicit costs.

Costs as Efficiency Costs

The cost of production varies as a firm changes its output. The cost corresponding to each output is defined in economics as an efficiency cost—in the sense that the expenditure by the firm is the minimum cost of producing the particular output. The notion of least cost can be clarified by bringing together the production possibilities and the financial constraints of a firm.

An isocost line is like the budget line of an individual consumer. A budget line shows the different combinations of goods a consumer can purchase with a given income to spend on them. An isocost line shows the different combinations of resources a firm can purchase with a given monetary cost outlay. Assume a firm uses two resources, A and B. Its total outlay equals the price per unit of A times the amount of A used plus the price per unit of B times the amount of B used. In symbolic notation:

$$p_a a + p_b b = \text{TC}$$

where a and b denote the quantities of A and B per unit of time, p_a and p_b represent the prices of A and B, and TC designates the total combined cost outlay on A and B by the firm.

The isocost line is depicted in Figure 10.1. Notice its similarity to the budget line of the consumer. If the firm uses zero units of B, then $p_b b = 0$

in the above formula, and $a = TC/p_a$. This is the point of intersection of the line with the horizontal axis. If $a = 0$, then $b = TC/p_b$, the intersection with the vertical axis. These and all other points on the line show the values of a and b that satisfy the above equation. Thus, for given prices of the resources and a given expenditure on them, the line shows the alternative combinations of A and B that can be purchased.

For a given total outlay on resources, it is assumed that the firm will attempt to obtain the greatest possible output. In terms of its isoquants this means it will move to the highest possible isoquant that its isocost line will allow. The firm seeks to maximize output subject to the isocost constraint.

Figure 10.2 brings together the firm's isoquants and isocost line. The firm will be on the highest isoquant permitted by its isocost line when the isocost

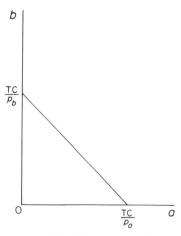

FIG. 10.1.   Isocost Line

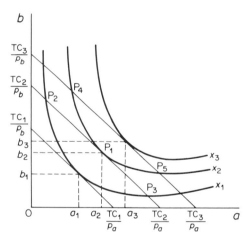

FIG. 10.2.   Least-Cost Combinations of Resources

line is tangent to an isoquant. Suppose first that the total cost outlay is to be TC_2. Then the firm will operate at point P_1, producing x_2 units by using a_2 units of A and b_2 units of B. Any other combination of A and B obtainable with an outlay of TC_2 at the given factor prices would leave the firm on a lower isoquant. Moving toward P_2 or P_3 means the firm would produce a smaller output at the same cost. Another way of saying this is that the given output of x_2 is produced at the least cost if a_2 of A and b_2 of B are used to produce it. Points like P_4 or P_5 entail the same output at a higher cost, TC_3 instead of TC_2.

The least-cost combinations of A and B for producing other outputs can also be seen from the diagram. At an outlay of TC_3, the least-cost combination of A and B for producing x_3 units of output is a_3 of A and b_3 of B. At an outlay of TC_1 the least-cost combination for producing x_1 is a_1 of A and

b_1 of B. Each tangency point yields an output and the smallest total cost of producing that output. The entire set of tangency points traces the firm's expansion path, showing a relationship between output and least cost.[3]

COST SCHEDULES AND COST CURVES

In the present chapter we are concerned only with the short run in which some resource inputs are variable and others are fixed. Often it takes considerable time to rent or construct a new building, to order machines built to specification, or to recruit skilled labor. Consequently, the short run is not defined in terms of a fixed number of days or years. If during any calendar period it is impossible for the firm to vary at least one resource input, the firm is said to be operating in the short run.

Sometimes fixed resources give rise to variable costs, or variable resources result in fixed costs. Land used by the firm may be fixed in amount. But if the rental contract specifies that the rent shall be based upon output, the fixed input will yield a cost that varies with output. On the other hand, more or less hours of secretarial labor can be used without alteration in the cost of secretarial labor as output varies, granted that the firm's secretaries are paid a fixed salary.

To simplify the discussion, it will be assumed that fixed resources result in fixed costs and variable resources result in variable costs. Variable costs are, therefore, the explicit and implicit costs of variable resources employed by the firm. The total quantities of fixed resources are sometimes referred to as the firm's scale of plant. Then, by definition, the scale of plant is not variable in the short run, and the cost of the plant is the firm's fixed cost.[4]

This distinction between fixed cost and variable cost forms the basis for the analysis of three cost concepts: total cost, average cost, and marginal cost.

Total Cost

Assuming a firm employs the two resources A and B, total cost was defined earlier as $\text{TC} = p_a a + p_b b$. By definition of the short run, not all resources are variable. Therefore, suppose we interpret B to mean the firm's scale of plant. That is, output can be varied only by using more or less of

---

[3] The slope of the isocost line is equal to minus the ratio of the price of A to the price of B (see discussion of the budget line in Chapter 5). In the previous chapter it was shown that the slope of an isoquant is given by $\text{MRTS}_{ab} = \text{MPP}_a/\text{MPP}_b$. Since, at the tangency point, the slope of an isocost line equals the slope of an isoquant, it follows that $\text{MPP}_a/\text{MPP}_b = p_a/p_b$. Rearranging this equation, we can write $\text{MPP}_a/p_a = \text{MPP}_b/p_b$. The firm will satisfy this condition at each possible output. To obtain any output at least cost, the marginal physical product of a dollar's worth of one resource must equal the marginal product of a dollar's worth of every other resource used.

[4] It is important to avoid thinking of the plant as the factory only. It is defined as the total quantity of all fixed resources, regardless of which resources these may be. In addition, the firm may have several factories, each in a different location. The firm's fixed plant will then include all of these factories if they are all fixed in size.

resource A in combination with a fixed amount of B. Let the fixed quantity of B per unit of time be represented by $\bar{b}$. We assume the price of A, $\bar{p}_a$, and the price of B, p_b, are constant; so let us draw bars over them also, giving $\bar{p}_a$ and $\bar{p}_b$ as the symbols denoting the given resource prices.[5] Since $\bar{b}$ and $\bar{p}_b$ are both fixed numbers, $\bar{p}_b\bar{b}$ is also a fixed number. This is the firm's total fixed cost, which may be expressed symbolically as TFC = $\bar{p}_b\bar{b}$. Regardless of the output produced by the firm, total fixed cost will remain a constant amount because the amount of B and its price are both constant.

The resource A is a variable input. Since the price per unit of A is assumed constant, total expenditures on A by the firm will increase as more A is used. Consequently, total variable cost is expressed as TVC = $\bar{p}_a a$. We see from this equation that total variable cost will rise as output is increased, for additions to output require additional units of A.

The breakdown of total cost into its fixed and variable components can be summarized schematically as follows:

$$\text{TC} = \text{TVC} + \text{TFC} = \bar{p}_a a + \bar{p}_b \bar{b}$$

Since in this formula only a is variable, total cost will change with changes in a. Changes in a are in turn dependent upon changes in output, so total cost can be related to output. Our next problem, therefore, is to discover the way in which total cost varies as output is expanded or contracted.

Table 10.1 shows the total fixed cost schedule, the total variable cost schedule, and the total cost schedule of a firm producing a commodity X. Column 1 records the variable amounts of resource A used to produce X,

Table 10.1

1	2	3	4	5	6
			TFC = $p_b\bar{b}$	TVC = $\bar{p}_a a$	TC =
a	$\bar{b}$	x	= \$10 × 30	= \$100 × a	TFC + TVC
0	30	0	\$300	\$ 0	\$ 300
$1\frac{1}{2}$	30	1	300	150	450
$2\frac{1}{2}$	30	2	300	250	550
$3\frac{1}{4}$	30	3	300	325	625
$3\frac{3}{4}$	30	4	300	375	675
$4\frac{1}{2}$	30	5	300	450	750
$5\frac{1}{2}$	30	6	300	550	850
7	30	7	300	700	1,000
9	30	8	300	900	1,200
12	30	9	300	1,200	1,500

[5] Taking the resource prices as constant is tantamount to assuming their prices are not affected by the quantity of resources purchased by the firm. In actuality this may not be true in some cases, e.g., a resource price may be bid up as the firm employs more of it. Nevertheless, we shall maintain the assumption of constant resource prices because this simplification greatly helps to clarify the nature of cost curves. Cases in which firms do affect resource prices, and the implications for cost analysis, will be discussed in Chapters 20–22.

while column 2 shows that the amount of B is fixed at 30 units per unit of time. In the third column the output of X per unit of time, x, obtained from each combination of a and b is presented. This is total physical product, so the first three columns actually demonstrate the firm's production function.

We assume the price of resource B is given as $10 per unit, yielding a total fixed cost of $300 shown in column 4. Though the price of A is assumed constant at $100 per unit, the amount of A used is not. Consequently, total variable cost, recorded in column 5, rises as x increases because a increases as x increases. Finally, in column 6 total cost is shown.

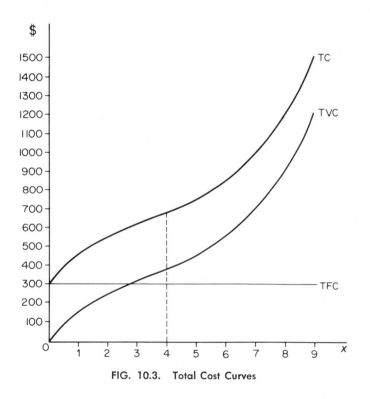

FIG. 10.3.   Total Cost Curves

From this schedule the costs can be plotted against output. In Fig. 10.3 the quantity of X per unit of time is measured on the horizontal axis, and costs in dollars are measured on the vertical axis. Since total fixed cost amounts to $300 regardless of the firm's output, the total fixed cost curve (labeled TFC in Fig. 10.3) is a horizontal line. It lies above the horizontal axis by a distance equal to $300 measured on the vertical axis.

Total variable cost rises as output increases. Notice that at first, up to 4 units of output, each successive unit increment in output raises total variable cost by *less* than the preceding increment. On the other hand, beyond 4 units of output each successive unit increment in output adds *more* to variable cost than does the preceding one. This is reflected in Fig. 10.3 by the downward concavity of the TVC curve to the left of 4 units on the horizontal axis and by the upward concavity of the curve to the right of 4 units.

This is where the production function once more enters the picture. *For the behavior of total variable cost follows directly from the law of diminishing returns.* The precise shape of the total variable cost curve depends upon the shape of the firm's total physical product curve. Examine Fig. 10.4, which depicts the total physical product curve, plotted from columns 1 and 3 of Table 10.1. Observe that the TPP curve is concave upward from zero units of A to $3\frac{3}{4}$ units of A and concave downward thereafter. At $3\frac{3}{4}$ units of A the firm passes from Stage I on its production function to Stage II, the stage of diminishing returns. Next examine Fig. 10.5, where the TVC curve is reproduced. Notice first that $3\frac{3}{4}$ units of A (given 30 units of B) yield 4

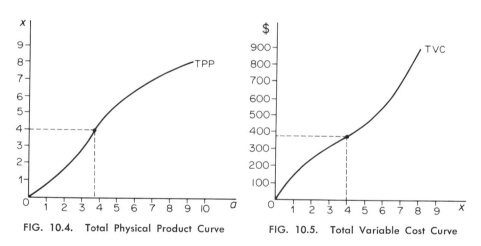

FIG. 10.4.   Total Physical Product Curve   FIG. 10.5.   Total Variable Cost Curve

units of X, as can be seen from Table 10.1. For outputs smaller than 4, less than $3\frac{3}{4}$ units of A are being used and the firm is in Stage I. Beyond 4 units of X, more than $3\frac{3}{4}$ units of A are employed and the firm is in Stage II. It is precisely because the TPP curve is at first concave upward and then concave downward that the TVC curve is at first concave downward and then concave upward. The quantity of A at which the TPP curve changes concavity produces the quantity of X at which the TVC curve changes concavity. Were output to be carried to its absolute maximum (the beginning of Stage III), the TVC curve would become vertical, for additional units of resource A cannot add to output, although they do add to cost.

It may be helpful to look at this cost behavior in another way. While in Stage I the firm is using A too sparsely in combination with the fixed amount of B. Thus A may represent too little labor combined with the fixed scale of plant, B. By adding more men, each one-man addition expands output by more than the previous one as cooperative effort and specialization of tasks facilitate the elimination of wasted motion. Each man adds $100 to total cost (the wage per week). Hence, by adding another man, cost rises by $100 while output per week rises by successively greater amounts. Each $100 addition to cost stretches output further as it were, for x is increasing faster than TVC. Then when the firm enters Stage II, each additional $100 spent on labor creates successively smaller additions to output. As a result, total variable cost will rise faster than output.

The last column in Table 10.1 shows total cost, the sum of total fixed and total variable costs at each level of output. In Fig. 10.3 the TC curve is obtained by adding to the TVC curve at each point a vertical distance equal to the height of the TFC curve above the horizontal axis. It follows that the TC curve and the TVC curve must have the same shape. The vertical distance between them at each output is a constant amount equal to total fixed cost. So any increase in output increases total cost and total variable cost by the same amount—another way of saying the TC and TVC curves have the same slope at each output.

Average Costs

The costs per unit of the commodity produced are classified as average fixed cost, average variable cost, and average cost. Average cost is the sum of average fixed costs and average variable costs. These cost concepts impart essentially the same information as the total costs, but the expression of costs in terms of averages rather than totals is more useful for the analysis of certain problems.

Average fixed cost is the fixed cost per unit of the commodity produced. It is computed by dividing total fixed cost by output. Referring again to resources A and B used to produce X, and assuming the quantity of B is fixed, we have

$$AFC = \frac{TFC}{x} = \frac{\bar{p}_b \bar{b}}{x}$$

where AFC signifies average fixed cost.

Average variable cost is simply the variable cost per unit of the commodity produced, and is computed by dividing total variable cost by output:

$$AVC = \frac{TVC}{x} = \frac{\bar{p}_a a}{x}$$

Here the symbol AVC denotes average variable cost.

Finally, average cost is the sum of average fixed and average variable costs. Total cost is divided by output to find average cost: $AC = TC/x$, where AC represents average cost. Since we know $TC = TVC + TFC$, we can write average cost as

$$AC = \frac{TVC + TFC}{x} = \frac{TVC}{x} + \frac{TFC}{x} = \frac{\bar{p}_a a}{x} + \frac{\bar{p}_b \bar{b}}{x} = AVC + AFC$$

From Table 10.1 the average cost schedules can easily be derived. Column 2 of Table 10.2 presents the average fixed cost schedule. At each output average fixed cost is computed by dividing total fixed cost, $300, by that output. The average fixed cost curve is plotted as AFC in Fig. 10.6, where the numerical scales on the axes are omitted for convenience. It is seen that average fixed cost must decline as output increases. Since total fixed cost is constant, a fixed amount of money is spread over more and more units as larger outputs are considered, so each unit of product bears a smaller share. Notice, however, that average fixed cost will never become zero—the AFC curve will never touch the horizontal axis. Regardless of how large x may become, the ratio $\bar{p}_b \bar{b}/x$ cannot become zero so long as neither p_b nor b is zero.

Table 10.2

1	2	3	4
x	$\text{AFC} = \dfrac{\$300}{x}$	$\text{AVC} = \dfrac{\text{TVC}}{x}$	$\text{AC} = \text{AFC} + \text{AVC}$
0	∞	∞	∞
1	$300	$150	$450
2	150	125	275
3	100	108.33	208.33
4	75	93.75	168.75
5	60	90	150
6	50	91.67	141.67
7	42.86	100	142.86
8	37.50	112	150
9	33.33	133.33	166.66

To obtain average variable cost the total variable cost of column 5 in Table 10.1 is divided by the quantity of the commodity produced. Column 3 of Table 10.2 shows that average variable cost declines at first as larger outputs are produced; it reaches a minimum and then increases with output thereafter. Average variable cost is plotted as the AVC curve in Fig. 10.6. And, again, it is the production function which imparts to the AVC curve its U shape. Just as the shape of the TVC curve depends upon the shape of the TPP curve, so the shape of the AVC curve is determined by the firm's APP_a curve. With resource A the variable input it has been shown that average variable cost may be written

$$\text{AVC} = \frac{\bar{p}_a a}{x}$$

which may be rewritten as

$$\text{AVC} = \bar{p}_a \cdot \frac{a}{x} = \frac{\bar{p}_a}{x/a} = \frac{\bar{p}_a}{\text{APP}_a}$$

Since the price of resource A is held constant, average variable cost varies inversely with the average physical product of A—AVC falls as APP_a rises and rises as APP_a falls. In our discussion of production functions it was demonstrated that as the input of A increases, hence as output increases, the average physical product of the variable resource rises at first, reaches a maximum and then declines. It follows that the average variable cost must fall, reach a minimum and then rise. The amount of A for which the APP_a curve is at its highest point produces the amount of X at which the AVC curve is at its lowest point.

The common-sense interpretation of this bit of algebra should be clear. Suppose once more that B represents a fixed plant and A represents labor. As the firm applies more units of labor the stage of increasing returns to labor is experienced at first. The output produced by one laborer is extremely small, but when another laborer is added the specialization of tasks and saving of energy permit output to more than double. Since the laborers are hired at a fixed wage rate, doubling labor cost (total variable cost) will more than double output. Therefore, the labor cost per unit of product (average variable cost) must decline; and this continues throughout Stage I of the production function. Eventually, however, Stage II will be reached in which the average physical product of labor declines. Doubling labor input, for example, will double total variable cost, but it will not double output. As a consequence the average variable cost will rise with output precisely because the average physical product of labor is declining. The law of diminishing average physical product in the short run might well be called the law of increasing average variable cost.

The third per-unit cost, average cost, is shown in column 4 of Table 10.2. It is computed in either of two ways: dividing total cost in column 6 of Table 10.1 by the quantity of X produced, or by adding columns 2 and 3 of Table 10.2. The average cost curve is labeled AC in Fig. 10.6. Because the AC curve is the result of summing vertically the AFC and AVC curves, it has a ∪ shape arising from the ∪ shape of the AVC curve. The vertical distance between the AC and AVC curves at each output is equal to the vertical distance between the AFC curve and the horizontal axis at that output. As one moves farther to the right the AC curve approaches the AVC curve because the AFC curve approaches the horizontal axis. But since the AFC curve never touches the axis, the AC curve never touches the AVC curve.

As larger outputs are considered the productive efficiency of the fixed resource B continually increases, i.e., the AFC curve slopes downward, while the efficiency of the variable resource increases at first and then declines. The AC curve reflects the combined efficiency of both fixed and variable resources. It slopes downward at first because the efficiencies of both types of resources are increasing. However, the efficiency of the variable resource reaches a peak and then declines, exerting a force that operates to turn the AC curve upward. In a sense the AVC curve "pulls" the AC curve upward along with it when it turns up. Though the variable resource becomes less

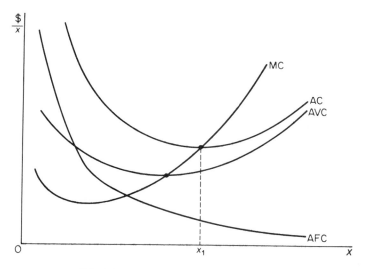

FIG. 10.6. Average and Marginal Costs

efficient, the fixed resource is still becoming more efficient. Hence, the upward pull of the AVC curve is counteracted by the downward pull of the AFC curve. These counteracting forces cause the AC curve to reach its minimum point at a greater output (farther to the right) than the output at which the AVC curve is at its minimum point.

Marginal Cost

Marginal cost of production is defined as the change in total cost that results from a small change in output. Usually the change in output is taken to be a one-unit increment. In terms of our symbolic notation $MC = \Delta TC/\Delta x$, where Δ again signifies "a change in." We have already seen that total cost is the sum of total variable costs and total fixed costs. Fixed cost does not change with changes in output, so the change in total cost must be entirely due to a change in total variable cost. That is, $\Delta TC = \Delta TVC$. Utilizing the definition of total cost introduced previously, we can write

$$ MC = \frac{\Delta(\bar{p}_a a + \bar{p}_b \bar{b})}{\Delta x} = \frac{\Delta(\bar{p}_a a)}{\Delta x} + \frac{\Delta(\bar{p}_b \bar{b})}{\Delta x} = \frac{\Delta(\bar{p}_a a)}{\Delta x} + 0 = \frac{\Delta TVC}{\Delta x} $$

The change in fixed cost with respect to a change in output is zero. Consequently, marginal cost does not depend in any way upon fixed cost.

Marginal cost is computed by dividing the change in total cost—or the change in total variable cost—by the unit change in output that gives rise to the cost change. With reference to Table 10.1, total cost is given in column 6. Each Δx is taken to be one unit since we are considering one-unit changes

Table 10.3

1	2
x	$\text{MC} = \dfrac{\Delta \text{TC}}{\Delta x}$
0	
1	$150
2	100
3	75
4	50
5	75
6	100
7	150
8	200
9	300

in output. The corresponding changes in total cost are shown in Table 10.3, and the marginal cost curve is plotted in Figure 10.6 where it is labeled MC.

Like the AVC and AC curves the MC curve is typically U-shaped. And just as the shapes of the AVC and AC curves depend upon the shape of the APP_a curve, so the shape of the MC curve depends upon the shape of the MPP_a curve. It has been shown that marginal cost is defined as

$$\text{MC} = \frac{\Delta \text{TVC}}{\Delta x} = \frac{\Delta(\bar{p}_a a)}{\Delta x}$$

which may be written

$$\text{MC} = \frac{\Delta(\bar{p}_a a)}{\Delta x} = \bar{p}_a \cdot \frac{\Delta a}{\Delta x} = \frac{\bar{p}_a}{\Delta x / \Delta a} = \frac{\bar{p}_a}{\text{MPP}_a}$$

The denominator in the last expression is the marginal physical product of the variable resource A. With the price of A held constant, marginal cost falls as the marginal physical product rises, and rises as the marginal product falls. The marginal physical product of A rises at first. Therefore, marginal cost must decline at first as output expands. After a point, however, the marginal product of A diminishes, so the marginal cost must rise, imparting to the MC curve its U shape. The amount of A at which the marginal physical product of A is a maximum produces the quantity of X at which marginal cost is a minimum. If the employment of A is carried far enough, its marginal product becomes zero, so marginal cost becomes infinite.

Marginal cost of production is entirely independent of fixed cost, so the MC curve bears no relation to the AFC curve. But average variable cost is related to marginal cost. When the MC curve is below the AVC curve, average variable cost is declining as output expands. When the MC curve is above the AVC curve, average variable cost is rising with larger outputs. The MC curve cuts the AVC curve at the minimum point on the AVC curve; when marginal cost equals average variable cost, average variable cost is neither increasing nor decreasing. Notice that it is not a question of whether the MC curve is sloped upward or downward that determines whether average variable cost is rising or falling. Rather it is a question of whether the MC curve is above or below the AVC curve.

A similar type of relationship was seen to hold between the marginal physical product of a variable resource and its average physical product. In the case of the firm's production function the MPP_a curve lies above the APP_a curve while the APP_a curve is sloped upward; the MPP_a curve intersects the APP_a curve when average physical product is a maximum; and it lies below the APP_a curve when the APP_a curve is sloped downward. The MC and AVC curves *look like* the MPP_a and APP_a curves turned upside down. The cost curves, however, are not simply the product curves turned upside down. The product curves are drawn with physical output measured on the vertical axis and physical input of the variable resource measured on the horizontal axis. Cost curves, on the other hand, are drawn with money costs measured on the vertical axis and physical output on the horizontal axis.

The MC curve intersects the AC curve at its minimum point also. It is below the AC curve when average cost is declining, and it is above the AC curve when average cost is rising. The explanation of this relationship is the same as that of the relationship between the MC and AVC curves. Because minimum average cost occurs at a greater output than that at which average variable cost is a minimum, the MC curve intersects the AC curve at a point farther to the right.

Short-Run Optimum Output

A firm's optimum output is defined as that output at which average cost is a minimum. In Fig. 10.6 an output of x_1 units is the firm's optimum output of commodity X. The per-unit cost of production is the smallest possible, given the fixed amount of resource B.

Suppose A represents variable labor and B the fixed scale of plant. If the firm produces x_1 units of the product, the cost of both inputs per unit of the product is smallest. This output is the firm's "most efficient" output in the sense that the firm's given scale of plant is being utilized most efficiently. At smaller outputs average cost is higher, which means that too little labor is combined with the fixed plant—too little in that there are too few laborers to permit effective use of the fixed resources. Expansion in the input of labor makes possible more efficient utilization of the plant with the result that cost per unit of product declines as more is produced. This continues up to what we call optimum output where average cost is least. If output were to be increased further by increasing the input of labor, there would be too many laborers combined with the fixed plant to keep average cost from rising, because the plant is utilized less and less effectively. Thus beyond x_1 units of output average cost continually rises as larger outputs are produced.

SHIFTS IN THE POSITION OF SHORT-RUN COST CURVES

In previous discussions it was shown that consumer demand for a commodity or a firm's production function can be expressed in symbolic functional notation. The same holds true for a firm's cost of production. In general, we can write

$$\text{TC} = f(x,\ p_a,\ p_b,\ b,\ \text{F})$$

to signify that short-run total cost is a function of, or depends upon, every variable inside the parentheses—output, x; the prices of resources, p_a and p_b; the amount of the fixed factor of production, b; and the firm's production function, F. The firm's total cost *curve* relates total cost to output, and is drawn under the condition that resource prices and the amount of B are conceptually held constant. Since the production function is taken as given, a total cost curve also assumes no change in the production function (no alteration in the relationship between inputs and output). Hence, the notation corresponding to the total cost curve may be expressed as follows:

$$\text{TC} = f(x,\ \bar{p}_a,\ \bar{p}_b,\ \bar{b},\ \text{F})$$

This expression in effect states that total cost varies with output for all other variables held constant. When this functional relationship between cost and output is plotted in a diagram, it yields the TC curve.

Recall the similarity in method used in the analysis of demand and production. In each case we have related the variable under investigation to a number of other variables. And we have held constant all but one of the determining variables in order to study the way in which the determined variable behaves when the one variable is increased or decreased. Therefore, from the above expression we can see that cost curves will shift when we allow for changes in the variables provisionally held constant. That is, by drawing the cost curves with resource prices, the quantity of B, and the production function given, we have been able to isolate the behavior of cost with respect to variations in output. Once the cost curves have been derived we are in a position to take account of changes in these other variables.

Consider first the amount of B employed. We must continue to hold it fixed in the short run, for if we were to vary b we would be talking about the long run by definition. In the short run b cannot be varied, so there cannot be any shift in the short-run cost curves from this source.

The same does not hold true, however, for the prices of A and B. They can change in the short run. Let us first examine the effect of some change in the price of B. If p_b rises, total fixed cost will rise for each possible level of output. In column 4 of Table 10.1 the price of B is $10 and the fixed amount of B is 30 units, giving $300 as total fixed cost. Were the price of B to change from $10 to $20, for example, total fixed cost would be $600 at each output. The new TFC curve is still horizontal in a diagram like Fig. 10.3, but it is drawn at a higher distance above the horizontal axis. Though total variable cost is unaffected, total cost is increased because TC = TFC + TVC and because TFC is larger at each possible output. The TC curve shifts upward by an equal distance at all points on the curve such that its slope remains exactly the same at all possible outputs. The upward shift of the TC curve equals the upward shift of the TFC curve. Naturally the AFC curve shifts upward also, but in contrast to the TFC curve the distance by which the AFC curve shifts upward is not the same at each output. (This can easily be verified by recomputing average fixed cost at each output under the assumption that the price of B is $20 instead of $10 and redrawing the AFC curve.) The AVC and MC curves are unaffected by a rise in the price of B, but the AC curve will shift upward when the AFC curve does so. Obviously just the opposite effects are produced by a fall in the price of B: the TFC and hence the TC curves shift downward; the AFC and AC curves also shift downward.

A change in the price of the variable resource A shifts the positions of the variable and marginal cost curves, but it has no effect on the fixed cost curves. Referring again to Table 10.1, but concentrating this time on column 5, we can see that a rise in the price of A from $100 to, say, $150 will raise total variable cost at each amount of A used. Thus it will raise total variable cost at each output. As a consequence the TVC curve in Fig. 10.3 shifts upward (and in general its slope will be altered at each point). Although the TFC curve is unaffected, the TC curve shifts upward by the same distance as the TVC curve at each output. Moreover, since total variable cost is higher at each output, so is average variable cost. That is, $AVC = \bar{p}_a/APP_a$, where APP_a is unchanged but p_a is conceptually held constant at a new higher amount, so AVC must be larger for each quantity of A and for each quantity of the product. It follows that average cost is also larger because $AC = AFC + AVC$, where AFC is unchanged and AVC is larger at each possible output. Therefore, the AC curve shifts upward by the same distance as the upward shift in the AVC curve at each output. Marginal cost is also raised at each output when the price of A rises, which can be seen from the marginal cost equation: $MC = \bar{p}_a/MPP_a$, where MPP_a is unaltered and p_a is held constant at a higher amount. The MC curve shifts upward such that it intersects the new (higher) AVC and AC curves at their minimum points. Of course, a fall in the price of the variable resource has just the opposite effects: the TVC, TC, AVC, AC, and MC curves all drop.

Finally, any change in the production function shifts the firm's cost curves by shifting the position of the product curves. Given the fixed amount of resource B, a more efficient production function, due for example to an improvement in technology, shifts the TPP curve upward, with a consequent upward shift in the APP_a and MPP_a curves as they are drawn in Fig. 9.2 of Chapter 9. When the product curves shift upward, the variable cost curves shift downward. The TVC, TC, AVC, AC, and MC curves all drop. Recall the cost definitions that linked average variable and marginal costs to the production function:

$$\text{AVC} = \frac{\bar{p}_a}{\text{APP}_a} \quad \text{and} \quad \text{MC} = \frac{\bar{p}_a}{\text{MPP}_a}$$

The improved technology makes APP_a and MPP_a larger for each possible amount of A employed. Since p_a is constant, this implies that AVC and MC must be lower for each amount of A used. And since a and x increase and decrease together, the higher APP_a and MPP_a must reduce AVC and MC at each output.

A shift in the short-run cost curves from this last source, alterations in the production function, is unlikely to be purely a short-run phenomenon. Most changes in the firm's production function are due to changes in the state of technology. And the effects of technological change are ordinarily put into operation when the firm is able to vary its scale of plant. For example, more advanced machines and equipment are introduced when the firm is replacing old ones and expanding its scale of operation. Thus technological change is better discussed in connection with the long run. More important in the short run are shifts in cost curves due to changes in resource prices. The assumption that resource prices are constant is merely a provisional assumption made for the sake of convenience. It permits one to draw a firm's cost curves and to see the effect of output on the cost of production, i.e., to see the way in which cost varies as production is increased or decreased. By then allowing resource prices to vary, their effect upon cost can be explained in terms of shifting cost curves.

PROBLEMS

1. In Problem 1 of Chapter 9 a firm's production function was presented and the average and marginal products of a variable resource A were computed. Assume the price of the fixed resource B is $10 and the price of A is given as $2.

(a) For the output range of zero to 443 units, construct a table in which you compute:

Total Fixed Cost
Total Variable Cost
Total Cost
Average Fixed Cost
Average Variable Cost

Average Cost
Marginal Cost (Divide the change in total cost by the corresponding change in output, i.e., the change in output need not be one unit.)

(b) Plot the TFC, TVC, and TC curves in a diagram as Figure 1.

(c) Plot the AFC, AVC, AC, and MC curves in a diagram as Figure 2.

(d) Explain why you could not have completed the table in part a without knowledge of the table in Problem 1 of Chapter 9.

(*e*) Explain why the AC curve reaches its minimum point at a larger output than that at which the AVC curve reaches its minimum point.

(*f*) Explain why the MC curve intersects the AC curve at its minimum point.

2. Explain the meaning of economic cost and provide an example of explicit and implicit costs other than the one discussed in the text.

SUGGESTED READING

J. M. Clark, *Studies in the Economics of Overhead Costs*, Chaps. 4–6. Chicago: University of Chicago Press, 1923.

G. J. Stigler, "Production and Distribution in the Short Run," *Journal of Political Economy*, XLVII (1939), 305–27. (Reprinted in *Readings in the Theory of Income Distribution*, pp. 119–42. Philadelphia: The Blakiston Co., 1946.)

11

Long-Run Costs
of Production

The long run is defined as a period of sufficient duration to permit variations in the inputs of all resources. In the case of two resources, A and B, used to produce a commodity X, both A and B are variable. The behavior of total cost emerges from Fig. 10.2 of the previous chapter. Each alternative total cost outlay determines a different isocost line, and the tangency points trace the relationship between output and least cost. For given equal shifts of the isocost lines (equal changes in total cost) the corresponding changes in output depend upon how far apart the isoquants are spaced, i.e., what returns to scale the production function displays.

Since B is no longer to be taken as fixed, there are no fixed costs of production; total cost and total variable cost are identical. It follows that average cost and average variable cost are also identical. The behavior of long-run cost as output varies can be described with reference to the long-run average and marginal cost curves of the firm.

AVERAGE COST

The long run is thought of as a series of alternative short-run situations. Corresponding to each short run is a fixed amount of at least one resource. The quantity of B may be fixed at b_1 units, giving rise to one short-run situation. Were B to be fixed at b_2 units, a second short-run results, and so on for other amounts of B conceptually held constant. The entire set of all these short runs makes up the long run, and the set of all possible short-run cost curves comprises the long-run cost curve.

To simplify matters and to gain insight into the process of long-run change, let us begin by supposing there are only three distinct short runs to be considered. In Fig. 11.1 the short-run average cost curve of the firm when b_1 units of B are being used is labeled AC_1. Let b_2 represent a greater quantity of B per unit of time. Then an alternative short run is that in which the firm utilizes b_2 units of B, generating another short-run average cost curve labeled AC_2. Therefore, if in fact the quantity of

B were fixed at b_2 units, the firm could vary output only by moving along AC_2. Likewise, AC_3 is the firm's short-run average cost curve when B is held constant at b_3 units.

We assume for any output the firm will want to produce that output at the smallest cost. Consider, then, an output of x_1 units in Fig. 11.1. In the short run with b_1 units of B and the short-run cost curve AC_1 the firm can produce x_1 units at a cost of \$225 per unit. However, with a larger quantity of B—with b_2 units of B—the average cost of this same output is higher, namely \$300. Therefore, given enough time to vary B, the firm would use b_1 units of B to produce x_1 units of X, having AC_1 rather than AC_2 as its short-run average cost curve. To produce x_2 units

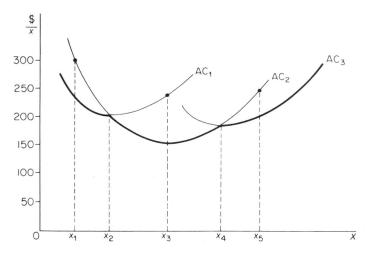

FIG. 11.1.   System of Three Short-Run Average Cost Curves

of X it would not matter whether the firm used b_1 or b_2 units of B, because the average cost is \$200 in either case. However, for outputs in excess of x_2 units the AC_2 curve is below the AC_1 curve. For example, x_3 is produced at a cost per unit of \$235 if b_1 units of B are used, while the same output would cost \$150 per unit if b_2 units are used. So the firm would utilize b_2 units of B to produce an output of x_3. Up to x_4 units of output average cost is least for b_2 units of B. At x_4 it does not matter whether the firm employs b_2 or b_3 units. But for outputs larger than x_4 the AC_3 curve lies below the AC_2 curve, indicating that cost is lower when B is expanded to b_3 units.

Since the long-run average cost curve depicts the lowest average cost of alternative outputs, it is comprised of the heavy, darker segments of the three short-run curves in Fig. 11.1. In the long run the thinner, lighter segments of the short-run curves become irrelevant because the firm can always move onto the long-run curve by varying the quantity of B—and this it cannot do in any one given short-run situation.

Internal Economies and Diseconomies of Scale

The behavior of long-run average cost as output expands depends upon the economies or diseconomies the firm may experience as it expands the inputs of all resources. When all resource inputs are varied, the firm's scale of plant is said to change. More of all inputs makes the scale of plant larger; less of all inputs makes it smaller. With reference to cost there are three outcomes that could occur when the scale of plant is altered.

An expansion in the scale of plant may cause long-run average cost to decline. Figure 11.2 again depicts three short-run situations for the firm. This firm is experiencing internal economies of scale from x_1 to x_2 units of output. Increasing the inputs of all resources shifts the short-run curves downward, resulting in a declining long-run average cost curve (denoted by LAC). Between x_1 and x_2 units of the product the firm can continue to reduce average cost by continuing to expand its scale of plant.

Declining long-run average cost is termed *internal* economies of scale because it results from some internal reorganization within the firm itself, and not from some forces outside the firm. Suppose labor and raw materials are variable in both the short and long runs. Assume the firm's factory and machines are fixed in the short run but variable in the long run. With a small plant few laborers will be hired, and each laborer will perform several different operations. It stands to reason that he will not be equally proficient at all of them. In addition it will take time and energy for him to transfer from one task to another. But with a larger scale of plant, division and specialization of labor become possible. If the firm employs more workers, each worker can perform the job at which he is most skilled. Specialization and division of labor (both manual and mental) eliminate lost time and wasted motion, increasing the productivity of each worker and thereby reducing average cost below that possible with the smaller scale of plant.

Furthermore, with a larger plant it is cheaper to use automatic machines, conveyor belts, and other tools of mass production. A bakery producing, say, 100 loaves of bread per day would surely not use much mechanized equipment such as automatic dough blenders, presses, or ovens, conveyor belts, and automatic packaging machines. It would be folly to do so, for the expense of operating such equipment with a small output would make the cost per loaf produced extremely high. In a small bakery it is cheaper to perform many operations by hand, and still average cost is comparatively high. An expansion in the scale of plant usually permits substantial reductions in average cost. Were the bakery to increase production to 5,000 loaves per day, then the scale of plant could be enlarged, mechanized equipment installed, and the cost per loaf of bread reduced significantly.

In addition to labor specialization and "automation" there are often cost savings due purely to size. One large factory building requires less building material than two small ones covering the same space; a conveyor belt four feet wide uses less lubricating oil, less motor power, and fewer supports than do two belts, each two feet in width and the same length as the wider belt; an electric motor of 400 horsepower requires fewer working parts than do two motors of 200 horsepower each. The costs

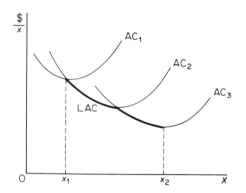

FIG. 11.2.   Internal Economies of Scale

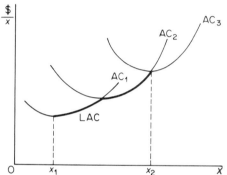

FIG. 11.3.   Internal Diseconomies of Scale

of construction and maintenance are less than proportionate to the size of these physical means of production. When an increase in the scale of plant entails an increase in the size as well as the number of inputs, these economies contribute to lower average cost.

Figure 11.3 represents the firm experiencing internal diseconomies of scale from x_1 to x_2 units of output. Increasing the inputs of all resources shifts the short-run cost curves upward, causing the LAC curve to be positively inclined. This means the firm can reduce its average cost by contracting rather than expanding its scale of plant.

The existence of internal diseconomies is a signal to the firm that it has passed the point at which further division of labor, mechanization, and size will reduce the cost per unit produced. What are the factors that contribute to a rising LAC curve? One may be the cost of transportation. For the scale of plant required to produce outputs in excess of x_1 units the firm might find that its product must be sold in a wider geographic market. Then the cost of transporting each unit of product increases as output expands. Contact of management with the day-to-day operations of the firm may become more remote, so there is duplication of effort. Delays in production scheduling and poor coordination among departments are costly. The saving in cost due to internal reorganizations is more than offset by increased paper work, travel expenses of salesmen, telephone bills, employee services, or just plain "red tape."

There remains one other possibility, depicted in Fig. 11.4. In this case the short-run average cost curves neither rise nor fall as the firm increases output from x_1 to x_2 units by expanding its scale of plant. Consequently, the LAC curve has been drawn as a horizontal line.[1] Either growth in the firm's scale of plant has no influence on any cost element, or the forces causing a reduction in cost exactly offset those

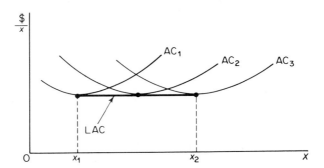

FIG. 11.4.   Neither Internal Economies nor Diseconomies of Scale

operating to raise average cost. There are no advantages to be gained from further specialization of labor. All workers are performing tasks sufficiently limited in scope so that increases in output merely require additional men doing the same task. And the best available types and sizes of capital equipment are employed and used most effectively. Expansions or contractions in the scale of plant yield no significant improvements in the internal organization of the firm.

The Generalized Average Cost Curve

A firm for which internal diseconomies set in at the very outset is extremely rare. Even more rare, indeed impossible, is a firm for which internal economies never come to an end. Typically, internal economies are experienced at first as all inputs are expanded. This continues up to a point, but after that point internal diseconomies set in. That is, considering all possible levels of output, the LAC curve is U-shaped.

The advantages of mechanization and labor specialization can be obtained in practically all productive operations, but these advantages cannot be reaped indefinitely as the firm's scale grows. Specialization of labor can be carried to the point at which monotony and deterioration

[1] The reason for drawing the LAC curve as a horizontal line, rather than tracing the lowest segments of each of the short-run curves, will be pointed out in the discussion in the next section.

of morale more than offset the gains, so that labor cost rises faster than output. Expansion in the size of capital equipment may no longer be feasible because machines of sufficiently large size to keep average cost from rising are simply not available. Or the firm's credit position may be such that it cannot finance the construction of a larger plant without paying a higher interest rate on borrowed funds. Even if these limitations did not restrict the firm, there would still exist the managerial problem. More complicated administration and control of intricate procedures lead to inefficiencies. The upshot is that at some size further expansions in scale lead to increased average cost.

In the final analysis, even assuming resource prices are not affected by a firm's increase or decrease of scale, the U shape of an LAC curve can be traced to the same forces that determine the U shape of any one AC curve—the characteristics of the production function. Indivisibilities generate increasing physical returns at first in the short run (the average physical product of the variable resource is rising). This causes short-run average cost to decline, given resource prices. Eventually a decline in the average physical product of the variable resource creates rising short-run average cost. And this latter phenomenon is due to the firm's inability to expand its fixed inputs. When we turn to the long run, it is also indivisibilities and resource limitations that impart to the LAC curve its U shape. Increasing *returns to scale* are explained by indivisibilities (see Chapter 9). It is precisely because the firm cannot continue to reduce all inputs proportionately when output is reduced that long-run average cost is forced to rise with contractions in output. Likewise, if the firm could continue to double all inputs, output would double too, and at given resource prices long-run average cost would remain unchanged. The long-run average cost rises after some point because of decreasing *returns to scale*, due in turn to limits on the availability of some inputs. Labor of the same quality as that previously used, for example, cannot be increased indefinitely. And there is some practical limit to the size of buildings and equipment. Thus, increasing and then decreasing returns to scale are reflected in declining and then rising long-run average cost.

The behavior of long-run average cost has been generalized to a U-shaped LAC curve, which is depicted in Figure 11.5. There is another respect, however, in which we can gain a more general perspective on long-run average cost. We have previously considered only three short-run situations. More generally, the long run includes more than three alternative short runs. The different amounts of B the firm can use, given sufficient time, may be indefinitely numerous. Figure 11.5 shows a large number of short-run curves and the resulting long-run curve. Even in this diagram not all the short-run alternatives are shown, for between each adjoining pair of short-run curves others may be drawn infinitesimally close to one another. Each very minute variation in the quantity of B used per unit of time creates a new short-run curve. The outer portions of all these short-run curves (like the heavy segments in Fig. 11.1) form the LAC curve. But since the AC curves are indefinitely close to one another, the LAC curve is tangent to an AC curve at each output. The LAC curve forms a lower boundary to the AC curves called an envelope curve.

At outputs smaller than x_3 units the firm enjoys internal economies of scale. Notice that the point at which the LAC curve is tangent to any one AC curve occurs to the left of the point at which adjoining AC curves intersect. That is, long-run average cost is smaller than short-run

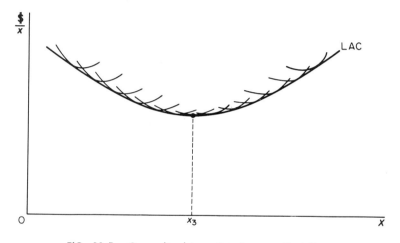

FIG. 11.5. Generalized Long-Run Average Cost Curve

average cost at the output for which the short-run average cost is a minimum. This means the firm can continue to reduce average cost by expanding its scale of plant. For outputs in excess of x_3 units the minimum point on each short-run curve occurs to the left of the point of tangency with the LAC curve. The firm can reduce average cost by contracting, rather than expanding, its scale of plant because it is experiencing internal diseconomies of scale. At x_3 units both economies and diseconomies are absent. Hence, if all possible short-run alternatives are considered, and if it were possible that internal economies and diseconomies are absent at all levels of output, then the firm's LAC curve would be a straight horizontal line.

The LAC curve in Fig. 11.5 is drawn symmetrically for convenience, and it should not be interpreted to mean that cost curves are in fact symmetrical. Nor does it mean that increasing long-run average cost sets in at the same scale of operation for every firm. The declining portion of the LAC curve may extend over a much greater range of output for one firm as opposed to another, even for firms in the same industry.

Firm I might have an LAC curve that appears as ⌣ ,
while Firm II's may appear as ⌣ . Indeed, it is even
possible that the LAC curve may appear as ⌣ for a
third firm. In general, all LAC curves are U shaped, though the minimum long-run average cost occurs at vastly different outputs for different firms.

MARGINAL COST

Long-run marginal cost is defined as the change in long-run total cost
in response to a small change in output. Figure 11.6 permits us to examine the relationship between the firm's long-run average cost curve,

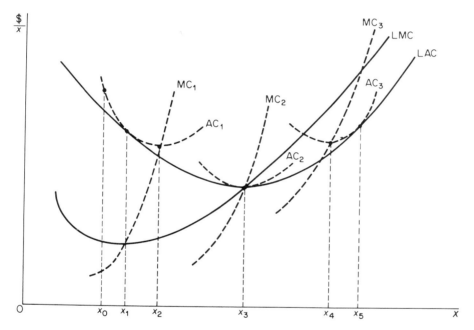

FIG. 11.6.   System of Short- and Long-Run Average and Marginal Cost Curves

LAC, and its long-run marginal cost curve, LMC. The short-run curves,
drawn as broken curves in the diagram, may be ignored for the moment.
The relation of the LAC to the LMC curve is formally the same as the
relation of an AC to an MC curve. When the LMC curve lies below the
LAC curve, the LAC curve is declining as output increases; when the
LMC curve is above the LAC curve, the LAC curve is rising with larger
outputs. Finally, the LMC curve intersects the LAC curve at the minimum point on the LAC curve, i.e., marginal cost equals average cost
when average cost is neither increasing nor decreasing.

This relationship between any marginal and average magnitude was seen to hold for the production function and the short-run costs. Of more interest to us now is the connection between short-run and long-run marginal cost curves. With the quantity of resource B fixed at b_1 units per unit of time, the short-run curves are labeled AC_1 and MC_1. Consider first an output of x_1 units. At this output, short-run average cost equals long-run average cost (the LAC curve is tangent to the AC_1 curve). Moreover, short-run marginal cost equals long-run marginal cost (the LMC curve intersects the MC_1 curve). To see why this must be, let us consider different outputs in the neighborhood of x_1 units. At x_0 the AC_1 curve lies above the LAC curve, which means that short-run *total* cost must exceed long-run *total* cost.[2] Next consider an output of x_1 units. At this output short-run average cost equals long-run average cost; thus short-run total cost equals long-run total cost. Notice, therefore, what this implies about marginal cost. In moving from x_0 to x_1, long-run total cost must increase by more than short-run total cost for each one-unit increment in output. That is, the long-run marginal cost curve lies above the short-run marginal cost curve to the left of x_1 units of output.[3]

Consider next a movement to the right, starting at x_1. Just the reverse ranking of long- and short-run marginal costs emerges. At x_1 units of output short-run total cost equals long-run total cost, as we have seen. For a one-unit increase in output the AC_1 curve rises above the LAC curve. It follows that short-run total cost rises more than does long-run total cost; so, by definition, the MC_1 curve must lie above the LMC curve. To summarize, in the neighborhood of x_1 units the LMC curve is above the MC_1 curve to the left of the point at which the LAC curve is tangent to the AC_1 curve; the LMC curve is below the MC_1 curve to the right of this point; and the LMC curve intersects the MC_1 curve at the output corresponding to the point of tangency.

Incidentally, observe that at x_2 units of output the minimum point on the firm's AC_1 curve is reached. The MC_1 curve cuts the AC_1 curve at this output—not at x_1 units where $MC_1 = LMC$. The optimum short-

---

[2] Let TC_1 denote short-run total cost for $b = b_1$. Then $TC_1 = AC_1 x_0$. Similarly, $LTC = LAC x_0$. Now since AC_1 is larger than LAC, it follows that TC_1 must be larger than LTC at x_0 units of output.

[3] To illustrate, suppose $x_0 = 100$ and that $AC_1 = 12$ and $LAC = 10$ for $x_0 = 100$. Then $TC_1 = 12 \times 100 = 1,200$ and $LTC = 10 \times 100 = 1,000$. Let $x_1 = 150$, at which output $AC_1 = LAC = 9$. Therefore, $TC_1 = LTC = 9 \times 150 = 1,350$. Take $\Delta x = x_1 - x_0 = 50$. Then

$$MC_1 = \frac{\Delta TC}{\Delta x} = \frac{1350 - 1200}{50} = \frac{150}{50} = 3$$

$$LMC = \frac{\Delta LTC}{\Delta x} = \frac{1350 - 1000}{50} = \frac{350}{50} = 7$$

The LMC curve lies above the MC_1 curve to the left of x_1.

run output for b_1 units of resource B is not an output at which the long- and short-run marginal costs are equal. Rather, long-run marginal cost is less than short-run marginal cost, indicating that output can be expanded at a smaller cost increment by varying all inputs than by varying only some of them.

Examination of the other two short-run situations depicted in Fig. 11.6 yields the same results. In each case the short- and long-run marginal costs are equal at that output for which short- and long-run average costs are equal. When b_2 units of B are employed, the MC_2 and AC_2 curves apply. At an output of x_3 units MC_2 intersects LMC, and also at this output the LAC curve is tangent to the AC_2 curve. To the left of this point the MC_2 curve lies below the LMC curve; to the right it lies above the LMC curve. Likewise, if b_3 units of B are used, the MC_3 curve inter- sects the LMC curve at x_5 units of output, where the LAC curve is tangent to the AC_3 curve. Notice again that the minimum point on the short-run average cost curve occurs at an output for which short- and long-run marginal costs differ. With b_3 units of B employed, the firm's short-run optimum output is x_4 units, while long-run marginal cost is above short-run marginal cost up to x_5 units.

The Long-Run Optimum

In Fig. 11.6 are shown three short-run optima—x_2, x_3, and x_4, each one corresponding to a different fixed scale of plant. The firm's long-run optimum output is defined as that output at which its long-run average cost is a minimum. The LAC curve reaches its lowest point at an output of x_3 units. This is also seen to be one short-run optimum, namely that corresponding to the employment of b_2 units of B, because at this output the AC_2 curve is also at its lowest point.

There are peculiar features of the long-run optimum. When the firm is producing its long-run optimum output, certain cost equalities are satisfied that do not hold for other short-run optima. In every short-run optimum, short-run marginal cost equals short-run average cost. In Fig. 11.6, $MC_1 = AC_1$, $MC_2 = AC_2$, and $MC_3 = AC_3$ at the three short- run optimum outputs corresponding to b_1, b_2, and b_3 units of resource B respectively. However, it is only when b_2 units of B are utilized that short- and long-run marginal costs are equal *and* each marginal cost is equal to short- and long-run average costs: $MC_2 = LMC = AC_2 = LAC$. Of all the possible short-run optima, only one is the firm's long-run optimum; one AC curve has a minimum point lower than the minimum point on any other.

Suppose a firm's factory building and equipment are fixed in the short run while labor services and raw materials are variable. Given sufficient time there are two ways the firm can vary output: (1) it can alter its inputs of labor and raw materials with the given scale of plant, or (2) it can vary its scale of plant by changing the inputs of all resources. Starting at an output like x_0 units average cost can be made lowest by producing x_2 units with the given plant size. But the firm's LAC curve is below its AC_1 curve at x_2 units of output, indicating that average cost can be further reduced by expanding it scale of plant. And this continues to hold true up to x_3 units. If instead the firm were to produce x_5 units, with the scale of plant corresponding to the MC_3 and AC_3 curves, average cost could be made lower by contracting output. With the same factory building and equipment average cost could be made lowest by reducing the inputs of labor and raw materials until x_4 units are produced. Nevertheless, this is the lowest average cost only if the scale of plant is not changed, for the LAC curve is below the AC_3 curve at this output. The firm can further reduce average cost by using a smaller factory building and fewer (and perhaps smaller) pieces of equipment. Contraction of output by reducing scale continues to lower average cost until the firm produces x_3 units with a scale of plant yielding MC_2 and AC_2 as the short-run curves. Once the firm is in this position, there is no way to reduce average cost, either in the short-run or in the long-run.

SHIFTS IN THE POSITION OF LONG-RUN COST CURVES

Long-run cost curves are constructed under the assumption that all resource inputs are variable. For a firm using resources A and B, both of which are variable, to produce the commodity X, the symbolic expression LTC $= f(x, p_a, p_b, F)$ states that long-run total cost is a function of the output of X per unit of time, x; the prices of resources A and B, p_a and p_b; and the firm's production function, F. The firm's long-run total cost curve depicts a relationship between cost and output, given resource prices and the firm's production function: LTC $= f(x, \bar{p}_a, \bar{p}_b, \overline{F})$. A change in total cost as output changes is shown geometrically by a movement along the firm's LTC curve. The same interpretation is given to the firm's long-run average and marginal cost curves; the behavior of long-run average cost and long-run marginal cost as output varies is revealed by movements along the LAC and LMC curves respectively. And these curves are drawn for constant resource prices and an unchanged production function.

Just as the short-run cost curves shift position when either a resource price or the production function is altered, so the long-run cost curves shift. In the long run there is no distinction between fixed and variable costs, of course. A rise in the price of either A or B will shift the LAC and LMC curves upward. A reduction in either one or both resource prices will shift the long-run cost curves downward. Anything that shifts the firm's production curves, such as a change in the state of technology, will in turn shift the firm's long-run cost curves. An improvement in the state of technology, for example, will cause the long-run cost curves to shift downward, while a deterioration in the state of technology shifts them upward.

CONCLUSION

In concluding this discussion of cost two important points warrant emphasis. First, a system of cost curves is intended to interpret geometrically a set of hypothetical propositions. Rather than stating what the firm's actual output is, a cost curve specifies the cost that would correspond to each one of a number of alternative outputs. Nor are the various outputs interpreted as chronologically succeeding one another; they are alternatives open to the firm at any given moment.

The proper conception of the short and long runs hinges on this interpretation of the cost curves. The short and long runs are not elapsed periods of time; they are ways in which the firm can view its alternatives at any moment. The short-run curves tell the firm how cost would vary if output were to be varied with at least one resource input fixed. The firm's long-run view permits it to see how cost would vary if output were to be varied by changing the inputs of all resources. And this long-run view is formulated by the firm at the moment for which the curves are drawn. The important point is that one should not regard a cost curve as a historical record of how cost has behaved in the past or how it will behave in the future. Both the short- and long-run curves are drawn for fixed resource prices and a given production function. And with the passage of time resource prices and technology can change, shifting the position of the entire set of cost curves.

Second, the firm's cost curves were obtained under the assumption that only two resources are employed. This simplified the presentation, but it does not hinder the validity of the conclusions about cost. The analysis of cost can be generalized to include any number of resources without altering the essential principles. Moreover, the theoretical principles of cost behavior apply to a firm producing more than one commodity, whether it uses two or more than two resources. The reason is that at the heart of cost analysis lie the law of diminishing returns in the short run and the law of diminishing returns to scale in the long run. And the essential features of these laws of production are not altered by the number of products produced or by the number of resources employed by a firm.

PROBLEMS

1. The following table shows a firm's output and average cost at each output for four different scales of plant.

Output per Day	Scale I Average Cost	Scale II Average Cost	Scale III Average Cost	Scale IV Average Cost
0	\$ ∞	\$ ∞	\$ ∞	\$ ∞
1	100	130	140	160
2	50	60	80	130
3	40	45	60	110
4	35	35	45	90
5	40	30	35	70
6	45	25	25	60
7	50	30	20	50
8	60	40	15	40
9	80	55	20	35
10	100	75	30	30
11	120	95	50	40
12	150	125	80	55

(*a*) Plot as Figure 1 the short-run average cost curves corresponding to each scale of plant.

(*b*) Construct a table showing four entries of the firm's long-run average cost schedule and approximate the firm's long-run average cost curve in Figure 1.

(*c*) What is the firm's optimum scale of plant? What is the firm's long-run optimum output? Explain your answer.

2.   If the prices of all resources are taken as constant to a firm and if the firm's production function shows constant returns to scale, what will be the shape of the firm's long-run average cost curve? Explain.

SUGGESTED READING

J. Viner, "Cost Curves and Supply Curves" in G. J. Stigler and K. E. Boulding, eds., *Readings in Price Theory*, pp. 198-232. Chicago: Richard D. Irwin, Inc., 1952.

A. Young, "Increasing Returns and Economic Progress," *Economic Journal*, XXXVIII (1928), 527–42.

Part IV

Product Pricing: Pure Competition

Equilibrium of the Firm

The firm's decision with respect to output is a problem of choice. Before one can determine which of the alternative outputs the firm will choose to produce, it is necessary that the firm's objective or goal be postulated. Once this is done, the output that satisfies that goal can be determined. And once the firm's output is determined, the cost of production for that output can be found from the cost curves. Knowledge of the combination of inputs used to produce that output is rendered by the production function.

It is instructive at this point to recall the analysis of consumption by a single consumer. The assumption that the consumer maximizes utility permitted us to find the quantity of each good he would consume at given prices and a given income. In the case of a single firm the same formal method is adopted. The firm is assumed to maximize total profit. Just as there is one combination of goods for which the consumer's utility is maximized, so there is one output at which the firm's total profit is maximized. Of all the different outputs the firm can produce, this is the one it will choose.

THE CONCEPT OF PROFIT

Total profit is defined as total revenue from sales minus total cost of production. Since total cost includes all contractual obligations of the firm, both explicit and implicit costs, total profit is a residual left over after all costs have been deducted from sales receipts. Should cost exceed revenue, profit will be negative—the firm will incur a loss. Therefore, the firm's objective is to maximize its profit, or minimize its loss if it cannot make a profit.

The recipient of a firm's profit is the entrepreneur. He is also the bearer of losses if the firm cannot show a profit. The possibility that a firm may experience a loss does not necessarily mean, however, that the entrepreneur as a person will have a zero or negative personal income. To illustrate, suppose we consider once more the case of the grocery entrepreneur discussed in Chapter 10. The firm's income statement is as follows:

Revenue from Sales		$50,000
Less: Costs		
Payment for merchandise	$40,000	
Rent for store space	2,000	
Clerk's wages	3,000	
Total Cost		45,000
Total "Profit"		$ 5,000

Recall that the owner of the store provided labor and capital services, the payments for which are implicit costs to the firm considered as an entity separate from the entrepreneur. If the grocer's wages for the labor amount to $3,000 and the interest on his capital is $1,500—both computed on the basis of opportunity cost—the firm's economic profit is $500. The owner in his capacity *as a supplier of resources* is said to earn $4,500 as contractual income *from this source*. In his capacity as entrepreneur he receives a residual income of $500.

Suppose, on the other hand, that the firm's implicit costs had amounted to $6,000. Let us say the owner's wages are $3,000 and the interest on his investment is $3,000. Then the firm is losing $1,000. The owner *as a person* would have the following income statement:

Wages as a supplier of labor	$ 3,000
Interest as a supplier of capital equipment	3,000
Profit as an entrepreneur	−1,000
Net Personal Income	$5,000

Of course a similar outcome would follow upon a drop in sales revenue while implicit and explicit costs remain unchanged.

There is an important reason why economists make this distinction between the contractual and residual components of an entrepreneur's income. If the firm is incurring a loss, the entrepreneur's income as a person is smaller than it could be if he gave up the firm and sold or hired his resources to some other firm. There is an incentive for this firm to pass out of existence. The previous example, in which the firm's implicit cost is $6,000 and profit is minus $1,000, leaves the entrepreneur with a personal income of $5,000. Were he to give up the firm and sell his labor and capital services to some other firm, his personal income could be $6,000. The reason is simply that the implicit costs of the firm, of which he is the recipient, are computed on the basis of opportunity cost. Similarly, if there are positive profits, an entrepreneur can enjoy a greater personal return here than elsewhere. Then there is an incentive for other entrepreneurs to enter this industry in the expectation that they too may obtain such gains. In short, the distinction between contractual and residual income has important implications for resource allocation in the economy.

REVENUE OF THE FIRM

A firm's profit takes into account the firm's revenue and its cost. The behavior of cost as output varies is independent of the degree of competition in the product market. The construction of a cost curve requires knowledge of the prices of resources used by the firm and the firm's production function. And the law of diminishing returns, which imparts a definite shape to the cost curves, applies to any type of firm. This is not true of the firm's revenue, however. Just as a firm's total, average, and marginal *cost* curves were constructed, so a set of total, average, and marginal *revenue* curves can be constructed. But the general shape and location of a revenue curve will be different for different degrees of competition in the product market.

Pure competition is a form of industrial organization with the following characteristics: (1) the product of each seller or firm is substantially the same as the product of any other firm in the industry; (2) each firm is small relative to the size of the whole industry, so that it cannot by its own operations influence the price of the product; (3) there are no restrictions on the freedom of new firms to enter the industry or for old firms to leave the industry. Though all firms operating together can alter the market price of the product by changing the total industry supply, no single firm can control the price by varying its output. Therefore, each firm must take the market price as given. Whereas the *market* demand curve is in general negatively sloped, the demand curve *faced by one firm* is infinitely price elastic. The firm views the demand curve for its output as a horizontal line, indicating that as far as the firm is concerned any amount it produces can be sold at whatever price is established in the market. In agriculture, for instance, a farm can sell any output it wishes to produce at whatever price is determined by the total U.S. and foreign demand and the total U.S. and foreign supply. Since it is only one of a very large number of producers, a single farm cannot obtain a higher price by restricting output. Nor can it depress the price by expanding output.

Let us proceed to this result by a less direct but more enlightening route. The total revenue of a firm is equal to the amount produced (and sold) multiplied by the price of each unit. Suppose a price of $10 is established in the market for a product X produced under conditions of pure competition. Let TR denote the firm's total revenue. Then

$$TR = \$10 \cdot x$$

where x represents the quantity of the product X produced by the firm per unit of time. Or, in general for a purely competitive firm, we can write

$$TR = \bar{p}_x x$$

where $\bar{p}_x$ denotes the constant price of X, whatever its numerical value may be.

The total revenue curve of the firm is depicted in Fig. 12.1 for $\bar{p}_x = \$10$. With the firm's production per unit of time measured on the horizontal axis, total revenue is represented by a straight line out of the origin with a positive slope.

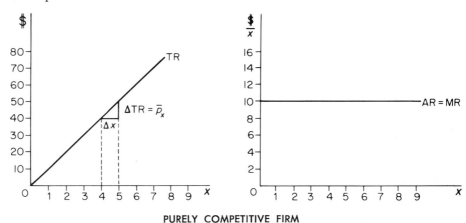

PURELY COMPETITIVE FIRM

FIG. 12.1.   Total Revenue Curve   FIG.12.2.   Average and Marginal
                                                      Revenue Curves

Average revenue is defined as revenue per unit of the product sold. It is computed by dividing total revenue by output:

$$AR = \frac{TR}{x}$$

When the price of X is $10, average revenue becomes

$$AR = \frac{TR}{x} = \frac{\$10 \cdot x}{x} = \$10$$

Or in general

$$AR = \frac{TR}{x} = \frac{\bar{p}_x x}{x} = \bar{p}_x$$

That is, average revenue at any output equals the price of the product at the output. Indeed, average revenue is simply another name for price when the price is viewed from the point of view of the seller. Under pure competition, with the price independent of the firm's output, average revenue or price is the same at every output. The average revenue curve of the firm, labeled AR in Fig. 12.2, is a horizontal line at a distance above the horizontal axis equal to the given price of $10.

Finally, marginal revenue is defined as the change in total revenue brought about by a small change in output, calculated by dividing the change in total revenue by the change in output that caused the change in revenue:

$$MR = \frac{\Delta TR}{\Delta x}$$

where the increment in x, Δx, is usually taken to be one unit. Under pure competition marginal revenue turns out to be equal to the (constant) price:

$$MR = \frac{\Delta TR}{\Delta x} = \frac{\Delta(\bar{p}_x x)}{\Delta x} = \bar{p}_x \cdot \frac{\Delta x}{\Delta x} = \bar{p}_x$$

Since the price neither rises nor falls as the firm produces more or less, the amount added to total revenue by selling one more unit is always equal to the price of that additional unit. Were the firm to increase output from one to two units, $10 would be added to the firm's total revenue; were it to increase output from two to three units, $10 is again added to total revenue. If output is expanded from 1,000 to 1,001, the one-unit increase in output would still add $10 to total revenue because the price is not altered by the size of the firm's output.

It follows that marginal revenue is equal to the given price regardless of the firm's output. Therefore, the marginal revenue curve is a horizontal line at a distance above the horizontal axis equal to the price of the product. In Fig. 12.2 the marginal revenue curve, MR, is a horizontal line at $10. The height of the MR curve above the horizontal axis is equal to the slope of the TR curve. With Δx equal to one, TR must always equal price so long as price is unchanged by the increment in x, as is indicated in Fig. 12.1. Moreover, since average revenue and marginal revenue both turn out to be equal to the given price, the AR and MR curves coincide.[1]

It is a simple matter to show that the demand curve faced by an individual firm is that firm's average revenue curve. A demand curve is defined in general as showing the quantity per unit of time that would be taken at each alternative price. Average revenue is price viewed by the seller. As far as the single firm is concerned there is only one price

[1] Marginal revenue at x_1 units of output equals the slope of the TR curve at x_1 units. Average revenue at x_1 units equals the slope of a line from the origin to the TR curve at x_1 units. But since the TR curve is itself a straight line out of the origin, a line joining the origin to a point on the TR curve must be coincident with the TR curve. Hence, the slope of this line (average revenue) equals the slope of the TR curve (marginal revenue) at any output. See the Mathematical Appendix.

or average revenue. But any quantity the firm might choose to produce would be taken by the market at that price. This, by definition, means that the firm's demand curve is its average revenue curve, and that the demand curve is therefore infinitely elastic.

SHORT-RUN EQUILIBRIUM

In the short run, output can be varied only by changing the quantity of variable resources the firm combines with a fixed quantity of others. This fixed scale of plant implies that a firm cannot leave the industry; for departure from the industry requires the departure of all its resources. In the same sense, entry into the industry implies a variation in the scale of plant. To enter or leave, a firm must have sufficient time to change its scale of plant from zero to some positive size or from some positive size to zero. Consequently, in the short run each firm's scale of plant is fixed, and there is a fixed number of firms in the industry. With the price of the product given and the scale of plant given, the decision problem of any one firm in the short run is that of choosing the output that maximizes total profit.

Profit Maximization: Total Curves

To find the firm's total profit at each output it is necessary that the firm's total revenue and total cost curves be brought together. These are labeled TR and TC respectively in Fig. 12.3. The total profit curve is also shown as TP, where TP = TR − TC. The vertical distance between the TR and TC curves is equal to the vertical distance between the TP curve and the horizontal axis.

Comparison of the TR and TC curves at each output reveals how total profit varies with output. Consider first an output of zero; total revenue is zero and total cost is equal to total fixed cost. Hence, total profit is negative, and the firm's loss is equal to its total fixed cost. For any output less than x_0 units the firm would incur a loss. The TC curve lies above the TR curve so that the TP curve lies below the horizontal axis, indicating negative profit. If the firm were to produce x_0 units, total profit would be zero because total revenue is exactly equal to total cost. Any output between x_0 and x_2 units would result in positive profits; x_2 units would make profit zero; outputs in excess of x_2 units would again cause the firm to experience a loss, and the loss becomes greater the larger is the output produced.

Though profit can be made by producing any output between x_0 and x_2 units, it is a maximum at x_1 units. The TP curve reaches its highest point because the distance by which the TR curve lies above the TC

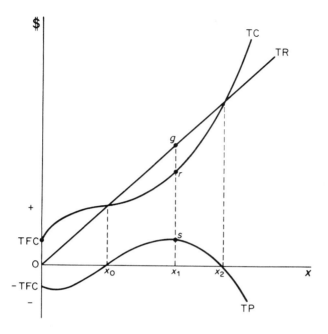

FIG. 12.3. Short-Run Equilibrium: Total Cost and Revenue Curves

curve is greatest at this output. The vertical distance from point q to point r is equal to the vertical distance from point s to the horizontal axis. Hence, x_1 units is the firm's short-run equilibrium output.

Profit Maximization: Average and Marginal Curves

Figure 12.3 contains all the information necessary to determine the firm's output. But for purposes of the analysis to be carried out in succeeding chapters it is very convenient to express the same conclusion in terms of the average and marginal curves. Figure 12.4 shows the short-run average and marginal cost curves of a firm; also drawn in the diagram are the firm's average and marginal revenue curves (which, of course, coincide). It is assumed that the price determined on the market is p_1, so the MR curve is drawn at a distance above the horizontal axis equal to p_1.

To maximize total profit the firm produces that output at which marginal cost is equal to marginal revenue. This output is seen to be x_1 units of the product—the same equilibrium output as that indicated in Fig. 12.3. In order to see why the firm will equate marginal cost to marginal revenue, consider any output less than x_1 units. If the firm were to expand output, the dollar amount added to total revenue is given

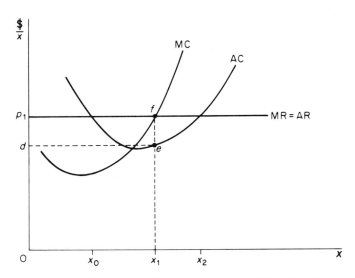

FIG. 12.4.   Short-Run Equilibrium: Average and Marginal Curves

by the MR curve; the dollar amount added to total cost is given by the MC curve. Since the MR curve lies above the MC curve, more would be added to revenue than to cost by increasing output. Total profit would increase. This holds true for any output short of x_1 units. The MC curve approaches the MR curve as output approaches x_1 units, but it remains below the MR curve. This means that the amount *added* to total profit becomes successively smaller. Though the amount added to profit becomes smaller, there is still *some* addition to profit. And to maximize profit the firm will continue to expand output.

At x_1 units of output, marginal cost is equal to marginal revenue. Why will not the firm produce a larger output? Consider an output one unit larger than x_1 units. The MC curve is above the MR curve, i.e., more is added to cost than to revenue by the one-unit increment in output. Consequently, total profit would shrink. The larger the output in excess of x_1 units, the more does marginal cost exceed marginal revenue, and the smaller total profit becomes. Therefore, total profit must be a maximum at the output at which the MC curve intersects the MR curve.

At the firm's equilibrium in Fig. 12.4 total revenue, total cost, and total profit can be determined. Average revenue or price is given by the vertical distance from the horizontal axis to the AR curve, or the distance x_1f. Total revenue equals average revenue times output, where output is shown as the horizontal distance $0x_1$. Consequently, total revenue equals x_1f times $0x_1$, which is the area of the rectangle $0x_1fp_1$.

Total cost is found in the same way. Cost per unit equals the vertical distance from the horizontal axis to the AC curve, x_1e. Total cost is average cost (x_1e) multiplied by output ($0x_1$), or the area of the rectangle $0x_1ed$.

The difference between the area of the rectangle $0x_1fp_1$ and the area of the rectangle $0x_1ed$ is equal to the area of the rectangle $defp_1$. This represents total profit. Or, one can approach the same result in a different way. Revenue per unit minus cost per unit equals profit per unit. Hence, average profit equals the vertical distance ef. Multiplying profit per unit by the number of units produced yields ef times de (where de equals $0x_1$), which is the area of the rectangle $defp_1$. It is easy, then, to see why profit is zero for an output of x_0 units or an output of x_2 units. Average cost is equal to price, so average profit, and therefore total profit, must be zero. Similarly, at all outputs less than x_0 or greater than x_2, average cost exceeds price, indicating that average profit (and total profit) is negative.

Notice it is not average profit that the firm maximizes. Since the product price does not vary with output, average profit is largest when average cost is smallest. At the minimum point on the AC curve, marginal cost is below marginal revenue. The firm can add more to revenue than to cost, and so increase total profit, by expanding output. There is no assurance that a purely competitive firm will produce its optimum output in the short run, given its invariable scale of plant. If positive total profit can be made, the profit-maximizing output will definitely be larger than the firm's optimum output.

Loss Minimization

There is no reason to assume that a firm must make a positive profit in the short run. It could happen, for example, that maximum total profit is zero. There may be one output at which average cost equals average revenue; while at all other possible outputs average cost exceeds average revenue. Then the best the firm can do is to prevent a loss by producing the output at which average cost and average revenue are equal. This could be represented in Fig. 12.4 by dropping the AR curve so that it is tangent to the AC curve at the minimum point on the AC curve. At the point of tangency, marginal cost equals marginal revenue, so profit is maximized. However, maximum profit is zero because it is seen that average cost equals average revenue. At any other output the AC curve lies above the AR curve.

Nor is there reason to assume that a firm must make even a zero profit in the short run. The firm would be forced to incur a loss if the AR curve lies below the minimum point on its AC curve. Should a firm be unable to make a profit, the best it can do is to minimize loss. The firm's decision will boil down to a choice between two courses of action. It can (1) produce some positive output at a loss or (2) discontinue production entirely. Regardless of the output produced, and whether it produces or not, the firm has a certain fixed cost that must be met. The short run presupposes a fixed scale of plant that gives rise to total fixed cost. If the firm produces nothing, variable cost is zero; it is obligated only for its fixed cost. If, on the other hand, the firm does produce some positive output, both fixed and variable costs are incurred. In order to minimize loss, therefore, the firm's decision will hinge on whether the revenue obtained from a positive output will more than cover its *variable* cost.

In Fig. 12.5 a firm's short-run average cost curve and its short-run average variable cost curve are shown. Let us suppose, first, that the

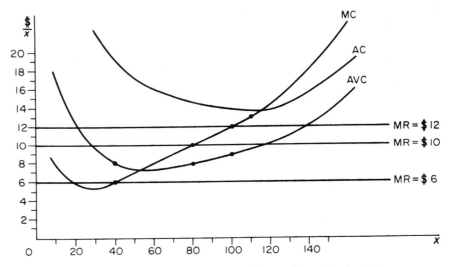

FIG. 12.5.   Short-Run Equilibria for Three Different Product Prices

given price of the product is $12. Faced with this price the firm must experience a loss, for average cost is greater than $12 at any output the firm might produce. Still, the loss is minimized by equating marginal cost to marginal revenue, that is, by producing an output of 100 units per unit of time. Any smaller or larger output would make the firm's loss greater. At 80 units of the product, for example, marginal cost is $10 and marginal revenue is $12. Expanding output by one unit would add $12 to revenue and $10 to cost, reducing the loss by $2. Likewise, at an output of 110 units, where marginal cost is $13 and marginal revenue is $12, a one-unit increase in output would increase the loss by $1.

Production of 100 units entails an average variable cost of $9 per unit; so total variable cost is $9 times 100, or $900. Total revenue is $12 times 100, $1,200. Now suppose the firm has a total fixed cost of $500. By producing 100 units, $900 of the $1,200 in total revenue can be used to meet its variable cost. The remaining $300 can be applied to fixed cost, leaving the firm with a minimum loss of $200. There is no other output (including zero output) at which the firm's loss can be made less than or equal to $200.

The same argument applies if the product price is $10. To minimize loss, the firm produces 80 units, at which total revenue is $800 and total variable cost is $640. From total revenue, $640 can be used to cover variable cost, leaving $160 to apply toward total fixed cost. This leaves a minimum loss of $500 − $160 = $340.

Finally, consider what the firm would do if the price were $6. By producing the output at which marginal cost equals marginal revenue (40 units), total revenue would be $6 · 40 = $240. But total variable cost would then be $8 · 40 = $320. Total revenue is not sufficient to cover total variable cost. Consequently, the firm loses $500 + ($320 − $240) = $500 + 80 = $580. By suspending production it could reduce the loss to $500. At zero output the firm has no revenue but it also has no variable cost, so the loss amounts to total fixed cost.

The foregoing illustrations may be generalized to a profit-maximizing rule for the firm under pure competition that takes into account both profit and loss. To maximize profit or to minimize loss the firm produces the output at which *marginal cost equals price if the price is greater than or equal to average variable cost at this output*. If the price is below average variable cost at the output for which marginal cost equals price, the firm will produce nothing. In the former case, total revenue is at least large enough to cover total variable cost. In the latter case, however, it will pay the firm to suspend production and meet its total fixed cost, for any positive output will result in a greater loss.

LONG-RUN EQUILIBRIUM

Whereas in the short run a firm can change its output only by varying the degree to which it utilizes a fixed scale of plant, in the long run the scale of plant can itself be varied. Alteration in the scale of plant means also that new firms can enter the industry and existing firms can leave. Withdrawal of a firm from the industry should not be confused with the firm's producing zero output. We have seen that a firm may choose to produce zero output in the short run in order to minimize loss. But even if, as a result of losses, the firm wishes to leave the industry, by definition of the short run there is not sufficient time to dispose of its fixed inputs. It is still a (nonproducing) member of the industry. By definition of the long run the firm does have sufficient time to dispose of its fixed plant. Then withdrawal from the industry is possible.

Figure 12.6 depicts the long-run equilibrium of a firm under conditions of pure competition. The same general principle for profit maximization applies in the long run. To maximize total profit the firm produces the output at which marginal cost equals marginal revenue, which of course equals average revenue or price. However, the relevant cost curves in this case are the long-run curves: long-run marginal cost is set equal to price. At the same time the profit-maximizing rule implies that a short-run marginal cost is also equal to price. For to each point on the LMC curve there corresponds one MC curve. The LMC curve is made up of the series of different possible MC curves, one drawn for each scale of plant.

Similarly, the LAC curve is composed of a series of different AC curves, with one AC curve corresponding to each scale of plant. Since,

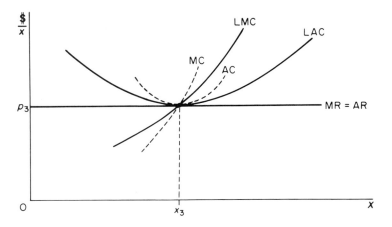

FIG. 12.6. Long-Run Equilibrium: Purely Competitive Firm

in long-run equilibrium, the firm operates at one point on its LAC curve, it must also operate at a point on one of its AC curves. That is to say, a long-run equilibrium is of necessity also some short-run equilibrium (though the reverse does not hold true).

There are two distinguishing features of a firm's long-run equilibrium under pure competition. First, total profit is zero. Long-run average cost is exactly equal to the given price, p_3, at the profit-maximizing output, x_3. Second, it follows from this that the firm's profit-maximizing output is also the long-run optimum output. The intersection of the LMC curve with the MR curve must occur at the output for which the LAC curve is tangent to the AR curve. With a horizontal AR curve, this point of tangency must be at the minimum point on the LAC curve (and at the minimum point on one AC curve). Thus, a product price determined by market forces beyond the control of the firm and the condition of zero profit force the firm (1) to utilize the optimum size plant and (2) to operate the plant so that average cost is the smallest possible.

Because optimum output is a result of zero profit, let us examine why profit must be zero in the long run for any firm under pure competition. Suppose, to begin, that firms in the industry are making short-run profits. Total revenue exceeds total explicit and implicit costs. Since costs are computed on the basis of the opportunity-cost principle, the rate of return to the owners of firms is greater than the maximum that could be earned elsewhere. As a consequence new firms will be attracted to this industry with the expectation that they too can reap profits. Existing firms in the industry cannot restrict freedom of entry; and as new firms come into the industry they add to the supply of the product flowing onto the market. With demand unchanged, a greater supply will depress the price of the product, reducing profit for all firms, old and new. In addition, these new firms will enter the market for resources—bidding for labor, raw materials, and capital equipment. This increased demand may raise resource prices, which, as we have seen in Chapter 11, will shift all firms' cost curves upward. The entry of new firms exerts one or both of two forces that squeeze profits: a fall in the AR curve of every firm and/or a rise in the LAC (and AC) curve.

This process will continue until total profit has been reduced to zero for each firm in the industry. As new firms enter and profits are reduced, but not to zero, there remains an incentive for more firms to enter—and thereby to reduce profits further. Only when profits have been eliminated, when the rate of return in this industry is equalized with alternative rates of return, will the entry of new firms cease. Then each firm will be in a position of stability, of equilibrium as pictured in Fig. 12.6, with no incentive to reallocate its resources.

Just the reverse process of adjustment to long-run equilibrium will follow if profits are negative. Losses in the short run can be minimized, but they can be avoided entirely in the long run. The firm has no fixed cost, and a price below minimum average cost implies that the rate of return to the entrepreneur is less than that obtainable elsewhere. So firms will leave this industry and the resources will be employed elsewhere. The withdrawal of firms decreases the supply of the product, raising the product price so that the AR curve faced by each remaining firm rises. Perhaps the decreased demand for resources will lower their prices, causing the cost curves of remaining firms to shift downward. One or both of these forces act to reduce losses. As long as losses are being incurred, even though they become smaller, firms will continue to leave. And the exodus will continue until the incentive to leave has been eliminated, i.e., until total profit is zero for all remaining firms.

As long as profits are being made or losses incurred, the firms cannot be in equilibrium. For either situation sets in motion forces that eliminate the profits or losses. The only stable long-run position is that in which there is no incentive for a firm to increase profit by either leaving the industry or altering its output. Since the product price is the same for each firm, the average cost of production *in equilibrium* must also be the same. *Identical average costs do not mean, however, that all firms have identical cost curves.* The *minimum* long- and short-run average costs are all equal to the same price, and so equal to each other.[2] Yet the minimum point on the LAC curve may occur at vastly different outputs for different firms.

Emphasis on the meaning of zero profit will bear repeating. Rather than zero income, zero profit means simply that no resource owner receives an extraordinary income relative to what he could earn by employing his resources elsewhere. The *marginal* return to all suppliers of resources is equalized in all alternative employments. There is no residual or additional income to be gained by switching resources from one use to any other. Neither does the long run imply that purely competitive firms are necessarily in long-run equilibrium at any given point in time. One might observe that a firm is making a profit and then, say, two years later, that it is still making a profit. Long-run equilibrium is a situation that firms are continually pursuing. During any given interval of time market forces are operating to move each firm toward its optimum output. But whether this zero-profit output is actually reached by each firm will depend upon whether revenue and cost curves are caused to shift before long-run equilibrium is attained. In a world of constant change and fluctuation, as a firm approaches optimum output that optimum itself may change. Then the firm pursues a new optimum under new revenue and/or cost conditions. Given stable cost and revenue curves and given sufficient time for adjustments in scale of plant, each firm in a purely competitive industry will indeed produce its optimum output.

---

[2] Equal long-run average costs for all firms rest upon the opportunity-cost principle. Cost inequalities in the short run are entirely possible. One firm may have lower cost curves than another (smaller cost of production *at each possible output*) because of superior management, a more favorable location, access to better capital equipment, or more liberal credit appraisals, etc. But in the long run other firms can take advantage of these profit-making conditions. They can bid for the services of superior management, relocate so as to gain better access to markets, or seek out the financial institutions that allow liberal credit terms. In doing so they will by their combined efforts, affect the prices of these resource inputs. Since costs include both implicit and explicit costs, and since the cost to one firm is the value of these resources to other firms by the opportunity-cost principle, the profit these factors can earn for one firm could be earned for another. And by seeking to take advantage of these resources services and thus affecting their value, cost differences will disappear in the long run if costs are calculated on the basis of opportunity cost.

PROBLEMS

1. A firm sells a product in a purely competitive market, where the product price has been established at $10. Complete the following table.

Output per week	Total Cost	Marginal Cost	Marginal Revenue
0	$ 400		
100	1,600		
200	2,600		
300	3,400		
400	4,000		
500	4,700		
600	5,500		
700	6,500		
800	7,500		
900	8,700		
1,000	10,200		

(a) Plot the marginal cost and marginal revenue curves as Figure 1. Determine the firm's equilibrium output.

(b) Why does not the firm produce 200 units of the product?

(c) Does your Figure 1 represent a short-run or a long-run equilibrium for the firm? Explain.

2. Explain the difference between a firm's suspending production (producing zero output) in the short run and the firm's producing zero output in the long run.

13

Derivation of
Industry Supply

The equilibrium output of a single firm is determined for any given product price. What this given price will be, however, depends upon the total market demand for the product by consumers and the total market supply by the industry. Construction of the industry supply curve is essential to the determination of equilibrium. Together with demand it establishes the market price, which in turn establishes the output of each firm, given its cost of production.

SHORT-RUN SUPPLY

A market demand curve for a product is the horizontal sum of the demand curves of individual consumers. Likewise, an industry or market supply curve is the horizontal sum of the supply curves of individual firms in the industry. The first step in constructing an industry supply curve, therefore, is to identify the supply curve of a firm.

Short-Run Supply Curve of a Firm

By definition, a supply curve is a locus of points depicting the quantity per unit of time that would be offered for sale at each possible price. Under pure competition a firm maximizes profit by setting marginal cost equal to a given price. The output at which this equality is satisfied is the output the firm would supply at that given price. Consequently by considering an entire system of alternative prices, rather than just one, the quantity offered for sale at each price can be found.

Figure 13.1 shows the marginal cost curve and the average variable cost curve of a firm producing commodity X. Four different alternative prices are considered. If the price were to be p_4, the output offered for sale by the firm would be x_4 units. Similarly, at a price of p_3, x_3 would be supplied; and at p_2, x_2 would be supplied. The price p_1 is below the average variable cost curve, indicating that the firm's loss can be mini-

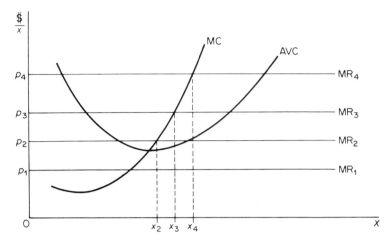

FIG. 13.1.   Supply Curve of a Firm Producing Commodity X

mized by producing no output. Hence, at a price of p_1, or any other price below the AVC curve, the firm would supply zero quantity.

The part of a firm's marginal cost curve that lies above its average variable cost curve is the firm's short-run supply curve, for this segment of the marginal cost curve shows the quantity that would be supplied at each price. For example, in Fig. 13.1, at a price of p_4, x_4 units would be supplied, at p_3, x_3 units, and so on. The quantity supplied by the firm is zero at any price below its average variable cost curve.

Short-Run Industry Supply Curve

The industry supply curve shows the quantity that would be offered for sale on the market by all firms in the industry at each possible price. Since the quantity offered by the industry as a whole is nothing other than the sum of the quantities offered by each of the member firms, the industry supply curve is the horizontal summation of the firms' individual supply curves.

For simplicity, let us assume there are three firms in a purely competitive industry producing the commodity X. The firms are labeled I, II, and III in Fig. 13.2, where the MC curve of each firm above its AVC curve is shown. If the product price were below $1, nothing would be produced by any of the firms. So zero quantity would be supplied by the industry. At $1, Firm I would supply 5 units. Because this price is below the average variable costs of II and III, they would still supply nothing. Therefore, the industry supply is the supply of Firm I. This holds true up to a price of $2, at which Firm II would also supply a positive quantity. At $2, for instance, Firm I would offer 20 units and Firm II would offer 10 units, making the quantity supplied by the industry 30 units. Between $2 and $3, the industry supply curve is the horizontal summation of the supply curves of I and II. Should the price rise to $3, Firm III would be able to cover its variable cost and so would offer 15 units. These 15 units are added to the units offered by I and II at a price of $3, namely 30 by I and 20 by II, so the quantity supplied by the industry at $3 is 30 + 20 + 15 = 65 units. Similarly, the quantity supplied by the

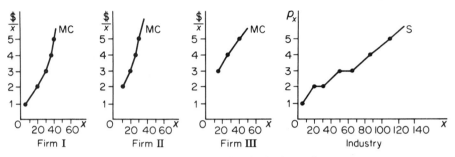

FIG. 13.2.   Summation of Individual Supply Curves

industry would be 85 units if the price were to be $4—that is, 35 units supplied by I, 25 by II, and 25 by III.

The short-run supply curve of the industry, labeled S in the diagram on the extreme right, is positively sloped, which follows from the positive slope of each firm's supply curve. Because in this simple illustration only three firms were taken into account, the curve S has horizontal segments, even though its overall slope is positive. The horizontal segments arise from the fact that as a firm makes its first positive contribution to industry supply, the quantity supplied by the industry undergoes a large increment. In reality, however, a competitive industry consists of many more than three firms. And this large number will iron out the "wrinkles" in the industry supply curve, leaving a relatively smooth positively inclined curve.

Industry Equilibrium

The final price that will prevail in the market depends, of course, upon demand as well as supply. When the demand curve is taken into account, the equilibrium price is determined by the intersection of the demand and supply curves. This price in turn establishes the actual quantity supplied by each firm.

Once again suppose there are three firms in a purely competitive industry producing a commodity X. Figure 13.3 shows the average cost curve of each firm as well as its marginal cost curve above average variable cost. The short-run industry supply curve S is again shown on

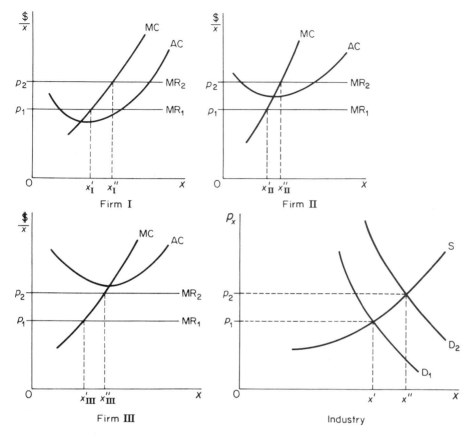

FIG. 13.3.   Industry and Firm Equilibria

the extreme right. Let us assume the market demand curve for X is D_1. Then the market price is p_1, in the short run, and the demand curve faced by each firm is perfectly elastic at a distance above the horizontal axis equal to the price.

The equilibrium quantity produced by Firm I is x'_I, that of Firm II is x'_{II} and that of Firm III is x'_{III}. The quantity supplied by the industry equals the quantity demanded by households, that is, x', which is $x'_I + x'_{II} + x'_{III}$. Notice that Firm I is making a profit since p_1 is greater than its average cost. Both Firms II and III incur a loss, but the loss is minimized in each case.

Now suppose that the market demand curve were D_2 instead of D_1. The equilibrium market price would be p_2, at which Firms I, II, and III produce x''_I, x''_{II}, and x''_{III} respectively. In this instance the demand curve faced by each firm taken separately is denoted by MR_2. The profit of Firm I is larger than it would be with a market price of p_1. Firm II is profitable, whereas Firm III is still unprofitable.

Changes in Short-Run Supply

Events leading to a change in short-run market supply are those causing a change in short-run marginal cost curves. In Chapter 10 it was seen that the marginal cost curve of a firm is constructed under the assumption of given (fixed) resource prices and a given production function. A change in the supply of any variable resource input used by the firms in an industry will change the price firms must pay for that resource. A rise in the price of any variable resource will shift the marginal cost curves of firms upward, while a drop in the resource price will effect a fall in the marginal cost curves. Geometrically speaking, an upward shift in an MC curve is equivalent to a movement to the left, for a larger marginal cost for each alternative output means a smaller output for each alternative marginal cost. Similarly, a downward shift in the MC curve is tantamount to a movement to the right from a geometric point of view. Since the industry supply curve is the horizontal summation of the MC curves, a rise in the MC curves implies a shift to the left in the industry supply curve. A fall in the price of a variable resource lowers the firms' MC curves; therefore, the industry supply curve shifts to the right.

Any alteration in the production function of a firm will also change short-run industry supply. A technological improvement may raise the marginal physical product of a variable resource. Suppose this is resource A. Then the entire MPP_a curve shifts upward—which, in turn, shifts the MC curve of the firm downward, leading to a shift to the right in the industry supply curve. A technological deterioration produces opposite effects, reducing the marginal physical productivity of some resources. And if a variable resource is thus affected, the firms' MC curves shift upward, and the industry supply curve shifts to the left.

These results can be conveniently summarized in symbolic notation. Let x_s denote the quantity supplied of a commodity X per unit of time by a competitive industry. The quantity supplied depends upon the price of X, the prices of variable resources employed by the industry, and the firms' production functions. Assuming the industry uses only one variable resource, call it A, and that the industry is comprised of n firms, the supply relationship can be written:

$$x_s = s(p_x, p_a, f_1, f_2, \cdots, f_n)$$

where p_x denotes the price of X, p_a the price of A, and the f's represent the firms' production functions. The industry supply curve relates the quantity supplied to the product price for given resource prices and given production functions:

$$x_s = s(p_x, \bar{p}_a, \bar{f}_1, \bar{f}_2, \cdots, \bar{f}_n)$$

In this expression the "bars" once more denote that p_a and all f's are conceptually held constant.

From the theory of the firm it is known that as p_x becomes larger, x_s also becomes larger: the industry supply curve is positively sloped. Since the industry supply curve is drawn for constant p_a and a constant f for each firm, a change in either or both will shift the supply curve. A given rise in p_a (to a higher level at which it is again held constant) will reduce x_s for any alternative p_x. Given the market demand curve, such as D_1 in Fig. 13.3, this shift of the industry supply curve to the left will raise the price of the product and decrease the quantity traded on the market. On the other hand, a fall in p_a will increase industry supply, which reduces the product price and expands the quantity of X exchanged on the market.

In general, an increase of the f's will increase x_s for each possible value of p_x. Greater productivity of the variable resource shifts the industry supply curve to the right, reducing the product price and increasing the quantity of X exchanged. A decrease of the f's has the opposite affects. Though it is certainly possible that technological changes can occur in the short run, generally they occur in the long run. It is when the scale of plant is altered that technological innovations that increase productivity are put into practice. Much more important in the short run will be the changes in product supply due to changes in resource prices, for the supplies of resources available to the industry can change radically in the short run.

Modification of the Firm's Supply Curve—A Digression

Strictly speaking, the short-run supply curve of a firm is that firm's MC curve above the AVC curve only in the absence of what are called *external* economies or diseconomies of production. Under pure competition one firm, operating alone, cannot alter resource prices by purchasing more or less as it expands or contracts output. Its MC curve would then be stationary, and in response to higher or lower product prices the firm would expand or contract output by moving along its MC curve. However, the higher or lower product price would cause not just one firm to change output but all firms in the industry. And all firms acting simultaneously can cause resource prices to change. Changes in resource prices that are a *direct result* of variations in industry output *in response to different product prices* are called *external* economies or diseconomies imposed by the industry as a whole upon each firm considered separately.[1] They are external to the firm in the sense that they are outside the control of any one firm.

Though we shall not go into the reasons at this point, an expansion of output by an industry can cause resource prices to fall. Suppose the product price rises. Each firm begins to increase output by moving along its MC curve. If this movement by all firms together causes resource prices to fall, each firm's MC curve shifts down. Instead of staying on its original MC curve the firm switches over to a higher point on the new, lower MC curve. In response to the higher product price, the firm's increase in output will be greater than it would be with no shift in its MC curve. This is called an external economy because the fall in resource prices is not internal to the firm's operations, i.e., it is not subject·to the control of the firm operating by itself. The firm's supply curve in this event is more price elastic than its MC curve. Therefore, the industry supply curve, obtained by summing these firms' supply curves, is *more* price elastic than the horizontal summation of stationary MC curves.

External diseconomies in the short run spring from increases in resource prices. Again suppose the product price rises. As each firm moves upward and to the right along its MC curve, the increase of industry output causes resource prices to rise. Therefore, each firm's MC curve shifts upward. Each firm switches over to a new, higher MC curve, and in response to the higher product price its increase in output will be smaller than it would be with no shift in the MC curve. Each firm's supply curve is less elastic than its MC curve. Consequently the industry supply curve is *less* elastic than the summation of stationary MC curves.

The possibility exists that some resource prices will increase while others decrease. Then the net effect may be to alter the shapes of cost curves somewhat and to cause some to shift up while others shift down, depending upon whether the resource-price increases or decreases are dominant. In any event, the industry supply curve will in general deviate somewhat from the horizontal summation of stationary MC curves.

The existence of external effects does not invalidate the analysis of the previous section. External economies or diseconomies arise from changes in resource prices that in turn result from *movements along* a given product supply curve in response to a higher or lower product price. Thus, changing resource prices are incorporated in such movements. But changes in resource prices discussed in the previous section are those due to changes in the supplies of resources to the industry. Consequently, a

---

[1] Going into finer detail, and being more precise, short-run external effects can be of two kinds—pecuniary and nonpecuniary. Changing resources prices due to variations in industry output, discussed above, are pecuniary in nature. Nonpecuniary effects are changes in firms' productions functions due to expansions or contractions of industry output in response to variations in the product price (consumer demand). These effects are less likely to occur than are pecuniary effects in the long run, and even less likely in the short run; I have therefore chosen to ignore them in the preceding discussions.

change in the supply of resource A, causing p_a to change, will shift the industry supply curve for a product X regardless of whether the supply curve for X allows for external effects.

External effects alter the degree of price elasticity of supply, but they do not change the slope of the short-run supply curve from positive to negative. Since we are interested in the direction in which price and quantity will move as the demand curve shifts, it is sufficient for our purposes to treat the industry supply curve as the horizontal summation of firms' MC curves above AVC. Though external effects can be ignored in the short run, the analysis of long-run supply is a different matter. As we shall see, external economies and diseconomies are an essential feature of the industry's long-run supply curve.

LONG-RUN SUPPLY

Under pure competition the long run is differentiated from the short run by three characteristics: (1) all resources are variable for each firm in an industry, (2) there is not a fixed number of firms in an industry, and (3) in long-run equilibrium every firm in an industry is making zero profit. These characteristics set the framework for analyzing long-run industry supply, but they are not enough in themselves to explain the nature of the supply curve. The slope and price elasticity of the long-run industry supply curve depend upon the presence or absence of external economies or diseconomies of production.

A Constant-Cost Industry

It is simplest to begin our analysis with the case in which external effects play no part. An industry characterized by the absence of external economies or diseconomies of production is called a constant-cost industry. Figure 13.4 consists of two diagrams; a firm producing commodity X is shown on the left and the market for X is depicted on the right. For our "representative" firm the long-run marginal cost curve has been deleted because it is not essential to the analysis and would unduly complicate the diagram. In order to derive the long-run industry supply curve for X we take some equilibrium position as a starting point. Granted that the market demand curve is D_1 and that the *short-run* industry supply curve is S_1, the price of X is p_1 and the quantity traded on the market is x_1 units. The firm is in long- and short-run equilibrium producing x_1' units and making zero profit.

Now suppose demand increases to D_2. In the short run the market price will rise to p_2, at which x_2 units are produced and consumed. Each firm moves upward and to the right along its MC curve; Firm I produces x_2 units, making a short-run profit. The existence of profits will attract new firms to the industry. As each new firm enters, the short-run industry supply curve must shift to the right. For instead of summing the MC curves of, say, 100 firms that comprised the industry at the initial equilibrium, the MC curves of 101 firms must be summed when one new firm enters. The MC curves of 102 are summed when two new firms enter, 103 when three enter, and so forth.

At the heart of the matter is the question of when the inflow of firms will cease. In principle, two things can happen as new firms enter. (1) The product price will obviously fall below p_2 as the short-run supply curve shifts to the right. (2) The cost curves of the firms could shift position. By definition of a constant-cost industry we rule out the second possibility. That is, we are concerned at this point only with an industry in which the cost curves do not shift as the industry varies output in response to a change in the product price. The restoration of (a new) long-run equilibrium requires

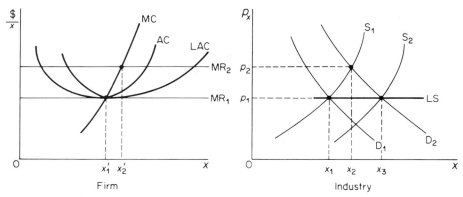

FIG. 13.4.   Long-Run Supply under Conditions of Constant Costs

that profits be once more reduced to zero. Hence, firms will continue to enter, shifting the short-run supply curve farther to the right, until it comes to rest at the position depicted by S_2. In the process, the product price falls and firms move back along their MC curves. Since the cost curves do not shift, profits are eliminated by causing the price to drop back to its original level, p_1. When this new long-run equilibrium has been reached, each firm that was originally in the industry will produce the same amount it did before the change in demand. Firm I will produce x_1' units, for example. But the industry as a whole supplies x_3 units, not x_1. The increase in long-run industry output is contributed entirely by the new firms.

The diagram on the right in Fig. 13.4 illustrates two points on the industry's long-run supply curve, the combination (p_1, x_1) and the combination (p_1, x_3). The entire long-run supply curve joins all points of long-run equilibrium that would be reached for all possible levels of demand. It is traced by the shifting short-run supply curve as firms enter or leave the industry.

The long-run industry supply curve, labeled LS in Fig. 13.4, is a horizontal line. It is infinitely price elastic. Though a change in demand will alter the short-run price of the product, the long-run price remains un-changed regardless of the direction or the degree of a change in demand.

An Increasing-Cost Industry

A long-run expansion or contraction of industry output in response to a higher or lower product price may cause the firms' cost curves to shift position. In this section we shall examine the case in which cost curves shift upward with output expansions and downward with con-tractions. The shifts in cost are due to forces external to the firm and are called external diseconomies of production. Thus an industry in which external diseconomies exist is termed an increasing-cost industry.

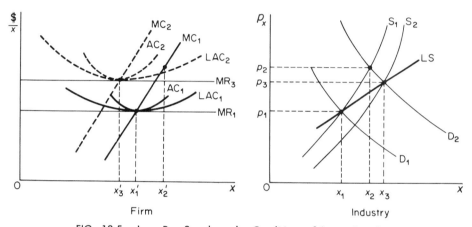

FIG. 13.5. Long-Run Supply under Conditions of Increasing Costs

Figure 13.5 again depicts an initial market equilibrium for a com-modity X and the corresponding long-run equilibrium of a "representa-tive" firm. Given the demand curve D_1 and the short-run industry supply curve S_1, the price is p_1 and the quantity x_1 is traded on the market. The firm is in long-run equilibrium producing x_1' units of X, the output at which long-run and short-run marginal costs are both equal to the price, and where profit is zero. Given the industry output of x_1 units, the cost curves are represented by LAC_1, AC_1, and MC_1.

As in the previous illustration, let the demand curve shift to D_2. The price rises to p_2 in the short run, at which x_2 units are supplied. In order to maximize profit each firm increases output by moving along its MC curve; in short-run equilibrium Firm I produces x_2' units, and a profit is being made. The entry of new firms, attracted by the prospect of profits, has the effect of shifting the short-run industry supply curve to the right, which in turn causes the price to fall below p_2. Moreover, in this case the entry of firms has the added effect of shifting the cost curves of all firms upward. Profits are subjected to a double squeeze—from above by a falling price and from below by a rising average cost. And this process will continue until profits have been eliminated. Then the entry of firms will cease, leaving the industry once more in long-run equilibrium.

The cost curves of Firm I shift up to the positions indicated by LAC_2 AC_2, and MC_2. This upward shift results in a new long-run price that exceeds the old equilibrium price. Although the entry of firms causes the price to fall from p_2, it does not return to its original level. The long-run equilibrium price p_3, following upon the short-run increase of supply to S_2, lies between p_1 and p_2. The output of Firm I is x_3' units, the output at which the LAC_2 curve is just tangent to MR_3. In Fig. 13.5, Firm I's output has decreased from x_1' to x_3' in the long run. This is not a necessary outcome however. Industry output will definitely increase. But whether the firm's output increases or decreases depends upon the way in which the cost curves shift upward. If the cost curves shift straight up, the firm's new long-run output will be equal to the old. If the cost curves move a little to the left as they shift upward, the firm's new long-run output will be less than the old. Finally, if they move a little to the right, the new output will be somewhat greater than the old.

The right-hand diagram in Fig. 13.5 again shows two points on the long-run industry supply curve, the combinations (p_1,x_1) and (p_3,x_3). The supply curve itself, shown as LS, is traced by all possible shifts in demand. For any increase in demand the short-run supply curve does not shift as far to the right as it would in the case of constant costs, because the cost curves of firms shift upward. Therefore, the long-run price rises. Similarly, a fall in demand reduces the short-run price. Losses motivate firms to withdraw from the industry and cost curves shift downward, so the short-run supply curve shifts to the left. In the new long-run equilibrium, profits are again zero, but at a lower price since the cost curves have been lowered. The short-run supply curve does not shift as far to the left as it would if cost curves were stationary.

The long-run industry supply curve is positively sloped in the case of an increasing-cost industry. Nevertheless, it is more price elastic than the short-run supply curve. A given increase in demand will raise the long-run price, but the price rise will be smaller than it is in the short run. Likewise, the price will fall less in the long run than it does in the short run for any given decrease in product demand.

A Decreasing-Cost Industry

The analysis of a decreasing-cost industry is formally much the same as that of the other two types. Because of what are called external economies of production, the cost curves of firms shift downward with expansions of industry output, and they shift upward with contractions. As before, we begin in Fig. 13.6 with an initial equilibrium. The price is p_1 and the quantity exchanged is x_1 units for a demand curve D_1 and a short-run supply curve S_1. Firm I supplies x_1' units of X for its given cost curves LAC_1, AC_1, and MC_1.

The increase of demand from D_1 to D_2 raises the price to p_2 in the short run, at which price the firm produces x_2'. Profits are being made, so new firms enter the industry, shifting the short-run industry supply curve to the right. Up to this point there is no difference between the three types of industry. The difference is centered on what happens to the cost curves of firms. In this case the entry of firms causes the cost curves to fall rather than to rise. The falling price tends to eliminate profits, but it is offset by falling average costs. As a result, profits must be reduced to zero by means of a fall in price to a level below p_1. Assuming that the cost curves of our "representative" firm drop from LAC_1, AC_1, and MC_1 to LAC_0, AC_0, and MC_0, the short-run supply curve must continue to shift until it reaches the position S_2. The long-run price is not only lower than p_2, it is lower than the initial long-run equilibrium price, p_1. This is the price, p_0, at which the MR_0 (or AR_0) curve is tangent to the (lower) LAC_0 curve. Only when the price reaches this level will the entry of firms cease.

In Fig. 13.6 the firm's long-run output increases from x_1' to x_3'. But again this is not a necessary outcome, even though the industry output definitely increases in the long run. Whether any one firm will produce more or less depends upon the way in which the cost curves shift down. A direct vertical shift will leave the firm's output unchanged. A slight movement to the left as the curves shift down will decrease the firm's long-run output, whereas a slight movement to the right will increase its output.

The combinations (p_1,x_1) and (p_0,x_3) are two points on the long-run industry supply curve. All possible shifts in demand reveal the entire supply curve, labeled LS. Increases in demand are followed by relatively large increases in short-run supply due to the downward shifts in cost curves. The shifts in short-run supply are larger than those that would occur if the industry were one of constant costs, and much larger than would occur if the industry were one of increasing costs. Any decrease in demand, followed by a drop in the short-run price, leads to the departure of firms from the industry and an upward shift in the cost curves

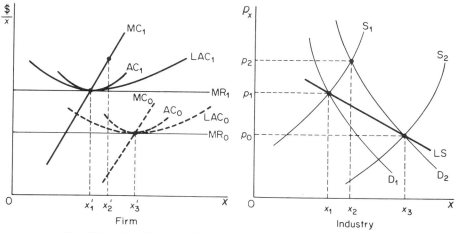

FIG. 13.6.   Long-Run Supply under Conditions of Decreasing Costs

of the remaining firms. Hence, the long-run price must rise to equal the higher average cost at the new long-run equilibrium.

The distinguishing feature of a decreasing-cost industry is a negatively sloped long-run supply curve. An increase in demand, though it raises price in the short run, reduces the long-run price, and vice versa for a decrease in demand. Incidentally, the supply curve's negative slope does not vitiate the notion of market equilibrium. The supply curve cuts the demand curve from below, a condition that is sufficient to make equilibrium a stable position. Given one demand curve and the long-run supply curve, the intersection point once attained will be maintained. At any quantity greater than the equilibrium buyers will pay less than the price needed to cover cost, so the quantity offered will decrease. At any quantity short of the equilibrium, buyers will pay more than enough to cover cost and quantity supplied will increase.

Sources of External Economies and Diseconomies

The effects of shifting cost curves on the industry long-run supply curve have been traced. In the short run, the industry supply curve must be positively sloped. Consequently any increase in demand will raise price and output, while any decrease in demand will reduce price and output. Whether this will happen in the long run depends upon whether the industry is one of increasing, decreasing, or constant costs. Since the long-run outcome on price and quantity exchanged depends upon the shifting of cost curves, it is natural that we inquire into the reasons for these cost changes. It has been stated that they are due to external economies or diseconomies of production, that is, to forces external to the individual firm. External effects are of two kinds: pecuniary and non-pecuniary.

Pecuniary External Effects. Shifts in the cost curves are brought about by changes in resource prices. Under purely competitive buying the amount purchased by a single firm will not affect a resource price, but the quantity bought by the industry as a whole may alter its price. The entry of new firms will result in an increased demand for resource inputs, and the withdrawal of firms will result in a decreased demand. Whether the industry will be one of increasing, decreasing, or constant costs will depend upon what happens to resource prices when the demand for them by the industry undergoes a change.

When pecuniary external diseconomies are present, resource prices rise as the industry expands output. Consider again the industry producing a commodity X. Suppose a resource A is used in the production of X and that this industry uses a substantial part of the total amount of A available in the economy. An expansion in the industry output of X requires an increase in the input of A. The entry of new firms into the industry and the expansion of output by those already in the industry increases the demand for A. If the supply curve of A to the industry is positively sloped, the price of A will rise. Obviously, this may also happen to the prices of other resources used by the industry. The rise in resource prices is a pecuniary external diseconomy imposed upon each firm by the industry as a whole as the industry expands output in response to a higher product price. A movement upward and to the right along the long-run industry supply curve for the product entails an upward shift in the cost curves of the individual firms.

When pecuniary external economies or diseconomies are absent, resource prices do not change. The industry in question might use only a small proportion of each resource total available to the economy. Then this industry bears the same relationship to all buyers of a resource that one firm bears to its own industry. The supply curve of each resource to the industry is horizontal. Since the industry uses but a relatively small quantity of each resource, it cannot affect any resource price by varying the quantity employed. As new firms enter the industry and others expand output, the industry demand for resources increases. As some firms depart and others contract output, the industry demand for resources decreases. But the resource prices are not changed. Consequently, cost curves do not shift. If other things remain the same, the industry will be a constant-cost industry.

When pecuniary external economies are present, resource prices fall as the industry demands more inputs in order to produce more output. Firms' cost curves shift downward. A contraction of industry output in response to a lower product price has the opposite effects. This could happen only if the industries selling resources to this industry were themselves decreasing-cost industries. An input A from the viewpoint of the industry producing X may be an output from the viewpoint of another industry producing A. For example, if A represents a fabric it is a raw-material input for the garment industry producing men's clothing X, but it is an output for the textile industry producing it. If the long-run supply curve of the industry producing A is negatively sloped, the price of A will fall when the industry producing X increases its demand for A. One might ask, however, what makes the resource industry one of decreasing costs. Does it in turn use resources that have negatively sloped supply curves? And if so, cannot the argument be carried back ad infinitum? The answer is that decreasing costs may be due to nonpecuniary as well as to pecuniary effects.

Nonpecuniary External Effects. Nonpecuniary external effects are changes in the production functions of member firms imposed on them by the industry as a whole. Average and marginal physical product curves may shift as a result of expansions or contractions of industry output. Shifts in the product curves in turn cause shifts in the cost curves, opposite in direction to the shifts in product curves.

Suppose several firms in the same industry are located in a given area. The entry of new firms to the area may cause waste-disposal problems. The volume of waste material, the result of the production process, may become too large to be handled by the public incinerators formerly used. Incinerators farther from the factories may have to be utilized, and more labor hours, truck depreciation, gasoline, etc., may be involved. This means that to produce any given output more resource inputs are required. Or the entry of new firms may result in traffic congestion in the area so that delivery trucks consume more gas, and more driver hours are required for the delivery of any given output. Other examples should be obvious. The essential point is that expansions of industry output in response to a higher product price can cause the average and marginal product curves of firms to shift down. These are technical or nonpecuniary diseconomies of production imposed on the firm by the industry, causing cost curves to shift up with expansions of output and down with contractions of output. Notice that these shifts in cost curves can occur even though resource prices are unchanged.

Nonpecuniary external economies have the opposite effects. The entry of new firms, increasing the size of the industry, may stimulate the development of transportation service into and from an area. Highways may be widened, thus reducing traffic congestion. An increase in the number of firms located on a river may lead the community to provide more efficient water purification, reducing the inputs firms formerly had to use to purify their water. In such cases the average and marginal physical product curves of the firms shift upward with industry expansion, shifting cost curves downward. Therefore, external economies that cannot be traced to lower resource prices are explainable by the development of improved market organization, transportation, etc., that arise from sources external to the individual firm.

Internal and External Economies Contrasted. Both pecuniary and nonpecuniary external effects may operate in the same direction, both tending to raise cost curves or both tending to lower them. Then again, they may not. If they operate in opposite directions, the net outcome will depend on which is the stronger influence. The absence of both pecuniary and nonpecuniary effects will make the industry a constant-cost industry. It will also be a constant-cost industry if these two effects are operative but exactly offset each other in such a way that the cost curves are left unchanged. The essential question, the answer to which determines the type of industry and thus the slope of the long-run industry supply curve, is whether the cost curves shift up, down, or not at all. If both external effects are present, but they operate in different directions, the stronger effect will determine the direction in which cost curves shift.

Increasing-cost industries appear to be the most common of the three types by far. Decreasing or constant costs are most likely to occur, if at all, when an industry is relatively young. If at an early stage in its development an industry does experience external economies of size, it may also go through a stage in which it is one of constant costs. But the available evidence suggests that as they become mature and firmly established, most industries become increasing-cost industries.

External economies of production, whether pecuniary or nonpecuniary, should not be confused with internal economies of scale, discussed in Chapter 11. Internal economies arise from the control of the firm over its own organization of resources. These internal effects impart a shape or slope to any given cost curve. By enlarging its scale of plant the firm may be able to reduce average cost. The LAC curve may slope downward to the right over a relatively large range of output. External economies, on the other hand, emerge from forces outside the control of the firm. They depend upon the size of the industry rather than the size of the firm. And they cause downward shifts in the position of the LAC curve. Regardless of the shape of the LAC curve, whether it reaches its minimum point at a small or a large output, external economies will shift its position as the entire industry expands or contracts output.

CHANGES IN LONG-RUN SUPPLY

If external effects are present, movements along a given industry supply curve incorporate some shifts in the cost curves of firms. The causal sequence runs like this. There is a change in demand. In response to the consequent change in price the industry moves along the supply curve to a new intersection point. This movement entails the entry or departure of firms and some shifting of cost curves. But these shifts in cost are the result of movements along the industry supply curve.

What, then, will cause a shift in the position of the long-run industry supply curve? First, a change in resource prices, not the effect of a movement along a given product supply curve, will shift cost curves and thus the long-run industry supply curve, whether the industry be one of increasing, decreasing, or constant costs. The causal sequence runs as follows. A change in the supply curve of a resource to this industry alters the price of that resource. This shifts the cost curves of the firms in the industry, upward if the resource price increases and downward if its price decreases. The industry supply curve for the product then shifts —upward to the left (a decrease in supply) if the resource price has risen, downward to the right (an increase in supply) if the resource price has fallen. In the former case the product price rises and the quantity exchanged on the market declines. In the latter case, the product price falls and the quantity traded increases. The shift in the long-run product supply curve is caused by a change in some resource price. This change in price has its source in the market for resources; in particular, it is due to a change in the supply of a resource.

Similarly, any technological change that shifts the physical product curves of firms up (or down) will shift their cost curves down (or up). The shift in cost curves in turn shifts the long-run industry supply curve for the product. Suppose a technological innovation increases the average and marginal productivities of some resource. The long- and short-run cost curves shift downward. Long-run industry supply increases, lowering the product price and increasing the quantity exchanged on the market, given no change in demand.

PROBLEM

1. Suppose an industry of 100 firms is purely competitive. Each firm has a given scale of plant such that total fixed cost for each firm is $100. Moreover, assume the total variable cost schedules are identical for all firms in the industry. The total variable cost schedule for any one firm is given in Table I below. Finally, the market demand schedule for the product is given in Table II.

Table I			Table II	
Output per Week	Total Variable Cost		Price	Quantity Demanded per Week
0	$ 0		$30	800
1	12		29	900
2	23		28	1,000
3	33		27	1,100
4	42		26	1,200
5	50		25	1,300
6	58		24	1,400
7	67		23	1,500
8	77		22	1,600
9	88		21	1,700
10	100		20	1,800
11	113		19	1,900
12	127		18	2,000
13	142		17	2,100
14	158		16	2,200
15	175		15	2,300
16	193		14	2,400
17	212		13	2,500
18	232		12	2,600
19	253		11	2,700
20	275		10	2,800
21	298			
22	322			
23	347			
24	373			
25	400			
26	428			
27	457			
28	487			
29	518			
30	550			

(*a*) Calculate the average variable cost, average cost, and marginal cost schedules for one firm. Plot these cost curves in one diagram as Figure 1.

(*b*) Plot the market demand curve as Figure 2.

(*c*) Draw the industry supply curve in Figure 2 (the sum of marginal cost curves), and find the equilibrium price and quantity traded on the market. Explain why these are the equilibrium price and quantity.

(*d*) Draw the demand curve faced by one firm in Figure 1, and find the equilibrium output of the firm. Explain why this is the firm's equilibrium.

(*e*) Given this initial equilibrium, suppose that the price of raw materials rises such that each firm's cost rises by $2 for each unit produced. Assume no other changes occur. Draw the new cost curves of the firm as Figure 3, and draw the new industry supply curve as Figure 4. Draw the market demand curve once more in Figure 4 and read off the new equilibrium price and quantity. Draw the firm's new demand curve in Figure 3, and find the firm's new equilibrium.

(*f*) Was each firm profitable prior to the rise in the price of raw materials? Explain. Is each firm profitable after the rise in the price of raw materials? Explain. If firms are now not profitable, what will happen in the long run? As compared to the price of the product in the short run, just after the rise in the price of raw materials, what will happen to the price of the product in the long run? That is, what determines if the product price will rise or fall in the long run?

14

Applications of
Cost and Supply

The analysis of cost and supply has been presented in the form of abstract principles. Because it is very general the theory covers a variety of situations. Such situations can be clarified and their consequences understood with the aid of price theory, appropriately adapted to the concrete conditions of an event. In this chapter the abstract tools of analysis will be applied to a few hypothetical problems that are designed to illustrate the operation of market forces. Then, the discussion will close with a brief examination of the statistical measurement of cost and supply.

THEORETICAL APPLICATIONS

Fixed Available Quantities

Some items offered for sale on a market are fixed in quantity. A particular house or a factory building cannot be duplicated—at least within a short period of time. The decision of a seller is not "how much to sell" but rather "to sell or not to sell." The same is true of a particular painting or a rare coin. The quantity supplied by a seller is a fixed amount and cannot be varied in response to variations in price, except that the item can be withdrawn from the market.

Less obvious examples of a fixed quantity can also be brought to mind. Retailers who have in stock a given amount of perishable foods must dispose of them before they spoil. In the very short run, before new deliveries can be made or previous orders canceled, there is a certain quantity that can be offered for sale regardless of the price. Besides physical perishability there are other factors that can induce the same supply conditions, for example, the effect of fashion upon prices asked by clothing retailers.

Any of these cases can be described by saying that the supply of the commodity is *perfectly price inelastic*; that is, the supply curve is a vertical line. In some instances there will exist what economists call a "reservation price" below which the seller or sellers would refuse to sell. These supply conditions can be illustrated with a general demand-supply diagram. Let the quantity of the commodity X per unit of time be denoted by x and its price by p_x in Fig. 14.1, where x_1 represents the fixed available amount in a particular market. The market supply curve is denoted by S, and three different demand situations are labeled D_1, D_2, and D_3. For simplicity we shall assume that all sellers of X have the same reservation price when we apply the diagram to a case of more than one seller. Thus, at any price below p_1 the sellers prefer not to sell (the quantity offered for sale per unit of time would be zero).

First, let the diagram represent an auction held in a particular community and let X be a certain type of antique chair. Set x_1 equal to 4, a

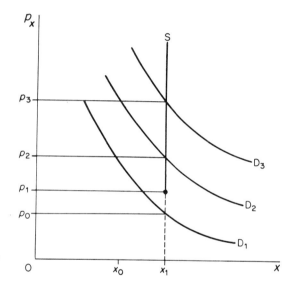

FIG. 14.1.   Fixed Available Quantity
of Commodity X

grouping of 4 matched chairs. Hence, all 4 chairs are to be auctioned at whatever price they will bring. The supply of chairs is fixed at 4 per day with a zero reservation price set by the seller, so the supply curve includes the broken segment and extends to the horizontal axis. Buyers bid against each other to reveal how much they will pay. If it should happen that prospective buyers do not value the chairs highly and the demand is that given by D_1, the price at which the chairs sell will be relatively low, namely p_0. A greater demand, D_2, would yield a price of p_2, while a still greater demand such as D_3 would result in a price of p_3. But no additional quantity would be traded at the higher price. In such a situation the supply condition alone determines what the quantity traded will be. And demand alone determines what the price will be if the commodity is to sell at a positive price.

It sometimes happens that sellers can sell part of their existing stock at a prevailing price but they cannot sell all of it. Assume retailers in a given market in May had on hand 500 summer dresses of which 100 are left in August. It is expected that they will be out of style next year. The dresses have been selling at $30 each during May, June, and July. Now sellers find that the dresses are not selling and that autumn styles must be introduced. How shall this situation be depicted? Let $p_3 = \$30$ and let the demand for these summer dresses, X, in August be represented as D_2. Demand was formerly larger, D_3, but as the summer draws to a close the demand curve shifts to the left. Set $x_1 = 100$, the fixed quantity remaining in August. The supply curve in August is the solid portion of S, indicating sellers have a common reservation price of p_1, say $15, which is what they could get if the dresses were returned to the manufacturer. If the price is kept at $30, with D_2 as the current demand, only a part of the remaining inventory could be sold, the quantity x_0. However, all of it could be sold if the price were reduced to p_2, which we may interpret as $20. And perhaps the sellers must reduce the price to $20 before September when the demand curve shifts even farther to the left to a position like D_1. For by then only a part of the stock could be sold at $20; on the remainder the sellers would have to accept their $15 reservation price.

Variable Quantities

Except in the case of some particular item like a rare coin or in the case of the shortest of short runs, more or less of a commodity will be supplied at various prices. The supply curve will not be vertical. Three different phenomena affect the conditions of supply and thereby change the price of the commodity.

A Specific Sales Tax. In discussing the incidence of a sales tax in Chapter 8 it was assumed that the imposition of a tax shifts the industry supply curve. Having formulated the theory of cost, and the dependence of supply upon cost, we are now in a position to examine how the tax will change supply.

Suppose the government imposes a tax of one dollar per unit on firms producing a particular commodity under conditions of pure competition. The short-run average and marginal cost curves of one firm are shown in the left panel of Fig. 14.2. On the right are shown the market demand curve by consumers, D_1, and the short-run industry supply curve, S_1. The price before the tax is $5, at which this firm supplies 8,000 units per month, and the industry is in short- and long-run equilibrium.

Let us first examine the short-run effects of the tax. The tax is collected from the firms by the government. For each unit produced the

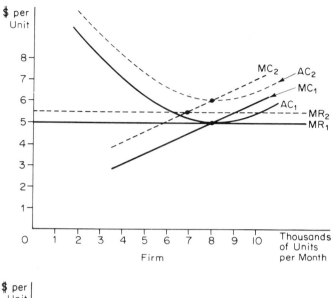

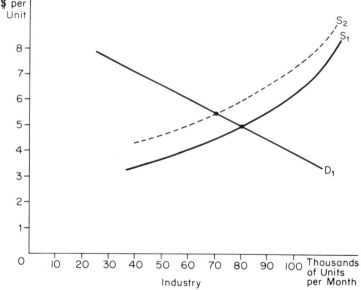

FIG. 14.2.   Short-Run Effects of a Specific Sales Tax

firm must add one dollar to its cost; average cost rises by one dollar at each output. Therefore, the firms' AC curves shift up by one dollar. Marginal cost also rises by one dollar at each output shifting the MC curves upward, as can readily be seen from the following example.

Before Tax				After Tax			
Output	AC	TC	MC	*Output*	AC	TC	MC
0	$—	$ 0	$—	0	$—	$ 0	$—
1,000	8	8,000	8	1,000	9	9,000	9
2,000	7	14,000	6	2,000	8	16,000	7
3,000	6	18,000	4	3,000	7	21,000	5
4,000	5	20,000	2	4,000	6	24,000	3

The average and marginal cost curves of a firm after the imposition of the tax are shown as the broken curves AC_2 and MC_2 in Fig. 14.2. Since the industry short-run supply curve is the horizontal summation of the MC curves of the firms in the industry, the industry supply curve shifts to the left. The decrease in supply from S_1 to S_2 raises the price to consumers, who in turn purchase a smaller quantity.

The extent of the price rise will depend upon the price elasticity of demand. However, price will not rise by the full amount of the tax, i.e., to $6, unless the demand curve is perfectly price inelastic. In this example the price rises to $5.50. As a consequence, individual firms will incur losses in the short run. For the firm depicted in Fig. 14.2 average revenue is below average cost, regardless of what output the firm might produce. And the firm minimizes its loss by producing 7,000 units per month.

To analyze the long-run effects of the tax, two additional aspects of the problem must be taken into account. First, since some firms are unprofitable, the departure of firms from the industry must be taken into consideration. Second, it must be decided whether the industry is one of increasing, constant, or decreasing costs, for this will determine the shape of the long-run industry supply curve. We shall suppose that this is a constant-cost industry. As a consequence, cost curves do not shift as firms depart, and the long-run industry supply curve is a horizontal line.

Though the firm's long-run cost curves are not shown in Fig. 14.2, they also are affected by the tax. Just as short-run average and marginal costs are increased by one dollar at each output, so the long-run average and marginal costs are increased by one dollar, causing the long-run supply curve to shift. In the left panel of Fig. 14.3 are shown the firm's long- and short-run cost curves after the imposition of the tax. After the tax, but before firms have had time to leave the industry, the firm in question operates at point q. Hence, the industry is at point Q on S_2 in the right panel.

At point Q the industry is not in long-run equilibrium, for profits (or losses) are not zero. As losses cause firms to leave the industry the short-run industry supply curve shifts to the left, beginning with the

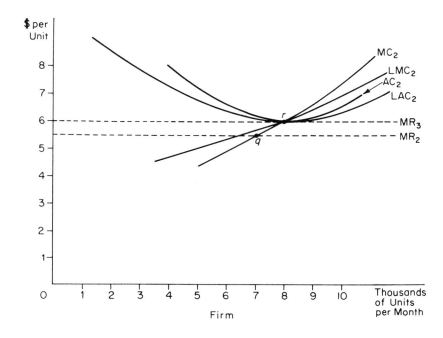

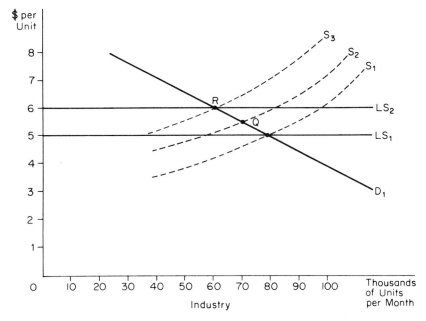

FIG. 14.3. Long-Run Effects of a Specific Sales Tax: Constant-Cost Industry

curve S_2. Since this is assumed to be a constant-cost industry, cost curves are not affected by the exodus of firms. Therefore, firms will continue to leave until the price rises to $6, eliminating the short-run losses of all remaining firms. In the new long-run equilibrium the firm pictured in Fig. 14.3 will operate at point r, and the industry will be at point R on the short-run supply curve S_3. The firm produces the same output produced before the tax, but the industry output is smaller because of the withdrawal of firms.

Notice that in the long run, the price has risen to $6. Although consumers pay only a part of the tax in the short run, those who continue

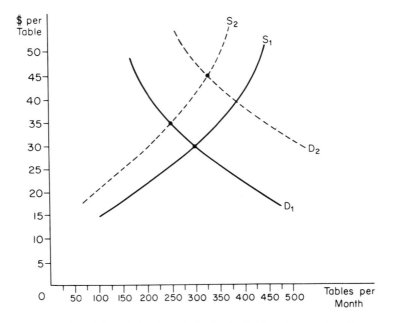

FIG. 14.4.   Market for Maple Coffee Tables of Given Quality

to purchase the product pay all of the tax in the long run. *However, this conclusion holds only if the industry in question is one of constant costs.* Analysis of the long-run outcome under increasing and under decreasing costs is left as an exercise at the end of the chapter.

Changes in Resource Prices. A change in the price of a resource, variable in the short run, will shift the short-run industry supply curve. Suppose the furniture industry approximates the conditions of pure competition and that each firm can purchase any quantity of maple lumber at a given price per square foot. The short-run industry supply curve for maple coffee tables of a particular quality is shown as S_1 in Fig. 14.4. The demand curve is given as D_1, so 300 tables per month are sold at a price of $30 per table.

Now suppose that a disease suddenly threatens maple trees, which requires that growers of maples incur greater costs to prevent infection. Let us assume this raises the price of maple lumber by a given amount per square foot. The higher price of lumber raises the marginal cost of producing maple tables. As the short-run marginal cost curves of the producing firms shift upward, the short-run industry supply decreases to S_2. With a higher cost of production, firms would be unwilling to offer any given quantity for sale unless they were to receive a higher price. The price rises to \$35, at which 250 tables per month are purchased by consumers. The extent to which the price rises depends upon the price elasticity of demand for maple coffee tables, which in turn depends largely upon the number and closeness of substitutes.

Whether, in the final outcome, the quantity of tables bought will decrease depends upon whether the demand curve for tables is stationary. Let us assume that because of a rise in consumer income, the demand increases at the same time that supply decreases. With a rise in income the demand curve shifts to D_2. The price of tables will rise still further— to \$45 in this example. Firms expand output, and the industry moves upward to the right along S_2, beginning at 250 tables per month. For any given increase in demand, how much the short-run price will rise, above \$35, depends upon the price elasticity of supply. We shall suppose that in this case the quantity supplied increases to 325 tables per month. Using the arc elasticity formula, the price elasticity of supply is seen to be

$$e_s = \frac{\dfrac{x_2 - x_1}{x_2 + x_1}}{\dfrac{p_2 - p_1}{p_2 + p_1}} = \frac{\dfrac{325 - 250}{325 + 250}}{\dfrac{45 - 35}{45 + 35}} = \frac{\dfrac{75}{575}}{\dfrac{10}{80}} = \frac{\dfrac{15}{115}}{\dfrac{1}{8}} = \frac{15}{115} \cdot \frac{8}{1} = \frac{120}{115} = 1.04$$

For each 1 per cent rise in price, the quantity supplied will increase by about 1.04 per cent. Generally, the more price elastic is the supply curve, the smaller will be the price rise following upon a given increase in demand, and the larger will be the increase in the quantity supplied.

The price elasticity of the short-run industry supply curve in turn depends upon the steepness of each firm's marginal cost curve. A firm's MC curve will be steeply inclined if the marginal physical product of the variable resource declines sharply as more of that input is used. Hence, if diminishing returns are felt strongly in an industry, the MC curves of firms will be relatively "steep," and the short-run industry supply curve will tend to be less price elastic. On the other hand, if diminishing returns occur very gradually as more variable resources are used, the MC curves of firms will be relatively "flat," and the short-run industry supply curve will tend to be more price elastic.

Technological Change.   Technological innovations ordinarily occur in the long run. The effect of such innovations is typically to shift upward the average and marginal physical product curves for resource inputs. This implies a downward shift in the long-run cost curves of the firms affected, and therefore an increase in long-run industry supply. Examples of such technological innovations are the introduction of electrically powered motors, automatic dishwashers, etc. To illustrate, let us examine the effects that may be expected from industrial uses of nuclear energy, once safety from radiation has been accomplished.

Consider three different purely competitive industries. The first produces a product, call it X, under conditions of increasing cost. The industry producing the second product, Y, is a constant-cost industry, while the third product, Z, is produced by a decreasing-cost industry. Initially, each product is produced by the use of conventional power. Then nuclear power is adopted, which raises productivity and shifts the cost curves of all firms downward. Long-run supply increases in

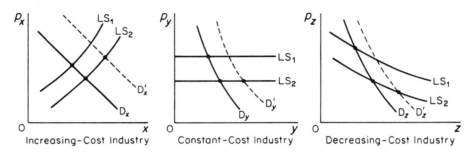

FIG. 14.5. Effects of Technological Innovation Followed by Increased Demand

each industry, shown as a shift from LS_1 to LS_2 in Fig. 14.5. Given the demand for each product—D_x for X, D_y for Y, and D_z for Z—the price of each product falls and the quantity exchanged increases. This holds true in all three industries, regardless of the shapes of the long-run supply curves.

The analysis so far isolates the effect of the technological innovation, given that other things do not change. Of course, other things may change, in which case their effects must be superimposed upon the effects of the technological innovation itself. Suppose that with increasing population and income the demand for each commodity increases—from D_x to D_x', from D_y to D_y', from D_z to D_z'—as shown by the broken curves in Fig. 14.5. The industries move along their respective LS_2 curves. The price of X rises to a level even higher than it was before the introduction of nuclear energy. The price of Y is unaffected by the increase in demand and remains at the price determined by the innovation. The price of Z falls even further.

As mentioned earlier, it is to be expected that most industries are increasing-cost industries, at least the well-established ones. The extent of the price rise following upon any given increase in demand will then depend upon the price elasticity of long-run supply. This in turn depends upon the magnitude of external diseconomies of production, the degree to which cost curves shift upward as new firms enter the industry. The greater the extent to which resource prices rise because of the increase in demand for them as new firms enter, and the more production curves shift downward because of external nonpecuniary effects, the more will cost curves shift upward. And the more cost curves shift upward, the less price elastic will be the long-run industry supply curve. Finally, the less elastic is the supply curve, the greater will be the rise in price for any given increase in demand.

Practical examples are numerous. These few illustrations are designed to indicate the lines along which a problem in pricing can be approached, organized in terms of demand and supply, and a price-quantity prediction made. Each force affecting product prices is categorized and interpreted either as a movement along a demand or supply curve, or as a shift in one or the other curve. It is important to distinguish between a movement along a curve and a shift in a curve, and to distinguish the forces that cause each, for the outcome depends upon whether a given action produces a movement or a shift. By classifying economic phenomena in these terms and tracing their consequences, our comprehension of the operation of markets is greatly enhanced.

STATISTICAL MEASUREMENT OF COST AND SUPPLY

Our primary concern is economic theory. Nevertheless, if the theoretical principles are to be regarded in proper perspective, some reference should be made to their empirical counterparts in the real world. After all, theory is a proffered explanation, and unless the explanation can find observable applications, there is no basis for judging its validity.

In Chapter 8 statistical measurements of demand are discussed. Cost and supply are also subject to quantitative measurement, and the statistical problems are similar to those encountered in the measurement of demand. Essentially, estimation of an industry supply curve consists of the following steps. (1) A sample of observations on price and quantity traded is collected. The sample may consist of a time series—a series of observations on price and quantity in the same place at different times—or a cross-section sample—a series of observations on price and quantity at the same time in different places. Regardless of which type of sample is used, each observed price-quantity combination is treated as an equilibrium combination. (2) The series is plotted to yield a graph. Each observed price-quantity combination fixes one point. Plotting the entire set of sample observations provides a scatter diagram to which a geometric curve may be fitted. This procedure is described in Chapter 8. (3) The empirical curve so obtained is used to estimate the "true" supply curve. If certain statistical conditions are met, the estimate will be reliable. This inference, that the empirical supply curve yielded by the sample is an estimate of the "true" industry supply curve, is probable. One can specify that the probability of being in error in making the inference is less than some (small) amount.

The same steps apply to productivity curves and to cost curves. The only difference lies in the data used. To measure a total product curve the observations would consist of output-input combinations, and to measure a total cost curve the observations would be comprised of cost-output combinations.

Problems of Estimation

As a rule economists are more interested in market supply than they are in the costs or the production function of any single firm. The cost curves of a firm would be of more interest to the firm itself. But since supply does depend upon cost, it is worth pointing out some of the main problems inherent in cost measurement.

Data on cost are scarce relative to market data. Much information bearing on cost is regarded by firms as confidential. Even where it is not confidential such information is often not of sufficient social interest to warrant publication. Suppose we consider a hypothetical firm whose figures on cost and output are available. What problems would arise in attempting to identify the firm's average cost curve?

A range of different outputs are recorded and the average cost corresponding to each output is known. Each output-average cost combination is one observation in the sample. When plotted on graph paper, the entire sample yields the scatter diagram shown in Fig. 14.6. Had the cost curve been perfectly stable, each point would lie on the same cost curve. But apparently the cost curve has not been perfectly stable. Movement from one observed point to another may have been solely a movement along a cost curve. On the other hand, such a movement may have involved a shift in the cost curve as well.

A curve fitted to the scatter (in such a way as to minimize the deviations of the points from the fitted curve) would have the U shape usually assumed in economic theory. If the deviations are small enough and if they are distributed in a certain way, the fitted curve will be a reliable estimate of the cost curve. But the deviations may be such as to greatly distort the estimate of the firm's cost curve.

In this connection, it must be recalled that a given cost curve is drawn for constant resource prices and a given state of technology. If significant changes in these determinants of cost have occurred, it is desirable that they be identified. Otherwise, it may be impossible to separate movements along a cost curve from shifts in the cost curve. Granted that all these changes can be identified and the data adjusted to remove their impact, the *adjusted* scatter of points will lie on one cost curve. This would be an ideal. Actually, some small deviations of the points from the fitted curve would persist. If for no other reason, then simply because of clerical errors in the recording of data. Such "errors" in estimating the cost curve will generally be of little importance if the impact of changes in resource prices and technological changes has been sufficiently removed. And the resulting cost estimate will be a close approximation to the "true" cost curve.

In order to obtain the firm's empirical marginal cost curve, it is not necessary that a new sample of marginal cost be collected. Once average

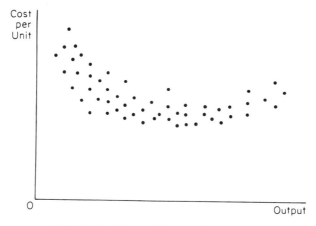

FIG. 14.6. Scatter Diagram of Average Cost

cost has been estimated, it can be multiplied by output to get the total cost curve. And from total cost the change in total cost in response to each change in output can be computed to reveal the firm's marginal cost curve.

Separation of the variables that cause shifts in a curve from those that cause movements along a curve is not peculiar to cost curves. The same problem is encountered in statistical estimation of supply curves. Assuming no errors have been made in collecting and recording the sample data, if the industry supply curve is perfectly stable and the market demand curve is shifting, the sample data when plotted will yield a set of points, all of which lie on the supply curve. This is shown in Fig. 14.7. The observed points P_1, P_2, and P_3 all lie on the supply curve S_1, traced by the demand curve as it shifts from D_1 to D_2 and then to D_3. The supply curve is then identified by the data. On the other hand, a shifting supply curve and a perfectly stable demand curve result in a set of points, all of which lie on the demand curve; and the demand curve is identified by the data. It sometimes happens that both curves have shifted. Suppose that supply changes from S_1 to S_2 to S_3 at the same time that demand changes from D_1 to D_2 to D_3. The points

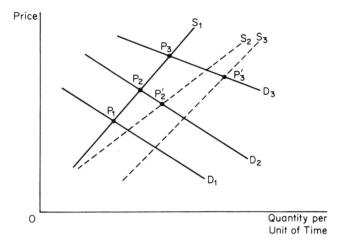

FIG. 14.7.   Empirical Observations Generated by Shifting Curves

observed in the sample will be P_1, P'_2, and P'_3. The scatter diagram is comprised of a mixture, revealing neither the demand curve nor the supply curve.

It rarely, if ever, happens that one or the other curve is *perfectly* stable. But sometimes one curve is much more stable than the other. If the supply curve is much more stable than the demand curve, the scatter of points given by the plotted sample data will approximate the supply curve. When both the demand and supply curves are highly unstable, the resulting scatter diagram may appear like that shown in Fig. 8.9 of Chapter 8. Then if one is to estimate the supply curve, the variables that caused the shifts in supply must be identified. Once this is done, and assuming it can be done, the impact of these variables can be eliminated. Then the adjusted data will reveal an approximation to the supply curve.

There are statistical techniques designed to eliminate from the data the impact of forces causing shifts in supply. The direction and the quantitative magnitude of these shifts, once determined and isolated, can in turn be measured. It must be pointed out, however, that these techniques are not always successful. Statisticians and economists are currently working to improve the techniques. As more powerful methods are developed and employed, it is to be expected that our knowledge of the quantitative properties of supply will be enhanced.

Examples of Empirical Research

More empirical studies have been conducted in the area of demand than in the area of supply. There are several reasons for this. First, actual instances of pure competition in the economies of Western countries are not abundant. Since the supply curve applies to a purely competitive industry, there are relatively few opportunities to observe industry supply curves. Second, the forces producing shifts in supply curves are often difficult to identify and quantify. Changes in resource prices do not pose many special problems. But the effects of technological innovations are frequently complex, difficult to pin down, and their influence varies from one firm to another. Third, the definition of what comprises an industry is necessarily somewhat arbitrary—a problem not encountered to the same degree in studies of demand. Though fewer in number than studies of demand, quantitative studies of supply have provided useful information.

Many attempts have been made to measure cost for various types of firms. Professor Joel Dean has made statistical cost studies of a furniture factory, a leather belt shop, a hosiery mill, a department store, and a chain of shoe stores.[1] His data consist of cost and output observations at monthly or fortnightly intervals covering periods of two, three, or four years. In the case of the furniture factory, for example, the most reliable estimate of marginal cost at the factory was a constant $1.12 per unit over the observed range of output. That is, the marginal cost curve was a horizontal line. The hosiery mill showed average cost declining with increases in output and marginal cost constant at about $2.00 per dozen pairs of hosiery, while the shoe stores displayed a U-shaped average cost curve and a rising marginal cost curve. A study of the cost of producing steel[2] based on annual data from 1927 to 1938 yielded declining average cost and constant marginal cost of approximately $56 per ton. On the other hand, a U-shaped average cost curve and a rising marginal cost curve gave the best fit to data on an electric light and power plant.[3]

Some empirical investigations bear out the theoretical assumption of U-shaped average and marginal cost curves. Other results appear to be at variance with this assumption. It must be kept in mind, however, that the available evidence is frequently not conclusive. In some instances tabulations on all the components of cost could not be obtained, so the investigator had to "make do" with a partial list of cost items. Second, although the data used in these studies have been "corrected" for changes in resource prices, some technological reorganizations may have occurred that could not be taken into account. Thus, it is questionable that shifts

[1] J. Dean, "Statistical Determination of Costs with Special Reference to Marginal Costs," *Studies in Business Administration*, VII (1936) ; "Statistical Cost Functions of a Hosiery Mill," *Ibid.*, XII (1941) ; J. Dean and R. W. James, "The Long-Run Behavior of Costs in a Chain of Shoe Stores," *Ibid.*, XIII (1942) ; "The Relation of Cost to Output for a Leather Belt Shop," National Bureau of Economic Research, Technical Paper No. 2 (December 1941) ; "Department Store Cost Functions," in *Studies in Mathematical Economics and Econometrics*, ed. Oskar Lange (London: Cambridge University Press, 1942).
[2] T. O. Yntema, *Steel Prices, Volume, and Costs*, United States Steel Corporation Temporary National Economic Committee Reports, II (1940).
[3] J. A. Nordin, "Note on a Light Plant's Cost Curves," *Econometrica*, XV (1947).

in the positions of cost curves have been completely eliminated. Finally, the observations may not have covered a sufficient range of output. For example, at outputs smaller than those observed, or outputs larger than those observed, marginal cost may show a radical departure from the straight horizontal line. Of course, it may indeed be true that average cost declines over a significant range of output for many firms—perhaps even for most firms. But this does not contradict the assumption of a U-shaped curve. For a U-shaped curve need not be symmetrical. Diminishing returns might not set in until the firm is very close to full capacity.

The existence of extensive and reliable data has attracted economists to the study of agricultural supply. Since agriculture is a purely competitive industry of national importance, it has provided an opportunity for significant statistical applications of the theory of supply. From a time series sample covering the years 1920-43 Professor Gerhard Tintner has estimated the supply curve of all agricultural commodities as a group.[4] The estimated supply curve is a straight line with a positive slope, so the price elasticity of supply is different at different points on the supply curve. Letting x represent an index of all agricultural output and p_x an index of price received by farmers, price elasticity of supply is given as

$$e_s = \frac{\Delta x}{\Delta p_x} \cdot \frac{p_x}{x}$$

From the sample, $\Delta x / \Delta p_x$, is estimated as 1.721. Hence, the elasticity is

$$e_s = 1.721 \frac{p_x}{x}$$

For any price and its corresponding quantity supplied, the price elasticity can be computed. At most of the observed points the supply is relatively price inelastic.

The supply curve and the price elasticity of supply for cotton in the United States was estimated by R. M. Walsh in 1944.[5] From a time series covering 1925-33, he estimates the price elasticity as approximately 0.22. Subsequent research by Marc Nerlove,[6] using more advanced techniques, indicates that the price elasticity for cotton is somewhat larger than 0.22. But it still turns out to be significantly less than unity. All studies on this commodity have yielded a supply curve that is relatively price inelastic.

[4] G. Tintner, "Multiple Regression for Systems of Equations," *Econometrica*, XIV (1946).
[5] R. M. Walsh, "Response to Price in the Production of Cotton and Cottonseed," *Journal of Farm Economics*, XXVI (1944).
[6] M. Nerlove, "Estimates of the Elasticities of Supply of Selected Agricultural Commodities," *Journal of Farm Economics*, XXXVIII (1956).

The examples of quantitative measurements suggest the kind of information that empirical studies may uncover. Just as the theoretical applications illustrate one way in which the theory of supply may be put to use, so the empirical applications illustrate the way in which abstract theory can be related to factual data. They convey the "experimental" or "applied" aspects of economics, in which theory is tested against observations and quantitative estimates are made.

Knowledge of the quantitative properties of supply is a great aid in the formulation of sound economic policy. It has a bearing on problems of taxation, the relative income shares of capital and labor, economic growth in industrially advanced nations as well as underdeveloped areas, and many other aspects of pricing and resource allocation.

PROBLEMS

1. Suppose the government imposes a tax of $1.00 per unit sold on a commodity produced under conditions of pure competition. The tax is collected from the sellers of the product. Trace the long-run effects of the tax on the price of the commodity and the quantity exchanged under each of the following assumptions:

(a) The industry is an increasing-cost industry.
(b) The industry is a decreasing-cost industry.

2. Suppose a commodity is produced competitively in the U.S. It is also produced competitively abroad. Demand and supply schedules for the product in the U.S. are presented in Table I. In Table II are shown the demand and supply schedules in the rest of the world.

Table I (United States)			Table II (Rest of World)		
Price	Quantity Demanded	Quantity Supplied	Price	Quantity Demanded	Quantity Supplied
$8.00	20	100	$8.00	40	200
7.50	30	90	7.50	50	190
7.00	40	80	7.00	60	180
6.50	50	70	6.50	70	170
6.00	60	60	6.00	80	160
5.50	70	50	5.50	90	150
5.00	80	40	5.00	100	140
4.50	90	30	4.50	110	130
4.00	100	20	4.00	120	120
3.50	110	10	3.50	130	110
3.00	120	0	3.00	140	100

(a) Plot the demand and supply curves in the U.S. as Figure 1. Plot the demand and supply curves in the rest of the world as Figure 2.

(*b*) Assuming free trade and no cost of transportation, the price in the U.S. will be the same as it is in the rest of the world. Find the equilibrium price. Find consumption and production in the U.S. and also in the rest of the world. Find the volume of trade between the U.S. and the rest of the world. Will the U.S. be an importer or exporter of this commodity?

(*c*) Now suppose the U.S. imposes a tariff of $1.00 per unit of the commodity imported into the U.S. Will the new equilibrium price in the U.S. be different from the price abroad? If so, by how much? What will happen to:

(*1*) Production in the U.S. and in the rest of the world,

(*2*) Consumption in the U.S. and in the rest of the world,

(*3*) The volume of trade between the U.S. and the rest of the world,

(*4*) The price consumers must pay for this product in the U.S.

SUGGESTED READING

K. Boulding, *Economic Analysis*, rev. ed., pp. 146–81. New York: Harper & Brothers, 1948.

L. W. Weiss, *Economics and American Industry*, Chaps. 2, 3, 4. New York: John Wiley & Sons, Inc., 1961.

J. Johnson, *Statistical Cost Analysis*, Chap. 4. New York: McGraw-Hill Book Company, Inc., 1960.

Part V

Product Pricing: Monopoly and Nonpure Competition

15

Monopoly

Monopoly is a market structure in which there is a single seller of a product. If we view the entire spectrum of market types, pure competition can be visualized as representing one pole and monopoly the opposite one. Whereas there are many sellers under pure competition, there is but one seller under monopoly. Where there exist many firms selling a standardized product, no one operating alone can significantly influence the price. A monopolist, on the other hand, differentiates his product from all others sold in the economy and exerts control over its price. His one-seller position can persist only if there are no good substitutes for the product he sells. Therefore, unlike the purely competitive firm, the monopolist must be able to prevent the entry of new firms that may be attracted to the industry by the profit he enjoys. Otherwise, he could not remain a monopolist.

Examples of pure monopoly are rare. Nevertheless, certain markets do approximate monopolistic conditions. Although it is not the only producer, a single firm may control 80 per cent or more of the total market supply. And though there are substitutes for its product, they may be very imperfect substitutes. In the United States local public utility companies come close to being pure monopolists. Others, such as the shoe machinery, aluminum, and nickel industries, have characteristics quite similar to pure monopoly. Entry of additional firms into the industry may be blocked for any one of several reasons. The existing firm may hold a patent or a license that prohibits duplication of its product, as in the case of the shoe machinery industry where one firm has held patents on virtually all types of manufacturing equipment. Or the firm may control supplies of raw materials, as one company did in the aluminum industry prior to World War II. However, it is not necessary that competition be prevented by a conscious device. The size of the market may not be sufficient to support two profitable firms. An additional firm might force total revenue below total cost for both firms.

REVENUE OF A MONOPOLIST

An approach to the theory of monopoly can be organized in the same way as that of the firm under pure competition. The monopolist is assumed to maximize total profit. Nothing new need be added to the theory of cost. Since the law of diminishing returns determines the shapes of a firm's cost curves, the U-shaped average and marginal cost curves are not affected by the existence or nonexistence of competition in the selling of products. Consequently, the cost curves of a monopolist have the same general appearance as those of a purely competitive firm. And, as before, we shall assume that any given set of cost curves is drawn for constant resource prices and a given state of technology.[1]

The possibility of product price control definitely affects a firm's revenue curves. Since a purely competitive firm is only one of many sellers, it can sell any output at the going market price; the entrepreneur views the demand curve *faced by the firm* as a straight horizontal line. In contrast, a monopolist, since he is the only seller, is faced with the market demand curve. The market demand curve and the demand curve for his output are one and the same thing. Therefore, the monopolist must lower his price in order to sell more. If he raises his price he will sell less, but his sales will not drop to zero because there are no other firms in competition with him selling the same product. Consequently, his average revenue will not be constant with respect to output, and it will deviate from marginal revenue.

Revenue Curves

The market demand schedule for a commodity X is shown by columns 1 and 2 of Table 15.1. Price multiplied by its corresponding quantity bought is the total expenditure on X by buyers. As the only seller, this is also the monopolist's total revenue, shown in column 3.

The monopolist's total revenue curve is plotted and labeled TR in Fig. 15.1. It is interesting to compare this curve with the TR curve of the purely competitive firm depicted in Fig. 12.1, Chapter 12. Notice first that the scale of operations differs for the two firms. Given the same market demand curve in either case (the same size of the market), the single purely competitive firm supplies but a small portion of the total industry output, so one is considering output units in the neighborhood

---

[1] If the monopolist can influence the prices of resources by varying the quantity he buys, the above assumption must be modified. Resource prices will change as the monopoly firm moves along its cost curves, and the supply curves of the resources rather than their prices are held constant for a given set of cost curves. However, this is a question not of monopoly selling on the product market but of monopoly buying on the resource market. The modification makes no essential difference in the theory of monopoly product pricing and output as presented in this chapter; it will be taken up in Chapter 21.

Table 15.1

1	2	3	4	5
Price of X	Quantity of X per Unit of Time	Total Revenue	Average Revenue	Marginal Revenue
p_x	x	$p_x x$	$\dfrac{p_x x}{x} = p_x$	$\dfrac{\Delta p_x x}{\Delta x}$
$10	10	$100	$\dfrac{100}{10} = \$10$	$\dfrac{100}{10} = \$10$
9	20	180	$\dfrac{180}{20} = 9$	$\dfrac{80}{10} = 8$
8	30	240	$\dfrac{240}{30} = 8$	$\dfrac{60}{10} = 6$
7	40	280	$\dfrac{280}{40} = 7$	$\dfrac{40}{10} = 4$
6	50	300	$\dfrac{300}{50} = 6$	$\dfrac{20}{10} = 2$
5	60	300	$\dfrac{300}{60} = 5$	$\dfrac{0}{10} = 0$
4	70	280	$\dfrac{280}{70} = 4$	$\dfrac{-20}{10} = -2$
3	80	240	$\dfrac{240}{80} = 3$	$\dfrac{-40}{10} = -4$
2	90	180	$\dfrac{180}{90} = 2$	$\dfrac{-60}{10} = -6$
1	100	100	$\dfrac{100}{100} = 1$	$\dfrac{-80}{10} = -8$

of 1, 2, 3, etc. For the same market demand curve, one firm supplying all of the output would be producing much more at each price. In Fig. 15.1 the units on the axis are 10, 20, 30, etc. This has been done to indicate that if one is contrasting the two different industrial structures as they would operate in the same market, the monopoly firm would be of larger size for any given total market supply.

More important is the difference between the shapes of the two TR curves. The competitive firm's TR curve is a straight line because the price is not affected by its output. The alteration in price is what im-

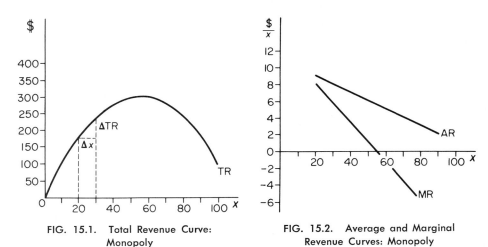

FIG. 15.1. Total Revenue Curve: Monopoly

FIG. 15.2. Average and Marginal Revenue Curves: Monopoly

parts to the monopolist's TR curve its concave shape. It is precisely because the price becomes lower with each successive increment in output that total revenue rises by a smaller amount for successive equal increments in output. As larger and larger outputs are considered, the TR curve rises at a decreasing rate, reaches a maximum, and then declines.

Average revenue is computed in column 4. When average revenue is plotted against output in Fig. 15.2, it becomes clear that the AR curve of a monopolist is nothing other than the market demand curve. It shows the average revenue or price the monopolist would receive at each possible quantity he might sell.

Column 5 of Table 15.1 records the firm's marginal revenue, and Fig. 15.2 depicts the marginal revenue curve, labeled MR. Whereas the MR curve coincides with the AR curve for a purely competitive firm (see Fig. 12.2), it deviates from the AR curve in the case of monopoly. With the exception of the first entry in Table 15.1, marginal revenue is below average revenue at each level of sales (the MR curve is below the AR curve). Moreover, the larger is the volume of sales, the greater is the amount by which marginal revenue falls short of average revenue. The fact that the MR curve lies farther below the AR curve as one moves farther to the right in Fig. 15.2 is but another instance of the general average-marginal relationship. In general, whenever the average is declining, the marginal must be below the average. Furthermore, if the average curve is a declining straight line throughout its entire range, as it is in Fig. 15.2, the marginal curve must be a straight line declining at a faster rate.

The vertical distance of the MR curve from the horizontal axis is equal to the slope of the TR curve. Since the slope of the TR curve becomes smaller as larger outputs are considered, marginal revenue must get smaller, so the MR curve must be declining. The TR curve reaches a maximum, at which its slope is zero. At this output marginal revenue is zero, and the MR curve intersects the horizontal axis. Thereafter, total revenue decreases as output increases; the TR curve is negatively sloped, making marginal revenue negative. Negative marginal revenue is indicated by the segment of the MR curve that lies below the horizontal axis.

These properties of the MR curve follow mathematically from the given form of the TR curve. It is instructive, however, to look into the economic reasons for the behavior of marginal revenue. Suppose the monopolist is selling 20 units of X. The demand schedule shows that 20 units will sell for $9 per unit. If the firm wishes to sell 30 units, it must reduce the price to $8. The additional 10 units sell for $8 each, and the firm must also reduce the price charged for its previous sales volume of 20 units. That is, the firm cannot sell 10 units at $8 and 20 units at $9; it must sell all 30 units at $8. The additional 10 units add $8 each, or $80, to the total revenue. But the previous 20 units must now be sold at $1 less, and a $1 drop in price for each of these units means total revenue falls by $20. The net effect is to add $80 to total revenue and to deduct $20, which increases total revenue by $60. Marginal revenue is the increase in total revenue ($60) divided by the increase in output (10), or $6 per unit sold. Marginal revenue is less than the price, $8, because the monopolist must reduce price on all units he sells.

Marginal Revenue and Demand Elasticity

The rate at which the TR curve rises, the output at which the peak occurs, and the rate at which the curve declines all depend upon the *extent* to which price falls as output increases. Since marginal revenue is equal to the slope of the TR curve, this is another way of saying that marginal revenue depends upon the price elasticity of demand. Recall the discussion of price elasticity in Chapter 6. It was demonstrated there that the direction in which total expenditures on a good change in response to a price decrease depends upon the price elasticity of demand. For any chosen point on the market demand curve for X:

If	*Then*
(1) Demand is relatively elastic	TE increases when p_x decreases
(2) Demand is relatively inelastic	TE decreases when p_x decreases
(3) Demand is of unit elasticity	TE is unchanged when p_x decreases

In this scheme, TE is used to represent total expenditures on X, and p_x the price of X.

Total expenditure on X is total revenue of the monopolist selling X, so whether total revenue increases, decreases, or remains unchanged depends upon the price elasticity of demand. Indeed, it can be shown mathematically that marginal revenue equals price plus the ratio of price to the elasticity at each output:

$$\text{MR} = p_x + \frac{p_x}{e_{p_x}}$$

where e_{p_x} denotes the price elasticity of demand for X.

In using this formula it should be remembered that e_{p_x} is a negative number. Consequently the term p_x/e_{p_x} will be a negative number, causing MR to be smaller than p_x. Moreover, the less elastic is the demand curve at any output, the closer is e_{p_x} to zero, and the greater is the amount by which MR falls short of p_x. A numerical example will help to clarify this last conclusion. Assume that at an output of 30 the price is \$8. If $e_{p_x} = -2$, then MR $= 8 + 8/-2 = 8 - 4 = 4$. If demand is more elastic, say $e_{p_x} = -4$, then MR $= 8 + 8/-4 = 8 - 2 = 6$. Marginal revenue is less than price in each instance. Yet it is closer to price in the case of the more elastic demand. At the infinitely elastic extreme, the case of the purely competitive firm, MR $= 8 + 8/-\infty = 8 - 0 = 8$, i.e., MR $= p_x$.

In Fig. 15.3 the line AB is a straight-line demand curve for X. It was shown

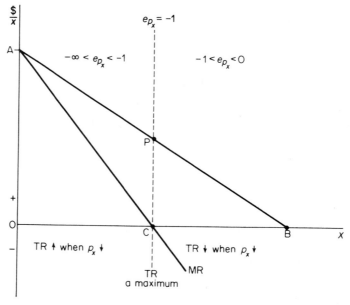

FIG. 15.3. Demand and Marginal Revenue

in Chapter 6 that a straight-line demand curve has certain elasticity characteristics. First, it is relatively elastic over half of the line and relatively inelastic over the other half. The distance 0C is half the distance 0B—C is midway between 0 and B. The point P is the point on the demand curve corresponding to the quantity 0C. Between points A and P on the demand curve, demand is relatively elastic. At point P it has unit elasticity. Between P and B it is relatively inelastic. Second, as one moves from A toward P, e_{p_x} approaches -1; at P it has unit elasticity; and as one moves from P toward B, e_{p_x} approaches zero. Hence, between A and P a one-unit increment in x will cause total revenue to increase. This, of course, means that marginal revenue is positive, as shown by the fact that the MR curve is above the horizontal axis. In terms of the formula, p_x/e_{p_x} must be less than p_x in absolute value and MR must be greater than zero. As e_{p_x} approaches -1, $(p_x + p_x/e_{p_x})$ approaches zero, so marginal revenue declines toward zero as an output of 0C is approached. At 0C, $e_{p_x} = -1$, so MR $= p_x - p_x = 0$; the MR curve cuts the horizontal axis. Finally, beyond 0C the demand curve is relatively inelastic. Thus, a one-unit increment in x causes total revenue to decrease, and the MR curve is below the horizontal axis. This is also shown by the formula. Disregarding its negative sign e_{p_x} is a fraction. Since p_x divided by a fraction is larger than p_x, then MR $= p_x + p_x/e_{p_x} < 0$.

From this analysis we can conclude that the marginal revenue curve must lie below the demand curve, regardless of whether the demand curve is a straight line. If the demand curve is a straight line, the MR curve will be more steeply sloped at each output; and it will intersect the horizontal axis midway between the origin and the point at which the demand curve intersects the horizontal axis.

SHORT-RUN EQUILIBRIUM

The determination of short-run price and output follows basically the same principles applied to the purely competitive firm. The firm is assumed to maximize total profit or to minimize total loss. The only essential difference is that the competitive firm decides its profit-maximizing output for a given market price, while the monopolist simultaneously determines both output and price. His ability to control price is not completely unrestricted, for the market demand curve tells him there is a maximum price consumers are willing to pay for any quantity. The monopoly problem reduces to a choice of output such that it maximizes profit or minimizes loss for a given demand curve rather than a given price.

Profit Maximization

If the total cost curve is combined with the total revenue curve in Fig. 15.1, the vertical distance between them yields total profit. The equilibrium output of the firm is that at which the total profit curve is a maximum. Although short-run output can be found by use of the total curves, this method is not convenient for showing the price charged or the market equilibrium. It is better to take the market demand curve directly into account, in order to show that the monopolist's output is such that the quantity demanded is equal to the quantity supplied on the market.

In Fig. 15.4 the firm's short-run average and marginal cost curves are depicted. The market demand curve, **D**, is also the firm's average revenue curve, **AR**. And corresponding to the average revenue curve is the marginal revenue curve, **MR**. Like the purely competitive firm,

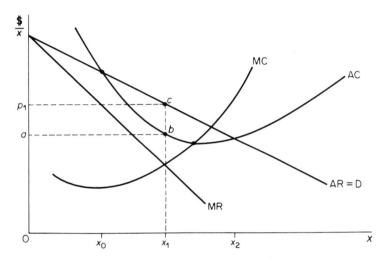

FIG. 15.4.   Short-Run Monopoly Equilibrium: Average and Marginal Curves

total profit is maximized at the output at which marginal revenue equals marginal cost, an output of x_1 units. At any output less than x_1, marginal revenue is greater than marginal cost. An additional unit of output adds more to total revenue than it adds to total cost. Total profit must increase, so it pays the firm to expand output. But the firm will not expand output beyond x_1 units because at larger outputs marginal revenue is less than marginal cost, causing total profit to shrink.

The market demand curve shows the maximum price consumers are willing to pay for each different quantity that might be offered to them. Since the monopolist has determined his output as x_1, the price he will charge is given by the demand curve, namely p_1. Price or average revenue is equal to the vertical distance x_1c. Total revenue is revenue per unit sold multiplied by the number of units sold (x_1c times $0x_1$), which equals the area of the rectangle $0x_1cp_1$. The cost per unit is given by the AC curve. For x_1 units produced average cost equals the vertical distance x_1b, and total cost equals the area of the rectangle $0x_1ba$. Finally, total profit, the difference between total revenue and total cost, equals the difference between the areas of these two rectangles, i.e., the area of the rectangle $abcp_1$.

Marginal cost is always positive, regardless of a firm's output. Marginal revenue for a monopolist, on the other hand, may be positive or negative, depending upon the level of output. We have seen that marginal revenue is related to the price elasticity of demand. Over the elastic segment of the demand curve marginal revenue is positive; over the inelastic segment it is negative. Since positive marginal cost is equal to marginal revenue in equilibrium, it follows that the monopoly equilibrium output will be on the elastic segment of the demand curve. In general, the demand curve is neither elastic nor inelastic at all points on the curve. Elasticity varies from one point to another. But the monopolist with positive marginal cost, if he produces any output, will produce an output corresponding to a relatively elastic point on the demand curve.

Loss Minimization

A monopolist, like a purely competitive firm, can incur a loss in the short run. Ability to exert control over the product price does not guarantee the monopolist a profit. Whether profit is made or not depends upon the relationship between demand and the monopolist's cost conditions. Should it happen that average revenue is not sufficient to cover average cost at any output, the best the monopolist can do in the short run is to minimize his loss.

Figure 15.5 depicts a loss situation. Given his cost curves, demand is not great enough to permit the monopolist to make a profit. At no point is the price large enough to cover average cost. By producing x_1 units, where marginal cost equals marginal revenue, and charging a price of p_1 his loss is minimized. Loss per unit is equal to the vertical distance de, and total loss is given by the area of the rectangle p_1def. Since price is larger than average *variable* cost at this output, the monopolist can cover his total variable cost and have something left over. Whatever is left over will contribute to the payment of his total fixed cost.

Suppose the demand curve were to shift to the left, so that the new MR curve cuts the MC curve farther down and to the left. At this point of intersection suppose further that price is below average variable cost (the AR curve is below the AVC curve at all outputs). At this output total revenue would fall short of total variable cost. The monopolist would lose an amount equal to his total fixed cost *plus* the difference between total revenue and total variable cost. But he can make his loss less than this by producing zero output. Then his loss equals his total fixed cost. Taking this and the previous case into account we can con-

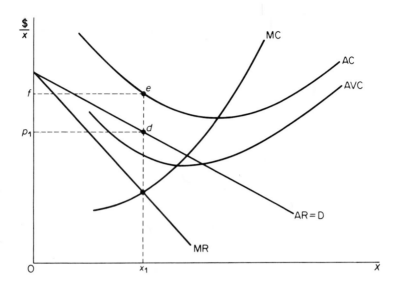

FIG. 15.5. Minimization by Monopolist

clude the following. To maximize profit or to minimize loss in the short run the monopolist will produce an output such that marginal cost equals marginal revenue if the price at this output is greater than or equal to average variable cost. If this price is less than average variable cost, he will utilize no variable resources and suspend production.

LONG-RUN EQUILIBRIUM

The long run is a period of sufficient duration to allow variations in all resource inputs. The monopolist can vary his scale of plant; he can operate with a plant of any desired size and he can withdraw entirely from production because he can dispose of his plant. In contrast to pure competition one cannot say a monopolist will build an optimal scale of plant; he will do so under certain conditions, but under other conditions he will build a plant of greater or lesser size. Neither is there any assurance that profit will be zero in the long run. Of course, profit will not be negative, of that we can be sure. For if his best prospect is a loss in the long run, the monopolist simply will not produce the product. A loss implies he could earn more by employing his resources in some other endeavor.

Though we can say profit will not be negative, we cannot say it will be zero. Profit will be at least zero and may be positive. Indeed, it is most likely that profit will be positive. With entry into the industry blocked, other firms attracted by positive short-run profit can be kept out. Thus, with the prevention of competition short-run profit can be ex-

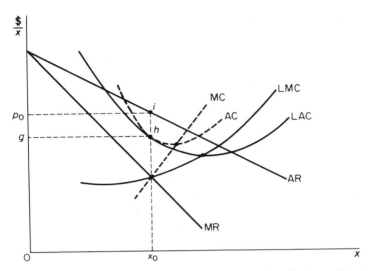

FIG. 15.6. Long-Run Monopoly Equilibrium: Less than Optimum Output

tended into the long-run situation. This profit is the incentive a monopolist has for protecting his monopoly position.

Two different possibilities are depicted in Figs. 15.6 and 15.7. In each case the monopolist maximizes profit by producing the output at which long-run marginal cost is equal to marginal revenue. Since the long-run equilibrium is also one short-run equilibrium, short-run marginal cost

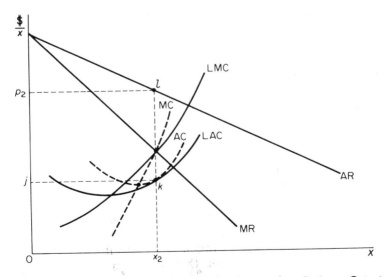

FIG. 15.7. Long-Run Monopoly Equilibrium: Greater than Optimum Output

is also equal to marginal revenue. Then it follows that long-run and short-run marginal costs are equal.

In Fig. 15.6 the market for the product is so limited that the MR curve cuts the LMC curve to the left of the minimum point on the LAC curve. Long-run equilibrium output is x_0 and the price is p_0. Total profit equals $ghip_0$. Since the firm will produce any output at the least cost, the AC curve is tangent to the LAC curve at x_0 units; this implies that MC = LMC, as demonstrated in Chapter 11. The most important characteristic of the diagram is the fact that output is less than optimum output. Not only does the monopolist utilize a smaller than optimum scale of plant, he does not produce the optimum output corresponding to the scale of plant he does use. The reason is that the market is not large enough (the demand curve does not lie far enough to the right) to warrant a greater output. It does not pay the firm to take advantage of internal economies of scale. As a result the average cost of production and the price are higher than they could be in a larger market. Public utility companies in small communities sometimes encounter this situation. The local market does not consume enough power to make the use of more efficient techniques profitable, or to promote the most efficient utilization of existing equipment, leaving the firm with excess capacity.

On the other hand, the extent of the market may be so large that it is profitable for a monopolist to expand his plant beyond optimum size. This situation is shown in Fig. 15.7. The long-run profit-maximizing output is x_2 and the price is p_2, yielding a total profit equal to the area $jklp_2$. The monopolist builds a larger than optimum scale of plant and operates it at a greater than optimum output for that plant size. It is more profitable for him to use a scale of plant that is less efficient than possible. The diseconomies of scale are more than compensated for by the additional revenue that accrues from larger output. This situation is most likely to occur when a monopolist produces for a national market.

It might happen that long-run profit-maximizing output turns out to be optimum output, granted that a particular combination of demand and cost conditions prevail. The MR curve must be such that it intersects the LMC and MC curves at the minimum point on the LAC curve. Then the firm will produce the output at which cost per unit is least. But this long-run equilibrium should not be confused with the equilibrium under pure competition. Unlike pure competition, there is nothing inherent in the structure of the market to guarantee optimum output. In a sense, it is accidental that profit-maximizing output is also optimum output.

Changes in Equilibrium

Strictly speaking, there is no industry or market supply curve in monopoly. The supply curve describes the quantity that would be offered at each different given price, whereas the monopolist simultaneously determines both quantity and price. This does not mean, however, that one cannot trace the effects of a change in demand.

Suppose the demand for a product X increases. If X is produced by a monopolist, his AR curve will shift to the right. At the same time, the MR curve also shifts to the right. At the old equilibrium, marginal revenue is now greater than marginal cost. Since the MC curve is positively inclined, the firm will expand output by moving upward and to the right along its MC curve. How far will it move? To the point on the MC curve at which the *new* MR curve intersects it.[2] Profit is again maximized for the new revenue conditions. The price, given by the new demand curve at the new output, will be higher, and the quantity exchanged on the market will be larger. A decrease in demand will have opposite effects.

Of course, if there is a radical change in the slope of the demand curve when it shifts, these conclusions may have to be modified. But in almost all practical situations they will hold true. The essential point is that it is possible, even in these rare exceptions, to find the price-quantity effects. Both the short-run and long-run effects can be traced for any imaginable shift in demand.

A change in resource prices or a change in the state of technology shifts the purely competitive industry supply curve. Although there is no industry supply curve under monopoly, the effects on cost of resource price changes or technological changes are known. So the direction in which the cost curves will shift is determinable. Suppose the supply of some variable resource increases so that its price falls, lowering the monopolist's AC and MC curves. Given the demand for his product, the new lower MC curve will intersect the MR curve at a new point, farther down and to the right of the old intersection point. To maximize profit under the new cost conditions, he will increase output and reduce price. As for changes in the state of technology, technological improvement shifts cost curves downward. Like a lower resource price, the effect will be to lower the product price and increase the quantity traded, assuming the demand curve to be unchanged. Technological deterioration has the opposite effects.

PRICE DISCRIMINATION

It is sometimes possible and profitable for a monopolist to charge different prices to different buyers of the same commodity. Electric power companies usually charge commercial users one price and households another. Sometimes, in the case of international trading, a company charges one price to domestic buyers and a lower price to foreign

---

[2] This analysis assumes the MC curve does not shift position in the process of output expansion. The stable MC curve follows from the assumption, made earlier, that resource prices are not affected by the monopolist.

buyers. Charging different prices to different buyers of the same good is called price discrimination, and two conditions are necessary in order that discrimination occur. (1) For price discrimination to be *possible,* the monopolist must be able to separate markets, such as the separation of the commercial market from the household market or the domestic market from the foreign market. Otherwise those who buy in one market at the lower price can engage in arbitage: buy at the lower price and resell in the higher-priced market, cutting into the sales volume of the monopolist and perhaps underselling him in the high-priced market. Separation does not necessarily mean geographic separation; it means any device that prevents this arbitage. (2) For price discrimination to be *profitable* the price elasticities of demand in the two or more markets

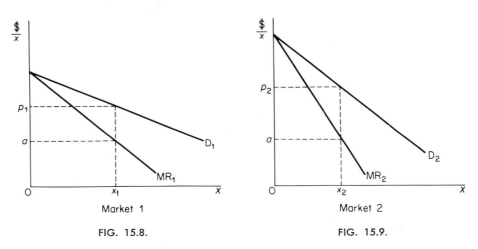

| Market 1 | Market 2 |
| FIG. 15.8. | FIG. 15.9. |

must differ. In particular, demand must be more elastic in one market than another at each possible price. The reason for this will become apparent as we go through the analysis.

In following a policy of price discrimination there are two decisions a monopolist must make. He must decide what his total output will be, and he must decide how this total output will be distributed among two or more markets. The price charged in each market is simultaneously determined when distribution among the markets is decided. As a first step in examining the problem, we shall consider only the question of revenue from each of two separated markets. Let the two markets for commodity X be denoted by 1 and 2. Figure 15.8 shows the demand curve for X and the marginal revenue curve in Market 1. The demand and marginal revenue curves for Market 2 are shown in Fig. 15.9. Assume for the moment that the marginal cost of production is equal to the vertical distance $0a$ (how marginal cost is determined will be discussed later).

Given that marginal cost is $0a$, how much will the monopolist sell in each market? And what price will be charged in each?

In order to maximize profit from any given volume of total sales, say x_3 units, the monopolist will sell a quantity in each market such that the marginal revenue in that market is equal to marginal cost. Therefore, assuming that marginal cost is equal to $0a$, he sells x_1 units in Market 1 and x_2 units in Market 2, where $x_1 + x_2 = x_3$.

To see why this sales distribution leads to maximized profit, imagine what would happen if the monopolist were selling one unit less in Market 1 and one unit more in Market 2. Remember that selling one less in Market 1 means he must sell one more in Market 2, and vice versa, because total sales are assumed given. If the monopolist were to sell one unit less in Market 1, he would be to the left of x_1 on the horizontal axis in Fig. 15.8 where marginal revenue is greater than marginal cost. Profit from sales in Market 1 would increase by increasing sales to x_1 units. At the same time, by selling one unit less than x_1, he must sell one unit more than x_2 in Market 2. Were he to do this, marginal revenue in Market 2 would be below marginal cost. Profit from sales in Market 2 are diminished. Thus, starting at x_1 units in Market 1 and x_2 units in Market 2, any diversion of sales from Market 1 to Market 2 must reduce profit. By the same reasoning, any diversion from Market 2 to Market 1 must reduce profit. Therefore, profit is maximized by distributing the total sales volume so that marginal revenue is the same in each market and equal to marginal cost.

It follows that prices will differ in the two markets. A price of p_1 is charged in Market 1 and a higher price, p_2, in Market 2. The price differential can exist only if the price elasticities of demand differ in the two markets. It has been shown that

$$\text{MR} = p_x + \frac{p_x}{e_{p_x}}$$

Since marginal revenue is the same in both markets, the same elasticities in both markets would yield the same prices. To illustrate, suppose marginal cost is $1. Then $\text{MR}_1 = \text{MR}_2 = \$1$ in order to maximize profit. Consider the following example:

At Each Price	*Market 1*	*Market 2*
Elasticity of $D_1 = -4$	$\$1 = p_x + \dfrac{p_x}{(-4)}$	$\$1 = p_x + \dfrac{p_x}{(-4)}$
Elasticity of $D_2 = -4$	$\$1 = p_x - \tfrac{1}{4}p_x$	$\$1 = p_x - \tfrac{1}{4}p_x$
	$\$1 = \tfrac{3}{4}p_x$	$\$1 = \tfrac{3}{4}p_x$
	$p_x = \tfrac{4}{3} = \$1\tfrac{1}{3}$	$p_x = \tfrac{4}{3} = \$1\tfrac{1}{3}$

The prices that maximize profit are both $1.33⅓. On the other hand, let demand in Market 1 be less price elastic:

At Each Price	Market 1	Market 2
Elasticity of $D_1 = -2$	$\$1 = p_x + \dfrac{p_x}{(-2)}$	$\$1 = p_x + \dfrac{p_x}{(-4)}$
Elasticity of $D_2 = -4$	$\$1 = p_x - \frac{1}{2}p_x$	$\$1 = p_x - \frac{1}{4}p_x$
	$p_x = \$2$	$p_x = \$1\frac{1}{3}$

The price charged is higher in the market with the less elastic demand.

So far we have been assuming the total volume of sales is given and that marginal cost is given as $0a$ in the diagrams. To complete the analysis, we must now ask how these are determined. It is revenue, not cost of production, that is affected by market separation. Cost of production depends upon total output. Figure 15.10 depicts the firm's marginal and average cost curves, where total output is measured on the horizontal axis. Also shown are the marginal revenue curves for both markets, MR_1 and MR_2. The curve labeled MR is the monopolist's marginal revenue derived from his total output *when he is properly distributing his output between the two markets*. It can be determined by summing horizontally the MR_1 and MR_2 curves. The monopolist produces that output, x_3, at which marginal cost equals marginal revenue from all sources. The output x_3 is produced at a marginal cost equal to $0a$, which is equal to MR, and also to MR_1 and MR_2.

In summary, the monopolist decides on total output by equating marginal cost to marginal revenue from all markets; he produces x_3 at which $MC = MR$. This is nothing more than the solution to the usual monopoly problem. But unlike the usual problem, the discriminating monopolist does not set one price corresponding to a single market demand curve. He makes the simultaneous decision on how to distribute sales among mar-

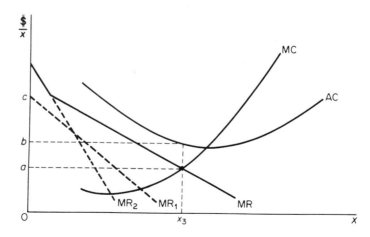

FIG. 15.10. Discriminating Monopolist: Total Output and Marginal Cost

kets and what price to charge in each. His average cost of production equals $0b$ in Fig. 15.10. Therefore, his average profit from sales in Market 1 is equal to the distance $(0p_1 - 0b)$; in Market 2 it is $(0p_2 - 0b)$. Total maximized profit is total profit from Market 1 plus total profit from Market 2, or $x_1(0p_1 - 0b) + x_2(0p_2 - 0b)$.

It should now be clear why the elasticities of demand must differ in two markets for price discrimination to be profitable, assuming that the markets can be separated. Separation may be due to transportation costs or tariff barriers. A monopolist, faced with a demand curve of a given elasticity on the domestic market, may find the demand curve on the foreign market more elastic. The presence of foreign competitors producing close substitutes makes buyers on the foreign market more sensitive to price changes. If he can convince the government to keep the products of foreign competitors out of the domestic market, by imposing on them a prohibitive import duty, he can charge a higher price on the domestic market—higher than the price at which he must sell on the foreign market.

The separation of markets need not be geographic. Monopolistic power companies can separate two markets by simply installing different meters, one with a rate for commercial users and another with a higher rate for households. It has been argued that different prices charged by medical doctors to different patients in the same city is another example of monopoly price discrimination. People with relatively high incomes tend to have a less price-elastic demand for medical services than do people with lower incomes. The fact that a license is needed to practice medicine means that those who are charged the lower price cannot resell the services they buy to others who pay a higher price. Thus, the two or more markets are effectively separated, and profit can be increased by discriminating price-wise between the two or more groups of buyers. The unwillingness of other doctors to engage in price competition permits the continuation of price discrimination by all who choose to follow the practice.

PROBLEMS

1. Suppose a firm has a patent on a particular product with exclusive rights to its production and sale. The demand schedule for the product by consumers is given in the following table.

Price	Quantity per Week	Price	Quantity per Week
$9.0	10	$6.5	60
8.5	20	6.0	70
8.0	30	5.5	80
7.5	40	5.0	90
7.0	50	4.5	100

(*a*) Compute the monopolist's total revenue, **average revenue**, and marginal revenue.

(*b*) Plot the firm's average revenue curve and its marginal revenue curve from an output of 20 units per week through 100 units per week. Label this Figure 1.

(*c*) The firm's long-run total cost schedule is presented in the following table.

Output per Week	Total Cost	Output per Week	Total Cost
0	$ 0	60	$370
10	110	70	440
20	180	80	525
30	225	90	630
40	260	100	750
50	310		

(*d*) Compute average cost and marginal cost.

(*e*) Plot the firm's long-run average and marginal cost curves in Figure 1.

(*f*) Find the firm's long-run equilibrium output, compute its total profit, and indicate total profit in Figure 1.

2.   Explain why a firm would not take advantage of an opportunity to become a monopoly if the demand for the product it would produce and sell is relatively price inelastic at all possible prices.

3.   Draw a diagram showing a monopolist in long-run equilibrium producing his optimum output. How does the equilibrium differ from that of a firm under pure competition?

SUGGESTED READING

J. R. Hicks, "The Theory of Monopoly," *Econometrica*, III (1935). Reprinted in *Readings in Price Theory.*

J. Robinson, *The Economics of Imperfect Competition*, Chaps. 2, 3, 15, 16. London: Macmillan & Co., Ltd., 1933.

16

Oligopoly

Certain industries, though not competitive in the strict sense, approximate the conditions of competition. Some firms are monopolists or they resemble closely the monopolist. Still other industries cannot be described by either of these theoretical "models." Among such mixed types the most important by far is oligopoly, a very prominent form of industrial organization in the United States today.

Oligopoly is an industry characterized by *few* sellers. Because of the small number of sellers the price a firm can charge depends not only upon its own output (as in the case of monopoly) but also upon the pricing and output policies of other firms in the industry. The decisions of sellers are *mutually interdependent*. Unless all sellers of a commodity enter into some form of cooperation, a particular seller cannot be sure that if he offers 100 units he can sell them at a price of, say, $1 each— even when the total market demand curve is given. The reason is that another seller may charge a lower price if he charges $1, cutting into his sales volume and forcing his sales below 100 units. Unlike the purely competitive seller or the monopolist the oligopolistic seller must be continually conscious of how he will be affected by the policies of others in the industry.

The demand curve faced by an oligopolist is negatively sloped, indicating that the firm exerts significant control over the product price. But the firm's average revenue curve is not the total market demand curve. Since there are other sellers in the industry, any one firm sells only a part of the quantity traded on the market. Furthermore, the location and slope of the firm's demand curve depend upon the decisions made by other firms in the industry. A change in their prices will shift the position of this one firm's demand curve and/or change its slope. If the firm in question knows how other firms in the industry will react to changes in its price and output, the demand curve faced by this firm is determined. Then the price and output that maximize profit can be unambiguously established. When the reactions of other firms are uncertain, however, the position and slope of any one firm's demand curve cannot be ascertained.

One must be careful to interpret correctly the economic meaning of few sellers. It cannot be said, for example, that seven sellers are few and seventeen are many. The economic definition of *few* versus *many* hinges on the mutual interdependence of their actions. When a change in price by one seller entails a significant reaction by others in the same industry, it is said there are few sellers in that industry. In contrast, many sellers (under pure competition) are defined as a number sufficient to render the decisions of any one seller independent of the decisions made by others. It is true that more firms in the numerical sense, other things being the same, diminishes the interdependence among firms. But one cannot simply draw a line at any one specific number and say fewer firms constitute oligopoly.

Since the decisions of each firm depend upon those followed by other firms in the industry, oligopoly presents one of the most important and challenging problems in price theory. No unified general theory, comparable to the theories of pure competition and monopoly, exists in contemporary economics. Diverse breeds of oligopoly have been found, each with its own peculiar attributes. Writers on oligopoly group these industries into convenient types. And various forms of classification exist, depending upon the nature of the problem to be analyzed. The following classification scheme will be adopted and we shall analyze each type in turn, proceeding from the most- to the least-determined market structure.

> Class I: Pure Oligopoly
> > (1) Formal Collusive Oligopoly
> > (2) Informal Collusive Oligopoly
> > (3) Noncollusive Oligopoly
> Class II: Differentiated Oligopoly

PURE OLIGOPOLY: SHORT-RUN ANALYSIS

In practice most oligopolists differentiate their products one from another. They rely on brand names, packaging design, advertising, etc., to distinguish their products and perhaps to permit the setting of different prices. But sometimes product differentiation is slight, as in the case of steel or cement. Consequently, it is instructive to analyze pure oligopoly under which products are assumed to be identical. The theory of pure oligopoly goes a long way toward explaining pricing and output in industries where product differentiation is weak. In addition, the theory sheds light on markets in which product differentiation is pursued on a large scale.

Pure oligopolies have been classified as collusive or noncollusive. By *collusion* is meant a form of cooperation among sellers, or coordination of their policies, in order to escape the uncertainties of mutual interdependence. The subtypes have not been listed under differentiated oligopoly in the classification scheme. In reality, these subtypes often apply to both pure and differentiated oligopolies. Nevertheless, by treating the subtypes under the simpler assumption of pure oligopoly exposition is greatly facilitated, and the effects of collusion under differentiated oligopoly can easily be inferred.

Formal Collusive Oligopoly

A cartel represents the most complete form of collusion. Firms enter into an explicit formal agreement by which the market is to be shared among them. If there is complete unity, so that their objective is to maximize the *joint profits* of all firms together, the cartel operates like a pure monopolist. A single decision-maker sets the market price and

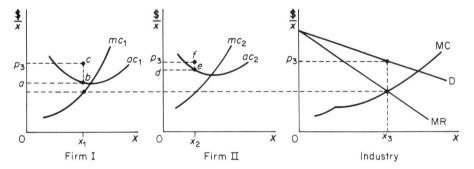

FIG. 16.1.   Cartel: Maximization of Joint Profits

the quantity offered for sale by the industry. Power to set the price and to determine industry output is surrendered to a central agency, output quotas are assigned to the firms, and all firms abide by the decision of the agency. The maximized joint (industry) profit is distributed among the firms on whatever basis has been adopted in the agreement.

For simplicity let us assume the cartel consists of a duopoly, i.e., an oligopoly of two firms. The firms produce the same commodity, called X. The cost curves of Firm I are shown in the left panel of Fig. 16.1; those of Firm II are shown in the middle panel. In the right-hand panel the market demand curve, D, is depicted. Corresponding to the market demand curve is the industry marginal revenue curve, MR, derived from the demand curve in the usual way. Finally, the panel on the right shows the industry marginal cost curve, MC, which is the horizontal summation of mc_1 and mc_2.

That the industry marginal cost curve is the horizontal sum of the firms' marginal cost curves follows from the profit-maximizing objective of the cartel. For each possible industry output the central agency should produce that output at the least possible cost. Cost is minimized for each output by allocating quotas to the member firms so that the marginal cost of one firm's output equals the marginal cost of the other firm's. Otherwise, the cost of the combined output is not minimized. For the agency could reallocate the same total output between the firms and reduce cost. For example, by taking one unit away from Firm I with a marginal cost of 10 cents and assigning it to Firm II with a marginal cost of 8 cents, total cost goes down by 10 cents and up by 8 cents, making total cost of the industry output lower. Thus, when the quotas are correctly distributed for each alternative industry output, marginal cost must be the same for each firm and total cost is least for that output. Since marginal cost must be the same for each firm, it follows that the industry marginal cost curve is the horizontal summation of the firms' marginal cost curves.

The cartel maximizes industry profit by producing x_3 units at which MC = MR and setting a market price of p_3. Firm I contributes x_1 units, the output at which MR = mc_1 (since MC = mc_1 at this output). Firm II contributes x_2 units, its output at which MR = mc_2. And $x_1 + x_2 = x_3$. It is easily seen that the market equilibrium is the same that would prevail under pure monopoly. The agency, acting with complete control to maximize joint profits for the two firms, operates just like a monopolist with two plants, each having a given marginal cost curve. The monopolist would assign quotas to the two plants in such a way that marginal cost is the same in both for any joint output. This minimizes the cost of each output he might produce. Then he produces the total output that equates marginal cost to his marginal revenue derived from the market demand curve.

Industry profit cannot be determined from the right-hand diagram alone. Total joint profit consists of the profit from Firm I's output plus the profit from Firm II's output. Given the price of p_3 at which each firm sells, Firm I generates a profit equal to the area of the rectangle $abcp_3$, while Firm II generates a profit equal to the area $defp_3$. The cartel profit is therefore the sum of these two areas.

This does not mean, however, that the owner of each firm necessarily receives the profit generated by his firm. How much each receives depends upon the prearranged contract among them. It is as if all profits generated by the member firms are pooled and the central agency then doles out shares on the basis of the agreement. Indeed, very inefficient firms could receive relatively large shares even though cost considerations alone would dictate that the firms should be shut down completely. This is most likely to happen if the central agency is a government body and political maneuvering determines the distribution of profits.

Cartels of this nature are very unstable. There is a strong incentive for some firms to break away from the cartel. In the illustration, Firm I generates more profit than Firm II. According to the agreement it may receive less. Since its costs are lower than those of Firm II, Firm I could increase the profit it receives by operating independently, selling at the same price as Firm II, and keeping all the profit it generates. Even in the event of no cost differentials an incentive to leave the cartel remains. With the rest of the industry abiding by the cartel price, a single independent firm would have a demand curve for its output that is more elastic than the industry demand curve in the neighborhood of the cartel price. For at a price slightly below the cartel price it can attract many of the cartel's customers, while at a price slightly above the cartel price it can sell little or nothing. As a consequence, marginal revenue for that firm would be higher than its marginal revenue if it remained in the cartel. Provided most of the other firms remain in the cartel, the firm that can successfully strike out on its own will have a greater marginal revenue, so its profit possibilities are enhanced. Therefore, unless the cartel can effectively police its regulations, there is a tendency for firms to break away.

The obstacles to rigid enforcement of cartel policies under joint profit maximization have led to another, more common, type of cartel. Firms enter into an agreement by which they share the market for the product, with each firm retaining its own profit. Under certain special conditions the *market-sharing cartel* will set the price and industry output at the same levels as a pure monopolist. Suppose again that there are two firms in the industry, but this time let them have identical costs of production. Assume they agree to share the market half and half at each possible price.

Figure 16.2 shows the cost curves of Firms I and II as the solid curves labeled *mc* and *ac* in the left panel and the center panel respectively. On the right is shown the market demand curve for the product X, labeled D. Since the firms agree to share the market equally, each will supply one-half of the quantity demanded at each possible price. In the right-hand diagram is drawn the curve *d*, which shows one-half the quantity

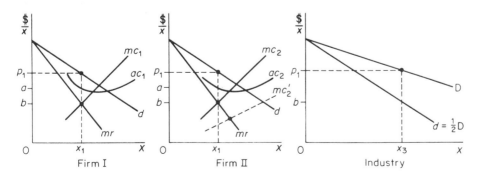

FIG. 16.2. Market-Sharing Cartel: Identical Cost and Equal Market Shares

demanded on the market at each price. It follows that the demand curve faced by each firm is equal to d; so d is drawn in the diagram for each firm. Corresponding to the firm's demand curve is its marginal revenue curve, denoted by mr, which is, of course, the same for each firm. Given the same marginal revenue curves and the same marginal cost curves, each firm will maximize profit at the same output, namely x_1 units of X. And since they produce a homogeneous product, both charge the same profit-maximizing price of p_1. The total quantity supplied on the market is x_3, which equals two times x_1. Moreover, since the firms charge the same price and have identical average costs, total profit is the same for both: the distance ap_1 times the distance $0x_1$.

The industry output x_3 and the price p_1 would be the same if the industry were monopolized. If one monopolist owned both firms, treating each as a different plant, his marginal cost curve would be the horizontal summation of mc_1 and mc_2. The monopolist is faced with the industry demand curve, and his marginal revenue curve is equal to curve d (see Chapter 15 on the relation of monopoly marginal revenue to market demand). Hence, the monopolist's marginal cost curve would cut his marginal revenue curve at x_3 units, the output at which marginal cost and marginal revenue are both equal to the distance $0b$. And the price charged would be p_1. Each firm maximizing its profit individually is tantamount to maximizing industry (monopoly) profit.

These conclusions hold only under the very unlikely conditions we have assumed, that cost and revenue conditions are identical for the two firms. Unless these conditions are satisfied the market-sharing cartel tends to be unstable just like the cartel under joint profit maximization. Suppose we retain the assumption of equal market shares but we drop the assumption of identical cost curves. Let the marginal cost curve of Firm II be mc'_2 rather than mc_2. To maximize its profit Firm II would prefer to charge a price lower than p_1 and to produce more than x_1 units. Should Firm II do so, Firm I, selling the same product, would be forced to reduce price also, and to accept a smaller sales volume. This would reduce, and perhaps even eliminate, Firm I's profit. With any cost differential the firm with the lower cost has an incentive to break the agreement of equal market shares. Then the firms may agree to share the market on some other basis, with the larger share going to the low-cost firm. Yet if Firm II's costs are lower than Firm I's for every output level, and if the total market is not too large, there is a temptation for Firm II to take over the market completely, to become a monopolist. Unless the other firm can by some device prevent this, the cartel is in danger of dissolution.

When a market-sharing cartel does persist, the market is usually shared on some basis other than cost. It may be split up into separate geographic areas, it may be shared in proportion to the size of firms independently of cost, or shares may be decided on the basis of political influence. Whatever criterion is adopted, the cartel has always to cope with conflicts of interest due to cost differentials, the failure of all firms to agree on changes in product design or production techniques, and encroachments of firms on the markets of others through accident or intent. Perhaps this explains why few cartels have been successful without the support of the police power of the state.

Informal Collusive Oligopoly

Informal collusion among oligopolistic firms may occur for two reasons. First, a cartel may not be possible because it is illegal or because some firms refuse to surrender completely their freedom of action. Second, in the absence of a cartel the firms may find it is in their mutual interest not to engage in price competition. When outright formal agreements are not in effect, firms can collude by covert "gentlemen's agreements" or by spontaneous coordination designed to avoid the effects of price wars. Foremost among these means of "playing it safe" is *price leadership*. One firm sets the price and all others follow, with or without a prior understanding. Various forms of price leadership have been practiced, and we shall analyze a few typical ones. Regardless of the type of price leadership, in adopting such a policy the firms in effect enter into a tacit market-sharing agreement.

Price Leadership by a Low-Cost Firm. Often the price leader is the firm with the lowest costs of production. We saw in the previous section that a conflict of interest arises whenever two or more oligopolistic firms have different costs. One way in which the conflict can be settled is to reach an explicit or implicit agreement about market shares in which the low-cost firm is allowed to set the product price. Economic theory cannot say how the firms will agree to share the market. Given any agreement with respect to market shares, the theory can determine the consequences for price, outputs, and profits. Figure 16.3 presents a situation in which the low-cost firm commands a greater share of the market.

The demand curve of Firm I, d_1, lies farther to the right than d_2, Firm II's demand curve. The market demand curve, the horizontal summation of d_1 and d_2, has been omitted to avoid cluttering the diagram. Firm I, the price leader, sets the price and output that maximize its profit: output x_4 at which $mc_1 = mr_1$ and price p_4.

Given the market shares, Firm II would prefer to produce an output x_2 and charge a price of p_5; for this price-output combination maximizes the firm's profit. By agreement, however, Firm I is the price leader. If Firm II were to refuse to go along and charge p_5 instead, the firm would lose all or most of its customers. Indeed Firm I could, by reason of its lower cost, engage in a price war that would likely drive Firm II out of existence. Why does Firm I not do so? Because it would leave Firm I with a monopoly subject to antitrust prosecution, or it could lead to

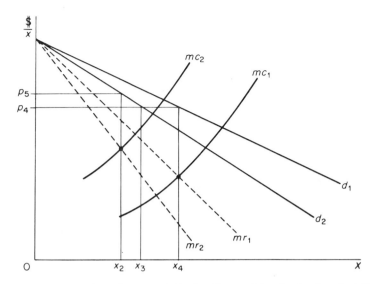

FIG. 16.3.   Duopoly with Unequal Market Shares: Price Set by Low-Cost Firm

losses by both firms for an extended period of time. To avoid these consequences the firms have tacitly agreed to let Firm I set the price. Therefore, Firm II has no recourse but to follow suit, to charge p_4 also.

The market will take $(x_4 + x_3)$ units at a price of p_4. Since Firm I supplies x_4 units, there remain x_3 units to be supplied by Firm II if equilibrium is to prevail. Granted that Firm II does supply the additional x_3 units, mc_2 is greater than mr_2. To avoid the possible outcome of a price war Firm II accepts a smaller profit than that obtainable purely on the basis of market shares. Firm II sacrifices revenue for the sake of security.

This is not the only conceivable outcome, however. Although Firm II agrees to let Firm I set the price, Firm II is under no compulsion to supply x_3 units. The firm can supply less than the market would take by simply not having the commodity available when the last buyers come for it. If Firm II decides to follow this procedure, an interaction between the firms will result that will generally change somewhat the equilibrium market price. The change in the equilibria of the market and the firms will depend upon the relative differences in cost between the two firms and the shape and position of the market demand curve.

Price Leadership by a Large Firm.   Some oligopolies are characterized by one giant firm and a number of smaller firms. The existence of the smaller firms is beneficial to the large one because they lend the appearance of a competitive industry and so help to keep the antitrust wolf away from the door. By a tacit understanding the large firm sets the product price and allows the smaller firms to sell whatever quantity they wish at this price. Then the large firm supplies the rest of the market.

If this practice is adopted, each small firm is confronted by a situation very similar to that of the firm in a purely competitive industry. The market price is given, and the firm can sell any quantity without affecting the established price. To maximize profit the firm produces that output at which marginal cost equals price.

The quantity supplied on the market at each possible price by all the small firms together can be determined by the same methods employed to derive the industry supply curve under pure competition. The marginal cost curves of the firms are summed horizontally. Figure 16.4 depicts the market demand curve, D, and the aggregate supply curve of the small firms, S_s.

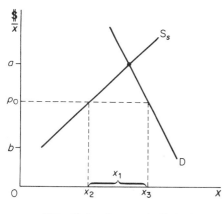

FIG. 16.4. Aggregate Output
of Small Firms

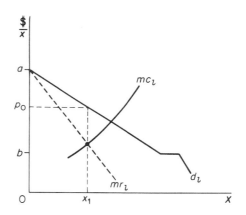

FIG. 16.5. Price and Output Set
by Large Price Leader

Unlike pure competition the intersection of the demand curve and this supply curve does not determine the price. The supply curve S_s does not take into account the output of the large firm. Because the large firm sets the price, it is necessary that the demand curve faced by the large firm be determined before the market equilibrium can be found. The large firm is assumed to supply whatever is not supplied by the small firms. The demand curve faced by the large firm is, therefore, simply the difference between what the market would take at each price (the curve D) and what the small firms would offer at each price (the curve S_s). The horizontal difference between D and S_s is shown as d_l in Figure 16.5, which represents the demand curve for the output of the large firm. At any price greater than or equal to $0a$ the quantity supplied by the small firms would be greater than or equal to the quantity demanded on the market. So the demand for the large firm's output would be zero. Below $0a$, at lower and lower prices the quantity demanded of the large firm becomes greater and greater. The distance between D and S_s in Fig. 16.4 equals the distance between the vertical axis and d_l in Fig. 16.5. At any price below $0b$, d_l becomes identical with the market demand curve because the small firms would suspend production entirely.

The revenue and cost conditions of the large firm permit us to determine the price it will set; and, together with the curves D and S_s of Fig. 16.4, the quantity traded on the market can be established. To maximize profit the large firm produces x_1 units at which $mc_l = mr_l$. The corresponding price is p_0. Figure 16.4 reveals that the small firms will supply the quantity x_2 at a price of p_0. At this aggregate output each firm is producing a quantity at which its marginal cost is equal to the given price. The quantity exchanged on the market is x_3 units, which of necessity equals the combined outputs of all firms: $x_3 = x_1 + x_2$.

The average cost curve of the large firm has not been drawn. By including its average cost curve the large firm's profit can be found, and from knowledge of their individual average cost curves the profits of all the small firms can be computed. These curves have been deleted to avoid undue complications in the diagrams.

Noncollusive Oligopoly

In the absence of any kind of collusion the individual firm is beset with a great deal of uncertainty. Ability to affect the product price coupled with mutual interdependence among the firms forces each one to eye his "competitors" when contemplating any action. The firms are like players in a chess game or generals in a military campaign. Each price-output decision resembles a tactical move within the framework of a broader strategy, always subject to the effects of a counterstrategy by the firm's rivals. Eventually the firms often settle for some type of informal collusion by price leadership. If they do not do so, and they are unwilling to engage in recurrent price wars, an equilibrium is possible even in the absence of collusion.

Recent attempts have been made to cast the oligopoly problem in terms of the behavior of participants in a strategic game. These efforts involve a departure from the conventional tools of marginal analysis, and we shall review them briefly in the following chapter. For the present, discussion will be limited to analysis of noncollusive oligopoly, using the familiar concepts of marginal cost and marginal revenue.

The Kinked Demand Curve.   It has been observed that under oligopoly product prices tend to be rigid or "sticky." A theoretical device introduced to explain price rigidity is the so-called kinked demand curve. The theory applies to oligopolies either with or without product differentiation, but for simplicity we shall treat it here under the condition of identical products. Two basic assumptions underlie the theory. First, without collusion the industry can and has attained a stable equilibrium. The second assumption refers to the way firms react to price changes by others in the industry. If one firm lowers its price, other firms are assumed to follow in order to preserve their shares of the market. That is, by cutting price any one firm cannot hope to do more than retain its former market share. On the other hand, if one firm were to raise its price, the others will not follow. Their feeling is that they can benefit by keeping their prices unchanged; for customers of the price-raising firm will shift to the other, now relatively lower-priced, firms. By raising its price the higher-priced firm will lose all or a substantial part of its share of the market.

The consequence of these two basic assumptions is to impart a sharp bend or kink to the individual firm's demand curve at the level of the exist-

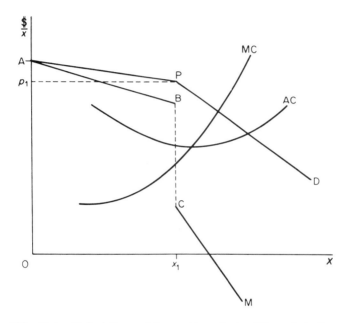

FIG. 16.6.   Kinked Demand Curve: Noncollusive Oligopolistic Firm

ing price. Such a kinked demand curve faced by the firm is depicted as the curve APD in Fig. 16.6. The point P is the point on the demand curve corresponding to the prevailing price p_1. At this point the price elasticity of demand changes radically. If the firm were to lower its price, others would do the same; so this firm would only retain its share of the market. Therefore, the segment PD has about the same elasticity as the market demand curve. In the event that this firm should raise its price above p_1, others would not follow, and the firm would lose a considerable portion of its former sales. The firm's demand curve at any price above p_1, the segment AP, has a much greater elasticity than the market demand curve.

The firm's marginal revenue curve corresponding to its kinked demand curve is shown as the curve ABCM in Fig. 16.6. Because of the kink in the average revenue curve the marginal revenue curve is *discontinuous* at the output x_1, where the kink occurs. It has a gap. The segment AB of the curve can be viewed as belonging to the AP segment of the average revenue curve, while the segment CM can be considered as belonging to the PD segment of the average revenue curve.

The cost curves are drawn such that the marginal cost curve passes through the discontinuity in the marginal revenue curve. This is almost necessarily what will happen. The marginal cost curve would have to be extremely high to cut the AB part of the marginal revenue curve, which is almost horizontal. Similarly, the marginal cost curve would have to be very close to the horizontal axis to intersect the CM segment. We can now see why the prevailing price of p_1 is an equilibrium for each firm. The price p_1 and the output x_1 are the firm's profit-maximizing price and output. At any output less than x_1 marginal cost is less than marginal revenue, so profit can be expanded by increasing output. Any output in excess of x_1 yields a marginal cost greater than marginal revenue, so an expansion of output beyond x_1 units would reduce profit. Thus, although the marginal cost curve does not intersect the marginal revenue curve in the usual way at x_1 units, this output is still the firm's equilibrium output.

The implications for price rigidity are by now apparent. With each firm operating on the discontinuous part of its marginal revenue curve, the product price will not change (or the change will be very small) in response to changes in either cost or demand. An extremely large change in cost is required in order that the MC curve intersect the AB or CM segments of the MR curve. Cost changes smaller in magnitude leave the MC curve within the discontinuous portion of the MR curve, so the profit-maximizing price and output remain unchanged. Similarly, a horizontal movement of the demand curve causes a stationary MC curve to pass through the discontinuous part of the new MR curve. Output varies but price remains constant. Changes in price can occur only if the shifts in cost or demand are made large enough. During declines in general business activity (recessions) some prices do not fall nearly as much as others, even when costs are decreasing. Though it does rest upon special assumptions about price reactions by rivals, the kinked demand curve hypothesis helps to explain why prices in the American economy are not as flexible as they might be.

PURE OLIGOPOLY: LONG-RUN ANALYSIS

Long-run output and long-run profit possibilities under oligopoly depend essentially upon the ease or difficulty with which new firms can enter the industry. In the long run each firm in the industry can vary its scale of plant. This is one source of variations in output and price. Another is the entry or withdrawal of firms. Conditions of entry vary from one oligopolistic industry to another; in some entry is completely free, in others it is partially blocked, and in still others it is totally blocked. The reasons for blocked entry are also variable. Since the presence or absence of free entry is central to the long-run analysis of oligopoly, our examination will proceed from three focal points: (1) free entry, (2) artificial barriers to entry, and (3) natural barriers to entry.

Free Entry

If profits are being made in the short run, other firms will be attracted to the oligopolistic industry. Under certain conditions freedom of entry will lead to a stable long-run equilibrium in which definite conclusions can be drawn with respect to price, industry output, the firms' scales of plant and their profit positions. Under other conditions not much can be said.

Let us consider first the effects of free entry on formal collusive oligopoly. Obviously, easy entry is destructive to the collusive arrangement. We have seen that in the short run a member firm has a strong incentive to break loose from the cartel, for by operating independently it can enhance its profit possibilities. The same is true of a prospective new entrant. By entering the industry but refusing to join the cartel, the firm will be faced by a demand curve more elastic than the cartel demand curve at the existing price. A more elastic demand means a higher marginal revenue at the existing price. Thus, by entering the industry but remaining outside the cartel, the firm can encroach upon the cartel profit—and perhaps eventually cause its collapse.

Even if entrants are accepted into the cartel, it is very likely that the cartel output would thereby increase, causing the market price to fall. If any profit remains, firms will continue to enter until profits are wiped out or some firms are bribed to produce nothing. In any event, the temptation to operate independently of the cartel and reap the advantages of a greater marginal revenue is strong. These dangers have motivated cartels to seek barriers to entry, which will be discussed in the following section.

We have seen that informal collusion involves some tacit agreement about market shares. When short-run profits are being made and no effort is made to prevent the entry of new firms, one or both of two effects will follow. Industry output will very likely, though not necessarily, change as new firms enter. Whether or not industry output changes, shares of this output must be assigned to these new firms at the expense of those already in the industry. Given any market demand curve, as additional firms are accepted into the collusive group, each firm, including eventually the price leader, will have its demand curve move farther and farther toward the left. As more firms share the given market each will be forced to accept a smaller share. Entry will continue as long as profits can be made, and the shrinkage of market shares will continue until profits are reduced to zero.

Assuming the industry attains a stable long-run equilibrium with free entry, the corresponding equilibrium of any one firm is shown graphically in Fig. 16.7. The firm's long-run average and marginal cost curves are depicted as *lac* and *lmc* respectively. The demand curve for its output, based upon its market share, is labeled *d*, to which corresponds its marginal revenue curve *mr*. Initially, we assume, the firm was making a profit that attracted new firms. As new firms enter they may bid up the prices of resources, causing the cost curves of all firms to shift upward. Whether or not this occurs, the firm's demand curve has shifted to the left as the market is shared among more firms. When enough firms have

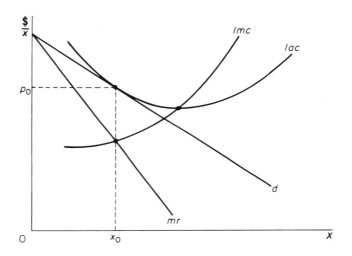

FIG. 16.7. Long-Run Equilibrium with Free Entry

entered, the demand curve faced by each firm will be tangent to its long-run average cost curve, profits will be reduced to zero, and entry will stop. The industry as a whole will be in equilibrium since no profits or losses occur to engender the incentive for entry or withdrawal.

The price of the product will be p_0 in the long run, at which price the firm in question produces x_0 units of the product X. Not every firm will produce the same output. What output each firm produces depends upon the market shares agreed upon (for given cost curves, it depends upon the location of the curve *d*). Nevertheless, it can be said that in this situation every firm will utilize a smaller than optimum scale of plant and produce a smaller than optimum long-run output with that scale of plant. Each firm's demand curve is negatively sloped, and so it must be tangent to the firm's *lac* curve where the *lac* curve is negatively sloped —that is, at a point on the *lac* curve to the left of its minimum point.

This analysis should not be taken to mean that informal collusive oligopolies will in fact attain a stable long-run equilibrium. Several modifying considerations cast doubt upon the likelihood of informal collusion and free entry existing simultaneously. Most important of all is the fact that, as in the case of formal collusion, freedom of entry is destructive to the collusive arrangement. Even with zero profits the incentive to entry may not be discouraged. A prospective entrant might challenge the price leader's authority, charge a price lower than that set by the price leader, if his cost position can stand it, in order to test the price leader's strength. Even in the absence of such a challenge freedom of entry is disadvantageous to the collusive group. Oligopolies often enter into collusion for the very purpose of making long-run profits. If free entry prevents this, the oligopoly must resort to devices that will discourage or prevent entry. Indeed, artificial barriers to entry are frequently the explicit means used to preserve the power of price leadership.

Finally, let us consider noncollusive oligopoly. In this connection we shall examine the long-run effects of free entry under the kinked demand curve hypothesis. The analysis is quite similar to the long-run equilibrium of the informal collusive oligopoly. With no collusion of any kind, and no natural barriers to entry, firms attracted by short-run profits will enter the industry. Given the market demand curve, additional entrants will cause the demand curve faced by any one firm to shift to the left, and perhaps cause cost curves to shift upward. One or both of these forces will continue until profits have been squeezed to zero. When this has occurred entry will cease.

Figure 16.7 may be used as a base to describe the long-run equilibrium. Instead of a straight line, the demand curve would show a kink at the price p_0, and the *lmc* curve would pass through the discontinuous part of the *mr* curve. The firm's long-run average cost curve is "tangent" to the firm's demand curve at the point of the kink, indicating zero profit at the firm's equilibrium output x_0. With a kinked demand curve the chances of a price reduction as new firms enter is slight; new firms will tend to set the same prices as the old firms. The point of the kink will move to the left, staying at the same horizontal level until it meets the *lac* curve. In long-run equilibrium each firm will utilize a smaller than optimum scale of plant and produce a smaller than optimum output for that scale of plant.

This analysis is subject to the same reservations as that of the short-run kinked demand curve analysis. It sheds some light on the long-run noncollusive oligopoly problem. But it assumes the attainment of long-run equilibrium based upon the postulate of a particular kind of expectations formed by firms. More generally, in the absence of collusion there will be as much uncertainty regarding the scale of plant as there is regarding short-run price and output policies. There is no definite reason to believe the firm will produce its optimum output in the long run. Nor can it be said that profits will definitely be zero. The firms may settle down to some mutually satisfactory position in which profits are not zero, but "fear of rocking the boat" leads none to alter its output. In such cases long-run price and output will be determinate. Or the firms may have recourse to collusion because their very existence is jeopardized by prospective entrants. Without a doubt, faced with such uncertainty, their incentive to collude and thereby prevent entry is considerable.

Artificial Barriers to Entry

Among artificial barriers the most secure protection against entry is that enforced or supported by the state. Exclusive franchises granted to firms by local or national governments are not uncommon. Public utilities are closely regulated through franchises and certificates of convenience and necessity. Transportation companies are often protected against competition on a local or national basis. Taxicab and bus services come under local jurisdiction, while the Interstate Commerce Commission regulates railroads and the Civil Aeronautics Board the air transportation field. Exclusion of rivals can be effected if the collusive oligopoly can obtain protection through control over the issuance of such franchises.

Another source of government support can be found in local or state licensing laws. Plumbers, barbers, and morticians come under local licensing regulations; state laws control the practice of medicine and the dispensation of alcoholic beverages. Local building codes are sometimes biased against manufacturers of prefabricated houses.

Less direct government support for restricted entry lies in the issuance and protection of patent rights to machines or production processes. Firms in the collusive group may be permitted to share in the patent right. Patented equipment can be leased to other firms by the holder of the patent or cross-licensing arrangements can be worked out, whereas these rights are denied to nonmember firms. Patents have given rise to many of the most important oligopolies in the United States: the industries producing cameras, rayon, radios, and electric lamps, for example.

The existence of patents, franchises, and licensing laws makes available to collusive oligopolies certain legal means for restricting entry. The question of the extent to which oligopolies have instigated these devices as tools of collusion and the question of the degree to which they have relied on these tools are both complex. The necessity for patent rights to reward the initiative of discovery has long been debated. There are also at least two sides to the question of the reason for and justification of building codes, licensing, and franchises. Nevertheless, it cannot be denied that these means have been used by oligopolies to prevent or curtail entry. Under the respectable guise of establishing and maintaining standards, oligopolies have often been the pressure groups that have initiated legislation that could be turned to their own collusive advantage.

Another artificial barrier against entry is control over supplies of raw materials. If a strategic raw material is necessary in the production of a commodity, competition can be suppressed by control over the source of the raw material. This device will be most successful when the raw-material source is geographically concentrated. Control over African diamond fields by De Beers Consolidated is perhaps the classic example. Other examples of controlled raw materials are nitrates, nickel, and radium. Weaker than the government-supported barriers, control over raw materials is subject to the threat of discovery of substitute raw materials or the development of substitute products not using the controlled raw material. Such discoveries and developments usually take time, however, and if competitors can be excluded even for five years profits may be enormous.

A third artificial barrier to entry is the threat of a price war. If its financial resources will sustain temporary losses, the cartel or price leader may frighten away prospective entrants by threatening to lower price sufficiently to make entry unprofitable. Thus, although the existence of profits makes entry attractive, actual entry would result in their disappearance. Because of the price policy of the oligopoly any firm entering the industry would find itself incurring a loss and would be forced to withdraw. The mere threat of such action will be sufficient to discourage a prospective entrant unless he possesses sufficient funds to withstand losses. The price policy of the Standard Oil Company in the late nineteenth century is a case in point.

Natural Barriers to Entry

In contrast to artificial barriers, which can be removed by appropriate measures, natural barriers are inherent in the nature of the industry. They can exist whether or not there is collusion. Although natural deterrents to entry may be, and often are, supplemented by artificial barriers, in some cases where collusion is absent firms can make long-run profits as a result of prevailing cost and revenue conditions.

An extremely large capital requirement is one important natural barrier. In the production of some commodities a very large and complex scale of plant is required to produce efficiently. As a consequence a vast initial outlay is required. The automobile industry is one example; the steel industry is another. In some instances, such as the cigarette industry, it is not so much the manufacturing plant as the advertising expenditures necessary to compete effectively with firmly established companies. If few prospective entrants can assemble the necessary funds, existing firms can enjoy long-run profits.

More important than capital requirements as a natural barrier is the size of the product market in comparison to the optimum size of plant for firms in the industry. It is possible that the market just will not support an additional firm even though those already in the industry have no cost advantage and are making long-run profits. To illustrate, let us consider two cases under some highly simplified conditions.[1] It is assumed a commodity X is produced by a noncollusive oligopoly. For convenience, we shall suppose the prospective entrant expects existing

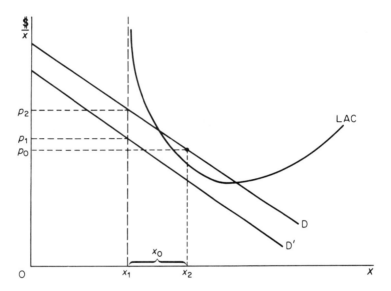

FIG. 16.8. Natural Barrier to Entry: Noncollusive Oligopoly

firms to maintain the same output if he should enter the industry. Consider first the market demand curve D in Fig. 16.8. The existing market price is p_2, at which the industry produces x_1 units. The prospective entrant, if he were to enter the industry, would have the long-run average cost curve LAC, which is assumed identical to the cost curves of all existing firms. With the output of the other firms given, his output would be added to the x_1 units. So if he enters, the industry output will exceed x_1. There is a range of output over which the demand curve lies above his LAC curve. Hence, he can enter and make a profit. Suppose his profit-maximizing output is x_0 units. Then the industry output becomes x_2 units, where $x_2 = x_1 + x_0$, and the price falls to p_0. At this output the entering firm is profitable, and so is every other firm since they all have identical cost curves. In this case, entry will occur.

[1] This illustration is based on an analysis by Professor Franco Modigliani. See F. Modigliani, "New Developments on the Oligopoly Front," *Journal of Political Economy* (1958).

Next, consider what would happen if the market demand curve is D'
instead of D. The industry output is again assumed to be x_1 units; the
price is p_1 corresponding to the demand curve D'. Since all firms have
average cost curves like LAC, it is seen that there are outputs for existing firms at which price exceeds average cost. The existing firms are
profitable. The prospective entrant, however, has no profitable output.
The relevant part of the demand curve, as far as he is concerned, is that
segment corresponding to the price p_1 and below. And no part of this
segment is above or equal to his average cost curve. Were he to enter,
his output would be added to x_1 and price would fall along D'. No price
on the demand curve covers his average cost. A price of p_0, for example,
could still be profitable to existing firms but not to him because he could
not sell enough at p_0 to cover his cost. Thus, in spite of the fact that existing firms are, and can remain, profitable, the prospective entrant would
incur a loss. In this case entry will not occur.

In the foregoing analysis it was assumed that the existing firms had
no cost advantage. All the more reason why entry will not occur if the
cost curves of the prospective entrant lie above the cost curves of existing
firms! The only condition under which entry would occur is if the prospective entrant has a substantial cost advantage, given the market demand curve D'. On the other hand, an expansion in the size of the market,
from D' to D, would permit entry as long as the prospective entrant does
not have too severe a cost disadvantage.

DIFFERENTIATED OLIGOPOLY

Oligopoly provides fertile soil for the cultivation of product differentiation. In the absence of collusion the dangers of price wars make firms
reluctant to encroach upon each other's market shares by lowering price.
But they have no inhibition against nonprice competition. Product differentiation by the use of brand names, advertising, product and packaging design, and other selling activities provides a safer way to increase
sales. These methods are safer primarily because reactions on the part
of rivals are likely to be less responsive and less disastrous. Selling
activities are easier to conceal in preparation and are less obvious in
their effects upon competitors.

Even in most types of collusive oligopoly nonprice competition is
prevalent. In a completely centralized cartel selling competition is unlikely to exist, except perhaps industry-sponsored sales programs designed to promote the product vis-à-vis the products of other industries.
In any other form of collusion, however, such as price leadership, the
firms may still vie with one another for larger shares of the market
through nonprice competition, while every firm accepts the price set
by the leader.

The Means of Product Differentiation

Product differentiation is intended to distinguish the product of one seller from those offered by other sellers in the industry. The products are sometimes basically the same. Yet if sales activities can convince the consumer that there are differences, he may be led to prefer one over the others. Thus, the direct objective is to create attitudes of differentiation in the mind of the consumer, whether or not the products do in fact differ. The ultimate objective, the intended result of successfully changing tastes, is a shift to the right in the demand curve faced by the single seller and to make it less price elastic. If successful, this will permit the firm to sell a larger volume at the same price as that charged by others (or perhaps at a slightly higher price) without the risk of a price war. Fundamentally, brand names are necessary to product differentiation. Otherwise, there is no way for the customer to identify readily the product of one seller and exercise his preference. All the means of product differentiation to be discussed presuppose the existence of brand names.

One very important means of product differentiation is advertising. Each seller attempts to attract customers to his particular brand name, although the brands may be physically no different. Patent medicines provide one example, especially simple drugs such as aspirin. Basically the products of all sellers must conform to government-controlled specifications. Some, perhaps, dissolve more quickly in a solution and some differ not at all. Still, certain nationally known sellers are able to attract and maintain a share of the market at a price much higher than the prices of other sellers in the industry. Sometimes one firm's attempt to capture a larger market share is anticipated by other firms, and they retaliate to protect their sales positions. The advertising campaigns cancel each other, leaving each firm with roughly the same share of the market and higher costs due to increased advertising expenditures. Once such rival advertising has begun, no single seller can afford to let up for fear of losing sales. Like Alice and the Red Queen in *Through the Looking Glass* they must keep running, as it were, just to remain in the same place. And the additional costs due to expanded advertising outlays lead to higher product prices. In the cigarette industry, for instance, larger and larger advertising expenditures have left the big three companies in about the same relative positions. Unless competitive advertising has the indirect effect of expanding the overall market, sales may remain approximately unchanged.

Another means of product differentiation, which goes hand in glove with advertising, is a change in product quality or design. Sometimes it takes the form of an alteration in a single product sold, and sometimes it takes the form of expanding the range of products offered by a single seller. The automobile industry provides an example of both forms. To attract customers, changes in design have been coupled with changes in quality, such as power steering, automatic transmissions, hi-fi radios in cars, etc. Then, too, each company has, over time, extended its "line" —offered automobiles in different price categories to appeal to a wider range of buyers. Similar examples can be found among electrical appliances (self-defrosting refrigerators), cigarettes (filters and menthol flavor), toothpastes (new flavors and additives) and in other industries. Whenever one firm has introduced a change in quality or design, others have imitated the change to protect their shares of the market. If the innovation is successfully imitated, the gains by the innovator are usually of short duration, and each firm ends up in about the same relative position. Sometimes consumers benefit by such product changes. If the change results in an improved product, consumer wants are usually satisfied more fully even though the product price rises. In other instances, however, the changes in quality are illusory: mere gadgets of questionable value or unwanted style changes. Then the effects are similar to retaliatory advertising. Firms engage in a race for style changes or obscure additives called something like "H-12" that add to cost but add little or nothing to the quality of the product while at the same time raising prices.

A third source of product differentiation is a change in packaging or labeling intended to make the product more attractive. Personal salesmanship is another. Few firms limit themselves to one or two of these selling activities. Most frequently they engage in all or almost all of them. Regardless of the promotional technique employed, innovations tend to be imitated or improved upon by other firms in the industry. Unless the overall market expands, the effect is to offset partially or completely the gains due to the innovation. In the final outcome the promotional costs are built into the cost structures of the firms, raising the prices of the products. Ultimately the consumer pays the cost of these activities whether or not they enhance consumer satisfaction.

Differentiation and Its Effects on the Market

Most of the short- and long-run analysis of pricing and output under pure oligopoly applies also to differentiated oligopoly, whether or not there exists collusion. The effects of uncertainty and the incentives for collusion persist. But certain features peculiar to differentiated oligopoly require modifications in the analysis.

First, with respect to product prices differentiation permits oligopolistic firms in the same industry to charge different prices. For if advertising, product design, and other selling activities can persuade consumers that a certain brand has advantages over others, the firm selling that brand will be able to command a higher price. Slight price differences can exist even under informal collusion; the price leader sets his price and others set theirs very close to it. The result is that there will be not one equilibrium market price but an equilibrium *cluster* of prices. Then changes in market demand, in factor prices or technology that affect all firms in the industry, will cause the entire cluster to rise or fall. There remains, however, the tendency toward price rigidity.

In the long-run, product differentiation provides an additional artificial barrier against entry into the industry. The commodity can become quite closely identified with the brand names of a few sellers. Consumers may be persuaded to refuse any but the "accepted" brands, so a prospective entrant must overcome prevailing public opinion. Over and above the barriers previously mentioned, this deterrent to entry operates in the automobile industry, the radio and television industry, the cigarette industry, and others. Indeed, advertising by trade associations encourages the purchase of standard brands as a criterion of quality. The more consumers can be oriented to the standard brands the smaller is the likelihood that a prospective entrant can encroach upon the long-run profits of the industry.

With respect to the scale of plant utilized by each firm in the long run, nothing more definite than that said about pure oligopoly can be inferred. Selling activities do definitely raise costs above what they otherwise would be, which affects the firm's long-run output decision. But whether a firm will be of optimum size, greater, or less depends upon its expected revenue in relation to cost. It can be said that, unlike pure competition, there is no automatic tendency for the firm to produce at the minimum point on its long-run average cost curve. Moreover, long-run profits are no less likely than under pure oligopoly.

The variety of products offered to consumers under differentiated oligopoly is greater than under pure oligopoly—or, for that matter, under monopoly or pure competition. The wider range of products appears to benefit consumers, other things being the same, since there is more opportunity for different individuals with varying tastes to satisfy their wants. Gradations of quality and style are suitable to a population with gradations in income and taste.

PROBLEMS

1. Suppose an oligopolistic industry is characterized by one large firm and 10 small ones, all producing the same product. The market demand schedule for the product is given in Table I below. Table II shows the marginal cost schedule of the large firm, and Table III shows the marginal cost schedule of one small firm. All 10 of the small firms are assumed to have identical marginal cost schedules.

Table I			Table II		Table III	
Price	Quantity Demanded per Week		Output per Week	Marginal Cost	Output per Week	Marginal Cost
$1.70	300		0	$—	0	$—
1.60	400		150	.85	10	.70
1.50	500		300	.90	15	.80
1.40	600		450	1.00	20	.90
1.30	700		600	1.10	25	1.00
1.20	800		750	1.25	30	1.10
1.10	900		900	1.40	35	1.20
1.00	1000		1050	1.60	40	1.30
.90	1100		1200	1.90	45	1.40
.80	1200		1300	2.40	50	1.50
.70	1300				55	1.60

Assume the large firm is a price leader, and it allows the small firms to sell all they wish at the established price. Find the price set by the large firm, its output, and the outputs of each of the 10 small firms.

2. The market demand schedule for a commodity is given in Table IV. The industry supplying the product is oligopolistic, and at present there are a given number of firms in the industry. They have set the price at $8 and their combined output is 1,000 units per month. No artificial barriers to entry exist, so another firm is considering entering the industry. The total cost schedule of this firm, should it enter, is presented in Table V.

Table IV		Table V	
Price	Quantity Demanded per Month	Output per Month	Long-Run Total Cost
$10	800	0	$—
9	900	100	800
8	1,000	200	1,200
7	1,100	300	1,350
6	1,200	400	1,400
5	1,300	500	1,500
4	1,400	600	1,620
3	1,500	700	2,100
2	1,600	800	2,800
1	1,700	900	4,050
		1,000	6,000

(a) If no other firms are contemplating entry, find the demand for the output of this prospective entrant on the assumption that firms now in the industry will not change price or output. Plot the demand for this firm's output and label the graph Figure 1.

(*b*) Could the prospective entrant produce any profitable output under these demand and cost conditions? If so, between what two outputs would the firm be profitable? Show this in Figure 1.

(*c*) Could the firm enter profitably by charging the price currently charged? If not, how low a price would it have to charge to make a profit?

(*d*) Assuming firms already in the industry would reduce the price to $6 if this firm were to enter, could the firm enter profitably? Explain and demonstrate your answer in Figure 1.

SUGGESTED READING

J. Bain, *Pricing, Distribution and Employment*, Chap. 6. New York: Henry Holt & Co., Inc., 1953.

W. Fellner, *Competition Among the Few*, Chaps. 1-7. New York: Alfred A. Knopf, Inc., 1950.

F. Machlup, *The Economics of Sellers' Competition*, Chaps. 1-5. Baltimore: The Johns Hopkins Press, 1952.

G. Stigler, "A Theory of Delivered Price Systems," *American Economic Review*, XXXIX (1949).

17

Experiments in
Oligopoly Theory

The preceding chapter began with the admission that no general theory of oligopoly has been developed by economists. Collusion lends an element of certainty to the conditions under which price and output must be decided by each firm. In turn, this greater certainty permits inferences about a determined market structure. Indeed, collusive forms of oligopoly can be treated as extensions of monopoly. Even then, however, a wide variety of industrial structures are possible, depending upon the specific forms that collusion may assume. Given a predetermined decision on the type of collusion, economic theory can only trace out its effects.

In the absence of collusion, mutual interdependence among firms leads to a high degree of uncertainty. Management must be constantly aware of the likely reactions of rivals to any change in the firm's policy. Since most products are differentiated, price changes are not the only moves that can bring retaliation. Advertising campaigns, alterations in product design or packaging, and expansion of the product line are part of a firm's arsenal of defensive and aggressive weapons. Moreover, each firm is in about the same position vis-à-vis others. Mutual interdependence—with decision makers trying to outguess one another—makes possible a complex web of tactics and countertactics that resist any systematic analysis.

In search of a more satisfactory resolution of these difficult problems, economists have adopted three different approaches. The first simply ignores interdependence as an intractable complication and seeks to examine alternatives to the assumption of profit maximization; a second approach attempts to find a systematic basis for predicting competitive reactions; a third calculates optimal strategies similar to those used in games of chance.

ALTERNATIVES TO PROFIT MAXIMIZATION

Empirical studies, founded upon the results of questionnaires and interviews, have not been able to identify a single goal for the firm to which business executives subscribe. Their responses indicate a desire to maximize profit—but also to maximize sales, to minimize cost, to maximize the firm's share of the market, and to maximize technological progress. Observers have recorded not only a multiplicity of objectives, but in many instances, the acceptance of two or more goals that are not mutually consistent. These observations have encouraged some social scientists to challenge the assumption of profit maximization.

In addition, it has been argued that the separation of ownership and management in large corporations is grounds for doubting the profit-maximizing assumption. Business executives who make the operating decisions of the corporation may well be motivated by other objectives of equal importance. For example, chief executives may be inclined to maximize the size of the enterprise under their control, or their free time, or their personal incomes in contrast to company profit.

Various empirical studies have been followed by theoretical investigations designed to explain behavior under noncollusive oligopoly. A variety of hypotheses have been developed, and most stress the multiplicity of products and resource inputs employed by each firm. In contrast to the single-product equilibrium of the firm (see Chapter 16), the multiproduct firm has more complex equilibrium conditions for profit maximization. Furthermore, it is alleged, an assumption other than profit maximization may provide a simpler explanation of the behavior of multiproduct firms.

Sales Maximization

One hypothesis states that firms seek to maximize the total dollar value of sales subject to the constraint that total profit must be at least equal to an acceptable minimum. The acceptable profit minimum may be specified as that satisfactory to stockholders. Both profit and sales are usually defined as averages over an extended time period. Expansion of sales consistent with acceptable profit is sometimes explained by the desire to enlarge the market share of the firm (which, in turn, may determine the prestige of the top echelon of management). The assumption of sales maximization has also been rationalized by the argument that management's salaries are related more closely to the size of the enterprise than to the profitability of the firm.

The implications of sales maximization, and its contrast with profit maximization, can be seen in Fig. 17.1. The total revenue, total cost, and total profit curves of the firm are labelled TR, TC, and TP respectively. For simplicity, these curves are drawn for a firm producing a single product, X.

Straightforward profit maximization determines an output of x_1 units at which total revenue (value of sales) equals the vertical distance OA. Unconstrained sales maximization occurs at an output of x_3 units. This is the output at which marginal revenue equals zero and total revenue is equal to the vertical distance OC. Now suppose that P_1 is the acceptable minimum profit level. Then the decision makers for the firm can maximize the value of sales and produce an output of x_3 units. If, however, P_2 is the acceptable profit

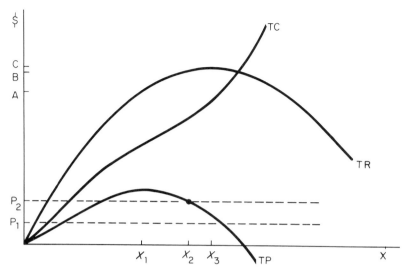

FIG. 17.1.   Sales and Profit Maximization

minimum, then an output of x_2 generates the largest total revenue consistent with the profit constraint, namely a total revenue equal to the distance OB.

By way of evaluation, what can be said about the hypothesis of sales maximization? First, unless the revenue and cost functions of individual firms can be measured (and most firms are reluctant to release the data for public inspection), there is no way to test this hypothesis directly against the alternative of profit maximization. Indeed, output and revenue may not differ significantly under the two assumptions. Second, the total revenue curve itself (and the total cost curve) can be affected by sales-promotion expenditures. The theory does not provide an explanation of advertising or other sales-promotion expenditures. Third, a relationship between the output of each firm and a determinate industry equilibrium has not been established. Finally, and most important, by ignoring the mutual inter-dependence among firms, the sales maximization theory fails to cope with the core problem of uncertainty under noncollusive oligopoly.

Satisficing and Simulation Theory

Professor Herbert A. Simon has introduced the concept of "satisficing" in place of "maximizing." [1] According to Professor Simon, firms might maximize profit—or even sales or another variable—if the modern world were simpler than it actually is. Recognizing the inadequacy of available data, the uncertain reactions of rivals, and the baffling complexity of the calculations needed, the typical firm has abandoned an attempt to compute

[1] Herbert A. Simon, "Theories of Decision Making in Economics," *American Economic Review*, XLIX (June 1959).

a unique optimum policy. Rather, firms try to define some broad criteria for satisfactory performance, that is, operational standards that will generate an acceptable long-run average profit and will protect the firm's potential for growth. Therefore, firms are said to satisfice instead of maximize if they seek to meet these standards of satisfactory performance.

Others have used this conceptual framework to build simulation models of business decisions. In place of an assumption about the objectives of the firm, this method begins by observing how decisions are actually made. Electronic computers are used to simulate the *process* by which decisions have been reached in the past, to feed in data relevant to new decisions, and to predict what those new decisions will be.

Since simulation models take into account a number of variables in addition to profit, and since these models have enjoyed considerable predictive success, they cast further doubt on the assumption that profit maximization explains the policies of business firms. Nevertheless, simulation is a predictive method rather than an explanation or theory of oligopoly. The relationship between one firm and others in the industry is not determined. Neither is the connection between the policy of one firm and the price-output position of the entire industry. The nature of mutual interdependence among firms is not demonstrated, and the conditions for attainment of a stable equilibrium in the industry are not determined.

PRICE REACTION

The achievement of a stable equilibrium in the industry depends upon whether the industry can attain a market position that is in some sense satisfactory to all firms. So-called *price reaction curves* have been used to demonstrate the nature of their mutual interdependence and the possibility of reaching an equilibrium. As presented here, these curves should not be viewed as a complete theory of noncollusive oligopoly. Rather they are intended to show, in somewhat more detail, the nature and consequences of interdependent price policies.

Suppose there are but two firms selling the same commodity X. Figure 17.2 presents two curves labeled I and II. On the horizontal axis are measured the possible prices that might be charged by Firm I. The different prices that might be charged by Firm II are measured on the vertical axis. A 45-degree line out of the origin bisects the diagram for purposes of reference. Along this line any value read off the vertical axis must necessarily equal the corresponding value read off the horizontal axis, i.e., the 45-degree line represents the locus of all points at which the two firms charge the same price.

Curve I, the price reaction curve of Firm I, is interpreted as follows. For each price II might charge, the demand curve faced by I lies in a given position. Thus there is a profit-maximizing price that I would prefer to charge, given its costs. For instance, if II were to set a price of $.20, Firm I would prefer to charge $.30. But if Firm II were to set a different price, Firm I's demand curve would shift position and its profit-maximizing price would change.

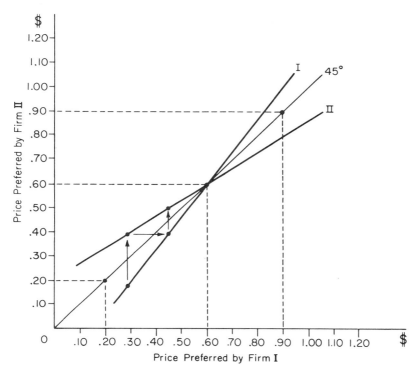

FIG. 17.2. Price Reaction Curves: Two Noncollusive Firms

The slope of Curve I is greater than 45 degrees, reflecting the assumption that at low prices set by II, Firm I would charge a higher price; while at high prices set by II, Firm I would charge a lower price. At low prices consumers are believed to be insensitive to price differences, so any loss of customers is more than offset by the higher price at which each unit is sold. Buyers are expected to be more sensitive when prices are high. The gain of a larger market share is more important than the loss of revenue due to a lower price on each unit sold.

Curve II has the same interpretation. The location of Firm II's demand curve depends upon the price charged by Firm I. Therefore, the profit-maximizing price for II varies with the price set by I. For the same reasons explained in the previous paragraph, curve II has a slope less than 45 degrees.

Where the two curves intersect, at $.60 charged by both, there is equilibrium. With both firms selling the same product they must charge the same price if equilibrium is to prevail. Suppose, to begin, that Firm II were to charge \$.20. Firm I then charges \$.30. When I sets a price of \$.30, Curve II indicates that Firm II would react by charging \$.40. At a price of \$.40 set by II, Curve I shows that Firm I will alter its price to \$.45. Again, II retaliates, and so on. As these reactions continue the firms move toward the intersection point in the direction of the arrows. Movement toward the intersection point also occurs at any price above \$.60. Only the intersection point is stable.

The assumptions regarding expectations that underlie the price reaction curves are restrictive to say the least. In addition, the curves themselves may shift position as the total market demand changes, as costs change, as new firms attempt to enter the industry, or as the existing firms jockey to capture greater market shares by nonprice competition. Nevertheless, price reaction curves are an aid to understanding the meaning and implications of interdependence.

THEORY OF GAMES

Under noncollusive oligopoly certain actions may be taken, not because they are immediately profitable in themselves, but because they ultimately improve the position of the firm relative to that of its competitors. Deliberate price cutting, although it may reduce current profit, is undertaken to drive out or to scare competitors. As a defense against possible moves by its rivals, the firm is led to undertake expensive precautions to insure supplies of raw materials in the event of a possible price war. Advertising campaigns, once begun, may be drastically revised in midstream in order to adjust to the countercampaigns of others. Expenditures on research and product development are sometimes stepped up or cut back; products are dropped from the company's line; sales techniques are imitated.

The kinds of actions a firm can take are numerous, and the possible reactions of others are complex. Because this uncertainty reduces the analytical effectiveness of the conventional tools of price theory, more promising methods have been sought in applications of modern probability theory. The oligopolistic firm finds itself in a position similar to that of a player in certain games, such as chess. The outcome of a move or action is probable, not certain, for the rival "player" may make any one of many countermoves. Nevertheless, it is possible to choose a strategy that will maximize the firm's *expected* return after the effects of his opponents' probable countermoves are taken into consideration.

The Certainty Model

In order to describe the strategy of game theory, let us first assume that each firm knows what the outcome will be if it adopts any one course of action and its competitors respond in a given way. For example, suppose the firm in question sets a price of $9.95 on the product, spends $500,000 on magazine ads, decides on a yellow package with a specific design, and retails the product through supermarket chains. Other firms set their prices, adopt advertising programs, choose their packaging designs, and follow given sales techniques. Under these circumstances, the firm is assumed to know with certainty what its share of the market will be. The firm also knows its total revenue, total cost, and total profit.

Other circumstances would result in different but known market shares and profits. If other firms were to change their policies—prices, advertising, packaging, etc.—the effects upon the given firm's market share and profit are assumed to be predictable with accuracy. Likewise, market shares and profits are known for each alternative pricing and sales policy that might be chosen by the firm in question.

Two-Person, Zero-Sum Game. For simplicity the analysis will be restricted to the case of duopoly (a two-firm industry). Furthermore, the goal of each firm is defined as a share of the market. The two firms are engaged in a struggle to obtain the largest possible slice of a given pie. A piece 10 per cent larger gained by one necessarily means the piece must be 10 per cent smaller for the other. Between them the two firms will divide 100 per cent of the market. The strategy of each is designed to maximize the percentage accruing to that firm and therefore to minimize the percentage of the market left for the other.

This game is called zero-sum because the *increment* in the market share to the *two firms combined* is zero. Whatever one gains the other must lose, so the net effect on the pair of them turns out to be zero. The zero-sum game applied to oligopoly assumes that actions taken by the firms will not change the absolute size of the market. As a consequence, their interests are diametrically opposed, and there is no incentive for collusion.

Let the two firms be designated as Firm A and Firm B, and consider the actions available to Firm A. Suppose there are q variables under its control. These variables include price, total advertising expenditures, distribution of advertising expenditures among different media, packaging design, other forms of sales promotion, product research, and whatever else has an effect upon the firm's market share. A strategy open to the firm is defined as a specific action that can be taken on each of the variables under its control. In symbolic language, let a_i denote the ith strategy of Firm A, where

$$a_i = (a_{i1}, a_{i2}, a_{i3}, \cdots, a_{iq})$$

represents a set of actions, one taken on each of the q variables under its control. Finally, let us assume there are n finite strategies that Firm A must choose among.

Similarly, allow Firm B to have r different variables under its control (as a special case r may be equal to q, but this is not necessary). The symbol b_j denotes the jth strategy available to Firm B:

$$b_j = (b_{j1}, b_{j2}, b_{j3}, \cdots, b_{jr}).$$

There are assumed to be m alternative strategies open to Firm B.

Payoff Matrix. Firm A must choose among n alternative strategies, while Firm B must choose among m alternatives. If A were to pick a particular strategy and B another one, a share of the market for each would be determined. Recall that if A's share is p per cent, then it necessarily follows that B's share is $(100 - p)$ per cent, for whatever value from zero to 100 p may assume. Therefore, by specifying the market shares of A corresponding to pairs of strategies on the part of A and B, the shares of B are simultaneously determined.

In general, the payoff in game theory is defined as the net gain (in whatever appropriate terms "gain" is specified) obtained by a player as the result of a pair of strategies, one chosen by each player. In this case of oligopoly the payoff is a share of the product market. A payoff matrix is an array of payoffs accruing to one player as the outcome of each possible combination of strategies selected by both players in the game. Let the general notation P_{ij} symbolize the payoff to Firm A if A adopts its ith strategy and B adopts its jth strategy. Then the payoff matrix is given as follows:

Firm B's Strategies

		b_1	b_2	b_3,	$\cdots$,	b_m
	a_1	P_{11}	P_{12}	P_{13}	$\cdots$	P_{1m}
	a_2	P_{21}	P_{22}	P_{23}	$\cdots$	P_{2m}
Firm A's Strategies	a_3	P_{31}	P_{32}	P_{33}	$\cdots$	P_{3m}
	$\vdots$	$\vdots$	$\vdots$	$\vdots$	$\vdots$	$\vdots$
	a_n	P_{n1}	P_{n2}	P_{n3}	$\cdots$	P_{nm}

If Firm A should decide upon strategy a_1, and if Firm B should counter with its strategy b_1, then the payoff to A is P_{11}. If, however, Firm B were to adopt strategy b_2 when Firm A selects a_1, the payoff to A is P_{12} rather than P_{11}. Still a third payoff, namely P_{13}, would result if B were to retaliate with strategy b_3, and so on.

Consider the second row of the payoff matrix; the same principle holds true. Given that Firm A has chosen strategy a_2, a series of m different payoffs might be realized by A, depending upon the counterstrategy followed by Firm B. This applies to each of the n different rows. In general, for any one strategy that A might pursue, the payoff to that strategy will depend upon what counterstrategy is selected by Firm B. Thus, the entire payoff matrix to Firm A consists of $n \times m$ payoffs.

We could just as easily have written out the payoff matrix for Firm B. But in the two-person, zero-sum game it is unnecessary. Since the two firms' payoffs sum to a constant total of 100 per cent, the payoff to B is $100 - P_{ij}$ for the combination a_i and b_j.

Equilibrium. A solution for Firm A is found in the so-called *maximin* strategy. Firm A's optimal strategy is that one which maximizes its payoff *on the assumption that Firm B will follow its own best possible counterstrategy.* Firm A considers strategy a_1, and across the top row in its payoff matrix identifies the smallest payoff, i.e., that corresponding to the best counterstrategy of B. Firm A repeats this identification of minimum payoffs in row 2, row 3, and so on, for all n of its alternative strategies. Finally, among these n minima, Firm A selects the maximum—the largest among the smallest. In effect, the firm is assumed to expect the worst, to value security, and to act accordingly.

What about Firm B? The opponent in the game must still choose an actual strategy. Firm B operates on an identical assumption that for whatever strategy B adopts, Firm A will pursue its best possible counterstrategy. We could calculate B's payoff matrix and proceed exactly as we did for A. However, as we have seen, the payoff matrix for A determines B's payoff matrix as well. Using Firm A's payoff matrix, B will consider each column rather than each row. For a given column, Firm B will identify the largest payoff to A because this is the smallest payoff to B. After identifying the m largest payoffs to A, one in each column, Firm B will decide upon the strategy that yields the smallest of these largest payoffs to A. Thus, Firm B's optimal strategy is called a *minimax* strategy. By minimizing the maximum payoffs to the other firm, B does in effect choose the largest among its own minimal payoffs.

Under certain mathematical conditions describing the form of the payoff matrix, the maximin strategy for one firm will generate a payoff which is 100 minus the payoff for the minimax strategy of the other firm. For example, suppose Firm A decides upon strategy a_3 because P_{32} is the largest among its minimum row payoffs. Firm A adopts a_3 on the assumption that if it does so, Firm B will select b_2. Firm B will indeed choose b_2 because $(100 - P_{32})$ is the largest payoff B can expect on the assumption that A pursues his best possible counterstrategy. Then a policy is determined for each firm, there is no incentive for change, and the industry reaches an equilibrium. It should be remembered that the conditions determining an equilibrium point on the payoff matrix are not always satisfied. Solutions to the game and strategy decisions can still be derived. However, the necessary discussion of utility theory and random selection of mixed strategies is beyond the scope of this book.

A Numerical Illustration. Suppose we have an extremely simple example of four strategies available to each firm. Product advertising can be concentrated on one of four media: billboards, magazines, radio, or television. The payoff matrix to Firm A is expressed in terms of its market shares:

Firm B's Strategies

		1	2	3	4
	1	35	25	(20)	40
Firm A's Strategies	2	25	(15)	35	[60]
	3	[40]	((30))	[50]	55
	4	(10)	20	15	30

Consider strategy 1 for Firm A. Firm B's best counterstrategy (strategy 3) yields a 20 per cent share of the market for A. If A were to adopt strategy 2, the best counterstrategy for B would be its policy 2, and Firm A would realize 15 per cent of the market. In response to its third strategy, Firm A expects B to follow its policy 2, so Firm A would have 30 per cent of the market. Finally, strategy 4 by A with the best retaliation available to B would realize 10 per cent of the market for A. The minimal payoff to A in each row is circled. Among these 4 minima—20, 15, 30, and 10—the largest is 30 per cent gained from strategy 3. Thus, strategy 3 is Firm A's maximin strategy. Next consider Firm B's decision. Examination of column 1 reveals that B's smallest market share, if (as B expects) Firm A follows strategy 3, would be 100, 40, and 60 per cent of the market in contrast to 65, 75, and 90 per cent, respectively, for adoption of strategies 1, 2, and 4 on the part of A. By identifying the largest number in column 1, Firm B ascertains its smallest market share corresponding to strategy 1. Following the identical procedure, 70 per cent in column 2, corresponding to counterstrategy 3 by A, is the largest share B can hope to gain; i.e., 30 per cent for A entails 70 per cent for B. For strategies 3 and 4 by Firm B, the best counterstrategies are 3 and 2 respectively by Firm A. The largest entry in each column is enclosed in a square. Among these 4 maxima—40, 30, 50, and 60—the smallest percentage of the market going to A (and thus the largest percentage going to B) results from adoption of strategy 2 by Firm B. Strategy 2 is Firm B's minimax strategy.

This payoff matrix allows a unique equilibrium solution to the game. Note that the maximin strategy of Firm A, strategy 3, assumes that Firm B would counter with its strategy 2. The minimax strategy of Firm B is indeed strategy 2, which is chosen on the assumption that Firm A would counter with its strategy 3. Under these circumstances, Firms A and B will decide upon strategies 3 and 2, respectively. There is no incentive for either firm to alter its strategy, and the market will be divided 30 per cent for A and 70 per cent for B.

The preceding outline of a two-person, zero-sum game assumed that the payoff for each pair of strategies is known with certainty. Although Firm A was uncertain as to how B would react to any strategy A might pursue and vice versa, both firms knew what the payoff would be if they each adopted a particular strategy. In effect, a firm was assumed to say, "I don't know how my rival will react to my decision; but if he reacts in a given way, the payoff to me is known." In other words, the uncertainty problem focused upon the two sellers. Uncertainty with respect to the reactions of consumers was ignored.

An added dimension of uncertainty is introduced when one recognizes that the payoff for a given pair of strategies is itself unknown. Without going into the theory of statistical decision making, it is not possible to present a thorough discussion of this problem. Nevertheless, a rudimentary treatment will help to illustrate the profound difficulties with which economists are confronted in attempting to develop a general theory of non-collusive oligopoly.

The Uncertain Payoff.   One way to cope with an uncertain payoff is to assume it is a random variable. Instead of a known number, the payoff is represented by a set of different numbers each having a specified probability that it will occur. For example, consider the payoff matrix for Firm A and, in particular, the cell corresponding to strategy a_1 by A and b_1 by B. The payoff is designated as P_{11} in general, and per cent of the market in the numerical illustration. This pair of strategies can be assumed to give rise to a probability distribution of market shares, rather than a known market share. There is a probability that the payoff will be 0 per cent of the market, another probability that the payoff will be 1 per cent, a third probability that it will be 2 per cent, and so on, to the probability that it will be 100 per cent. For selected percentage shares, the probability distribution can be set out in the following scheme:

That P_{11} will assume a value of	*has a probability of*
0 per cent	0
10 per cent	1/20
20 per cent	1/20
30 per cent	2/20
40 per cent	3/20
50 per cent	5/20
60 per cent	4/20
70 per cent	2/20
80 per cent	1/20
90 per cent	1/20
100 per cent	0

The chances are about 1 in 20 that the combination a_1 and b_1 will yield either a 10 per cent or 20 per cent share of the market to Firm A. There is about 1 chance in 4 that this strategy combination would capture half the market, but there is no likelihood at all that the counterstrategy of B would allow A to drive B out of existence and become a monopolist. There is, however, a relatively small chance that A could dominate the market. On the other hand, the probability is zero that B's strategy b_1 countered by A's strategy a_1 would permit B to take over the entire market.

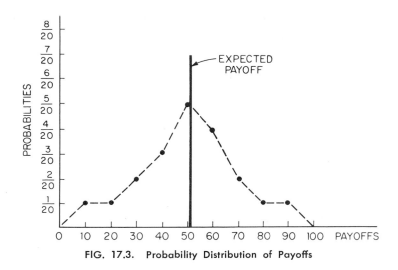

FIG. 17.3.   Probability Distribution of Payoffs

The payoff probability distribution is plotted graphically in Fig. 17.3. On the horizontal axis are measured market shares and on the vertical axis the probabilities. The coordinates of each point show the payoff and its corresponding probability. The broken curve joining the points is a linear interpolation of the probability distribution for market shares not recorded in the table.

The probability distribution charted in Fig. 17.3 rises to a peak and declines thereafter. There is no necessity, however, that the graph of the distribution have this particular shape. Moreover, different strategy combinations may give rise to radically different distributions. Some may be peaked at relatively small payoffs, while others are peaked at relatively large payoffs. Some may have no discernible peak. The important point is that the decision process is made more complex by the necessity of coping with an entire array of probable payoffs rather than a single known payoff, even for a given pair of strategies.

The Expected Payoff.   If we were to reconstruct the payoff matrix under these conditions, the matrix would show a probability distribution in each cell rather than a number like P_{11}, P_{32}, or P_{nm}. Instead of $n \times m$ different payoffs, the matrix would display $n \times m$ different probability distributions.

Consequently, in order to make the problem manageable, and in order to determine a solution, each distribution is reduced to some single number representative of that distribution. A given probability distribution has several parameters or constant characteristics of the distribution. These include the mathematical expectation of the distribution, or the average of the payoffs in the probability sense; the variance of the distribution, its degree of dispersion about the expectation; the skewness of the distribution, or the degree to which it "trails off" in one direction or the other; the most probable payoff, or that corresponding to the peak of the distribution; and the range of the distribution, in this case from 0 to 100 per cent of the market. Together these parameters describe closely the form of the probability distribution. Any one of the parameters is a constant for a particular distribution, and any one could be selected as an indication of what the distribution "looks like."

It has been suggested that the mathematical expectation of the payoffs, the average of the payoffs in the probability sense, be defined as the expected payoff and that the expected payoff replace the known payoff assumed in the previous model. The expected payoff is the weighted average payoff, where the weight attached to each probable payoff is the probability of its occurrence. For the scheme set out as an illustrative distribution, the expected payoff is

$$\begin{aligned}
\mathrm{EP}_{11} = {} & 0(0) + 1/20(10) + 1/20(20) + 2/20(30) + 3/20(40) + 5/20(50) \\
& + 4/20(60) + 2/20(70) + 1/20(80) + 1/20(90) + 0(100) \\
= {} & 50.5 \text{ per cent.}
\end{aligned}$$

The expected payoff is indicated in Fig. 17.3 by the heavy vertical line.

Given this change, the payoff matrix appears as before, except that the known payoff P_{ij} is replaced with the *expected* payoff EP_{ij}. Each cell in the matrix contains an expected rather than a known payoff. Proceeding as before, each firm maximizes its expected payoff on the assumption that its competitor will adopt its best possible counterstrategy. Firm A's optimal strategy is a maximin strategy, while Firm B's optimal strategy is a minimax strategy. As before, these optimal strategies will, under certain conditions, yield a unique solution and an industry equilibrium. The only procedural difference is that the firms maximize expected rather than certain payoffs.

The postulate that firms maximize the expected payoff in a probability distribution of payoffs implies some assumptions that are not likely to be satisfied in practice. First, the zero-sum game implies that both firms form the same probability distribution of payoffs. Each distribution is objective (as opposed to subjective) in the sense that the distribution (if not the payoff) is known to each firm. The distribution is determinable on the basis of some objective evidence. Second, there is an implied assumption that firms maximize utility and that the utility of any payoff to the firm is proportional to the payoff. The latter condition is highly restrictive.

Evaluation

Has game theory produced a general theory of noncollusive oligopoly? Unfortunately, the answer is "no." Two-person games can be expanded to any number of players that computers can handle. The sheer magnitude of players and strategies puts a strain upon results that can be reasonably well interpreted. More important, the zero-sum aspect of the game requires that the behavior of firms has no impact on their combined payoff. Real economic situations are rarely of this type. Strategies of firms increase or decrease both the absolute size of the market and the profits of all firms in the industry taken together.

There is in the literature of game theory an extensive system of analysis of nonconstant-sum games. However, little applicability to noncollusive oligopoly has been feasible. Some insights have been gained, and partial predictions of behavior have emerged. Nevertheless, a comprehensive analysis has not been possible.

CONCLUSIONS

We have reviewed three approaches to noncollusive oligopoly. The brief review is not intended to be a comprehensive investigation of new experiments in oligopoly theory. Its purpose is to impart an understanding of the problem and to serve as an introduction to theoretical methods that have been suggested to cope with the problem.

Three different approaches have been outlined. The first ignores mutual interdependence among firms and centers on alternatives to profit maximization as a basic theoretical postulate. The assumption of sales maximization and simulation models have not provided a satisfactory explanation of noncollusive oligopoly. Price reaction does little more than elaborate the nature of mutually interdependent decision making on the part of firms. Game theory, although it holds some promise for a theoretical breakthrough, does not in its present state of refinement offer a general theory of noncollusive oligopoly.

It would seem appropriate to close this chapter by stressing the admission made at the outset. Economists have not been able to develop a general theory of noncollusive oligopoly. Since oligopoly is a dominant form of industrial organization in the American economy, the absence of satisfactory theory leaves an important gap in the tools of economic analysis. Only further research—perhaps in statistical decision theory and related fields—will determine whether this gap will be closed in the near future.

SUGGESTED READING

William J. Baumol, *Business Behavior, Value and Growth*. New York: The Macmillan Co., 1959.

R. M. Cyert and J. G. March, *A Behavioral Theory of the Firm.* Englewood Cliffs, N.J.: Prentice-Hall, Inc., 1963.

R. D. Luce and H. Raiffa, *Games and Decisions, Introduction and Critical Survey.* New York: John Wiley & Sons, Inc., 1957.

J. C. C. McKinsey, *Introduction to the Theory of Games.* New York: McGraw-Hill Book Co., 1952.

18

Monopolistic Competition

The foregoing lengthy treatment of oligopoly will be offset by a brief consideration of monopolistic competition. Though it does provide insights into one variety of partial competition, the theory of monopolistic competition encounters severe limitations, which will be reviewed in this chapter. An industry classified as monopolistically competitive has two essential characteristics. First, there are many firms in the industry, and we have seen that "many" firms as opposed to "few" means the policies of any one firm are independent of those followed by others in the industry. In this respect the firm is similar to the purely competitive firm. Second, a firm differentiates its product from those of other firms in the industry. In effect it has a monopoly over a brand name, a product design, or a type of service accompanying the product. This element of monopoly permits the firm to exercise some control over price. Thus arises the strange conjunction of terms, "monopolistic competition."

THEORY OF THE FIRM

The theory of cost applicable to other market types also applies to the monopolistically competitive firm. On the revenue side it differs from firms operating under other industrial structures. Rather than a large share of the market, or complete control of the market, it is product differentiation that permits a firm to raise price without losing all of its sales. Because some consumers view one product as somehow different from others and prefer it over others, they will continue to purchase the product even at a higher price. And if one firm lowers its price, some additional buyers may be found, thus expanding sales over and above the increased purchases on the part of confirmed customers. Product differentiation need not entail a physical difference among commodities. It is sufficient that consumers regard the products as different, whether or not they are in fact. As a consequence, advertising and other sales promotion efforts will play a part in the activities of a firm. Indeed, differentiation may depend only upon the personality of the seller—he may

pat little kiddies on the head or offer them lollipops. Regardless of the
source of an imagined or real product differentiation, the seller is provided with a degree of price control.

Nevertheless, the demand for any one seller's product, though it is not
infinitely price elastic, is assumed to be "very" price elastic. The existence of a large number of firms suggests there are many substitutes for
any one firm's product, and products cannot be differentiated to the
extent that consumers make no price comparisons. For other firms can
simulate mysterious ingredients, imitate services, or duplicate claims
of superiority, leading to greater price consciousness by consumers. Independent price setting implies that each firm does not expect its competitors to follow price changes. As a consequence, any one seller will
tend to lose substantial sales if he raises price, and he can gain substantial sales if he reduces price. The exact degree of price elasticity
depends primarily upon the strength of product differentiation.

Short-Run Equilibrium

The short-run analysis of a monopolistically competitive firm follows
closely the analysis of monopoly or oligopoly. The formal difference in
graphical presentation centers on the price elasticity of the firm's demand curve. Figure 18.1 depicts the short-run equilibrium of a firm
producing a commodity X. In order to maximize profit the firm produces
x_0 units, the output at which marginal cost equals marginal revenue.
Corresponding to this output the firm sets a price of p_0, regardless of the

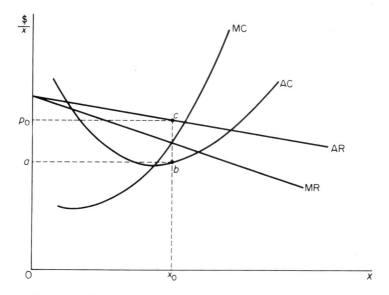

FIG. 18.1. Short-Run Equilibrium: Monopolistically Competitive Firm

prices charged by other firms, yielding a total profit equal to the area of the rectangle $abcp_0$.

As under any other industrial structure, a firm may well incur a loss in the short run. Had the demand for its product been such that price is less than average cost, but greater than average variable cost, at the output where MC = MR, then the firm would minimize its loss by producing that output. And if price is even below average variable cost at the output where MC = MR, the firm would suspend production. But it would not leave the industry because by definition of the short run the firm does not have sufficient time to divest itself of its fixed plant.

The firm may attempt to expand its profit or avoid a loss through advertising or other promotional efforts designed to influence demand. If successful, these activities will shift the demand curve to the right and perhaps make it less price elastic. Then the analysis of price and output is formally the same as that of differentiated oligopoly.

Long-Run Equilibrium

Whether the firm's long-run output is such as to yield a positive profit depends upon the conditions of entry. Ordinarily, monopolistically competitive industries are assumed to be characterized by complete freedom of entry. Since there are a large number of firms, effective collusion is extremely difficult to enforce. When profits exist and potential entrants believe they too can enjoy profits, entry will be attempted. As they enter, newcomers encroach upon the markets of existing firms, causing the demand faced by each firm to decrease. The average revenue and marginal revenue curves of any one firm shift downward and to the left.

Costs may also be affected by incoming firms. Like the case of pure competition (or oligopoly if entry is not blocked) industries can be classified according to increasing cost, constant cost, or decreasing cost. When the entry of new firms causes resource prices to rise, for example, and cost curves of all firms thus shift upward, the industry is one of increasing cost. If cost curves do not shift, the industry is classified as a constant-cost industry. In the extremely unlikely case of falling resource prices as new firms enter and bid for their services, the cost curves of all firms shift downward and the industry is one of decreasing cost.

It is to be expected that the typical industry is one of increasing cost. So as cost curves shift upward they tend to squeeze existing profits. At the same time, and regardless of the cost outcome, firms' average revenue curves will shift downward and to the left, tending to squeeze profits further. As long as any profits remain, the prospect of a higher return relative to alternative employments of resources provides an incentive for additional entrants. Therefore, when long-run adjustments are complete, profits will be zero for all firms. Likewise, losses will create an exodus of firms because their rate of return is lower than elsewhere.

The withdrawal of firms allows for increased demand faced by remaining firms and perhaps some cost decrease. The incentive to withdraw will cease only when losses have been eliminated and each firm is making zero profit.

The long-run equilibrium of one firm is presented graphically in Fig. 18.2. Zero profit implies the firm's long-run average cost equals its average revenue; that is, its LAC curve (hence, also its AC curve) is tangent to its AR curve at an output of x_1 units. The firm's long-run optimum output is x_2 units in Fig. 18.2. Of course, with a negatively

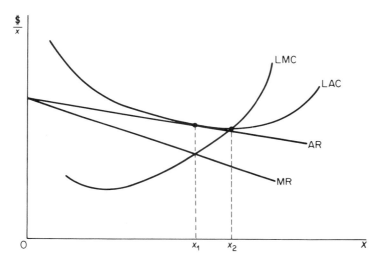

FIG. 18.2.   Long-Run Equilibrium: Monopolistically Competitive Firm

sloped average revenue curve, zero profit in turn implies that each firm will utilize a scale of plant smaller than its optimum plant size, and it will produce a smaller than optimum output with this plant. Therefore, free entry leads to excess capacity on the part of each firm. In comparison to pure competition, if firms have the same cost under either structure, it takes a greater number of firms to supply a given quantity for the market than would be required under pure competition. This outcome is sometimes described by saying monopolistic competition leads to an excessive number of firms.

The theory of monopolistic competition has been applied primarily to the retail trade. The very high rate of mortality of stores in some lines of retailing, especially in the first two or three years of operation, suggests a chronic tendency for excessive entry of new firms. Capital requirements are relatively small, so it is easy for hopeful entrepreneurs to enter, causing losses for many others. Long-run equilibrium may be a long time in coming, if ever it is reached. For the realization that others are making profits, or the belief on the part of prospective entrants that they can fare better than those already established, creates a situation conducive to excessive entry and a continual fluctuation in the number of firms. Although such practices are not common, this chronic tendency to excessive entry may motivate existing firms to erect barriers to further entry. The formation of a trade association with political influence might be sufficient to instigate legislation regarding licensing practices. Alternatively, legislation could take the form of Fair Trade Laws, which in effect prevent price cutting and other "unfair practices" in order to protect "small business" so existing firms may realize a "fair and reasonable profit." Or, in the absence of concerted effort, the strength of reputation built up by some firms may create such strong consumer preferences that entry is discouraged. Consumer good will can be used as a weapon to prevent encroachment upon a firm's market.

Whenever entry is effectively blocked, some firms may well enjoy a profit in the long run. The long-run equilibrium of such a firm is formally the same as that of an oligopolistic firm with successful barriers to entry. The output at which long-run marginal cost equals marginal revenue is also an output at which average revenue exceeds average cost. As in the case of oligopoly, no definite inference can be drawn regarding the firm's scale of plant. Its plant may be of optimum size, smaller than optimum, or greater than optimum, depending upon the demand conditions it faces.

THE INDUSTRY

As in differentiated oligopoly, product differentiation poses special difficulties in presenting a graphical analysis of the industry. The meaning of an industry supply curve is ambiguous to say the least. The product sold by one firm is not the same as that sold by another. Hence, summation of their outputs does not add up to the same thing. Unless all these similar but different products—such as laxatives, which are sold in pills, powders, pastes, and liquids—can be reduced to some common denominator, one is plotting essentially different and nonadditive quantities on the horizontal axis. The same difficulty arises in the concept of market demand and the demand faced by each individual firm. The market demand curve is presumably the demand for the output of the entire industry—again, a combination of products measured in different units. What relationship this market demand has to the demand faced by one seller is not clearly established.

A similar difficulty arises in handling the concept of price. No single price prevails in equilibrium. Each seller sets his own price, not greatly different from the prices charged by others. Aside from the problem of defining an industry supply curve or a market demand curve when there exists no one price to plot against quantity, there is the added difficulty that the market equilibrium will show not a single price but a cluster of different prices.

The cluster of "close" prices arises from the assumption that differentiated products are nevertheless close substitutes. Substitutability limits the seller's discretion in price setting and makes the demand for his output close to infinitely elastic. The more elastic are the demand curves faced by individual sellers, the closer will their prices tend to be.

The adjustment to long-run equilibrium with freedom of entry parallels that of pure competition. The difference arises in the slight negative inclination imparted to the firm's demand curve under monopolistic competition. Because of the entry of additional firms motivated by existing profits, the purely competitive short-run supply curve shifts to the right, driving down the market price and so the price at which each firm can sell. In the monopolistically competitive industry there is no single industry price. Indeed, as firms enter and industry output expands, there is no guarantee that the demand faced by each one firm must likewise decrease. Where demand does decrease for a single firm, one must think in terms of a decreasing demand situation rather than a decreasing product price. In viewing the market as a whole, "price" must be construed as a cluster of prices moving up or down in response to changes in consumer income or changes in cost of production. But how the individual firms' prices will move within this cluster is not known.

LIMITATIONS AND ADVANTAGES OF THE ANALYSIS

The careful reader will have noticed that I have been using several vague terms in describing monopolistic competition. If it is granted that precision is a virtue in theoretical reasoning, the theory of monopolistic competition can lay little claim to virtue. The limitations of the theory are essentially these:

(1) The industry is said to have *many* sellers. How many must there be to warrant classifying an industry as monopolistic competition rather than as differentiated oligopoly? Presumably the question might be answered by classifying an industry as monopolistic competition when the number of firms is large enough to render their pricing and output policies independent. For the functional definition of *many sellers* is that number required to eliminate interdependent pricing policies. But product differentiation itself implies some consciousness of rivals' reactions. It is questionable that a large number of close intraindustry substitutes does not in turn entail awareness of (dependence upon) the prices other sellers are charging as well as the sales promotion in which they engage.

(2) How elastic must a firm's demand curve be in order to be called "very" elastic? In particular, how elastic must it be as compared to an oligopolistic firm? As compared to a competitive firm?

(3) No precise meaning can be given to the industry supply curve or to the market demand curve. Moreover, the relation-

ship between a single firm's demand and supply and the market demand and supply is not established.

(4) Some writers have regarded the assumptions of free entry and product differentiation as incompatible. It is argued that strong consumer preferences for brand names are themselves restrictions upon entry.

There is no doubt that the theory furnishes a detailed description of those industries in which product differentiation occurs, in that it recognizes small monopoly elements and the consequent different but almost equal prices charged by various sellers. But it provides few new analytical tools. Since the theory of pure competition is a great deal more precise, some economists prefer to classify an industry as purely competitive for analytical purposes if the industry approximates pure competition more closely than it does oligopoly. That is, one would abstract from the effects of product differentiation if the interdependence among firms in the industry appears weak enough to warrant it. On the other hand, when the purely competitive model is not appropriate, the industry is classified as differentiated oligopoly. Then the logical difficulties inherent in the dual assumptions of product differentiation and independence are overcome. Of course, the problem of formulating a more satisfactory theory of differentiated oligopoly still remains.

On the credit side of the ledger, the theory of monopolistic competition (by laying stress upon product differentiation) has performed the service of introducing more explicitly into price theory the role of the product itself as an economic variable. What a consumer purchases is not just a physical item but a "package" consisting of the item and associated services—warranties, service contracts, more courteous customer attention, etc. The relevant price is then the price of the package. Though the portion of the total price attributable to greater convenience or reliability can sometimes be identified, the analytical implications and new vistas opened by this recognition have not yet been fully exploited. Second, the definition of an industry has been challenged and therefore subjected to greater scrutiny. Rather than a collection of firms producing a homogeneous product, some degree of diversity must be allowed. As a consequence, the industry as a distinct and manageable theoretical concept is in need of some reworking.

SUGGESTED READING

E. H. Chamberlin, *The Theory of Monopolistic Competition*, 7th ed., Chaps. 4, 5. Cambridge: Harvard University Press, 1956.

F. Machlup, *The Economics of Sellers' Competition*, Chaps. 6, 7. Baltimore: The Johns Hopkins Press, 1952.

L. W. Weiss, *Economics and American Industry*, Chap. 9. New York: John Wiley & Sons, Inc., 1962.

19

Applications of Monopoly and Nonpure Competition

The American economy is a mixed economy. Some of its industries are competitive, others are regulated monopolies, and many of its most important industries are oligopolies. This chapter will be devoted to a few theoretical applications designed to illustrate how price theory can help to resolve issues of public policy and to point out additional directions in which the general theory can be taken. Also, some empirical evidence on oligopolistic practices and industrial concentration in the United States will be briefly presented and discussed.

THEORETICAL APPLICATIONS

Comparison of Competition and Monopoly

It used to be said that monopolies are undesirable because they restrict output and charge high prices. On the basis of common sense the argument might appear reasonable enough. Vaudeville thrived on jokes about senile capitalists who wanted to corner the market on llama manure, or some such commodity, in the prospect of making a quick fortune—and certain comic strips elaborate on the theme even today. Actually, the assertion of restricted supply and a higher price is a comparative statement. It implies a smaller output and higher price as compared to some other market structure, say a competitive one.

At first glance the argument appears plausible. A competitive firm in long-run equilibrium produces the output at which both marginal and average cost equal price. A monopolist produces the output at which marginal cost equals marginal revenue, where marginal revenue is below price. If the two firms were to produce the same output at the same marginal cost, it would follow that price must be higher under monopoly. Or, if they were to charge the same price, output must be smaller under monopoly. The defect in this argument is that comparison of the two firms is invalid. A competitive firm supplies only a small share of the market while a monopolist supplies all of the market. It is like comparing a firm whose output of a given commodity is in the neighborhood of 1,000 units per unit of time with another whose output of the same commodity would be around 30,000 units. For this reason it is not the competitive firm but the competitive industry that should be compared with monopoly.

To permit price and output comparisons we must consider a given commodity produced under alternative market structures. We ask: What would be the product price and output if the industry were organized competitively? What would price and output be if it were monopolized? Since it is one and the same commodity, market demand can be taken as the same in either case. Then, given demand, it is the supply curve of the competitive industry or the marginal cost curve of the monopoly that determines equilibrium so that legitimate comparisons can be made. To begin, suppose the industry is made up of several physical plants. If they are individually owned, each plant constituting a firm, no one can control price. On the other hand, if they are centrally owned, they comprise one firm and the single owner–decision maker can control price. Moreover, assume all plants are operating in the short run. The competitive industry supply curve is the horizontal summation of the marginal cost curves of the individual firms. We have seen in Chapter 16 that a monopolist owning many plants would distribute output shares among them in such a way that the marginal cost curve of the monopoly is the horizontal summation of the marginal cost curves of the plants. Horizontal summation of plant marginal cost curves in either case therefore permits direct comparison of market equilibria under the alternative forms of industrial organization.

Now we can go into the geometry: Fig. 19.1 depicts the market demand curve for the product X, labeled D. The curve S represents the short-run market supply curve if the industry were competitive. Consequently, the product price under competition would be p_1 at which x_1 units are produced and consumed, with each firm producing the output at which marginal cost equals price. Since the curve S is the horizontal summation of firms' marginal cost curves, it would also be the marginal cost curve of the monopolized industry. The difference is that the monopolist would consider his marginal revenue curve corresponding to the market demand curve, the curve labeled MR in the diagram, and equate marginal cost to marginal revenue. To maximize profit the monopolist would produce x_0 units and charge a price of p_2.

A higher monopoly price and smaller output hinges on the assumption that costs are unaffected by the form of industrial organization. Transfer from atomistic to centralized ownership, or the reverse, is assumed to have no effect upon production functions or resource prices—no quantity discounts in the buying of raw materials for instance. If cost does indeed depend upon the form of ownership, the outcome might be different. Lower cost under competition would enforce the argument that price is

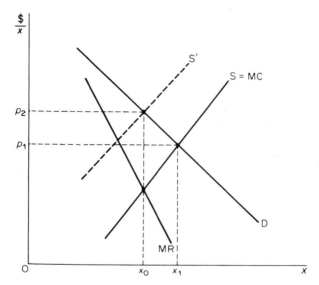

FIG. 19.1.   Comparison of Competition and Monopoly Under Identical Short-Run Costs

lower and output greater under that market structure. For the competitive supply curve would lie below and to the right of the monopoly marginal cost curve, yielding a price below p_1 and output greater than x_1. However, costs might be higher under competition. Then the outcome depends upon how much higher they are. The competitive industry supply curve would lie above and to the left of the monopoly marginal cost curve. Nevertheless, the competitive price might still be lower than p_2 and output greater than x_0. Only if costs are so high relative to monopoly that the competitive supply curve lies above and to the left of the curve S' in the diagram will the competitive price be higher and output smaller.

This analysis suggests there is a *tendency* for price to be higher and output smaller under monopoly. But the argument is by no means conclusive, especially when one considers the long run. It is entirely possible that production of the commodity is characterized by internal economies of scale over a very large span of outputs. If these economies of scale extend far enough, so that long-run average cost declines up to the quantity that would be demanded by the entire market, the industry in question is called a *natural monopoly*. Such a situation is depicted in Fig. 19.2. The production function for any one firm that might produce the commodity X shows increasing returns to scale over a very wide range relative to the size of the market. Long-run average cost declines as greater quantities are produced up to the output of x_3 units per unit of time. The market demand curve, represented by D in the diagram, indicates that one firm could supply the entire market and still be in the stage of declining average cost. Then a monopolist would equate long-run marginal cost to marginal revenue, producing x_2 units and charging a price of p_2. In contrast, if there were many competitive firms supplying the market, each one must produce a small share at comparatively high average cost. For instance, one competitive firm might be able to produce at most x_1 units at which average cost is substantially higher. In order to cover cost and remain in existence, the competitive firms would have to receive a price significantly higher than p_2.

There are two aspects of production conditions conducive to natural monopoly. The first is that price would be lower and output and consumption greater under monopoly than under competition. The second,

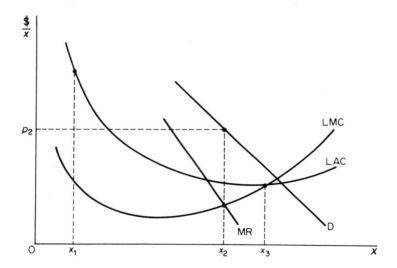

FIG. 19.2. Comparison of Competition and Natural Monopoly

not unrelated to the first, is that such a situation is inconsistent with long-run competitive equilibrium. For if all potential firms have long-run average and marginal cost curves like those in Fig. 19.2, the industry will naturally gravitate to monopoly. That firm with cost curves of the same general shape as the others but lying below the curves of the other firms could drive the rest out of existence by cutting price to a level that would not permit the others to cover costs. And there is an incentive for this firm to do so because it enjoys cost reductions as it absorbs the vacated shares of others. Even if the cost curves of all firms were identical (of the same shape and positioned at the same height at all points) one would eventually take over the entire market. The incentive to increase output would result in a race to see which firm could first reach the output x_2, after which it would be unprofitable for another to enter the industry. Therefore, in the nature of the situation there is nothing but the size of the market to limit the size of the firm. Of course, in the absence of any public regulation, firms might form a collusive oligopoly to avoid the risk of any one being driven out. Then average cost would be higher for each and price would be higher than the pure monopoly price. However, the incentive for any one to expand output is still present, so the oligopoly would tend to be unstable.

Practical examples of natural monopoly often appear in public utilities. Imagine, for example, the cost of providing telephone services to a city on a competitive basis. Each competitive firm would have to erect its own poles, string its own wires, provide its own switchboards and teams of operators, engage in maintenance and repair of its own facilities, etc. In the extreme, one would be unable to see the sky for all the wires stretched overhead, and only the birds would reap benefits. A single monopoly can string one set of wires, centralize switchboard operations, and avoid duplicate transportation to areas where breakdowns occur. As a result, telephone services can be supplied at a much lower cost per message. Though there are striking cost advantages to natural monopolies, there may also be extremely large profits. This is one of the main reasons why public utilities are regulated by government agencies as to the prices they can charge in the United States.

Consideration of natural monopoly makes it quite clear that monopolies do not necessarily restrict output and raise price as compared to competition. This is not to say there are no arguments against monopoly on grounds of economic efficiency. It can be shown that unregulated monopolies do misallocate productive services on the resource markets of the economy. But discussion of this effect must await the theory of resource pricing, the theory of general equilibrium, and the principles of welfare economics to be presented later in the book. At this point it might be noted that other objections to monopoly have been raised. It has been alleged that monopolies are undesirable because they contribute to extreme inequality in the distribution of income in society, because they may retard technological advance in the absence of competitive incentives, and because there are political objections to their existence in a democratic society. These assertions are not demonstrable within the framework of price theory, however, so we shall not pursue them further.

Oligopoly Spatial Location

Our examination of product pricing has for the most part ignored an aspect of firm behavior, namely, geographic location of its plant. The various aspects of spatial analysis will first be presented against a general theoretical framework involving simplifying assumptions. With this model as background material it is possible to examine locational decisions in either competitive or noncompetitive markets. Nevertheless, I shall restrict the discussion to oligopoly location.

In Fig. 19.3, the area enclosed by the polygon ABCD represents a spatial market. Assume there are two firms supplying the market with a given product. Firm I is located at point B; Firm II at point D. Suppose their identical products sell for $1 at the production points B and D respectively. Customers are distributed over the entire market area, so the price at the geographic point of purchase includes the cost of transportation. This cost is assumed to be one cent per mile on each unit transported. Since the distance from point B to point A is assumed to be 75 miles, a buyer located at A pays $1 plus transportation cost of $.75, or $1.75, if he buys from Firm I. He is located the same distance from D so he would pay the same price were he to buy from Firm II. A buyer located at point C is in the same situation. At point M (50 miles from either B or D) a buyer pays $1.50 regardless of the firm from which he buys because he is equidistant from B and D. In fact, the vertical line

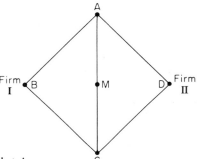

FIG. 19.3.   Geographic Market Area

AMC might be called the boundary of indifference, for all buyers located on the line pay the same delivered price, whether they purchase from one or the other firm. All located to the left of AMC are closer to B and pay a lower delivered price if they purchase from Firm I. All to the right of AMC pay a lower price by purchasing from Firm II. If we assume buyers are perfectly responsive to price differences, the market will be shared on this basis: the area of AMCB for Firm I and the area of AMCD for Firm II.

To set the stage for applications consider a unilateral price reduction. Suppose Firm I reduces its nondelivered price from $1 to $.80. The effect is to shift the boundary of indifference to the right. At point A, for example, the delivered price of Firm I is ($.80 + $.75) = $1.55, while the price charged by Firm II remains at $1.75. At point M, Firm I's delivered price is $1.30 as compared to Firm II's $1.50. The new boundary will be a hyperbola rather than a straight line. But the important point is that the unilateral price cut shifts the boundary of indifference to the right, resulting in a transfer of some but not all of Firm II's customers.

This simple theory sets the basis for interpretations of actual pricing policies. First to be noted is that pure competition does not require that all firms "post" the same price. It is final prices, net of all extras, that are equated. In this connection the transportation cost is one such extra. In applications to noncollusive oligopoly it should be recalled that pricing policies of firms are interdependent, so in the illustration given, Firm II may retaliate by reducing its nondelivered price. What is significant for market shares is the difference in delivered prices.

Let us examine first the decision of a firm contemplating location of a new plant in a given market area. Suppose Firm I has a retail outlet at point B from which it supplies the entire market area ABCD. Firm II is another firm in the noncollusive oligopoly, and it attempts to capture a share of this spatial market. Where in the market area shall it locate its retail outlet? Obviously, Firm II will want to obtain as large a share as it can. This will be accomplished by locating as near as possible to point B and still maintain enough difference so that buyers sensitive to transportation cost will not be indifferent between the two outlets. Firm II will seek to locate close to point B but to the right. Then transportation cost will be less to all buyers located to the right of Firm II's outlet, and these comprise by far the largest share of the market. Firm II could sell at the same nondelivered prices as Firm I and still offer lower delivered prices. In the case of retail stores the transportation cost must be correctly interpreted. Buyers come to the store but they pay transportation cost in the form of automobile or bus transportation, time consumed in travel, and nonpecuniary disadvantages associated with "bucking traffic."

By the same reasoning it can be shown that a third firm would try to locate its outlet close to the first two, and a fourth close to the other three. Indeed, they would tend to congregate regardless of where in the area the original firm was located (the principle of grouping does not depend on the assumption that Firm I located on the edge of the market). Minimization of locational differences due to transportation cost, correctly interpreted, goes a long way toward explaining the formation of the downtown shopping center. It is also significant that the recent trend toward suburban shopping plazas has been characterized by grouping according to plaza, with close competitors gravitating to the same plazas. Another application is to be found in the growth of "discount houses" selling appliances, jewelry, clothing, etc. Not only do new firms spring up in the cities where others are already located, they also tend to locate in the same sections of the cities—even to the extent of congregating within a radius of a few miles. For purposes of oligopoly product pricing the minimization of locational differences is much like the minimization of other product differences. Minimization of difference—to make the product as much like others as possible without destroying any distinctiveness—helps to explain why brands of cigarettes or makes of automobiles are so much alike. Sellers attempt to attract others' customers by making products (or locations) similar to those of others. But at the same time they utilize brand names and certain "extras" to permit consumer identification of their product.

Let us now turn the application of spatial analysis on its head and consider location for a firm that is a buyer rather than a seller. If the firm in question is a manufacturing firm, for instance, the location decision for its plant will take into account not only its closeness to customers but also its closeness to sources of raw materials. For a component of cost is the cost of transporting raw materials to the point of manufacture. Plant location is partly the result of balancing the forces that draw the firm to the consuming centers and the forces drawing it to the raw material centers. How important transportation cost is depends upon this cost per unit relative to the market value per unit or price of the item in question. Generally, for products or resources with high value per unit weight or volume—such as jewelry, paintings, or girdles—the transportation cost is not a dominant cost factor. For those with low value per unit weight or volume—coal, wheat, dog food— transportation cost will assume more importance.

Many manufacturing operations consist of transforming a bulky, heavy raw material into a product having greater value per unit of bulk. Then high transportation cost of the raw material will attract firms to the raw material source. Suppose the raw material source is located at point M in Fig. 19.3, and the market for the final product is given by the area of ABCD. Firms in this case will tend to converge in the neighborhood of M. An example can be found in the steel industry. When rich ores are available, the bulkiest raw material in steel manufacture is coal. Therefore, the steel industry at first congregated near the coal fields. Then as the richer ore deposits began to be exhausted and poorer ores of smaller value per unit of bulk had to be used, there emerged a tendency for the steel industry to establish new plants near the ore fields and to transport the coal there.

EMPIRICAL APPLICATIONS

Basing-Point Pricing

The so-called basing-point system of pricing provides an actual historical example of oligopoly behavior related to spatial theory as presented in the previous section. Prior to about 1900 steel firms usually quoted prices on the mill base system. The price was quoted at the mill, and the buyer paid the quoted price plus the transportation cost from the mill to the place of delivery. At this time the steel industry was essentially a noncollusive oligopoly. Price cutting was frequently practiced. In terms of Fig. 19.3, the point B might be Pittsburgh and point D Chicago. A firm in Pittsburgh by cutting price hoped to push the boundary of indifference to the right, toward Chicago, and thereby acquire a number of customers who had previously purchased from Chicago firms. Sometimes retaliation led to price wars as firms attempted to retain their market shares.

In order to escape the effects of retaliatory price cutting, a form of collusion, known as the basing-point price system, was introduced. Delivered prices were quoted on the basis of "Pittsburgh plus," i.e., the Pittsburgh mill price plus transportation cost from Pittsburgh to the buyer regardless of the firm from which he bought. For instance, a Chicago steel mill would charge a buyer in Indiana the Pittsburgh mill price plus freight charges from Pittsburgh to Indiana even though the steel was shipped from Chicago. The result was that all firms in the industry charged the same delivered price at any given geographic point. In other words, a form of price leadership was established with the United States Steel Corporation as leader in order to do away with spatial price competition.

As a consequence of identical delivered prices, firms had to accept varying nondelivered or mill prices. Firms in Pittsburgh received the same price at the mill no matter where they sold. Firms elsewhere received one price at the mill when they sold to buyers between their mill and Pittsburgh. However, they received a higher price when they sold to buyers on the other side. To illustrate, suppose Pittsburgh is at point B in Fig. 19.3. A firm located at M and selling to a buyer between B and M would receive as a delivered price the Pittsburgh mill price plus freight charges from B to the buyer. The actual freight charges would be from M to the buyer. Suppose, instead, that the firm at M were to sell to a buyer at point D. The seller would receive the Pittsburgh price plus freight charges from B to D. Actually, the freight charges are from M to D, just half the distance. So the seller located at M has a price advantage by selling to buyers located to the right of M. The effect of the basing-point system was a division of the market in a way that would discourage any one firm from attempting to increase its share by a small amount of price cutting. Western firms were not likely to compete for sales in the eastern area because they brought a lower net price as compared to western sales. So market shares were established by a special form of collusive pricing.

Concentration Ratios

Since oligopoly is an important form of industrial organization in the United States, many attempts have been made to measure the degree of oligopoly. One possible measure is fewness of firms in the numerical sense. The concentration ratio for an industry is the share of total product shipments controlled by the four largest firms in the industry. Statistics from which concentration ratios can be computed are available for all manufacturing industries, though not for most other enterprises. These industry ratios can be compared to yield relative indicators of the degree of centralized production.

Table 19.1 shows concentration ratios for a sample of eight industry groups. From an empirical viewpoint, industries can be defined narrowly or broadly, and there is no single dividing line that must apply. Some of the industries in Table 19.1 are defined more broadly than others. Where grouping has been done, the concentration ratio shown is a weighted average of the ratios for more narrowly defined industries within the group. Table 19.1 also shows the average rates of return on owner's equity after taxes for the same industry groups. This rate of return is a rough measure of profit, but more in the accounting sense than in the economic sense.

Table 19.1

Concentration Ratios and Rates of Return on Equity for
Selected Industry Groups (in Per Cent)

Industry	Concentration Ratio, 1954[a]	Average Rate of Return on Equity, 1949–58[b]
Motor Vehicles	95%	16%
Tobacco Manufacturers	76	10
Primary Metal Industries	57	11
Rubber Products	55	12
Chemicals and Allied Products	52	13
Furniture and Fixtures	18	9
Apparel and Other Fabricated Textile Products	14	6
Lumber and Wood Products	10	9

[a] Source: *Concentration in American Industry,* Report of the Subcommittee on Anti-Trust and Monopoly, Senate Judiciary, 85th Congress, 1st Session, 1957.
[b] Source: *Quarterly Financial Reports, United States Manufacturing Corporations,* FTC–SEC.

The industry groups have been divided into a set of five with comparatively high ratios and another set of three with relatively low ratios for purposes of comparison. One feature of the data worth noting is the higher rate of return in the more concentrated industries, which may well be due to some extent to oligopolistic practices. Indeed, from these limited observations there appears a strong correlation between rate of return and degree of concentration.

These data are meant to be illustrative rather than definitive. Caution is necessary if one is to avoid jumping to unwarranted conclusions. First, there are only eight observations presented in Table 19.1, so to infer a general relationship between concentration ratios and rates of return on the basis of this small sample would be illegitimate. Second, the concentration ratio is not the only, nor always the best, measure of degree of oligopoly. It covers only the four largest firms and tells nothing about the division of output among the remaining firms in the industry. Even a more detailed description of the distribution of shares among all firms in the industry would not be a foolproof indicator of oligopoly. Other criteria such as restrictions on entry, evidence of price leadership or other collusive practices, and types of advertising are also meaningful and should be taken into account.

Given these limitations of the concentration ratio, one might wonder why it is used in economics. In spite of shortcomings the concentration ratio is still a helpful, if rough, indicator. Used in conjunction with other aspects of the industry it can tell us something of the characteristics of concentrated production. More important for our purposes, it points out some of the problems and future prospects of empirical research. Unlike empirical demand studies, for example, in which demand functions can be estimated statistically from observations on consumption, prices, and income levels, measures of oligopoly must often use indirect approximations that do not correspond closely to the theoretical concepts. Indeed for the social sciences generally, nonavailability of data corresponding precisely to theoretical concepts often makes necessary the use of rough approximations based on some indirect experimentation procedure. Refined theory and inaccurate data cause problems of interpretation because even when the data are adjusted to yield more meaningful information, this may not be sufficient to test the theory or to measure its quantitative properties. Hopefully, more advanced data collection methods will reduce the obstacles to empirical research in the future.

PROBLEM

Assume a firm located in Maryland sells its product for $1.00 in the Southeast and for $1.30 in the Northeast. Suppose someone asserts that the firm is engaging in monopoly price discrimination. What factors would you take into account if you were to embark on a study intended to determine whether or not the assertion is true? Explain how each factor has a bearing on the truth or falsity of the assertion.

SUGGESTED READING

W. Adams, *The Structure of American Industry*, 3rd ed., Chaps. 4, 8, 11, 13, 14. New York: The Macmillan Company, 1961.

C. L. Harriss, *The American Economy*, 4th ed., Chaps. 5, 6, 7, 23, 24. Homewood, Ill.: Richard D. Irwin, Inc., 1962.

L. W. Weiss, *Economics and American Industry*, Chaps. 5, 6, 7, 8, 11. New York: John Wiley & Sons, Inc., 1961.

Part VI

Resource Pricing and Income Distribution

20

Purely Competitive
Resource Markets

Throughout the discussion of product pricing the question of resource pricing has been creeping in through the back door, which is not at all surprising since the two are intimately connected. Together with a firm's production function, resources prices determine costs of production, and costs affect commodity prices to the extent that they influence product supply. But the causal relationship works the other way as well. The conditions of product demand exert an influence on resource demand and so affect resource prices. The demand for resources is a derived demand—derived from demand for the product.

Like product markets, resource markets may also be competitive or noncompetitive (i.e., in reality they more closely approximate one or the other type). The following scheme displays the combinations possible.

	Resource Market		Conditions on the Product Market
	Sellers	*Buyers*	
Type I	Competitive	Competitive	Competitive Product Selling
Type II	Competitive	Competitive	Noncompetitive Product Selling
Type III	Noncompetitive	Competitive	Either
Type IV	Competitive	Noncompetitive	Either
Type V	Noncompetitive	Noncompetitive	Either

In principle, a given resource market may be characterized by competition on the part of both buyers and sellers, on the part of one but not the other, or on the part of neither. Moreover, the degree of competition on the resource market is not determined solely by the presence or absence of competitive product selling. Competition or monopoly in one market does not necessarily entail the same type of structure in the other market. The present chapter is devoted to Type I: competitive resource and product markets.

Chapter 21 will single out the other types for investigation. Since we are interested in the question of the pricing of resources and their allocation among different *industries*, our orientation will be that of resource demand by a given industry and resource supply to a given industry.

RESOURCE DEMAND

The fundamental starting point for any problem in pricing is shown in Fig. 2.2 of Chapter 2. There it was seen that households demand products and supply resources. Firms, on the other hand, supply products and demand resources. Utility analysis formed the central axiom of consumer demand, and it will provide the theoretical core of labor supply. Production analysis, the firm's production function, formed the central axiom of product supply. Likewise, it will also stand at the heart of resource demand.

Theory of the Firm

Pure competition in any resource market is defined formally in the same way as pure competition in any product market, except that the firm is a buyer rather than a seller. Since the single firm is but one of many buyers, the resource price is beyond its control. The selling of a resource is also assumed to be competitive, so no one seller can affect the price. Since aggregate market forces determined by all buyers and sellers acting together establish the resource price, the decision of a single firm reduces to the quantity it will employ.

Conditions of Profit Maximization. As in all previous discussion the firm is assumed to maximize total profit.[1] Our earlier examination of the firm's output decision raised the question "How much is added to cost and how much to revenue by a one-unit increase in output?" The analogous question here is "How much is added to cost and how much to revenue by a one-unit increase in a resource input?" If an additional unit of the resource adds more to revenue than to cost, the firm's profit will increase; if it adds more to cost than to revenue, profit will decrease.

This "addition to total cost by a small increase in a resource input" has been given a label. It is called the *marginal factor cost* of the resource or factor of production. In symbolic notation for a factor A the expression

$$\text{MFC}_a = \frac{\Delta \text{TC}}{\Delta a}$$

is read: the marginal factor cost of A is the change in the firm's total cost, ΔTC, which results from an increment in the employment of A, Δa. Normally, Δa is taken as equal to one. Similarly, a concept has been devised to

[1] Obviously, if the firm's goal is profit maximization, this goal applies to resource buying no less than to product selling. We are merely continuing to trace the consequences of the assumption, this time with reference to buying decisions rather than selling decisions.

describe changes in total revenue due to changes in the employment of a resource. For resource A,

$$MRP_a = \frac{\Delta TR}{\Delta a}$$

states that the *marginal revenue product* of A is defined as the change in total revenue, ΔTR, corresponding to an increment of A, Δa, where Δa is equal to one.

For any type of firm, whether it buys resources competitively or not, profit maximization entails the equating of these two magnitudes. That is, it can be shown that the marginal factor cost of any one resource will rise, or at least remain constant, as more of that resource is employed. The marginal revenue product of any resource, on the other hand, will decline as more is used. Consequently, if marginal revenue product exceeds marginal factor cost, the firm will expand its employment of the resource because this means more is added to revenue than to cost, thus increasing profit. In the process of expansion, marginal revenue product declines. However, as long as it is greater than marginal factor cost, by continuing to expand employment of the resource, the firm can still increase profit (even if by a smaller amount).[2] Expansion of the input will cease at that quantity of the input for which marginal factor cost equals marginal revenue product. Why? Because a further addition of the input would cause marginal revenue product to fall below marginal factor cost, thus shrinking profit. It follows that the firm's equilibrium employment of any one resource, again call it A, is that quantity at which

$$MFC_a = MRP_a$$

Let us proceed to this result more slowly. In particular, for the remainder of this chapter we shall limit ourselves to the study of a firm that buys its resources competitively. From the viewpoint of the firm the price of each resource is given. Suppose a particular resource A has an established price of \$2. Employment of one more unit will add \$2 to the firm's total cost regardless of how much or how little the firm employs. Expansion of a from 1 to 2 units raises total cost by \$2; expansion from 1,000 to 1,001 likewise raises cost by \$2. Since the resource price is viewed by the firm as constant, at any quantity of A it is precisely an amount equal to the given price that is added to total cost by a one-unit increase in A. Therefore, the marginal factor cost of A becomes a constant equal to the given price of A:

$$MFC_a = \bar{p}_a$$

where the bar signifies that the price of A is constant.

---

[2] Note the similarity to output decisions. As long as marginal revenue exceeds marginal cost, additional output adds more to revenue than to cost, increasing profit. With marginal cost rising and marginal revenue falling or constant, it pays to expand output even though a smaller amount is added to profit.

The behavior of marginal revenue product as the firm varies its employment of A can be seen most clearly by treating it as a process in two steps— by conceptually isolating two things that really happen simultaneously. First, when one unit of A is added there will be some change in output, given the amounts of other resources used. But this is nothing other than the marginal physical product of A. Second, there will be a change in the firm's revenue resulting from the sale of the additional output, and this is by definition the firm's marginal revenue. Putting these two steps together we have

$$\text{MRP}_a = \frac{\Delta x}{\Delta a} \cdot \frac{\Delta \text{TR}}{\Delta x} = \text{MPP}_a \cdot \text{MR}_x$$

where x denotes the quantity of the product X produced by the firm.

Not only resource buying but product selling on the part of the firm is assumed to be purely competitive. Consequently, marginal revenue in this case is equal to price, viewed as constant by the firm. Now comes more terminology! When MR_x is replaced by p_x, instead of the general term *marginal revenue product* (which applies whether marginal revenue is constant or not) the term *value of the marginal product* is applied. That is,

$$\text{VMP}_a = \text{MPP}_a \cdot \bar{p}_x$$

where the bar denotes that the product price is constant.

Here is where we once more encounter the law of diminishing returns. The MPP_a may at first increase as a increases, but after some point it will decline. Therefore, VMP_a must also decrease. What emerges for the firm purchasing A competitively is a constant marginal factor cost and diminishing value of marginal product. Its equilibrium condition becomes

$$\bar{p}_a = \text{MPP}_a \cdot \bar{p}_x$$

The quantity of A at which this equation is satisfied is the quantity that will be employed at the given price of A.

Before proceeding to a discussion of resource demand one important caution should be mentioned. It would be a mistake to interpret this equilibrium condition as something different from the profit-maximizing condition described earlier in connection with product pricing. It is the same condition, merely looked at from a different angle. To demonstrate, recall the discussion of marginal cost in Chapter 10. With A treated as the variable input and B a fixed input, it was shown that marginal cost turns out to be equal to the given price of A divided by the marginal physical product of A:

$$\text{MC} = \frac{\bar{p}_a}{\text{MPP}_a}$$

In order to maximize profit the firm produces the output at which $\text{MC} = p_x$.

Therefore p_x can be substituted for MC in the above expression, yielding

$$p_x = \frac{\bar{p}_a}{\text{MPP}_a}$$

But notice this is nothing other than a way of rewriting the firm's equilibrium condition with respect to the employment of A (rewritten by dividing both sides of that equation by MPP_a).

Indeed, for several variables inputs (call them A, B, C, etc.), the expression

$$\frac{p_a}{\text{MPP}_a} = \frac{p_b}{\text{MPP}_b} = \frac{p_c}{\text{MPP}_c} = \cdots = p_x = \text{MC}$$

is a general statement of profit maximization by a competitive firm. Equating marginal cost of output to marginal revenue is tantamount to equating marginal factor cost to marginal revenue product for each input used. One implies the other. The firm's equilibrium output entails a unique combination of inputs used to produce that output. In connection with resource pricing we are concentrating on the quantities of resources employed rather than the output produced.

Resource Demand.   Symbolically, for a firm using two resources, A and B, purchased competitively to produce a product X sold competitively, the equilibrium conditions are written

(1) $$\bar{p}_a = \text{MPP}_a \cdot \bar{p}_x$$

(2) $$\bar{p}_b = \text{MPP}_b \cdot \bar{p}_x$$

We shall assume provisionally that the quantity of B is fixed at b_1 units. With A the only variable input, the firm need only consider equation (1). The problem becomes one of finding out how the firm will vary its input of A as the price of A is allowed to vary. This is equivalent to asking how the value of the marginal product of A changes as the firm varies its input of A.

Column 1 in Table 20.1 shows various alternative inputs of A, and column 2 records the total output corresponding to each possible quantity of A combined with the fixed quantity of B. In other words, columns 1 and 2 record the firm's total product schedule. Column 3 is the marginal physical product schedule of A; it reveals that MPP_a rises at first, reaches a maximum at 2 units of A, and declines thereafter. In other words, it states the law of diminishing returns. Column 4 indicates that the product price is given as $2, independent of the firm's output. Finally, column 5 records the computed value of the marginal product of A. It is this that is to be equated to the price of A. Thus, if the price of A were $4, the firm would employ 8 units of A per day because this is the quantity of A that maximizes profit or minimizes loss.

Instead of a single given price of A, consider alternative prices with which the firm might be faced. By equating the value of the marginal product of

Table 20.1

1	2	3	4	5 = 3 × 4
Quantity of A per Day *a*	Total Output per Day *x*	Marginal Physical Product of A MPP*a*	Product Price *p_x*	Value of the Marginal Product of A VMP*a*
0	0		$2.00	
1	4.5	4.5	2.00	$ 9
2	9.5	5.0	2.00	10
3	14.0	4.5	2.00	9
4	18.0	4.0	2.00	8
5	21.5	3.5	2.00	7
6	24.5	3.0	2.00	6
7	27.0	2.5	2.00	5
8	29.0	2.0	2.00	4
9	30.5	1.5	2.00	3
10	31.5	1.0	2.00	2
11	32.0	.5	2.00	1
12	32.0	0	2.00	0

A to the price of A, by satisfying equation (1), that is, a quantity of A is determined for each different price. Prices of $1 through $10 are measured on the vertical axis of Fig. 20.1. The quantity of A per day is measured on the horizontal axis, and the curve labeled VMP$_a$ is a plot of the quantity that satisfies equation (1) at each price. When the firm enters the stage of diminishing returns, the curve becomes negatively sloped. At each point on

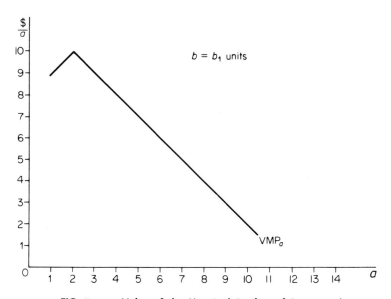

FIG. 20.1.   Value of the Marginal Product of Resource A

the VMP_a curve the firm is in equilibrium. Starting at any one point on the negatively sloped segment, if the price of A were to fall, equation (1) would no longer be satisfied. Since the product price is constant, the firm can restore equilibrium only by reducing MPP_a. This can in turn be done only by moving downward and to the right along its MPP_a curve, thus increasing a.

If the firm uses only two inputs, *and if* the quantity of B is in fact fixed so the firm is in fact operating in the short run, *then a VMP_a curve is the firm's demand curve for A*. For with all other inputs fixed this curve shows the quantity of A employed at each alternative price of A.[3] Its negative slope can be traced to the law of diminishing returns. The faster is the rate of diminishing returns (the steeper is the firm's MPP_a curve) the less price elastic will be its demand curve for A. With a given drop in p_a it takes a smaller increase in a to get MPP_a down far enough to restore equilibrium.

This "general" conclusion, however, must be qualified. For one thing, we must consider the firm's long run when all inputs are variable. For another, it requires that *all* other inputs be fixed. A firm using three inputs (say A, B, and C) will be in the short run if C is fixed even though both A and B are variable. Since the analysis gets more complex as we allow for more variable resources, let us approach the problem by retaining the assumption that two inputs are used. If we then allow both A and B to be variable, we are in effect discussing the firm's long-run demand for both A and B. But nothing is lost by concentrating on A because the same arguments apply to B.

With both A and B variable the equilibrium quantities of A and B must be such as to satisfy both equations (1) and (2). And, in deriving the demand curve for either input, allowance must be made for variations in the other. Choosing A for analysis, Fig. 20.2 reproduces the VMP_a curve already obtained in Fig. 20.1. It is, of course, drawn for B fixed at b_1 units. Suppose the price of A is \$7, at which price the firm employs 5 units of A and b_1 units of B because these are the values of a and b that satisfy equations (1) and (2). The firm is at point P_1.

Now suppose the price of A were to drop to \$6. The firm can be viewed as it it moves along this VMP_a curve, using 6 of A and b_1 of B. This alteration in a would restore equality in equation (1). However, and this is where the analysis differs from the previous case, the increase in a will have an effect also on equation (2). We saw in Chapter 9 that the marginal physical product curve of any one resource is drawn for a fixed amount of others. The resource B has an MPP_b curve drawn for a fixed quantity of A. The marginal physical product of B that satisfied equation (2) at the starting point (with p_a = \$7) was obtained as the point on the MPP_b curve corresponding to $b = b_1$. This entire MPP_b curve was drawn for $a = 5$. Now when a changes, B's product curve will shift position, and this throws the second equilibrium condition out of balance. If A and B are complementary re-

---

[3] Strictly speaking, outputs beyond the shutdown point (where MC = AVC) are required if the firm is to employ any A at all. Since the MC curve is positively sloped over this relevant output range, the VMP_a curve must be negatively sloped. So the positively sloped segment can be ignored.

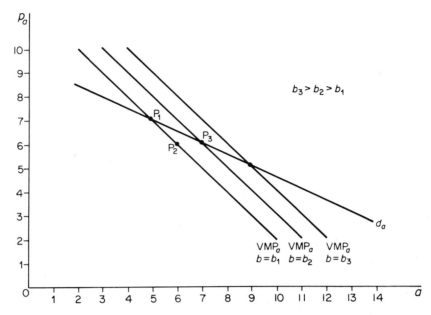

FIG. 20.2.   Demand Curve for Resource A by a Single Firm: A and B Complementary Inputs

source inputs, an increase in the use of A will shift the entire MPP_b curve upward, i.e., MPP_b becomes larger for $b = b_1$.

Let us assume A and B are complementary inputs. Then the process goes something like this. Initially, the price of A is \$7, the product price and the price of B are given, and the firm employs 5 units of A and b_1 units of B. Now the price of A falls to \$6.

> STEP I: Since p_a is lower and p_x is constant, equation (1) is no longer satisfied for $a = 5$. To restore equilibrium MPP_a must be reduced. With diminishing returns the firm moves along its MPP_a curve to $a = 6$, where $MPP_a = 3.0$ and $VMP_a = \$6$ (see Table 19.1).
>
> STEP II: As a is increased from 5 to 6, this shifts the MPP_b curve upward. Equation (2) was satisfied for $b = b_1$, but now MPP_b is higher for $b = b_1$. With p_b and p_x unchanged, MPP_b is too high and equation (2) no longer holds.
>
> STEP III: To restore equation (2), MPP_b must be reduced by moving downward and to the right along the new higher MPP_b curve, i.e., by increasing b. This in turn shifts the MPP_a curve upward, which means the firm moves over to a new VMP_a curve, one lying farther to the right in Fig. 20.2.

As a consequence of this series of interactions the firm will move, not to point P_2, but rather to a point like P_3 on a higher VMP_a curve. It is only with a greater quantity of B, and therefore with more than 6 units of A, that equations (1) and (2) are again both satisfied. In this example, b increases from b_1 to b_2 units when the price of A drops from \$7 to \$6, and the employment of A rises by more than one unit (it rises from 5 to 7 rather than 5 to 6). The demand curve for A when B is also variable is not a VMP_a curve. In the diagram it is the curve labeled d_a, which passes through higher and higher VMP_a curves as lower prices of A are considered. Consequently, it is more price elastic than any one VMP_a curve at any given price of A.

The same analysis holds if A and B are substitutes rather than complements in production. Only one modification is required: as a is increased the MPP_b curve shifts *downward* instead of upward, causing *less* of B to be used, with the effect that VMP_a curves lying farther to the right in Fig. 20.2 are drawn for less B, not more B. A diagram like Fig. 20.2 still applies. The firm's demand curve for A passes through successively higher VMP_a curves as lower prices of A are considered, but each higher VMP_a curve entails a smaller quantity of B.

What is the essential point of the analysis? Simply this: Any demand curve (for a product or resource) is defined as a locus of points showing the quantity taken at each price, given other *prices* among other variables. But a VMP_a curve holds constant not only the price of B but also its quantity. Consistent usage of the term *demand curve* requires that a resource demand curve be drawn for constant prices, not quantities, of other resources unless their quantities are in fact fixed. Therefore, the demand function for A on the part of the firm is written symbolically as

$$a_d = d(p_a, p_b, p_x, f)$$

where a_d denotes the quantity of A demanded and f denotes the firm's production function. Since the quantity demanded depends upon all the variables in the parentheses, the notation corresponding to the demand curve is

$$a_d = d(p_a, \bar{p}_b, \bar{p}_x, \bar{f})$$

As usual, the bars over the variables mean those variables are held constant, giving a relationship between a_d and p_a. Changes in these "barred" variables will shift the demand curve for A. In the *special* case in which b is in fact fixed, b is also included as a "barred" variable, yielding one VMP_a curve as the demand curve for A.

By the same reasoning we also obtain the firm's demand curve for B:

$$b_d = d(p_b, \bar{p}_a, \bar{p}_x, \bar{f})$$

Indeed, the entire explanation could just as well have been carried through for B instead of A. Nothing is changed by substituting the letter B for the letter A.

Beyond questions of consistent language, there are more substantive reasons for conceptually holding other resource prices constant on a given demand curve. They concern the effects of substitutes and complements in production. We shall postpone this topic until we come to examine the industry. Before leaving the firm that sells its product competitively, however, we should pay deserved attention to the case of more than two variable inputs. The foundations are already laid. Unless one makes very broad resource classifications, such as capital and labor, the firm will be viewed as employing several inputs. Suppose we consider three variable inputs: A, B, and C, where A and B are complementary inputs and A and C are substitutes. The firm might use other inputs as well, but if so they are assumed to be fixed. Let the price of A fall, so the firm moves downward to the right along a VMP_a curve (drawn for given amounts of B and C). Increased input of A shifts the MPP_b curve upward and the MPP_c curve downward. Given the product price, the VMP_b curve shifts to the right and the VMP_c curve to the left, so more B and less C are used at their given prices. Both of these changes, more B and less C, shift the MPP_a curve upward and the firm moves to a new VMP_a curve lying farther to the right. The resulting secondary increase in a again affects b and c. When all these complementary and substitute effects have worked themselves out and the firm once more reaches an equilibrium position at the lower price of A, it will employ more A, more of any resources complementary with A, and less of any resources that are substitutes for A. A rise in the price of A will have just the opposite effects. These readjustments and recombinations of resources are effects *internal* to the firm. The final outcome, concerning the demand curve for any one resource, is that it deviates from a value of marginal product curve in the way indicated in Fig. 20.2. Movements along the demand curve for any one resource allow for adjustments in the quantities of other variable inputs but not their prices.

Theory of the Industry

The problem of arriving at a resource demand curve for a single firm, and the equally important problem of identifying the variables held constant on a given demand curve, took into account only those reactions regarded as *internal* to the firm. In this connection, recall the discussion of competitive product pricing. There it was shown that attainment of an industry product supply curve required a consideration of *external* effects. It should come as no surprise, therefore, that the industry demand curve for a resource must also take account of effects external to the firm but internal to the industry.

Resource Demand. Because the firm is small relative to the size of the industry, one can draw a firm's resource demand curve under the assumption that the product price is given. But since the industry taken as a whole does indeed influence the product price, the industry demand curve cannot take the product price as constant. As a resource price changes and all member firms respond to the price change, the entire industry expands or contracts output and the product price in turn changes. This is an effect external to any one member firm, causing the resource demand curves of all firms to shift position as the entire industry varies output in response to a lower or higher resource price.

In the left panel of Fig. 20.3 is drawn the demand curve d_a, one firm's demand curve for the resource A. In the right panel is depicted the demand curve for A by the industry, D_a. Suppose, to begin, that the price of A is p_1. The equilibrium quantity employed by the firm is a_1 units, and the industry employs a_4 units—the sum of the quantities employed by all member firms.

What would happen if the price of A should drop to p_0? By reference to the left panel it is seen that the firm would increase employment from a_1 to a_3 units *if the product price were to remain constant*. In actuality, as this firm begins to expand its input of A and other firms do likewise, the industry output will increase. That is the lower resource price causes cost curves to shift downward, thus shifting the industry supply curve of the product to

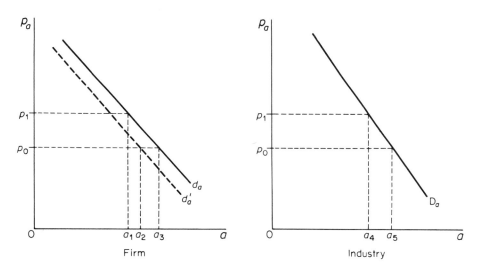

FIG. 20.3.   **Firm and Industry Demand Curves for a Resource**

the right. Given the market demand curve for the product (negatively sloped, of course) the product price will drop. As the product price begins falling the resource demand curves of the individual firms begin shifting to the left. Why? The value of the marginal product is smaller for any given quantity of A ($\text{VMP}_a = \text{MPP}_a \cdot p_x$ and p_x is lower, so VMP_a is smaller at any given quantity of A).

These are the external effects. In response to a lower resource price, as all firms simultaneously increase their resource inputs and hence output, they impose external effects upon each other, effects that must be taken into account in determining the final outcome for the industry. In Fig. 20.3 we assume the firm's demand curve shifts from d_a to d_a'. Given the fall in price from p_1 to p_0, the firm re-establishes a new equilibrium at a_2 rather than a_3 units because of the consequent fall in the product price. The industry demand curve for A takes into account this restricted expansion of a. At p_0

the industry employs a_5 units of A—the sum of quantities like a_2 rather than a_3. Movements along the industry demand curve for a resource incorporate effects internal to the industry but external to any single firm, thus allowing for shifts in the demand curves of the member firms.

To emphasize the distinction, let us put the subscript I on the resource demand functions of Firm I using A and B to produce X:

$$a_d = d_{\mathrm{I}}(p_a,\ p_b,\ p_x,\ f_{\mathrm{I}})$$

$$b_d = d_{\mathrm{I}}(p_b,\ p_a,\ p_x,\ f_{\mathrm{I}})$$

Here f_{I} denotes the production function of Firm I. For the industry as a whole the product price, p_x, is replaced by the *market demand curve* for X, D_x. The industry resource demand functions are written:

$$a_d = d(p_a,\ p_b,\ D_x,\ f_{\mathrm{I}},\ f_{\mathrm{II}},\ \cdots)$$

$$b_d = d(p_b,\ p_a,\ D_x,\ f_{\mathrm{I}},\ f_{\mathrm{II}},\ \cdots)$$

They include the production functions of each of the firms in the industry. The corresponding notations for the industry resource demand *curves* install bars over all variables but p_a in the parenthesis of the first expression, and over all but p_b in the second. This is tantamount to saying that the industry demand curve for any one input allows for external effects on the firms. For it allows the product price to change as one moves along an industry resource demand curve. But these price changes are those that occur by moving along the product demand curve because the product demand curve is conceptually held stationary.

This is not just an academic exercise in logic, for some rather important practical consequences follow. Since the product demand curve is negatively sloped, so must the demand curve for each resource be negatively sloped. Moreover, the price elasticity of the industry demand curve for any one resource depends upon the price elasticity of the market demand curve for the product. Price elasticity also depends upon the rate of diminishing returns in the industry. But given the production functions of the member firms, the more price elastic is the demand for output the more price elastic will be the industry demand for inputs. The more price elastic is the demand for the product the smaller will be the fall in the product price when the product supply increases because of a lower resource price. Therefore, the smaller will be the leftward shift of individual demand curves, which is the force operating to restrict employment expansion. Likewise, a given rise in a resource price will generate a larger decrease in employment the more price elastic is the product demand curve.

Changes in Resource Demand. To ask what changes resource demand is to ask how the variables held constant on a demand curve will cause the demand curve to shift. First, an increase in consumer demand for the product of the industry will increase the demand for all inputs used to produce the product. The product price faced by each firm rises; in turn the value of the marginal product of each resource rises. At any given resource price the firm will wish to employ more. Since the resource demand curves of each firm shift to the right, so will the industry demand curve.

Second, a change in the production functions of the firms will change resource demand. Unlike a change in product demand, a technological change that alters production functions will not necessarily operate in the same direction for all resource inputs. Generally speaking, a change in the state of technology that raises the marginal physical productivity of all resources will also increase the industry demand for all resources. For if the marginal physical product curve of each shifts upward, VMP curves shift to the right, the demand curves of each firm shift to the right, and the industry demand curves shift to the right. Nevertheless, in some instances, for some types of technological change, the marginal physical product curves of some resources may be lowered, even though others are raised. Then the industry demand for those resources will decrease while the demand for others increase. Is not the popular notion of "technological unemployment" therefore subject to analytical interpretation?

Third, changes in the prices of other resources will alter the demand for one. How demand changes is a question of complements and substitutes in production. Consider two inputs A and B. If they are complements in production (raw material and labor for example), then a lower price of B will increase the demand for A, and vice versa. As the price of B falls and the industry moves downward to the right along the demand curve for B, more of A will also be employed at any given price of A. Hence, the demand curve for A shifts to the right. On the other hand, if A and B are substitutes in production (some types of machines and labor, or two different kinds of labor), then a lower price of B will decrease the demand for A, and vice versa. Notice that the treatment of complements and substitutes in production is logically and conceptually the same as the treatment of final products that are complements or substitutes in consumption.

RESOURCE SUPPLY

In order to analyze resource supply in a competitive market it is useful to distinguish between human and nonhuman resources, for their determinants of supply differ. Nonhuman resources are either produced by some other firms (tools, power, raw materials, etc.) or they are "natural" resources that are not produced in the narrow sense of the word. However, even these so-called natural resources do entail costs: improvement and maintenance of land to make it fit for productive use, control and pumping of water for productive operations, etc. Consequently, the theory of cost and product supply is applicable. The services of human resources are generally termed labor. And the question of greater or smaller quantities supplied hinges on considerations other than cost of production.

Nonhuman Resources

At the outset it is important to recognize one distinction being made. Since we are ultimately interested in the allocation of resources among industries, discussion of resource demand focused on the demand by one industry—even though there may be other industries demanding the same resources in the same market. The related task in connection with supply is to determine the supply to that one industry in order to find the industry equilibrium. Given the supply conditions of individual sellers, there will result a total supply to the entire *market*, i.e., a supply to all buyers regardless of industry—regardless of the products resource buyers produce. From this market supply the supply curves pertaining to each industry can be derived.

A particular item may be regarded as a resource input from the viewpoint of one firm, yet it is regarded as a final output by another. With slight modifications the theory of product pricing applies. If the industry producing, say, B is purely competitive, the theory of the competitive firm sets the foundation for market supply. Instead of calling the product X, as we did in Chapters 12 and 13, we merely designate it as B. It follows that the short-run supply curve of an individual producer of B is that firm's marginal cost curve above average variable cost. The short-run supply curve to the *market* as a whole is the horizontal summation of all the firms' marginal cost curves, so the short-run market supply curve of B is positively sloped. Whether the long-run supply curve of B is positively sloped, horizontal, or negatively sloped depends upon whether the competitive industry producing B is one of increasing cost, constant cost, or decreasing cost respectively. In short, the theory of a competitive industry provides the analysis of supply to the resource market as a whole.

Next, what about the supply to one industry, the industry producing X, for example? This is where the "slight modifications" enter. Given the supply curve of the industry producing B, the supply curve to the entire resource market, what will be the supply curve of B to the industry producing X? As we saw in Chapters 12 and 13, the supply curve to the market is drawn for given prices of the resources used by the industry producing B and a given state of technology in the industry producing B. In addition to these variables the supply curve of B to one industry (such as that producing X) holds constant the price of B paid in other industries buying B as an input. Suppose, for simplicity, we assume there are only two other industries purchasing B in the resource market: the industry producing Y and the industry producing Z. Then the supply curve of B to the industry producing X holds constant the price of B in industry Y and the price of B in industry Z.

To determine the shape of the supply curve to industry X, two cases must be distinguished.

> CASE I.   Industry X is so small relative to the size of the re-
> source market that the price of B is not affected by a change in
> the employment of B by industry X. Then industry X is like a

single competitive firm facing the product market or, more exactly, like a single consumer in the product market. The price of B is given to the industry as a whole as well as to each firm in the industry. This is another way of saying the supply curve of B to the industry X is infinitely price elastic (horizontal) regardless of the shape of the supply curve of B to the resource market as a whole.

CASE II. Industry X is sufficiently large relative to the size of the resource market, so the supply curve of B to industry X may be taken as having the same general shape as the supply curve of B to the entire resource market. As a consequence, if the industry producing B is in its short-run position, the supply curve of B to industry X is positively sloped. In the event that the industry producing B is a constant-cost industry, the long-run supply curve of B to the market is horizontal and so is the long-run supply curve to industry X. If the industry producing B is an increasing-cost industry, its long-run supply curve to industry X is positively sloped, and it is negatively sloped if the industry producing B is a decreasing-cost industry.

Human Resources

Human resource services are supplied directly by households. Since the theory of utility explains a single household's allocation of its income among various commodities, it is only one small step to the utility analysis of labor supply. One person can supply more or less labor only by varying the hours he works. If *leisure* is defined as nonworking time including sleep, then given the number of hours in a day (or week or year), when one works more hours he does so at the sacrifice of leisure time. Indeed, leisure is a kind of "commodity." Satisfaction obtained from the time people have to amuse, enjoy, and educate themselves is no less relevant than the satisfaction obtained from salami sandwiches. Such items as Ping-Pong tables, cigars, or haircuts are procured by exchanging money income for them over the counter, so to speak. Leisure as a consumer good differs only in the way it has to be bought. One gives up income, but it is done by working fewer hours at remunerative employment. The exchange of money for a good is still there, hidden by the way the transfer is accomplished.

A utility comparison can be made between leisure on the one hand and the bundle of all other consumer goods on the other. Consider a laborer employed in a given industry. What he consumes, excluding leisure, can be represented by his money income at given product prices, because with given product prices his bundle of real goods will increase or decrease as his money income rises or falls. Figure 20.4 depicts the person's preferences for leisure and all other goods, represented by money income. On the vertical axis is measured leisure in hours per day. The horizontal axis measures money income per day from employment. Sticking with our assumptions of Chapter 5, the utility indifference curves are the usual kind: negatively sloped, convex to the origin, and nonintersecting. Likewise, as before, the individual is assumed to maximize total utility subject to a constraint.

The "budget constraint" must take account of the price of leisure. The price or cost per unit of leisure is the wage rate, because the amount of income given up to get one hour of leisure is the wage rate obtainable from working one hour. The constraint expresses the combinations of income and leisure attainable at a given wage rate. Suppose the prevailing wage rate is $2 per hour, yielding the budget line labeled I in Fig. 20.4. If this laborer works

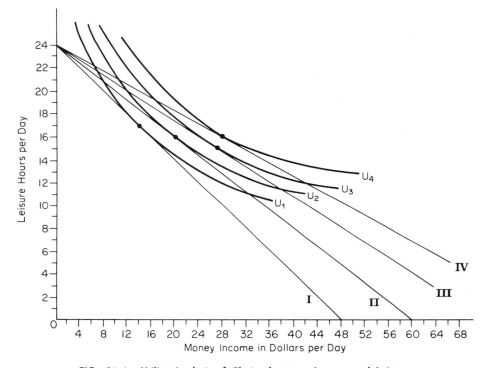

FIG. 20.4. Utility Analysis of Choice between Income and Leisure

zero hours, he can have 24 hours of leisure but no money income. So the line intersects the vertical axis at 24 hours, the upper limit of attainable leisure hours per day. At the other extreme, if he consumes no leisure (works 24 hours per day at $2 per hour), he can earn $48 per day. He can also choose any other combination on the line, such as 14 hours of leisure and $20 of income from 10 hours of work. The rate at which he can substitute leisure for income (the slope of the budget line) is determined by the prevailing wage rate.[4]

[4] The slope of the budget line equals minus the ratio of the price of income to the price of leisure (the wage rate). But since the price of income is equal to unity (the price of a dollar of income is a dollar), the wage rate alone determines the rate of substitution.

Given this wage rate, the individual maximizes utility by choosing 17 hours of leisure per day and $14 money income. In other words he works 7 hours per day. This may seem strange considering that employment contracts usually stipulate the length of the working day. But keep in mind that the units on the axes could just as well have been expressed in hours per year and yearly income, so the worker can choose to work 7 hours per day on the average by means of absenteeism. By the same interpretation the analysis applies to salaried personnel who can vary their working hours by absenteeism and nonpaid vacations. It is only the degree of flexibility in the choice of working hours that is affected by an employment contract.

Suppose, now, that the wage rate changes. If it rises to $2.50, the constraint will shift to the position labeled II. By working 24 hours and taking zero hours of leisure, the attainable money income becomes $60; for 10 hours of work and 14 hours of leisure the attainable income is $25 instead of $20, and so on. But the new line is not parallel to the old one. It rotates counterclockwise through the same point on the vertical axis, for the upper limit of attainable leisure is still 24 hours per day. Given his preferences, the laborer maximizes utility by choosing 16 hours of leisure and $20 per day money income. A rise in his wage rate means that leisure becomes more expensive relative to other goods, so other goods (money income) are substituted for leisure in his consumption pattern.

The same effect follows a rise in the wage rate to $3, yielding constraint III. But when the wage rises to $3.50 (constraint IV), utility maximization occurs at the combination of 16 hours leisure and 8 hours work, giving him $28 money income. How is the choice of more leisure explained? Note that a higher wage rate gives more *real* income for any given number of hours worked. Beyond some point the person chooses to take some of this higher real income in the form of leisure. He can have more of other goods without working more hours; indeed, he may actually work fewer hours because he regards the money income earned from fewer hours as sufficient to purchase the quantity of other goods he prefers. He can afford to take more time off. Another way of saying this is that he regards leisure as an inferior good at any wage rate up to $3. As his real income rises he consumes less leisure. But at higher real incomes he views leisure as a superior good; he consumes more of it when his real income rises.

Since hours of leisure and hours of work are simply two sides of the same coin, an individual's supply schedule of labor follows directly from the utility analysis. He can vary his labor offering to an industry only by varying the hours he will work at alternative wage rates. Table 20.2 records his choice at each wage rate, and is therefore his supply schedule of labor to the industry in which he is employed. Below $3 he supplies more hours at higher wage rates. Above $3 he supplies fewer hours at higher wage rates.

Diagrammatically, utility analysis gives rise to the famous *backward bending* individual supply curve of labor as depicted in Fig. 20.5. Given his employment in the industry in question, the individual's supply curve is posi-

Table 20.2

Wage Rate	Hours of Work per Day = 24 − Hours of Leisure
$2.00	7
2.50	8
3.00	9
3.50	8
4.00	7

tively sloped up to the wage rate W_1. At higher wage rates it is negatively sloped. This is not meant to imply that all individual supply curves change slope at the same wage rate. For some it may occur at a vastly higher or lower wage than it does for some others, depending upon their relative preferences for leisure and other goods.

Nor does utility analysis imply that the supply curve of labor faced by the industry as a whole must be backward bending, for the supply to the industry includes variations in the number of workers as well as variations in the hours supplied by each. We may safely assume the industry does affect the wage rate by the quantity of labor it employs. Then if the number of workers employed by the industry were fixed, the supply curve to the industry would be the horizontal summation of individual supply curves. Granted that the individual supply curves are backward bending, so too would the supply curve to the industry be backward bending above some wage rate, perhaps a very high one. However, allowance for increased numbers of workers applying for employment as the wage rate rises makes it highly probable that the supply curve to the industry will be positively sloped. A change in hours of labor supplied to the industry depends upon a change in hours by those already employed and upon a change in the number employed. Even if each worker already employed were on the backward bending segment of his supply curve, an increase in number of workers would tend to expand the total hours supplied to the industry as a higher wage

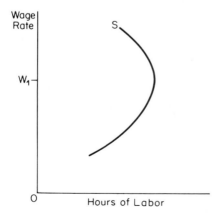

FIG. 20.5. Individual Labor Supply Curve

rate is offered. Therefore, we shall assume the supply curve of a particular type of labor to an industry is positively sloped.

Allowances for changes in the number of workers as one considers movements along a supply curve to the industry raises the question of the conditions of constancy under which it is drawn. For one thing, the size of the labor force is held constant. Here, since we are focusing on a particular type of labor as a resource input, the labor force refers to an available pool of this type, such as machinists, market research analysts, or managers. In turn, the size of this labor force depends heavily upon population and the prevailing level of education in society. The available labor force plays a role similar to the supply to the entire resource market in the case of nonhuman resources. An expansion in the labor force will tend to increase the supply to each industry that uses this type of labor as a factor of production, i.e., it tends to, rather than does, increase supply because some industries might be unaffected. Very likely most industries would experience an increase in labor supply as the labor force grows. But some may not, depending upon occupational choice by individuals as they enter the labor force and the non-pecuniary attractiveness of work in different industries.

In addition, the supply curve to one industry holds constant conceptually the wage rates paid in other industries for the same type of labor. It is only as the wage rate rises in one industry relative to the wage rates paid in others that labor will be attracted to the industry in question. A change in wage rates paid in other industries will shift the supply curve to the one in question: to the left as other wage rates rise and to the right as they fall. The degree to which the supply curve shifts depends upon the degree of inter-industry labor mobility. In general, the more mobile is this type of labor, the greater will be the shift of the supply curve in response to changes in wage rates paid elsewhere. Moreover, the more mobile is this type of labor, the more wage elastic will be the supply curve to the industry in question as workers transfer employments in response to wage differentials.

Summary of Resource Supply

Let A represent a certain type of labor whose price, p_a, is a wage rate per hour. Let B represent a nonhuman resource input whose price is denoted by p_b. For simplicity, assume the industry producing a product X uses only two inputs, A and B, which are purchased and sold competitively. Moreover, suppose there are only two other industries that employ these same resources, namely, the industry producing Y and the industry producing Z. The supply functions to X for A and B respectively are expressed symbolically as follows:

$$a_s = s(p_a^X,\ p_a^Y,\ p_a^Z,\ L)$$

$$b_s = s(p_b^X,\ p_b^Y,\ p_b^Z,\ S_b)$$

Here a_s denotes manhours of labor supplied and b_s the quantity of B supplied per unit of time. In the first expression the superscripts X, Y, and Z on p_a mean that the prices are interpreted as the prices of A (the wage rates) in those industries respectively. The term L denotes the available labor force or quantity of this type of labor. In the second expression the superscripts refer to the prices of B in the respective industries, and S_b signifies the supply *curve* of B to the entire resource market.

The symbolic notations corresponding to the supply *curves* of A and B to the industry are:

$$a_s = s(p_a^X, \bar{p}_a^Y, \bar{p}_a^Z, \bar{L})$$
$$b_s = s(p_b^X, \bar{p}_b^Y, \bar{p}_b^Z, \bar{S}_b)$$

where the bars again mean the variables are held constant.

Of course, the impact of a change in any barred variable is interpreted in terms of a shift in the position of the supply curve. As L increases, the supply curve will shift to the right unless the industry is completely immune to an increased labor force, which is very unlikely. Likewise, a drop in p_a^Y or p_a^Z, given L, will increase the supply of A to industry X, and a rise in either or both will decrease the supply. The same effect holds for changes in p_b^Y or p_b^Z on the supply curve of B, given S_b. Finally, an increase in S_b, a shift to the right in the supply curve of B to the entire resource market will shift the supply curve to the right for industry X. Incidentally, the supply curves of B to industries Y and Z will also shift to the right, lowering p_b^Y and p_b^Z as well as p_b^X, given that demand curves are negatively sloped. But the net outcome will still be an increased supply to the industry X.

INDUSTRY EQUILIBRIUM

Now that the details of industry demand and supply have been presented, it is time to tie up loose ends. We shall concentrate on one resource at a time and on the determination of equilibrium for that resource in one industry. We shall also examine the simultaneous equilibrium position of a single demander and a single supplier of the resource in question.

Nonhuman Resources

Let B again designate the nonhuman resource in question, employed by the industry producing and selling a product X competitively. In discussing the equilibrium price and employment of B in industry X, we assume the competitive industry producing B is in long-run equilibrium.

CASE I.   If the industry producing X is only one of a very large number of buyers, purchasing B in a national market, for example, it may be so small relative to the size of the market that the industry cannot affect the price of B. The supply curve of B to the industry is infinitely price elastic, and the quantity employed by the industry is determined by the intersection of the industry demand curve with the horizontal supply curve. Under these conditions, a change in the demand for B on the part of industry X will have no effect upon the price of B.

CASE II. From an empirical viewpoint, unless very detailed industry classifications are used, most defined industries will likely be large enough to exert an influence on the resource market. Even in this instance, however, a resource price will be unchanged by an alteration in demand if the competitive industry producing B is a constant-cost industry. For them the supply curve of B to the entire resource market will be horizontal, and we may take the supply curve of B to any one industry as horizontal also. The only difference from Case I is that the supply curve of B to the entire resource market is also horizontal in this instance, whereas it need not be in Case I.

But suppose that the industry producing B is an increasing-cost industry, so the supply curve of B to the resource market and the supply curve to industry X are both positively sloped. The middle panel of Fig. 20.6 represents the industry equilibrium, given the industry demand curve (the un-

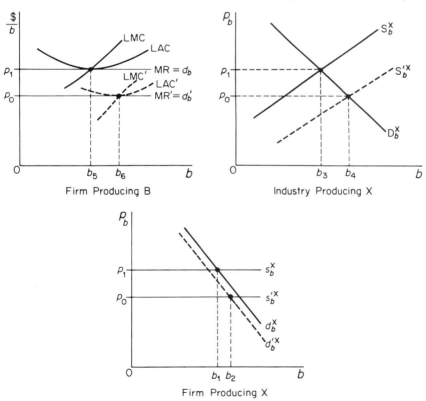

FIG. 20.6. Equilibrium Positions for a Resource B Produced Under Conditions of Increasing Cost

broken curve D_b^X) and the supply curve to the industry (the unbroken curve S_b^X). The equilibrium price of B is p_1 and the quantity used by the industry is b_3 units. Though the price of B is affected by changes in industry employment, it is not affected by any one firm producing X. Hence, the supply curve faced by one firm is still infinitely price elastic even though the supply curve to the industry is positively sloped. The supply curve of B to one firm in the industry X, the unbroken curve s_b^X in the right panel, is horizontal at the given price of p_1. With a demand curve d_b^X the firm maximizes profit by utilizing b_1 units of B. Shown in the left panel is one firm in the industry producing B. Like any purely competitive firm, the demand curve for its output (d_b in the diagram) is infinitely price elastic at the established price. Given its long-run cost curves, this firm produces b_5 units in order to maximize profit.

To illustrate a change in the industry equilibrium, assume there occurs a technological innovation in the industry producing B, and that the cost curves of all member firms shift downward. For instance, the cost curves of the firm depicted in the left panel drop from LAC and LMC to LAC′ and LMC′. As costs fall the long-run supply curve shifts to the right, to $S_b'^X$. The larger supply of B lowers the price to p_0 at which the industry X employs b_4 units. The single firm producing B reaches a new long-run equilibrium at b_6 units of output, where profit is again zero. What about one of the firms producing X? The supply curve of B faced by the firm is still horizontal, of course, but it is drawn at a height equal to the new price. In the right panel of Fig. 20.6 the supply $s_b'^X$, drawn for $p_b = p_0$, results in an increase from b_1 to b_2 units of B on the part of the firm. At b_2 units the firm's demand curve $d_b'^X$ intersects the new supply curve faced by the firm, i.e., at b_2 units the value of the marginal product of B equals the price p_0. (Query: Why does the demand curve of one firm shift to the left as a movement occurs along the industry demand curve for B?)

Finally, suppose the industry producing B is a decreasing-cost industry. The long-run supply curve to the market and to the industry X are negatively sloped. The equilibrium price-quantity combination is once more that at which quantity demanded equals quantity supplied, and the industry equilibrium is depicted in the middle panel of Fig. 20.7. Demand by the industry, D_b^X, and supply to the industry, S_b^X, determine a price of p_2 and industry employment of b_3 units. In the right panel it is seen that a single firm, confronted with a horizontal resource supply curve at a height equal to the price p_2, employs b_1 units. A single supplying firm, shown on the left, is in equilibrium at b_5 units of output.

Under these supply conditions an increase in the demand, a shift from D_b^X to $D_b'^X$, will have the effect of reducing the price of B. Following the increase in demand, short-run profits will attract additional firms to the industry producing B. As these firms enter, costs decrease because of economies internal to the industry but external to any one firm, as described in Chapter 13. At the new equilibrium price of p_1, the single producer of B supplies

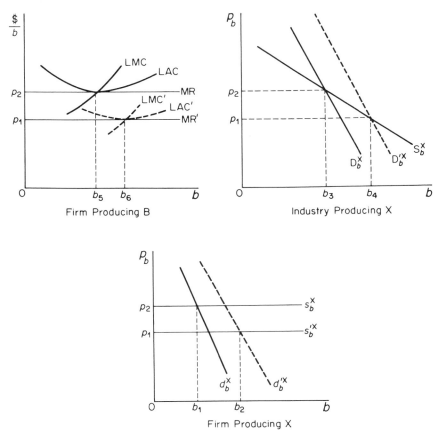

FIG. 20.7. Equilibrium Positions for a Resource B Produced Under Conditions
of Decreasing Cost

b_6 units. Since the price falls to p_1, the new supply curve faced by one firm producing X is infinitely price elastic at p_1. Given the firm's increase in demand (from d_b^X to $d_b'^X$) its employment of B expands from b_1 to b_2 units.

Human Resources

If a type of labor is bought and sold competitively, the same theoretical principles apply. In Fig. 20.8 the quantity of labor per unit of time is signified by a, and its wage rate by p_a. The middle panel again portrays the industry equilibrium: the price of labor or wage rate is p_2 and the quantity employed is a_2. Since one firm producing X cannot affect the price of labor, the supply curve to one firm is infinitely price elastic at the given price. A single firm with demand curve d_a^X is depicted in the right panel. Faced with the horizontal supply curve s_a^X, the firm employs a_1 units of this type of labor, where $p_a = \text{VMP}_a$. Likewise, an individual supplier cannot by his own actions influence the wage rate, so he views the demand for his labor as infinitely price elastic at whatever wage rate is established in the market. An individual supplier is shown in the left panel of Fig. 20.8. Given his supply curve, s_a, and the demand curve he faces, d_a, the individual supplies a_3 units.

Just as for nonhuman resources, the consequences of any change can be found. An increase in supply will lower the wage rate and increase employment, and a decrease in supply will have the opposite effects. An increase in

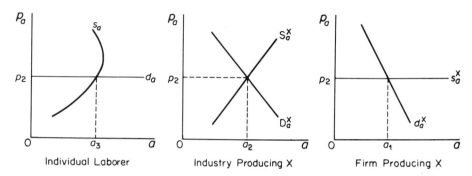

FIG. 20.8. Equilibrium Positions for a Particular Type of Labor

demand will raise the wage rate and expand employment, whereas a decrease in demand will lower the wage rate and reduce employment. Simultaneous changes in demand and supply may also occur, and the effects of one can be superimposed on the other to discover the net outcome for the industry.

PROBLEMS

1. Several variable inputs are used in the manufacture of clothing, which we shall assume is sold competitively under conditions of increasing cost. Among the resource inputs used by the clothing industry are raw material fabrics. Suppose fabrics are also bought and sold competitively, and are produced under conditions of increasing cost. For each of the following changes, trace the effects on the price and the quantity of fabrics used in the clothing industry:

(a) Decreased consumer demand for clothing.
(b) A technological innovation in the manufacture of clothing such that the marginal physical productivity of raw material fabrics rises.
(c) A reduction in the cost of producing fabrics (average and marginal cost curves of firms producing fabrics drop).

SUGGESTED READING

T. Scitovsky, *Welfare and Competition*, Chap. 7. Homewood, Ill.: Richard D. Irwin, Inc., 1951.

D. H. Robertson, "Wage Grumbles" in *Readings in the Theory of Income Distribution*, pp. 221–36. Philadelphia: The Blakiston Co., 1946.

G. J. Stigler, "The Economics of Minimum Wage Legislation," *American Economic Review* (1946).

C. L. Harriss, *The American Economy*, 4th ed., Chap. 27. Homewood, Ill.: Richard D. Irwin, Inc., 1962.

21

Noncompetitive Markets

Much of the groundwork for analysis of noncompetitive markets has already been laid. A firm's profit-maximizing condition with respect to a given resource A,

$$\text{MFC}_a = \text{MRP}_a = \text{MPP}_a \cdot \text{MR}_x$$

is quite general. One special case has been discussed—that called Type I at the outset of Chapter 20, in which p_a was substituted for MFC_a and p_x for MR_x. This chapter will analyze the remaining four types.

NONCOMPETITIVE PRODUCT SELLING

The market structure characterized as Type II is one in which the resource market is competitive on the part of both buyers and sellers, but the product market is not purely competitive. For a firm employing resources A and B to produce X, the equilibrium conditions are

$$(1) \quad \bar{p}_a = \text{MPP}_a \cdot \text{MR}_x$$

$$(2) \quad \bar{p}_b = \text{MPP}_b \cdot \text{MR}_x$$

Marginal revenue from the sale of X, MR_x, declines as larger outputs are produced, i.e., as larger quantities of inputs are employed.

Let us once more choose A for analysis and begin by assuming the quantity of B is fixed at b_1 units. In order to maximize profit the firm will employ the quantity of A at which equation (1) is satisfied. Table 21.1 illustrates the way in which the marginal revenue product of A varies as alternative employments of A are considered. Columns 1, 2, and 3 display the law of diminishing returns. The product price is recorded in column 4. Each entry shows the price at which the corresponding output can be sold; in other words, columns 2 and 4 together represent the demand schedule for the firm's output. Total revenue is computed in column 5 and marginal revenue in column 6. Finally, column 7 records the computation of the marginal revenue product of A. Therefore, if the price of A were to be $38, the firm would employ 3 units of A per day. Were the price of A to be $14, the firm would use 5 units of A per day.

Table 21.1

1	2	3	4	5 = 2 × 4	6	7 = 3 × 6
Quantity of A per Day	Total Output per Day	Marginal Physical Product of A	Product Price	Total Revenue	Marginal Revenue	Marginal Revenue Product of A
a	x	MPP_a	p_x	TR_x	MR_x	MRP_a
0	0			0		
1	10	10	$10.00	$100	$10.00	$100.00
2	22	12	7.00	154	4.50	54.00
3	32	10	6.00	192	3.80	38.00
4	40	8	5.40	216	3.00	24.00
5	46	6	5.00	230	$2.33\frac{1}{3}$	14.00
6	50	4	4.76	238	2.00	8.00

One aspect of Table 21.1 that differentiates it from Table 20.1 is the source of a declining marginal revenue product. Whereas the declining VMP_a of Table 20.1 was due entirely to diminishing returns, the declining MRP_a can be traced to two sources. Diminishing returns are reinforced by a declining marginal revenue. With only two inputs and with the quantity of B fixed, columns 1 and 7 comprise the firm's short-run demand schedule for A. A marginal revenue product curve for A is the firm's demand curve for A. Its negative slope is traceable to diminishing returns in the firm's production function and to a negatively sloped marginal revenue curve for output.

Suppose now that B is also variable; the firm is operating in the long run or it is in the short run with some third resource input fixed. Corresponding to each quantity of B is one marginal revenue product curve for A. Thus, in Fig. 21.1, MRP_a for $b = b_1$ is one possible marginal revenue product curve for A, MRP_a for $b = b_2$ (b_2 greater than b_1) is another, and so on. The curve labeled d_a is the firm's demand curve for A under the assumption that A and B are complementary inputs.

The reasons the demand curve is negatively sloped but more price elastic than any one marginal revenue product curve at a given price follow closely the reasons given in the case of purely competitive product selling. Starting at the equilibrium point P_1, let the price of A fall.

STEP I. Equation (1) is no longer satisfied at the initial quantity of A. To restore equality a is increased in order to reduce MPP_a. As a is increased and output expands MR_x also declines. The firm moves from P_1 to P_2 in Fig. 21.1.

STEP II. Two effects on equation (2) follow. By assumption of complementary inputs the MPP_b curve shifts upward, rais-

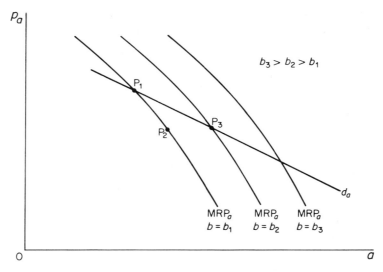

FIG. 21.1.   Demand Curve for Resource A by a Firm Selling Its Product Noncompetitively

ing MPP_b for $b = b_1$. In addition, MR_x is reduced. Unless these effects exactly offset each other, b must be varied because p_b is constant. Otherwise (2) is not satisfied. In this case the net effect of the increase in a is to raise the MRP_b and so increase the quantity of B employed.

STEP III.   This increase in b in turn reacts on MPP_a and MR_x, shifting the MPP_a curve upward and further reducing MR_x. Assuming the net effect is to raise MRP_a, there will be a further increase in a.

When all such interactions have worked themselves out, the firm moves to point P_3, where equations (1) and (2) are again both satisfied. In response to the lower price of A the firm uses more A and more B. Of course, had A and B been substitutes, the increase in a entailed by moving from P_1 to P_3 would result in a *downward* shift in the MPP_b curve, reducing the quantity of B used. Then the demand curve for A passes through MRP_a curves drawn for successively *smaller* quantities of B. A fall in the price of A generates more A and less B as A is substituted for B in production.

Again the conclusions regarding demand curves for both A and B can be summarized as follows:

$$a_d = d(p_a, \bar{p}_b, \overline{MR}_c, \bar{f})$$
$$b_d = d(p_b, \bar{p}_a, \overline{MR}_c, \bar{f})$$

These expressions, corresponding to resource demand curves, differ from the competitive ones in only one way. Here, MR_c is taken to mean the firm's marginal revenue *curve* for output, not marginal revenue at any one given output. On movements along one or the other resource demand curve the dollar magnitude of marginal revenue, MR_x, will vary. By moving along a resource demand curve the firm alters its output and thus moves along its marginal revenue curve. The curve itself, called MR_c, however, is assumed to be stationary.

It is not inconceivable that monopoly product pricing may persist even with competitive resource buying. Though a pure monopolist is the only buyer of resources in *this* industry, he may have to compete with other buyers belonging to other industries, so the resource price is beyond his control. In this event a process of aggregation from the firm to the industry is not needed. Demand for resources on the part of the firm is identical with demand on the part of the industry.

An oligopolistic industry may likewise purchase at least some resources competitively. With more than one firm in the industry, aggregation is relevant to the identification of industry demand. The resource demand curve of a single firm is drawn for a given marginal revenue curve, which implies a given share of the product market. If this share for each firm remains constant, the industry demand curve may be taken as the horizontal summation of the demand curves of the member firms. If, however, the firms jockey for position whenever resource prices change, the winners experience a shift to the right in their marginal revenue curves while the losers suffer a shift to the left. With marginal revenue curves shifting about, horizontal summation is impossible. Since it seems safe to assume that firms do not struggle for larger market shares *in response to changes in resource prices*, the industry demand can be closely approximated by horizontal summation. But one additional variable, the distribution of market shares, must be held constant on the industry demand curve.

The difference between Types I and II bears upon demand. For the remaining market types the supply conditions on the resource market are affected. Analyses of Types III, IV, and V will be carried out in terms of one input called B, regarded as a nonhuman, produced resource. Some of the general principles of noncompetitive resource pricing are applicable to human resources as well. Others must be modified somewhat when it is a question of labor markets, but we shall leave these modifications for the succeeding chapters.

MONOPOLY IN THE RESOURCE MARKET

Monopoly analysis, whether it refers to a product or a resource market, is governed by the same theoretical principles. A single seller controls supply and simultaneously determines output and price. In other words, the theory of monopoly product pricing is applicable to resource pricing without drastic alterations.

In order to isolate the effects of monopoly, it is assumed that the buying side of the resource market is purely competitive. In addition, we shall assume at first that there is only one industry using B as a factor of production. This simplifying assumption provides a convenient starting point. It means we can treat the market demand curve for B as identical to the demand curve of this industry. In the left panel of Fig. 21.2 is depicted the demand curve for resource B on the part of the competitive industry producing a commodity X, labeled D_b^X. Also shown is the marginal cost curve of the monopolistic producer of B. Since the monopolist faces a negatively sloped demand curve, he will maximize profit by equating marginal cost to marginal revenue. Thus he supplies b_3 units of B and charges a price of p_3.

The equilibrium position of a single buyer is illustrated in the right panel of Fig. 21.2. With a demand curve d_b^X, and with a perfectly price-elastic supply

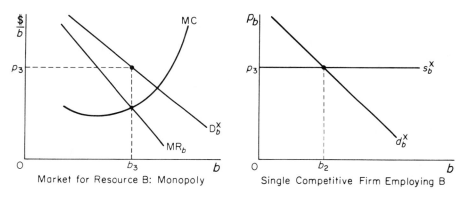

Market for Resource B: Monopoly   Single Competitive Firm Employing B

FIG. 21.2.

curve, s_b^X at a price of p_3, the firm's employment of B is b_2 units. Notice that the equilibrium representation for a single buyer is formally no different from that existing under pure competition on both the buying and selling sides of the resource market. However the resource price is determined on the market, a single firm takes the price as given and equates marginal revenue product to the established price. In contrast to a purely competitive resource market, the monopolist sets the market price, but the buying firm nevertheless faces a perfectly price-elastic supply curve.

We are now in a position to branch off into variations on this basic theme. Rather than one industry employing B, suppose there are several; say the competitive industries producing commodities Y, Z, etc., are also users of B. Then the monopolist has a market demand curve that is the aggregate of the demand curves of each of the buying industries. Corresponding to this aggregate demand curve is the monopolist's market marginal revenue curve. By equating his marginal cost to marginal revenue, the total output of B is determined. Now another question arises. Will the monopolist charge the same price to all users of B? This question is left as an exercise for the reader, with still another question put forth for consideration. What are the conditions under which the seller will engage in monopoly price discrimination?

The analysis summarized in Fig. 21.2 also provides a springboard into oligopoly pricing of resources. In place of a pure monopoly we can consider the case in which the industry producing B is comprised of few firms with the consequent interdependence of pricing and output policies. Then, as long as the buying side of the resource market is purely competitive, the theory of oligopoly product pricing is directly applicable.

MONOPSONY IN THE RESOURCE MARKET

Monopsony is monopoly turned on its head, so to speak—a single buyer rather than a single seller. Again we shall focus on price control existing on one side of the market, this time by assuming the selling side is purely competitive. As the only buyer, a monopsonist faces the entire market supply curve for the resource in question, once more denoted by B. The shape of this market supply curve is traceable to the cost conditions prevailing in the competitive industry producing B. We shall assume that the industry producing B is the typical kind, an increasing-cost industry (the other cases are easily inferred from the analysis of this one). Unlike a competitive resource buyer, a monopsonist thus faces an upward sloping supply curve because he exercises control over the market price.

To obtain greater quantities of the resource per unit of time, the monopsonist must pay higher prices. The price of a resource is another way of saying the *average* resource or factor cost from the viewpoint of the buying firm. Since this average factor cost is not constant, but rather rises as more is employed per unit of time, it follows that marginal factor cost will deviate from average factor cost, being higher than average factor cost at any one quantity of the input.[1] The connection between the resource price and its marginal factor cost is illustrated in Table 21.2. Columns 1 and 2 together comprise the market supply schedule. Column 3 records the firm's total cost of the resource; that is, column 3 is total cost of production if we assume for simplicity that there is only one input used (allowing for other inputs does not essentially change the argument). Finally, column 4 shows the computed marginal factor cost at each quantity of the resource that might be employed.

---

[1] The relationship is analogous to that between average revenue and marginal revenue or average cost and marginal cost. If the average is constant, then average equals marginal. But if the average is rising, marginal must exceed average.

Table 21.2

1	2	3 = 1 × 2	4 = Δ3/Δ1
Quantity of B per Unit of Time	Price of B (Average Factor Cost of B)	Total Cost of B	Marginal Factor Cost of B
b	p_b	bp_b	$\Delta TC/\Delta b$
1	$1.00	$1.00	
2	1.20	2.40	$1.40
3	1.40	4.20	1.80
4	1.60	6.40	2.20
5	1.80	9.00	2.60
6	2.00	12.00	3.00
7	2.20	15.40	3.40
8	2.40	19.20	3.80
9	2.60	23.40	4.20
10	2.80	28.00	4.60

Perusal of the table immediately demonstrates that marginal factor cost exceeds price at each possible quantity of B. To explain the economic reasoning behind this outcome, suppose the firm were to increase its employment of B from 4 to 5 units. The fifth unit must be purchased at a price of $1.80, whereas the 4 units formerly used were obtainable at $1.60 each. However, to obtain 5 units, the firm must pay $1.80 *to all 5 units*. Not only the fifth but also the "previously used" other 4 must be paid a higher price. Therefore the cost of employing the other 4 units has risen by $.20 per unit, an increment to total cost of $.80. Added to this is the $1.80 that the fifth unit costs, making the addition to total cost equal to $.80 plus $1.80 or $2.60.

A graphic presentation of marginal factor cost is included in Fig. 21.3. The market supply curve is labeled S_b in the right panel of the figure. Derived from this supply curve is the marginal factor cost curve, MFC_b, which lies above the supply curve and is more steeply sloped. The demand curve for B by the monopsonist is designated D_b. From previous analysis it is known that, with other variable inputs, there is a marginal revenue product curve passing through each point on the firm's demand curve. Since the monopsonist maximizes profit by equating marginal factor cost to marginal revenue product, he will employ that quantity of B at which the MFC_b curve intersects the demand curve; for only at this point of intersection is $MFC_b = MRP_b$. Hence, b_1 units are employed.

The price of B is set by the monopsonist, but he will not pay the price corresponding to the intersection point, i.e., he will not pay a price equal to the distance $0m$ in the diagram. The market supply curve specifies the price at which each quantity of B would be offered for sale. And for the quantity b_1, the supply curve indicates that suppliers would accept a

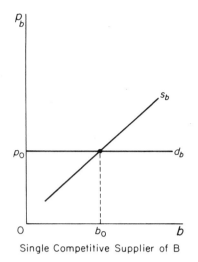

Single Competitive Supplier of B

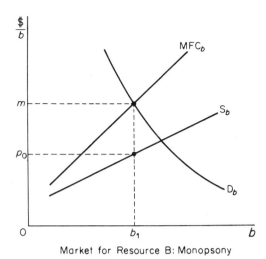

Market for Resource B: Monopsony

FIG. 21.3.

price of p_0. In order to maximize profit the monopsonist will therefore pay the lowest resource price he can. Consequently, he sets the price at p_0.

The equilibrium of one competitive supplier is presented in the left panel of Fig. 21.3. Because a single seller cannot affect the price, the demand curve faced by any one—shown as d_b in the diagram—is perfectly price-elastic at the established market price. With a supply curve s_b the individual seller in question supplies b_0 units per unit of time.

Monopsony in the purchasing of resources has sometimes been designated as *monopsonistic exploitation*. Specific meaning can be attributed to the notion of exploitation by a comparison of monopsony with pure competition. Under competition each firm employs any one resource up to the point at which the marginal revenue product of the resource equals its price. The resource owner receives a price equal to what any one unit of the resource contributes to the firm's total receipts. Indeed, if the product market is also competitive the resource owner gets paid a price equal to the value of that resource's contribution to output. Under monopsony, on the other hand, the resource owner receives a price lower than what any one unit contributes to the firm's total receipts, and the differential is a source of profit to the firm at the expense of the resource supplier. In the equilibrium depicted in Fig. 21.3, the resource B has a marginal revenue product equal to m, whereas the payment to the resource owner is p_0, less than m.

Monopsony analysis is not restricted to produced, nonhuman resources. It can occur for this type of input, of course. For example, when a very large manufacturer purchases certain specialized parts from a number of small suppliers who sell their entire outputs to this one user, the buyer possesses monopsony power. Or conditions of monopsony may be approximated when these competitive sellers supply other firms as well but rely to a great extent upon the orders received from one large purchaser. In the case of human resources monopsony may arise for a variety of reasons. The notorious "one company town" is an example. If one employer dominates a geographically restricted labor market *and* if the inhabitants are not mobile, the employing firm may well be in a monopsony position—in the short run at least. Another source of monopsony power in labor markets is a specialized characteristic of the labor used. A special type of skill may be developed to meet certain requirements of the firm (some types of entertainers come to mind), where the particular skill has little or no other productive usefulness. Or married females who work part time at certain jobs may permit the employer to pay them less than their marginal revenue product. Essentially, in all such cases the maintenance of monopsony power is possible only if the resource owners feel there is a lack of alternative employment opportunities.

As the foregoing discussion suggests, a particular situation may not disclose monopsony in its pure form. Oligopsony may be more closely approximated, with or without collusion among the few buyers. But the fundamental principles of resource pricing remain much the same.

BILATERAL MONOPOLY

To complete the circuit, one other market situation remains, namely, the absence of competition on both sides of the resource market. A market structure in which there exists monopoly on the selling side and monopsony on the buying side is called bilateral monopoly. In pure form a single seller deals with a single buyer, and in nonpure form collusive oligopolists deal with collusive oligopsonists. The outcome of such a situation can be seen by putting together the two preceding types of market control.

Consider first the monopolist. He is in a position like that depicted in Fig. 21.2, facing a negatively sloped demand curve. Given his marginal cost curve, the monopolist would maximize profit by equating marginal cost to marginal revenue. This "most preferred position" of the monopolist is reproduced in Fig. 21.4, where it is seen that he would seek to sell b_3 units of B at a price of p_3 in order to maximize profit.

Next, consider the monopsonist. He can be regarded as viewing the seller's marginal cost curve as his, the buyer's, *average* factor cost curve. Why? Because at any given or fixed price he might offer, the seller would supply the quantity indicated by this curve; that is, if the buyer were to offer a fixed price, the seller could maximize profit only by equating marginal cost to this price. Thus with reference to Fig. 21.3 the seller's marginal cost curve is like S_b in the right panel. So there

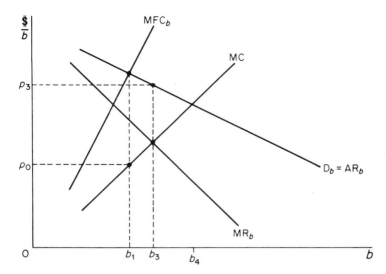

FIG. 21.4. Market for Resource B: Bilateral Monopoly

will be a marginal factor cost curve based upon the seller's marginal cost curve. This marginal factor cost curve is shown as MFC_b in Fig. 21.4. Consequently, the monopsonist maximizes his profit by equating marginal factor cost to marginal revenue product, yielding his "most preferred position." He will seek to purchase b_1 units of B at a price of p_0.

The price under bilateral monopoly is said to be indeterminate, for the seller seeks to set a price of p_3 and the buyer a price of p_0. The final outcome depends upon the relative bargaining strengths of the two traders. The stronger is the monopolist, the closer the price will be to p_3; and the stronger the monopsonist, the closer it will be to p_0. The negotiated price will doubtless lie somewhere between p_3 and p_0, but exactly where the price will settle cannot be determined by the theory.

Joint profits of the two firms would be maximized at a quantity of b_4 units. Here marginal revenue product equals marginal cost, where a single owner of both firms would operate. Given the disagreements over price, there exists a strong incentive for the two firms to merge or to collude in order to maximize joint profits. Thus bilateral monopoly is probably an unstable form of industrial organization.

COMPARISON WITH PURE COMPETITION

Will the price and employment of a resource be any different under pure competition than under monopoly or monopsony? It is not possible to answer this question unless some assumptions are made about the position of industry demand and supply curves in the resource market.

A competitive demand curve might lie in a position different from that yielded by monopsony. In turn, this difference would require that the very organizational structure of the industry itself influences the production functions of the member plants or the demand conditions for the commodity produced. Centralization or decentralization of ownership, other things the same, would have to result in economies or diseconomies of production, for instance.

Figure 21.3 provides a convenient starting point for comparison. Suppose the monopsony were to consist of several plants centrally owned so there is one decision maker, but the entire firm sells its output on a competitive product market. And suppose the monopsony generates the resource demand curve D_b. Let us also assume that if the monopsony were converted to pure competition on the resource market by means of legal proceedings the resulting resource demand curve would be no different. This is equivalent to saying that decentralization of plant ownership—each plant separately owned, comprising a separate firm, and no one able to affect significantly the resource price—would have no effect upon plant production functions or revenue conditions. The assumptions are made in order to isolate the effects of monopsony as opposed to other determinants of resource demand. Then, granted an unchanged demand curve D_b, direct comparisons can be made. For with the selling side of the resource market also competitive and yielding a supply curve S_b in Fig. 21.3, the industry equilibrium will occur at the intersection of the demand and supply curves. As a consequence, the price of B will be higher than p_0 and the quantity of B employed by the industry will be greater than b_1 units because the individual firms will carry employment to the point at which the price of B equals the value of its marginal product.

Let us next turn to the selling side of the market, where Fig. 21.2 provides the basis for comparison. Suppose the monopoly producing B were converted to pure competition. Moreover, assuming the monopoly marginal cost curve is the horizontal summation of the marginal cost curves of a number of plants and that these plant cost curves are not affected by the conversion to separate ownership, then the competitive supply curve of B can be taken as identical to the former marginal cost curve. Given the competitive resource demand curve D_b^X, the equilibrium price and quantity traded are determined by the intersection of the MC and D_b^X curves. Hence the price of B will be lower than p_3, and the quantity employed will be greater than b_3 units because the supplying firms will carry the production of B to the point at which marginal cost equals price.

Under the conditions assumed, the results can now be combined. A monopolist would charge p_3 for b_3 units traded, whereas a monopsonist would pay p_0 for b_1 units traded. Under competition the price of B would lie between these two "extremes," and the quantity of B employed would be larger than would occur under either monopoly or monopsony. Control over supply raises the price above its competitive level (in favor of the seller) whereas control over demand depresses the price below its competitive level (in favor of the buyer).

EPILOGUE ON COST OF PRODUCTION

In Chapters 10 and 11 the method of drawing a firm's cost curves under the assumption of given (constant) resource prices is tantamount to assuming an individual firm faces a perfectly elastic supply curve for each of its variable inputs. Resource prices are not affected by the firm's output; or, to put it another way, they are not affected by the quantities of inputs employed by the firm. Having analyzed noncompetitive resource markets, attention can be given to the question of how cost curves are altered when this condition on the resource market is no longer fulfilled.

Monopoly in the selling of resources changes nothing. True, the resource price level established on the market may be different from that prevailing under competitive resource selling, but as long as there is competition among the buyers, it still follows that changes in the output of any one firm have no significant effect upon resource prices. So the firm's cost curves are correctly drawn for constant resource prices.

A monopsonist in the resource market faces not a given price but a given supply curve. It follows that variations in the firm's output, requiring variations in the quantities of inputs used, will necessarily entail resource price changes. Suppose the firm producing a commodity is a monopsonist in the market for an input B. Let the demand for his product increase. In order to maximize profit the firm will expand output. When it does so, the firm increases its demand for B and the price of B changes. Therefore, in constructing the firm's cost curves, allowance must be made for the changing price of B as the firm moves along its cost curves. If the supply curves of inputs are positively sloped, a secondary force—in addition to diminishing returns—tends to raise average and marginal costs as output increases. Consequently, even if the firm experiences increasing returns to scale in its production function (leading by itself to declining long-run average cost), the rising resource prices operate to raise long-run average cost. The existence of elements of monopsony power on the resource market is further support for the proposition that average and marginal cost curves are U-shaped.

Actually, consideration of monopsony permits a broader rule regarding cost behavior. In general, regardless of the degree of competition on the resource market, the cost curves of a single firm are drawn under the assumption of *given resource supply curves* faced by the firm. In one special instance of the rule these supply curves are all horizontal, in which case a given resource supply curve is equivalent to a given resource price.

The theory of resource pricing also reveals the source of pecuniary effects external to a firm but internal to an industry. Putting aside nonpecuniary effects, whether an industry producing a commodity X is one of constant cost, increasing cost, or decreasing cost depends upon how resource prices change as the industry expands or contracts output. As the market demand for X increases, the consequent expansion in industry output entails an increase in the demand for resource inputs. What happens to resource prices (therefore, what determines the slope of the long-run supply curve of X) depends upon the slopes of the resource supply curves to the industry. If the supply curves of *all* resources to the industry are horizontal, then resource prices will be unchanged, cost curves of the firms producing X will not shift, and the long-run industry supply curve of X will also be horizontal. If, however, the resource supply curves are positively sloped, expanded demand will raise resource prices, cost curves of the firms will shift upward, and the long-run supply curve of X will likewise be positively sloped. Negatively sloped resource supply curves to the industry will cause resource prices to fall, and thus cause cost curves of the firms to drop, as the industry expands output in response to an increase in demand for X. Consequently, the long-run industry supply curve of X will in turn be negatively sloped. Naturally, some resource supply curves may be positively sloped while others are negatively sloped and still others are horizontal. Then the net effect of changing resource prices will determine whether firms' cost curves rise or fall as the industry expands output. It was argued in Chapter 13 that most industries, especially mature ones, are very likely to be increasing-cost industries. The reason should now be apparent. Supply curves of most types of labor are almost certain to be positively sloped. Some industries producing nonhuman resources may be in a short-run position, so their supply curves are positively sloped. Therefore, even if some few resource supply curves are negatively sloped or horizontal, the net effect of changing resource prices will likely be an upward shift in cost curves, generating external diseconomies in the industry producing the commodity X.

PROBLEMS

1. A firm has committed 10 units of capital inputs to the production of fountain pens. The price per unit of capital is $88.50. Also, the firm can hire any number of hours of labor at a given wage rate of $2.40 per hour. The firm's engineering division has provided information on the total product schedule, and its marketing division has provided information on total revenue from sales. These data are presented in the following table.

Hours of Labor per Week	Output of Pens per Week	Total Revenue
0	0	$ 0
100	100	550
200	220	1,150
300	330	1,555
400	430	1,955
500	520	2,270
600	600	2,510
700	670	2,685
800	730	2,805
900	780	2,880
1,000	820	2,920
1,100	850	2,935
1,200	870	2,935

(a) Compute the firm's (1) marginal physical product schedule for labor, (2) marginal revenue schedule, (3) marginal revenue product schedule for labor.

(b) Compute the firm's demand schedule for labor, and draw its demand curve as Figure 1.

(c) Find the equilibrium prices of capital and labor and the amounts of each employed by the firm. Represent the firm's equilibrium employment of labor by drawing the supply curve of labor to the firm in Figure 1.

(d) What is the firm's equilibrium output? What is the firm's total profit at this output? For what quantity of labor employed is total profit equal to zero?

2.   Suppose a firm sells its output on a competitive product market. The existing product price is $2. However, the firm is a monopsonist in its purchase of a resource input B. The supply schedule of B faced by the firm is presented in columns 1 and 2 below. The firm is in a short-run position with all other inputs fixed, and its total expenditure on these inputs is $1,000. The marginal physical product of the variable input B is shown in column 3.

1 Quantity of B per Unit of Time	2 Price of B	3 Marginal Physical product of B
100	$1.00	
200	1.10	1.05
300	1.20	1.00
400	1.30	.95
500	1.40	.90
600	1.50	.85
700	1.60	.80
800	1.70	.75
900	1.80	.70

(*a*) Construct a table that includes all the relevant variables and find the equilibrium price of B and quantity employed. Explain why this is the equilibrium.

(*b*) Show the equilibrium graphically as Figure 2.

(*c*) Suppose consumer demand for the product increases such that the product price rises to $2.75. Find the new equilibrium price and employment of B. Show it graphically in Figure 2.

(*d*) Suppose the supply of B decreases such that each quantity of B would be supplied at a price $.60 higher than the former price. Using the original demand schedule (ignoring the change postulated in part c) find the new equilibrium, explain how you found it, and show it graphically in Figure 2.

SUGGESTED READING

W. H. Nicholls, *Imperfect Competition Within Agricultural Industries*, Introduction and Chaps. 1-3. Ames, Iowa: The Iowa State University Press, 1941.

W. Adams, *The Structure of American Industry*, 3rd ed., Chaps. 3, 7, 11, 12. New York: The Macmillan Company, 1961.

22

On Wages and Rent

The preceding two chapters presented the theory of resource pricing within a general framework. Although the basic analysis is applicable to any resource, different factors of production possess special characteristics that warrant further discussion. The classical economists treated resource payments under the triumvirate of Wages, Interest, and Rent. Because interest theory is properly a matter of macroeconomics, only wages and rent will be examined in more detail.

WAGES

I might just as well begin this discussion of labor markets with a frank admission. The theory of labor demand stands up well under critical evaluation, but the theory of labor supply, as presented, leaves something to be desired.[1] The rigorous fashion in which the theory of resource demand has been formulated is not yet possible in the theory of labor supply. At bottom, supply is partly determined by nonpecuniary variables that often become recalcitrant to systematic theory and measurement. Nevertheless, the situation is by no means hopeless. We can show how pecuniary and nonpecuniary characteristics other than the wage rate exert an influence on the supply curve of labor to an industry, i.e., how they shape or shift the supply curve of labor.

Labor Unions

The theory of resource pricing helps to explain, in part at least, the economic consequences of organized labor. The development of labor unions usually results in labor-management negotiations, so the wage

---

[1] Indeed, it might be said that the two weakest areas of contemporary microeconomic theory are oligopoly product pricing and labor supply. Current research efforts are being directed toward these difficult problems, and the student of today who becomes the economic theorist of tomorrow will, let us hope, shed additional light on them.

rate is determined by what happens over the bargaining table. When the wage rate is set by negotiations between a single union and a group of employers representing the entire industry, the labor market is essentially one of bilateral monopoly. As a matter of fact there is a remarkable similarity between an entrepreneurs' cartel in the product market, which we have seen is much like a pure monopoly, and a labor union in the resource market. Both attempt to fix the price (wage rate), to exclude rivals (control membership by closed or union shops), and to suppress substitutes (labor-saving techniques of production).

Because of this analogy, attempts have been made to devise theories of union activity based on maximizing behavior, but they have not met with marked success. To the extent that unions are monopolies—i.e., control labor supply and by means of such control exert an influence on the wage rate—for analytical purposes they might be treated in the same way as the monopoly case discussed in the previous chapter. However, a monopolistic seller of a produced, nonhuman resource can be assumed to maximize profit—an assumption that will not do in the case of unions. A maximization theory must postulate some magnitude that the union is assumed to maximize. At first glance it might appear that the wage rate fills this need. Not so. As a rule, by maximizing the wage rate the union can only expect a reduction in employment because labor demand curves are negatively sloped. For the same reason the alternative goal of maximizing union membership and thus employment may lead to the necessity of accepting a lower wage rate. A maximum wage bill or payroll (wage rate per hour times number of hours worked) may also entail acceptance of a lower wage rate or drastic reduction of employment, depending upon the wage elasticity of the labor demand curve. Because of these conflicting goals it has been customary to assume that high wages and large employment are simultaneously sought. Then the outcome is less determinate, for wages and employment hinge upon how much value the union attaches to each. Sometimes the political role played by unions has received special attention. The union is regarded primarily as a political association whose aim is to effect legislation favorable to the "labor movement."

As a matter of historical record some unions have been effective in raising wages and others have been rather weak. Most successful have been those that can rigidly control the number of workers through apprenticeships, seniority rules, or closed shops. Craft unions of skilled workers such as printers are a case in point. More recently the giant industrial unions and the amalgamations of craft and industrial unions have adopted similar practices. Nevertheless, there are many unions, especially smaller ones, that have not been successful in raising wages. Their lack of success is due in large part to conditions prevailing in the industries involved: an easy substitution of capital for labor, too large a number of employers geographically dispersed, a highly mobile work force, and the absence of long-term worker commitments to the job (compare unions of salesgirls and unions of locomotive engineers).

Whatever the ultimate goals of labor unions, one aspect of union behavior is clear. Effective organization of employees results in higher wage demands on the part of the union. The higher wage demand following upon the union organization is obviously understandable since it is one of the prime attractions for membership. In order to discover the effects of such demands, let us study the proposition in the language of economic theory. Suppose, first, that the labor market in question was purely competitive prior to the establishment of a union. Figure 22.1 depicts the competitive industry demand curve for labor, D_L, and the competitive labor supply curve, S_L. The wage rate is determined as W_1, and there are H_1 hours of labor employed in the industry.

Now assume the labor force is effectively organized so that the union can control the labor supply. Aside from other facets of the employment contract, such as the introduction of safety measures and coffee breaks, the union can present (and historically has presented) the following bargain to employers: We offer you labor services at a certain higher wage rate, but if you do not accept this rate your employees will strike. In other words, the union offers the industry a horizontal supply curve at a wage rate above the prevailing one. For, in effect, the industry can hire any quantity of labor at the wage rate insisted upon but zero quantity at any lower rate. The initial demand may be greater than the union expects to get, and the final wage realized may be a compromise. Still, the compromise must be above the former wage if the union is to maintain membership. Let W_2 in Fig. 22.1 represent the final offer made by the union, so the curve S'_L represents the new labor supply curve to

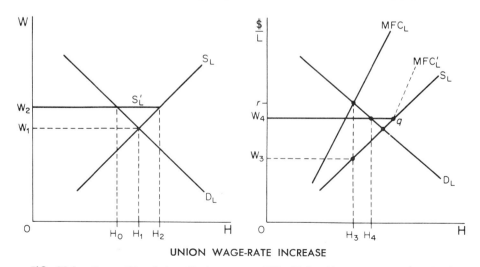

UNION WAGE-RATE INCREASE

FIG. 22.1.   Competitive Labor Market   FIG. 22.2.   Monopsonistic Labor Market

the industry. Observe that the new supply curve is horizontal up to the point at which it reaches the old supply curve and then coincides with the old one. Either supply curve depicts the minimum wage at which each quantity of labor would be forthcoming. Since the workers would not supply a quantity greater than H_2 hours without a higher wage offer prior to the establishment of the union, they will not do so now. The union bargains for the minimum wage rate, and it is up to the workers to decide if they will work more hours at a higher rate.

The union scale of W_2 is higher than the previous equilibrium, so firms will employ fewer hours of labor. H_0 hours are employed at a wage rate of W_2. Although those workers who remain employed receive a higher wage, displaced workers must seek other jobs. If they enter nonunionized labor markets, they will tend to increase the supply and depress the wage rate there. As a consequence, workers who gain from unionization do so at the expense of others. And if *all* other labor markets were also unionized, limiting membership to keep the wage rate up, the net effect would be to engender unemployment in the economy.

The extent to which employment declines in the industry shown in Fig. 22.1 depends upon the elasticity of labor demand. The more wage elastic is the demand curve, the greater will be the percentage decrease in employment. In particular, if the demand curve is relatively wage elastic between the rates W_1 and W_2, then the decline in employment will more than offset the increase in the wage, so the total wage bill will decrease also. A condition most favorable for union wage bargaining is a very inelastic industry demand curve for labor, for in this case a wage increase will lead to a relatively small drop in employment and an expansion of the total wage bill. In turn, the labor demand curve will be less elastic the less elastic is the consumer demand curve for the industry's product and the more difficult it is to substitute capital for labor.

The foregoing analysis points up some of the difficulties faced by union policy makers. It also goes a long way toward explaining why some unions have advanced so-called featherbedding techniques to prevent or to slow down the substitution of capital for labor (witness the insistence on firemen in diesel locomotives, for example). It also helps to explain why unions have in some cases supported employers or cooperated with them in endeavors to render the product demand curve less elastic (the union label on clothing is a case in point). Certainly it is possible that simultaneous increases in demand can offset the unemployment effect, but this happy accident is not the result of unionization; rather, it is in spite of it. In any event, the existence of artificial devices aimed at reducing unemployment suggests that the happy accident has not always been realized.

Union organizers and officials would be the first to challenge the assumption of pure competition in labor markets. Although they have not used the same language, union organizers have argued that labor markets are monopsonistic. The argument often runs as follows. Prior to union organization a single employer hiring many workers put each worker in the position of a competitive seller, while the employer, acting as one buyer facing many sellers, could set the wage on a take-it-or-leave-it basis. These are the grounds for claiming equal bargaining power. There may be substantial merit in the argument, at least if it is applied to a period of sixty years ago. It is a question of fact, and whether or not it is true today or has been recently in a significantly large number of instances, let us examine the effects of unionization in a monopsonistic labor market.

Figure 22.2 shows a competitive supply curve of labor, S_L. The single buyer, having a demand curve D_L, faces the supply curve and thus considers the marginal factor cost curve of labor, labeled MFC_L in the diagram. To maximize profit the employer equates marginal factor cost to marginal revenue product, hiring H_3 units at a wage rate of W_3. As before, given effective union organization the union insists upon a higher wage rate. Suppose the union succeeds in raising the wage to W_4, making the labor supply curve horizontal up to the point q. On the horizontal portion of the supply curve, marginal factor cost equals average factor cost (the wage rate). Under these new conditions the firm maximizes profit by equating the new marginal factor cost to marginal revenue product, which means the firm hires H_4 units of labor at a wage rate of W_4. The effect of unionization is to offset the labor "exploitation" that has been occurring because of monopsony, for wages and employment both increase and each worker gets paid a wage equal to marginal revenue product.

It follows that the unemployment effect necessarily results only if the labor market approximated pure competition prior to unionization. But even with monopsony the new wage must be no greater than r in the diagram—the dollar value per unit of labor at which the former marginal factor cost equaled marginal revenue product. If the union effects a wage rate greater than r, unemployment will result. Hence, if the labor market is monopsonistic and if the union scale does not exceed r with a stationary labor demand, the union can simultaneously increase the wage rate and employment.

Minimum-Wage Legislation

A public policy that can be analyzed with the aid of price theory is American minimum-wage legislation. During the past quarter-century, four national minimum-wage laws have been enacted. In effect they require that all employers whose products are traded in interstate commerce shall pay an hourly wage no lower than that stipulated by the law. Since some commodities, especially personal services, do not enter into interstate commerce, not all workers are covered by the legislation. Such laws are apparently an attempt to raise the incomes of workers who receive less than the contemplated minimum. A question arises as to whether they are successful in accomplishing this end, and if so to what extent.

Figures 22.1 and 22.2 provide a geometric illustration of the analysis. Suppose, first, that an industry affected by the law (one that employs workers covered by the legislation) purchases labor services in a competitive market. The prevailing wage rate for unskilled workers is, say, W_1 in Fig. 22.1, at which H_1 hours of labor are employed. Let us assume this wage is below the minimum set by law; the law forces all firms to pay at least W_2. Interpreted geometrically the supply curve for this type of labor becomes horizontal at a height equal to the distance $0W_2$ up to the quantity L_2 after which it coincides with the old supply curve. The new higher wage will have two effects that cooperate to reduce employment to H_0 hours.

First, the higher wage rate increases the cost of production, raising cost more the greater is the amount of labor used relative to other resource inputs. The upward shift in cost curves causes a decline in industry output, given no change in product demand. This effect, in itself, tends to reduce the employment of all inputs. But in addition, for any given level of output, even the now smaller one, firms will substitute other inputs for the now more expensive unskilled labor. Since nonhuman capital inputs and skilled workers become cheaper relative to unskilled labor, they are substituted for the labor affected by the law. Together these two reactions explain the movement upward and to the left along the industry demand curve for covered labor.

Displaced workers seeking jobs elsewhere thus increase the supply and depress the wage rate in some other industries. Because all industries so affected by the law will be experiencing the same kind of unemployment, the increase in labor supply is most likely to occur in uncovered industries. Hence, any increase in the wage rate paid by firms whose products are traded in interstate commerce will be at the expense of workers hired by firms whose product market is "local."

These conclusions hold only if the labor market is indeed competitive. If on the other hand the labor market is monopsonistic, then the unemployment effect need not follow. An industry may hire many unskilled married females, each of whom supplements the primary income provided by her husband as head of the household. Given that there are few other employment opportunities for unskilled females and that the household does not rely upon the wife's income for survival, conditions tend to be favorable for monopsonistic hiring practices. Geographic immobility may also force workers into a position of accepting a wage rate less than their marginal revenue products. Let Fig. 22.2 represent such a situation, where the wage rate is W_3 and H_3 units of labor are employed. Now suppose the firms are affected by a minimum-wage law raising the wage rate to W_4. Essentially, the law eliminates monopsonistic exploitation. To maximize profit the firms will equate marginal revenue product to the new marginal factor cost, and employment increases. Unless the minimum wage exceeds r in the diagram, the unemployment effect in this industry and the depressed wage rates in uncovered industries do not occur.

Whether the labor markets affected by legislation are competitive or monopsonistic is a question of fact. The available evidence, though scanty, suggests that some are not competitive. However, others appear to be—the cigar industry, sawmills, processed waste, and the hosiery industry, especially those member firms located in the South. It should come as no surprise that different reactions have been observed in different industries following upon enactment of minimum-wage legislation.

On-the-Job Training

On-the-job training is a popular employment feature in modern American industry. Training programs vary from one industry to another and lead to diverse results. Nevertheless, among them are common characteristics, which I have ignored in the general presentation of resource pricing. To demonstrate, suppose a firm is operating in competitive product and resource markets. When a firm engages in job training, there is no reason to expect that the standard equilibrium condition will prevail during the training period. Both the employer and the worker expect to gain in the future because of greater productivity. Since both may expect to benefit in the future, a question arises as to the cost of training and who will bear this cost. Appropriate modifications in the general theory can be made in order to analyze the problem.

For the sake of simplicity, assume all other resources are fixed so the value of marginal product curve for a specified type of labor constitutes the firm's demand curve. Figure 22.3 depicts the demand curve, labeled VMP_a for a type of labor denoted by A. Let a_1 represent the number of hours currently employed per unit of time for a single worker (we might measure a in hours per day and set a_1 equal to 8 hours per day). If there is no on-the-job training, then for a_1 hours the worker will receive a wage rate per hour equal to w_1. Suppose instead that a training program is in effect; part of the work day will be spent in training activity, making the worker's current productivity lower than it otherwise would be. This lower productivity is accepted by the employer and the worker because of the prospect of greater productivity leading to a value of marginal product in excess of w_1 at the termination of the training program. Reduced present productivity can be represented by drawing the VMP_a curve lower, as VMP'_a in the diagram, so it intersects the supply curve at a wage rate equal to w_0. The difference between w_1 and w_0 can be taken to represent the current cost of training. From the viewpoint

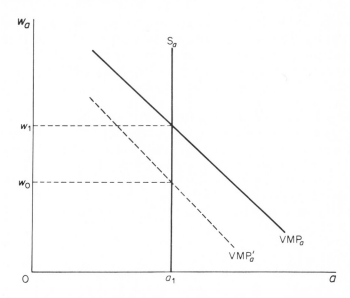

FIG. 22.3. Demand of Firm and Supply of Labor by Single Worker: On-the-Job Training

of the worker, w_1 is what he could earn currently if he undertook no training. Thus if he were paid w_0, the foregone income would mean he bears the full cost of the training. Likewise, from the viewpoint of the employer the dollar amount per hour equal to w_1 is the value of the marginal product in the absence of training—the addition to total revenue of the firm—whereas the amount w_0 is a smaller addition to total revenue. Hence, if the firm were to pay a wage rate of w_1 while the addition to total revenue yielded by the worker equals w_0, then the firm would bear the full cost of training. In general, the cost of training will be shared between the worker and the employer, with one or the other bearing the full cost as special cases.

How the cost is shared depends upon the nature of the training. Three cases can be distinguished. The first is completely specialized training that can be used to raise future productivity only in this particular firm. Since the training will have no effect upon the worker's productivity elsewhere, the future wage rate he could command from employment in another firm is left unchanged. In this case the firm would be willing to pay the full cost of training. The employer will pay the same wage rate that the worker could earn currently elsewhere, namely, w_1, because the firm can recapture this cost in the future from greater worker productivity.

The second case lies at the other extreme. The training is completely general in the sense that it raises the worker's productivity in similar firms by as much as it does in the firm in question. Then the value of the worker's marginal product rises by as much elsewhere as it does here, so the wage rate he can command elsewhere also rises. Since the employer stands to lose his "investment," he will be unwilling to bear any of the cost. The worker, whether he remains with the firm or transfers employment after completion of the training program, is sure to gain. In order to establish equilibrium with the existence of such a training program, the worker must be willing to accept a wage rate of w_0 during the training program. In effect, this case is identical to a situation in which the worker receives his general training (equally usable in several employments) outside the firm and pays for it himself.

More common than either of these extremes is on-the-job training that is only partly specialized. Training will raise the worker's productivity in other similar employments but not by as much as it does in the firm offering the training. Numerous examples could be cited: medical and dental receptionists, sales clerks, bookkeepers, even assembly-line production workers. Part of the acquired knowledge is transferable to other employments, but, because of special features of the product or peculiar ways in which operations are performed in the firm, the usefulness (rise in productivity) is greater in the firm offering the training program. Since the training does indeed increase the worker's alternative earnings, he must be willing to absorb some but not all of the cost. The employer is also willing to bear some of the cost—the same fraction of the cost that he expects to recover in larger future revenues because of the higher productivity in this firm relative to others. What proportions of the training cost are borne by worker and employer will differ from one firm to another, depending upon the fraction of cost the firm expects to recapture. In all such cases, however, the wage rate during the training period will be above w_0, the worker's actual value of marginal product during the training period, but below w_1, his potential value of marginal product during the period were there no training program.

The Increase in White-Collar Workers

Casual empirical observations suggest an increase in the number of persons employed in white-collar jobs as opposed to blue-collar jobs. Although casual impressions are often refuted by a more systematic examination of data, in this instance the impression is verified. Column 2 of Table 22.1 shows the total number of all workers employed in American manufacturing industries from 1947 through 1960. In column 3 are recorded the number of production workers over the same period, while column 4 presents the number of nonproduction workers. Most of the latter are persons engaged in executive positions, selling or buying, advertising, research, clerical posts, and so on—what are commonly designated as white-collar jobs.

Comparison of columns 3 and 4 shows a slight decline in the number of production workers and a steady increase in the number of nonproduction workers. More revealing are the percentages listed in column

Table 22.1
United States Employment in Manufacturing Industries, 1947–60

1	2	3	4	5
Year	All Employed Workers	Production Workers	Nonproduction Workers	Nonproduction Workers as Percentage of All Workers
1947	16,256[a]	13,176	3,030	18.9%
1948	16,455	13,233	3,222	19.6
1949	13,892	11,368	2,524	18.2
1950	15,827	13,133	2,694	17.0
1951	15,948	12,997	2,951	18.5
1952	16,778	13,560	3,218	19.2
1953	17,301	13,852	3,449	19.9
1954	16,007	12,612	3,395	21.2
1955	17,006	13,440	3,566	21.0
1956	17,238	13,465	3,776	21.9
1957	16,783	12,896	3,889	23.2
1958	15,795	11,981	3,814	24.1
1959	16,280	12,274	4,006	24.6
1960	16,165	12,071	4,094	25.3

[a] All employment figures in thousands.
Source: U.S. Department of Labor, *Employment and Earnings* (monthly).

5, where the number of white-collar workers is computed as a percentage of all employed workers. The upward trend of white-collar jobs is quite apparent, rising from around 19 per cent to about 25 per cent of all employed workers.

Annual average earnings in both production and nonproduction jobs have risen since World War II, but earnings in nonproduction jobs have increased relative to earnings in production jobs. The interpretation of the table suggested by these data is a greater increase in the demand for nonproduction workers, and a movement upward and to the right along the supply curve. There appears to be little shifting of occupations by those already in the category of blue-collar jobs. Rather, the movement along the supply curve of nonproduction workers has occurred primarily by more entrants into the labor force choosing white-collar employments. A greater number of new entrants seem willing to undertake the education and training necessary for these positions; this is doubtless a function of rising family income and wealth in the economy.

Wage Rate Differentials

If all labor were homogeneous, if all labor markets were competitive, if nonpecuniary characteristics of employment were everywhere identical, and if workers were perfectly mobile among industries and regions, then we should expect to find that wage rates would be the same in all industries. We do not live in such a world, of course, so wage rates vary significantly among industries. This fact is brought out in Table 22.2 where average hourly earnings are computed for seven selected industries. The industries are listed in order of increasing magnitude of the hourly wage rate. The lowest, $1.70 per hour, was found in the textile industry, while the largest in the group, $2.69 per hour, appears in the transportation equipment industry.

What are some of the factors that help to explain these wage differentials? There are many, and it is useful to treat them under three headings: equalizing differences, noncompeting groups, and incomplete adjustments to changes in demand and supply.

Table 22.2
Average Hourly Earnings for Production Workers
in Selected U.S. Industries, 1959

Industry	Hourly Earnings
Textile Mill Products	$1.70
Furniture and Fixtures	1.84
Food and Kindred Products	1.92
Fabricated Metal Products	2.29
Chemicals and Allied Products	2.55
Printing and Publishing	2.59
Transportation Equipment	2.69

Source: U.S. Department of Commerce, *Annual Survey of Manufactures*, 1959 and 1960.

Equalizing differences in wage rates are those monetary differentials that compensate for nonmonetary characteristics of employment. Even if all workers were completely mobile and markets were competitive, the fact that workers have different tastes for nonpecuniary employment conditions would lead to wage rate differentials. The less attractive jobs would have to offer greater monetary returns in order to offset nonmonetary disadvantages. If this were the only economic force determining wage rate differentials, then the differences in wages between two industries could be taken as a measure of the monetary equivalent attached to nonmonetary differences between jobs. The wage differentials are equalizing in the sense that workers can be assumed to equalize total net returns from employment, including monetary and nonmonetary returns.

In addition to these equalizing differences, wage rates will diverge because of forces giving rise to noncompeting labor groups. Two groups of workers may be considered as noncompeting if for any reason they do not vie for the same jobs. Differences in natural ability and training is one source of noncompeting groups. Workers in one industry paying a relatively low wage may be unable to obtain employment in another industry paying a higher wage, because a job in the second industry requires skills that these workers cannot attain or cannot afford to learn. Besides differences in ability and training there may exist discrimination. Certain firms belonging to a high-wage industry may discriminate by color, age, or sex in their hiring practices. Then a worker with the requisite ability may still not qualify as a competitor for the high-wage job. Unionization in a high-wage industry can operate in a similar way. In order to protect its members from the effects of a larger labor supply, the union may be able to enforce a union shop and control union membership. Thus it can restrict competition by limiting membership. Labor immobility is still another force generating noncompeting groups. Workers whose families are established in the community are often reluctant to move to another geographic area in order to take advantage of a higher wage. In turn, immobility is due not only to the money and psychic costs of movement, but also to ignorance of the availability of employment and income opportunities elsewhere.

Finally, wage-rate differentials can be traced in part to incomplete adjustments to changes in demand and supply. Acquisition of skills, geographic movement, etc., all take time. So even if wage differences among industries were eventually eliminated or reduced, at any point in time observed differentials would be larger than would prevail in long-run equilibrium.

ECONOMIC RENT

Economic rent has its roots in classic economic theory. Many writers in the early nineteenth century singled out land as possessing special characteristics. As might be expected of that period in history, land was viewed primarily as an input for agricultural production. Land rent was explained by differential returns on various grades of land. As long as the demand for output is small only the best quality is used, and its price is just sufficient to cover average cost, i.e., the price per acre is equal to the cost per acre of making the land fit for production. Since the land is of high quality, this cost is relatively low. As the demand for output expands with increases in population and income, the demand for land as a factor of production likewise expands. But after a while the land of best quality is exhausted, so land of secondary quality (requiring a higher cost to make it productive) is brought into use. As demand continues to grow, third-quality land is used, and so on. Rent was defined as the payment per acre to the owner of land in excess of the minimum price that is necessary to bring forth that acre of land. As such, rent is equal to the amount by which the price of land exceeds the average cost of making it available.

Figure 22.4 depicts the demand for and supply of land according to

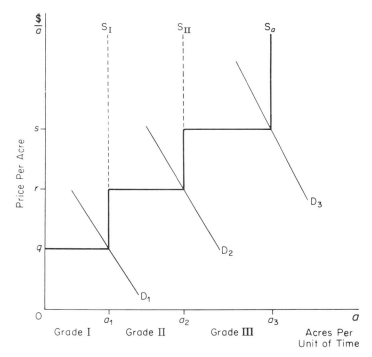

FIG. 22.4. Classical Theory of Land Rent

the classic analysis. As demand increases up to D_1, only Grade I land is used; its average cost is equal to the distance $0q$ and that is the price paid. Because all land in this class is of the same prime quality, all acres earn the same price. From zero to a_1 acres is so-called marginal land with this state of demand. Between D_1 and D_2, second-quality land, Grade II, is also used. The expansion of demand bids up the price of land to $0r$, just enough to cover the average cost of Grade II land. The owners of Grade I land receive a rent equal to the distance qr, but owners of Grade II obtain no payment above average cost. Given this state of demand, Grade II is marginal land, so its owners receive no rent. Notice that the rent paid to owners of Grade I land is a residual, a kind of windfall traceable to the increase in demand. By the time demand has risen to D_2 a total of a_2 acres are in use and all of Grade II land is employed. Finally, between D_2 and D_3 the price of land rises to $0s$, and Grade III with an average cost equal to $0s$ is forthcoming. In this state, Grade III is marginal (no rent) land, while Grade II receives a rent equal to the distance rs and Grade I a rent equal to qs. According to the classic theorists the differential rents vary directly with the quality of land.

Somewhat later this same analysis was applied to other types of nonhuman capital, and the residual payments were called *quasi-rents*.

It was argued that a machine, for example, may be fixed (not transferable to another employment) in the short run. If the owner of the machine receives a price because the machine has a positive productivity in its present use, this price will exceed its "average cost." Average cost was defined on the basis of the opportunity-cost principle. Since the machine is not transferable, its maximum return in an alternative employment is effectively zero. Thus its opportunity cost is zero, and any payment to the owner possesses the characteristics of land rent as expounded by classic theory. Thus quasi-rent was deemed to be a short-run phenomenon because the machine could be transferred elswhere in the long run.

Today's economists do not single out land, or for that matter machines, as being a resource whose owners are paid a rent. The concept has been generalized. The modern notion of *economic* rent is applicable to any type of productive input, human or nonhuman. It is defined as a payment to the resource owner in excess of that resource's opportunity cost. The question of whether a given resource payment is to be regarded as rent does not depend upon whether the productive services are contributed by land, machines, or workers. Rather, it hinges on the degree of specialization of the resource. Three cases can be distinguished: (1) completely specialized resources that have productive use in only one employment, what are called *specific* inputs; (2) completely unspecialized resources that are equally productive in other employments; (3) partially specialized resources that are very productive in one employment relative to all others.

Degrees of Specialization

We begin with specific inputs. One example is land that is under water but that contains an oil pool. It is useful in the production of oil but for no other purpose. Another example is a remote island usable only as a weather station, or perhaps as a refueling station for airplanes. Also included in this category would be the nontransferable machine giving rise to quasi-rents.

In order to be a specific input the resource must be available in a fixed quantity. More exactly, there is some fixed maximum amount of the productive service. Moreover, its cost is zero in that employment in which the resource is productive. That is, earnings from alternative employments are zero because the resource is productive in one and only one use. By the opportunity-cost principle its cost in this one use must therefore be zero. A specific input can be described geometrically as having a vertical supply curve extending from the horizontal axis. In the left panel of Fig 22.5, the specific resource A has a maximum of a_1 units per unit of time. The supply curve S_a is interpreted as horizontal along the horizontal axis up to a_1 units at which it becomes vertical. The

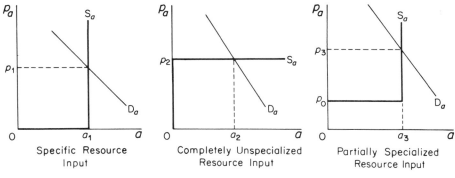

FIG. 22.5.

demand for A is shown as D_a, resulting in a price of p_1.

The resource A has zero opportunity cost and yet it is paid a price of p_1. The price paid to the resource owner is entirely economic rent since rent is defined as a price in excess of opportunity cost. This rent is a pure residual. If demand were to decrease the price would fall, but a_1 units would still be made available. Only if demand fell so far as to intersect the horizontal segment of the supply curve would rent go to zero, because the price has fallen to zero. Hence, in the case of a specific input there would be limited employment even if it were free. Why? Because it has no paying alternatives.

At the other extreme is the case of a completely unspecialized resource. The situation is depicted in the center panel of Fig. 22.5, where the resource in question is again called A. Any resource owner can obtain a price in an alternative employment equal to p_2. Since units are freely transferable and useful elsewhere, the resource must be paid at least p_2 in this employment. Otherwise, all units would move elsewhere. On the other hand, with perfect mobility, if the price were the least bit higher in this use, all units would flow into employment here. This is merely another way of saying its supply curve, S_a in the diagram, is horizontal at a height equal to p_2. Under these conditions the resource will be paid p_2—a price exactly equal to its opportunity cost—so no part of the price constitutes rent.

Neither completely specialized nor completely unspecialized resources are common. More often a productive service will be partially specialized, having a productivity higher in one use than it has in any other. A good example is the celebrated movie star, whose talent (or figure) may make her productivity high and enable her to earn $100,000 a year as an actress. It is not strange to find that her next most productive employment may be that of a nightclub waitress, where her productivity would bring an income of $8,000 a year. An executive in a public relations firm, because of his talent for public persuasion, may be able to command a salary of $40,000, whereas his highest alternative income would be as a salesman at \$10,000 a year. Closer to home is the illustration of a dog catcher who earns \$3,000 a year; his next most productive employment may be as a college professor at \$2,800 a year.

A partially specialized resource is illustrated in the right panel of Fig. 22.5, where the maximum available quantity of A is a_3 units per unit of time. The highest price paid in alternative employments is p_0 Consequently p_0 is the opportunity cost of its use in this employment. The supply curve S_a is horizontal at a height equal to p_0 up to the maximum available quantity, at which it becomes vertical. Because the resource is very productive in this use the demand curve D_a lies far to the right and intersects the supply curve on the vertical segment, making the price p_3. Of this total price, p_0 is opportunity cost and p_3 minus p_0 is economic rent, again a pure residual.

It is not necessary that a partially specialized resource have a supply curve that is horizontal and then vertical at the maximum available quantity. This procedure was followed in the diagram in order to emphasize the portion of the resource price designated as rent and the other portion designated as opportunity cost. Instead, the resource owner may offer more units of the productive service at higher prices, giving rise to a positively sloped supply curve. At the price p_0 the supply curve will reach the vertical axis, and will coincide with the vertical axis at all prices lower than p_0 because p_0 represents the resource's opportunity cost in this employment. In general, any supply curve not horizontal must entail rent as part of the resource price.

Social Rent and Individual Cost

In the discussion of economic rent, general terms like *employment* and *use* have been deliberately chosen in preference to terms like *employment by a firm* and *employment by an industry*. The reason is that rent from the viewpoint of society or an industry is not necessarily rent from the viewpoint of an individual firm. To illustrate, consider an entertainer who can play the guitar and "render" a song in a way that can be imitated but not duplicated. Suppose his income as an entertainer is \$100,000 a year. He has a very large marginal revenue product in the entertainment industry because his services are in great demand by teen-agers. Assume that his greatest alternative earning is \$5,000 a year as a truck driver. The social cost, the cost to the entire economy, of utilizing his services in the entertainment field is an opportunity cost, namely, the value of the maximum alternative product he could have produced. This cost by assumption is \$5,000. Likewise, the cost to the entertainment industry is his opportunity cost. Therefore, from the viewpoint of society or the industry, \$95,000 of his income is economic rent. In diagrammatic terms the supply of his services to the entire industry might be like the curve S_a in the right panel of Fig. 22.5.

The industry, if it acted as a unit, could employ these services for, say, $1 above the $5,000 that constitutes his greatest alternative earning. That is, the demand curve could be pushed to the left until it intersected the supply curve just a mite above the horizontal segment, and the industry could still obtain his services. Why, then, does the demand curve intersect the supply curve far above the horizontal segment? The answer is that member firms in the industry compete with one another for these services. No Las Vegas nightclub, for example, could expect to obtain his services without paying what others would offer. Competition among the member firms forces the demand curve to the right, pushing the resource price above the industry opportunity cost. The supply curve *faced by any individual firm* is horizontal at a height equal to the price established by the intersection of the industry demand and supply curves.

Therefore the individual firm considers the entire resource price as cost and not rent, even though the price is partly rent from the viewpoint of society and the industry. Moreover, this cost to the firm is truly an opportunity cost. Opportunity cost to the firm is the maximum this resource could earn in any other firm in the industry, not the maximum it could earn in another industry.

The Specific Sales Tax Once More

The economic effects of a sales tax imposed upon a commodity have been discussed in Chapter 8 and again in Chapter 14. A tax of a fixed amount per unit of the good sold, collected by the government from firms, is regarded by the firms as an addition to cost of production, thus shifting the average and marginal cost curves upward by the amount of the tax. The industry supply curve shifts to the left, raising the product price and reducing the quantity exchanged on the market. It was seen that the incidence of the tax depends upon the price elasticity of the product demand curve. The more inelastic is the demand curve, the larger is the proportion of the tax paid by consumers.

This attempt to pass the tax on to consumers is called an attempt to pass the tax *forward*. But in addition the firm will try to shift the tax *backward*. That is, the firm will try to avoid paying the tax by passing the burden on to the factors of production it purchases. The rise in cost causing a decrease in industry output means the firms in the industry will want to employ fewer resource inputs at any given resource prices. Consequently, the industry demand curve for each resource will shift to the left. The extent to which the price of a resource falls determines the extent to which the owner of that resource will bear the burden of the tax.

Take a simple example in which the industry employs two resources, A and B. The supply curve of A to the industry is assumed to be infinitely price elastic; that of B is assumed to have zero price elasticity. When the industry demand for resources decreases following upon the tax, the price of A remains unchanged even though less A is employed in this particular industry. Units of A receive the same price and so bear none of the tax. Note the formal similarity to a horizontal product demand curve whereby consumers pay none of the tax. The supply curve of B is vertical, so the price of B will fall when demand decreases. Resource B is a specific input, and *its share of the tax is tantamount to a reduction in the economic rent* received by the resource owner. Indeed, for any resource whose supply curve to the industry is not horizontal, the tax will fall upon economic rent.

The less price elastic is consumer demand for the product, the larger is the share of the tax borne by consumers; the greater is the degree to which firms can shift the tax forward. Likewise, the less price elastic is a resource supply curve to the industry whose product is taxed, the larger is the share borne by the resource owner. Firms are more successful in shifting the tax backward the less price elastic are resource supply curves to the industry.

Rent and Profit

In explaining product pricing the firm was assumed to maximize total profit. Profit, like rent, is a pure residual, and it is natural to pose the question of a possible relationship between the two. Since profit applies to an individual firm, its relationship to rent must mean a relationship to rent paid by the firm, not the industry. Some writers have tended to identify profit and rent. Under assumed certainty, i.e., assuming cost and revenue are known and not subject to unforeseeable fluctuations, it is argued that the firm maximizes rent. I have adopted a different course because there is a conceptual distinction between profit and rent. First, profit is a total dollar magnitude whereas rent is a dollar payment per unit of a resource input; the two are not expressed in identical units. More important, the firm is regarded as an intermediary between product and resource markets, an entity different from the resources hired by the firm. Profit is the dollar magnitude this entity seeks to maximize. In contrast, the conceptual orientation is different in the case of rent; rent is a payment by the firm to the owner of a resource supplied to the firm.

Nevertheless, the two are not unrelated. Granted that a firm is profitable, the entrepreneur "takes home" this profit as personal income. In the short run, fixed inputs in effect have vertical supply curves to the firm, and variable inputs have horizontal supply curves. The fixed resources thus give rise to rent. Since the assets the entrepreneur owns are not transferable in the short run, and since their services do have market prices, he takes account of these prices in determining the implicit costs of the firm. If profit is positive, he receives a contractual price for his own resources plus a rent per unit of self-owned resources in his capacity of residual income recipient. This rent is the attraction for others to become residual income recipients.

In the long run, the resulting competition for self-employed resources bids up their market prices, so opportunity cost rises. Eventually, rents in a competitive industry are reduced to zero. Because all resources are transferable in the long run, their supply curves are horizontal to the firm at the new market prices. The entrepreneur receives for his self-employed resources a price equal to opportunity costs. Under monopoly, however, self-employed resources can command a price in excess of opportunity cost even in the long run. A monopolistic firm is a source of long-run rent for owners of self-employed resources.

PROBLEMS

1. Assume an industry is competitive in both product and resource markets. The industry is faced by infinitely price elastic supply curves of all resources except executive personnel, for whom there is a positively sloped supply curve to the industry. Each additional executive hired by this industry raises the annual salary of all executives by $50. Each firm in the industry has one executive and produces 100 units of the product per year at the minimum point on its long-run average cost curve.

Suppose the demand curve for the product of this industry has a price elasticity of unity (equals minus one), and 10,000 units per year are produced by the industry at $100 per unit. Then the government levies a tax of $3 per unit of the product sold.

(a) Show why the product price will rise to $102 and the industry output will be 9,800 units per year in the long run.

(b) Suppose instead that the product demand curve faced by the industry were infinitely price elastic. Allowing for long-run adjustments, by how much will the annual salaries of executives change in this industry after the $3 tax is levied?

2. Suppose there is a competitive industry where the product price is $5. There are 20 firms in the industry. Of these, 19 firms, by maximizing profit in the short run, produce at an average cost of $5, so profit in each of these is zero. The remaining one firm, when it maximizes profit, can produce at an average cost of $4.50, so it makes a profit of $.50 on each unit produced. This short-run profit is due to the superior ability of the entrepreneur in the profitable firm, and he receives a rent on the resources he owns. In the long run every firm in the industry must make zero profit. Explain how the profitable firm ends up with zero profit in the long run, assuming the personal income of this entrepreneur remains the same in the long run as it was in the short run.

SUGGESTED READING

L. W. Weiss, *Economics and American Industry*, Chap 10. New York: John Wiley & Sons, 1961.

D. McCord Wright ed., *The Impact of the Union*. New York: Harcourt, Brace & Co., Inc., 1951.

W. D. Grampp and E. T. Weiler, *Economic Policy*, 3rd ed., Chaps. 10, 11. Homewood, Ill.: Richard D. Irwin, Inc., 1961.

M. Friedman and S. Kuznets, *Income from Independent Professional Practice*, Preface, Chaps. 3, 4. New York: National Bureau of Economic Research, 1945.

D. A. Worcester, "A Reconsideration of the Theory of Rent," *American Economic Review*, XXXVI (June 1946), 258-77.

K. E. Boulding, "The Concept of Economic Surplus," *American Economic Review*, XXXV (December 1945), 851-69.

23

Human Capital

The theory of resource pricing, like the theory of product pricing, has focused upon the price of a flow variable. For instance, a wage rate is the price of a flow of labor services (dollars per hour of labor services employed). A raw material price is quoted as dollars per quantity used per period of time. Equipment input is priced as the value of equipment usage, a service measured in such units as machine hours per year.

A related question centers upon the value of a stock. What is the value of a machine itself in contrast to the services per time period rendered by the machine? These services can be viewed conveniently as a stock embodied in the machine and released in the form of a flow as the machine is used in production. Land provides another illustration—the value of the land itself versus the value of its use (the monthly or annual rental price). Finally, what is the value of the stock of labor services embodied in a human being and forthcoming as a flow in actual employment?

Traditionally, capital theory has been concerned with the value of a capital stock and the relationship between this value and the value, or price, of the service flow. Stock-flow distinctions recognize the fact that a given piece of capital equipment has a durable productive life extending well beyond any one time interval (such as a year), during which its services are priced by the market. Therefore, capital theory addressed itself to a critical question left unanswered by the usual demand–supply analysis of resource flows. What are the determinants of the capital investment decision? Under what circumstances will firms add to the stock of plant and equipment?

Within the past decade a similar approach has been suggested for human resources. If the stock of labor services embodied in a person can be construed as a stock of human capital, then certain actions can be interpreted as investments in human capital. Decisions that affect the quantity or quality of the labor–service flow over extended future periods, through improved skills or knowledge, are viewed as the result of a deliberate investment. Before examining the causes and effects of such investments, however, we shall trace briefly the theory of investment in nonhuman capital, for the more recent departure in the analysis of human behavior leans heavily upon concepts developed as part of the earlier theory.

INVESTMENT IN NONHUMAN CAPITAL

The decision of a firm to invest in new plant or equipment is a profit-maximizing decision. It hinges upon the return expected from the capital equipment. But this return has two aspects. First, since capital equipment will have a useful life stretching over many years, it is an *expected* return accruing to the firm over several years in the future. Second, investment decisions entail a choice among alternatives. Thus the return is a comparative return, considering alternative uses to which funds can be allocated.

The Present Value of an Asset

If one were to lend $100 for a year at an interest rate of 5 per cent per year, he would get back at the end of the year his $100 of principal plus $5 in interest payment, or a total of $105. Put arithmetically, the final repayment is

$$\$100 + .05 \ (\$100) = \$100 \ (1+.05) = \$105$$

Instead of taking repayment, suppose one could let the loan run for a second year at the same interest rate. Then at the end of the second year he could collect $105 plus 5 per cent of $105, or $110.25. That is

$$\$105 + .05 \ (\$105) = \$105 \ (1+.05) = \$110.25$$

Notice, however, that the $105 in this formula was obtained from the first one: $105 = $100 (1+.05). Therefore, by substituting this expression for $105 in the second formula it can be written

$$\$105 \ (1+.05) = [\$100 \ (1+.05)] \ (1+.05) = \$100 \ (1+.05)^2 = \$110.25$$

If the loan were made for three years, final repayment would amount to $100 (1+.05)^3 and by extension a loan for t years will pay back $100 (1+.05)^t at the end of t years.

Now let us turn the question around. Instead of asking what one would get back in a year if he were to lend $100 today, we can ask, "If one gets back $105 in one year at 5 percent interest, what is today's value of that claim?" Obviously the answer is $100. In terms of the arithmetic formula, $100 = $105/(1+.05). The present value of $105 one year hence is $100. In a sense, $100 today is equivalent to $105 in a year, because if $100 were loaned for a year it would bring $105. The *present value* of a given amount to be received one year later is equal to that amount discounted by $1/(1+.05)$ where .05 is the interest rate and $1/(1+.05)$ is called the discount rate. In this example the discount rate is .9524 when rounded to four decimal places. A sum of money one year hence is worth today approximately 95 per cent of that sum.

Likewise, we can ask: "What is the present value of $110.25 two years from now?" With an interest rate of 5 per cent the answer is $100 because $110.25/(1+.05)^2 = $100. In general, the present value of a given amount R to be received t periods into the future is given by $R/(1+i)^t$ where i denotes the interest rate per period.

So far we have been dealing with a given amount to be received in one period sometime in the future. Rather than one claim collectible at a particular future date, a bond represents a series of claims collectible at different times in the future. A bond is essentially an I.O.U.: a promise to pay made by the issuer. When a bond is issued, let us suppose it has attached to it a set of coupons. Owners of bonds are coupon clippers. In each year the owner (a creditor) clips a coupon and sends it to the issuer (a debtor), who then pays the amount specified on the coupon. When no coupons are left the bond reaches maturity and is cashed in by the owner for its par value. When it is first issued, and at each date thereafter while it is traded on the bond market, the bond will have a value or price. This value is the present value of the sum of all the discounted returns to be paid in each future year plus the discounted maturity value.

Let R denote a fixed dollar amount to be paid by the borrower (issuer) in each year. This is the fixed dollar amount specified on each coupon. Let the interest rate be represented by i. Then our previous discussion indicates that the present value of R one year hence is $R/(1+i)$; the present value of R two years hence is $R/(1+i)^2$. If the bond has a duration of n years, the last coupon is worth today $R/(1+i)^n$. The bond also has a maturity value signified by P, and the present value of this repayment is $P/(1+i)^n$. As a consequence, the present value, V, of the bond is

$$V = \frac{R}{(1+i)} + \frac{R}{(1+i)^2} + \frac{R}{(1+i)^3} + \cdots + \frac{R}{(1+i)^n} + \frac{P}{(1+i)^n}$$

It is the discounted stream of future net returns plus the discounted maturity value.

The present-value formula for a bond indicates that there is an inverse relationship between the market value of a bond and the interest rate. Whenever V is rising, i is falling and vice versa. The reason is that R and P are fixed. When a bond is first issued, its face value is specified and the dollar payments to be made each year are fixed. However, the bond may have a duration of 100 years or more (n usually is quite large). For many years prior to its maturity date the bond will be traded on the bond market, and its ownership will be transferred to different people as they vary their security portfolios. Consequently, its price may fluctuate daily as conditions of demand and supply change on the bond market. What this means is that the "effective" interest rate, not that quoted on the face of a bond, is changing in the opposite direction.

The Marginal Efficiency of Investment

A firm, when contemplating capital expansion, must decide whether it is profitable to borrow the funds necessary to purchase additional capital equipment. If borrowing is unnecessary, if the firm already possesses the funds, it must decide whether it is more profitable to use the funds for capital expansion or for the purchase of some existing asset, such as the outstanding bond of another firm or a government bond. The investment decision is therefore a choice among alternatives based upon returns and costs expected from each possible action.

Since an entrepreneur purchases a machine with a view to its profitability, and since the machine has a long-run useful life, he must consider the contribution to profit rendered by the machine in each of several future years. There are three components of this profitability: the addition to total revenue in each year, the number of years involved, and the current cost of the machine.

The decision to purchase a machine is a marginal decision; it is a question of whether or not to add an item of capital equipment to the firm's total capital stock. Hence, the entrepreneur will want to know how much of the addition to total revenue is attributable to the machine as opposed to the other inputs with which it is combined to produce output. If the machine is purchased, it would in any one year be combined with labor and raw materials to yield output. From the sales proceeds of the output must be deducted these other costs (wages, costs of raw materials, cost of electrical power, etc.) in order to arrive at the *net* return attributable to the machine. In any one future year the size of this net return depends upon the physical productivity of the machine, the price at which the output produced with the aid of the machine can be sold, and the amount of these other costs. In turn the price of output and the other costs depend upon conditions in the product and resource markets. And since any one year is a future year, these market conditions are uncertain. As a consequence the entrepreneur must form an expectation of what the net return will be in any one year.

Having formed an idea of the return, the entrepreneur must next determine the useful life of the machine, for this will establish the number of years over which a return can be expected. Suppose it is anticipated that the machine will last for five years. Given the entrepreneur's expectations, we denote the series of net returns as R_1, R_2, R_3, R_4, R_5.

The above R's are a series of additions to total revenue attributed to the machine. To determine its expected profitability account must be taken of the cost of the investment. Suppose the purchase price of the machine is given, established by the market and beyond the control of a single firm. This purchase price is designated as O (for outlay). There is, however, another less obvious cost, and this is where the interest rate enters the picture. There is a cost involved in the use of money. An entrepreneur contemplating the purchase of a machine has two choices open to him. Since he cannot obtain the machine without money, he must borrow the necessary funds or draw upon his own accumulated financial reserves. If he borrows he must pay the current rate of interest on a loan of the necessary duration. Then as he receives the revenue from sale of the output produced with the machine, he can repay the principal and interest on the loan. But even if he does not have to borrow, the interest is still a cost. Why? Because if he did not purchase the machine, he could lend his funds by, say, purchasing a bond, which would yield him an interest income based upon the current rate of interest. By the opportunity-cost principle, the interest income foregone by purchasing a machine is properly a cost of its purchase. Thus, whether or not he had the funds on hand, the entrepreneur will count the interest as a cost and add this to the purchase price in order to determine the full cost of an additional machine.

In deriving cost and expected return one arrives at the core of the investment decision. If expected return exceeds cost, the firm will purchase the machine. For this means the firm could borrow funds equal to its purchase price, repay the loan plus interest, and still expect to have something left over. Or with the funds already on hand there is a greater return expected from using them to buy a machine rather than another asset. If cost is greater than expected return, the firm will not do so; it will not borrow the necessary funds or, if it has them, it will lend them out rather than use them to purchase the machine because the interest income from such an action exceeds the net income expected from the machine. Fundamentally, the decision is a choice among alternative forms of assets. It is the net return on a machine compared to the net return on other forms of assets, such as bonds, that determines the choice.

From this general description, the investment decision can be explained in more formal terms. Whether the firm were to purchase an interest-bearing asset or a machine, the outlay must be made in the present whereas the returns accrue in the future. The cost of borrowing can be expressed as a percentage of the funds borrowed, namely, the interest rate. The percentage rate of return on the purchase of a bond is also the interest rate. Hence, whether the firm must borrow or not, the prevailing interest rate will influence its investment decision. If the interest rate is 4 per cent, while the firm's expected percentage rate of return on investment is 3 per cent, it will not borrow the funds to carry out capital expansion. Assuming the firm has the funds, an interest rate of 4 per cent represents the return from purchase of a bond. And again the firm will not invest. On the other hand, an expected return of 6 per cent on capital expansion, with an interest rate of 3 per cent, will induce the firm to invest whether or not it must borrow the funds. The problem, then, is to specify the firm's expected percentage rate of return on investment in order to compare it with the interest rate.

In contrast to a bond the dollar amount to be received from a piece of capital equipment is not the same in each future year. Let R_t denote the dollar earnings expected of a machine in future year t. This return is that obtained from the sale of its output after deducting other operating costs. A series of annual returns can be expected, but they will vary depending upon expectations of changes in wage rates, other operating costs, and the demand for output. If the machine has a productive life of n years, the stream of expected net returns can be represented by R_1, R_2, ..., R_n. At the end of the n years the machine will have some scrap value, which we signify by G. The present value of this stream of returns plus scrap value is determined by the firm's expectations and its discount rate. The discount rate assumed to be chosen by the firm is the rate that will make the present value equal to the purchase price of the machine. Why this rate is used will become clear in a moment.

Let O represent the market price of a machine, which is known to the firm. The *marginal efficiency of investment*[1] is denoted by r where

$$O = \frac{R_1}{(1+r)} + \frac{R_2}{(1+r)^2} + \frac{R_3}{(1+r)^3} + \cdots + \frac{R_n}{(1+r)^n} + \frac{G}{(1+r)^n}$$

That is, the marginal efficiency of investment is defined as a per cent that determines the discount rate $1/(1+r)$ that makes the present value equal to the purchase price of the machine. As such, r is a *rate* of net return, or a return over cost, contributed to the firm by the machine. In this formula O is known by the firm; all R's and G are given by the firm's expectations. Therefore, the formula can be solved for r.

Suppose a machine costing $1,000 has an expected life of five years. If a firm must borrow the $1,000 it will have to pay an interest rate of, say, 4 per cent per year. Now if r equals 6 per cent, this means the firm could borrow the thousand dollars, make interest payments and repay the principal at the end of five years, and still expect to have something left over from the net proceeds earned by the machine. Clearly it is profitable to borrow for the purpose of capital expansion.

For a firm with the $1,000 on hand the interest rate represents a 4 per cent rate of return from purchase of a bond. Since r equals 6 per cent, use of the $1,000 to purchase a machine brings a greater net return. It pays to invest in the machine rather than the bond.

We can also look at it in a slightly different way. Assuming that the R's are the same for each alternative and that G = P, then r greater than i means that V is larger than O. To get the same net dollar "profit" takes a greater outlay on the bond than on the machine. Regardless of

---

[1] The discount rate is sometimes called the *marginal efficiency of capital*, the term used by J. M. Keynes when he introduced this theory of investment in 1936. See J. M. Keynes, *The General Theory of Employment, Interest and Money* (New York: Harcourt, Brace & Co., Inc., 1936), p. 135.

how we look at it the marginal efficiency of investment is the net percentage rate earned on investment capital, and when this rate exceeds the prevailing interest rate it is profitable to purchase additional pieces of capital equipment.

The Investment Demand Schedule

The investment demand schedule is a relationship between aggregate investment and the interest rate. To explain this relationship it is convenient to begin by assuming the interest rate is 7 per cent and the marginal efficiency of investment is 10 per cent. Under this condition firms have an incentive to increase investment. As they do so the marginal efficiency of investment will decline for two reasons. First, the R's, the net dollar returns in each year, decrease as investment expands. There are three forces which cooperate to produce this effect. As the number of machines and other pieces of capital equipment expand, their marginal physical products decline. Also, as output expands because of increased inputs of capital, product prices fall (given the demand for consumer goods). Moreover, greater demand for labor and other inputs combined with the additional capital tends to raise their prices, thus operating to reduce the net returns from sale of the product. Besides a decrease in the R's, the expanding demand for capital instruments tends to raise their prices. And a rise in O pushes r even lower.

In general, a drop in the R's and/or a rise in O cause r to decline as investment increases. At first r may fall to 9 per cent, then 8 per cent. But as long as this expected rate of return exceeds the interest rate of 7 per cent, it is still profitable to expand investment. Therefore, investment will continue to increase until r has been reduced to 7 per cent. When this happens, there is no longer an incentive to increase investment, for a further expansion of investment would push the marginal efficiency of investment below the interest rate. The equilibrium level of investment is that at which $r = i$.

Given an initial equilibrium with $r = i = .07$, investment will remain at its equilibrium level as long as the interest rate and expectations do not change. We now ask what would happen if the interest rate were to decrease from 7 to 5 per cent. Obviously, with r equal to 7 per cent, firms are not in equilibrium, so investment will increase. When it does, r falls as described above. Investment expands until the marginal efficiency of investment is equal to 5 per cent, at which the new equilibrium amount of investment is greater than the initial equilibrium amount. Notice that it is a change in the interest rate that disturbs the initial equilibrium. The fall in the interest rate causes investment to increase, and the increase in investment in turn pulls the marginal efficiency of investment down to equality with the lower interest rate.

An investment demand curve is depicted as the unbroken curve I_D in

Fig. 23.1. For the present, the broken curve I'_D is to be ignored. On the vertical axis are recorded alternative interest rates, and aggregate net investment is measured on the horizontal axis. The investment demand curve I_D is a locus of points showing the equilibrium amount of investment corresponding to each possible interest rate. Since the alternative amounts of investment determined by the curve are equilibrium amounts, this means that for a given interest rate the corresponding investment is that at which $r = i$.

From the diagram it is seen that net investment would be zero if the interest rate were to be i_1. There would be no net additions to the capital stock, and firms would be merely replacing capital equipment as it wears out. At an interest rate of i_3, investment is equal to I_3 because this is the investment flow at which $r = i_3$. The capital stock is being increased by I_3 units per period of time, which is the flow of net output of capital goods. If the interest rate were to fall to i_2, then investment would expand from I_3 to I_4. In the process of moving downward to the right along I_D, the marginal efficiency of investment declines until it is equal to the new lower interest rate.

The investment demand curve is drawn under the condition that firms' "profit" expectations are conceptually held constant. Recall that the R's are defined as *expected* net returns. A more or less optimistic outlook on the future by entrepreneurs may be interpreted as a larger or smaller R_t for each future year t. Expectations of product demand and cost

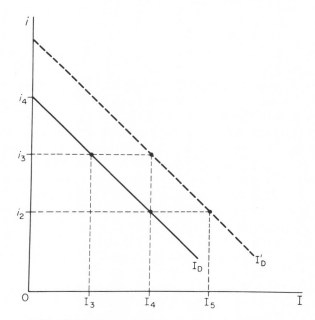

FIG. 23.1. Aggregate Investment Demand Curves

conditions in the long run may be such as to yield greater or smaller net earnings to be obtained from a machine or other piece of capital equipment. Since these expectations are of a subjective and psychological nature, it is not surprising that the investment demand curve is subject to rather violent shifts.

INVESTMENT IN HUMAN CAPITAL

Statistical studies have attempted to measure the contributions made by different resource inputs to the growth in national output. An aggregate production function is specified for the entire economy: national output as a function of the employment of land, physical reproducible capital, and man-hours of labor. If the various studies using modifications of this basic production function did successfully explain all determinants of economic growth, the quantitative expansion of inputs over time would account for the quantitative expansion of output. Instead, these studies have shown that actual increases in national output are larger than the increases explained by greater inputs of capital and labor.

The large unexplained component of economic growth has been attributed to two causes. Technological innovation has improved the quality of capital equipment, thus raising the productivity of capital. In addition, the labor force has improved in quality, so the productivity of labor has likewise increased. The latter is described as the result of investments in human capital in the expectation that such an approach will not only help to solve many of the puzzles of aggregate economic growth but also further our understanding of resource allocation.

The Concept of Human Capital

Economists have long known that people are an important part of a nation's wealth. Yet economists have been reluctant to explore the implications of human beings as wealth. One important reason is that men differ from all other forms of wealth. Unlike property or marketable assets, a man is much more than a means of generating goods and services. Man is a moral being and, if he is a free agent, the economy should serve his ends. Nevertheless, recognition that man is, among other and perhaps more noble things, a storehouse of productive services has led to a new stress upon the way in which he enlarges or improves his capacity as a unit of economic wealth.

In the past, expenditures by households have typically been treated wholly as consumption expenditures. Exponents of the human-capital approach have called attention to the fact that some household expenditures are comparable to those made by firms as capital investments. Expenditures on education and regional migration are cited as examples of household expenditures that are more properly to be regarded as investments, for these expenditures have the effect of raising productivity and future income.

People invest in themselves. By doing so, they promote more rapid national economic growth. These investments also affect the allocation of resources in the economy and the distribution of national income.

Some expenditures that raise human productivity and income are public; they are not drawn directly from the personal incomes of families. Public health services and "free" education are financed by public expenditures underwritten ultimately from taxes. But this is also true of nonhuman capital. So-called social overhead capital—public roads, dams, and parks—is financed in the same way.

What types of expenditures may be classified as investments in human capital? Probably the most important are expenditures on formal education at the elementary, secondary, and higher levels. Formal education, among its other effects, does impart skills and knowledge that raise economic productivity and earnings. One estimate suggests that the stock of education in the American labor force in 1956 was more than eight times greater than the stock in 1900. In comparison, the stock of reproducible physical capital rose only about four times during the same period.[2] Moreover, the average percentage return from expenditures on formal education has been about equal to that on investments in honhuman capital.[3]

Formal education is not the only means of acquiring skills that raise productivity. On-the-job training (including craft apprenticeships) and study programs for adults constitute another form of investment in human capital. To the extent that these measures raise labor productivity (see Chapter 22), they increase the rate of growth of output in a way no different basically from expenditures on more or better machinery. Although it is extremely difficult to measure the magnitude of such investments, expenditures for on-the-job training alone have been placed well above $15 million per year in the United States.

Relocation to take advantage of changing job opportunities is a third major category of self-investment. Migration may include not only a movement from one area to another but also a shift from one industry or occupation to another as the structure of the economy changes. Reallocation of resources from less productive to more productive employments raises the growth rate of national output. From an individual's perspective, decisions to migrate may be conceived of as investments with long-term returns to the prospective migrant. Since migration decisions are similar to investment decisions described in the previous section, they are properly regarded as investments in human capital. The 1960 Census of Population shows that Americans are a mobile people. In a single year, between 1949 and 1950, over 6.3 million persons migrated from one county to another; about one-third of them moved to a noncontiguous state. Over a five-year interval,

[2] T. W. Schultz, "Education and Economic Growth" in H. G. Richey (ed.), *Social Forces Influencing American Education* (Chicago: The University of Chicago Press, 1961).

[3] G. S. Becker, *Human Capital. A Theoretical and Empirical Analysis, with Special Reference to Education* (Princeton: Princeton University Press, 1964).

between 1955 and 1960, almost 28 million persons five years of age or older (17 per cent of this population) migrated to a different county; approximately half moved to a different state.

Finally, health facilities and services have an influence on human productivity. Better diet and health care affect not only life expectancy, physical stamina, and vigor but also—so the psychologists tell us—mental alertness and emotional stability. Private and public expenditures on health, broadly interpreted, therefore act to raise the productivity of the labor force.

It is apparent that investments in human capital are expenditures tied to an employment situation, in contrast to pure consumption expenditures. Economic decisions on whether to undertake additional formal education hinge on the educational requirements for different jobs. Returns on the investment are a function of the expected future earnings associated with alternative jobs and the costs of undertaking the education. Again, migration is a movement from one employment situation to another, with different earning possibilities to be compared against the cost of movement. Consequently, whether the analysis is applied to education, training, migration, or any other form of investment in human capital, it will be useful to describe the anticipated returns and costs in terms of employment opportunities.

Employment Choice

A person's choice of employment can be viewed from two angles: (1) choice of an occupation, and (2) choice of an industry in which that occupation will be practiced. Of course, for some occupations such as high school teaching or nursing the question of alternative industries in which the occupation might be practiced is irrelevant. The essential feature of this choice, at least occupational choice, is that it entails a long-term personal investment. Rewards hinge not only on the current wage rate but also on the anticipation of a series of future returns—both pecuniary and nonpecuniary—over one's expected lifetime.

Let us first consider the pecuniary returns associated with a given occupation practiced in a given industry. We shall call this occupation-industry combination an *employment opportunity*. Suppose a person were to consider the future monetary prospects accruing to him from each employment opportunity. In any future year he will expect some gross income, including the monetary value of fringe benefits such as company contributions to insurance, a pension plan, and so on. However, for practically all employment opportunities there will be some expenses to be incurred: for education or training, tools and equipment, uniforms, travel. And these will vary from one employment opportunity to another. Thus, for any one employment opportunity there will be an expected *net* income (gross income minus expenses) in each of several future years. This string of future expected net monetary returns constitutes what we call an *expected income stream*.

What are some of the forces that will affect the expected income stream? The current wage rate per hour worked, for one thing. But also there are many others: an expectation of future changes in the wage rate; hours worked per year, which depend upon seasonal fluctuations in output of the industry; the industry trend of growth or decline, and the extent to which it is affected by recessions or depressions; the time pattern of the person's productivity (how it varies with age); pension income; and the size and time pattern of expenses. Although the income stream will vary in appearance from one employment opportunity to another, it may nevertheless be instructive to ask what a "typical" expected net income stream would look like. In Fig. 23.2, age is measured on the horizontal axis; on the vertical axis is measured the expected annual net income that would accrue to the person if that employment opportunity were chosen. Net income is regarded as zero up to the age a_0, which may conveniently be taken as the age of minimum education required by law. The subsequent segment of negative net returns refers to the period of training when expense outlays—for tuition, books, tools, equipment, and the like—are likely to exceed any positive gross income earned. Thereafter, in general, net income becomes positive, rises to a peak, and then decreases with age because of declining productivity.

If a person with given abilities and wealth were to consider one such expected income stream for each employment opportunity, then he would be faced with the problem of choosing among them. That is, choice of an employment opportunity is tantamount to choice of an expected future income stream. Some of these opportunities, hence some of the income streams, will be regarded as irrelevant. People differ, of course, in mental and physical abilities, specialized skills, degree of knowledge of

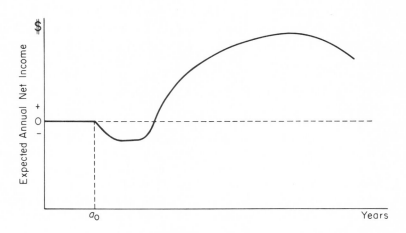

FIG. 23.2. Hypothetical Expected Net Income Stream

the market, wealth, and cultural background. Thus the entire set will be narrowed down to those that are considered to be feasible objects of choice. Once this restriction is made, choice among the feasible set will be influenced not just by the relative magnitudes of expected income but also by the nonpecuniary attributes of each employment opportunity: prestige; the desire to be one's own boss; attractiveness of the kind of work; climate, if this influences industry of employment; and so forth. In other words, people take account of both monetary and nonmonetary rewards to be derived from each employment opportunity. As a consequence, income streams will be ranked according to one's preferences, not necessarily in order of magnitude, and his choice will be based on the ranking. This is simply another way of saying that each person may be assumed to have a utility function. To each employment opportunity he regards as feasible he attaches a personal utility based on both pecuniary and nonpecuniary returns. The employment opportunity chosen is the one that maximizes his utility.

Investment Schedule

The theory of employment choice has not been refined to the point at which nonpecuniary variables have been included in a systematic way. Perhaps a more definitive theory must await interdisciplinary endeavors that incorporate not only economic theory and method but also contributions from psychology and sociology. Unlike investments in nonhuman capital, the theory of investment in human capital does not permit a prediction about an *equilibrium* rate of return or level of investment (see Fig. 23.1). Like the theory of nonhuman investments, however, a formulation of returns and costs is possible. A mechanism is thereby provided by which returns and costs can be estimated.

Two cautions are in order. In the present stage of development of the theory, only the economic aspects of the investment decision can be determined from it, not the "solution" of a final employment choice. Secondly, the question of the most relevant and accurate measure of the rate of return on investment is the subject of considerable debate. Keeping these cautions in mind, the following presentation is intended to be general enough to be applied to a variety of different human-investment problems and to indicate clearly the extent to which the formulation borrows from the theory of investment in nonhuman capital.

To keep the analysis simple, we shall consider only two employment opportunities. Let Q_t represent the earnings expected in year t from one employment opportunity, and let P_t represent the earnings expected in year t from the second employment opportunity. The difference between the two, $R_t = Q_t - P_t$, is the expected gain from transfer from the second to the first employment. Assume also that a person's expected work horizon is n years, i.e., $t = 1, 2, 3, \ldots, n$. Thus in each of the n future years some gain or loss would occur from being employed in the first rather than the second employment. The present value of this stream of expected future returns is

$$V = \frac{R_1}{(1+r)} + \frac{R_2}{(1+r)^2} + \frac{R_3}{(1+r)^3} + \cdots + \frac{R_n}{(1+r)^n},$$

where r is an "internal" or subjective per cent that determines the discount rate $1/(1+r)$.

Suppose that V is positive, so that the first employment opportunity carries greater expected earnings over the individual's working life. However, in order to take advantage of these greater earnings, an investment expenditure equal to O is necessary in the present. This outlay may be needed for additional formal education if the first employment carries a higher requirement of educational attainment. It may, however, represent the cost of job training or migration from one region to another, as the case may be. Whatever the form of investment, the internal or subjective rate of return (comparable to the marginal efficiency of investment in nonhuman capital) can be computed by setting V equal to O. With the cost of the investment, O, known, and expected future earnings, the R's, given, the percentage value, r, can be computed.

There are two routes that can be taken once the value of r is determined. One might be called the personal orientation. Statistical age–earnings profiles can be obtained for those who have undertaken the investment in question and for those who have not. The difference at each age yields R. For a person of a given age, the value of R at each future age provides an empirical estimate of expected future earnings that would be the result of self-investment. Having calculated the cost of the investment, O, the "marginal efficiency of investment" can be approximated for those who are in a position to undertake the investment. If r exceeds the interest rate, i, then the investment is profitable. The potential investor could borrow funds equal to the cost, O, make interest payments, repay the principal after n years, and still enjoy a financial gain. Alternatively, r greater than i means that the net return from human investment is greater than the return from asset accumulation in the form of bonds or other marketable securities yielding the interest rate i.

If, and only if, it could be assumed that human-investment decisions are based solely upon pecuniary returns, could one proceed along lines similar to investments in nonhuman capital. By aggregating individual investment expenditures, one could obtain an investment demand schedule like that in Fig. 23.1 and determine an equilibrium given by $r = i$. Few, if any, economists are willing to do so, however. The theory specifies only a mechanism for determining whether it pays in strictly pecuniary terms to carry out self-investment. You, the reader, can calculate your expected earnings after receipt of a bachelor's degree, the earnings you would expect as a secondary school graduate, the cost of your college education, and thereby the economic rate of return from an investment in college education. Also, by estimating your *net* earnings (gross income minus investment costs) in each year and selecting an appropriate discount rate, you can estimate your economic worth as the present value of the future net income stream. Query: How much life insurance are you willing to purchase now? How much would you purchase five years from now if you were married and had two children at that time?

A second orientation is that of national production and aggregate economic growth. By using the same procedures, the national average percentage rate of return can be calculated for each type of investment in human capital. These rates of return are used as partial evidence of the effects of such investments on the output of the country. The rates can be compared with each other and with the rate of return on investments in nonhuman capital to help determine which kinds of investment contribute most to economic growth. Comparative rates of return are useful in arriving at public policies on economic growth that affect shares of the nation's total resources directed toward one purpose or another.

Pros and Cons

The human-capital approach to resource allocation has been criticized on several grounds. First, in the case of private expenditures, it is difficult to separate total household expenditures into pure consumption and pure investment. In fact, many family expenditures include both components (direct satisfaction or utility from health and education, for example). Second, even if it were possible to isolate consumption from investment, it is not possible to assign a specific return to a specific type of investment. Instead, it is argued, any measurable return is the composite effect of all investment expenditures taken together. Third, some have alleged that the approach is ill-advised because it fails to give sufficient weight to nonpecuniary or noneconomic aspects of human goals and behavior. Finally, the statistics (estimates of future expected earnings and the discount rate), because they are so imperfect, may be misleading.

In spite of these criticisms, the human-capital approach has many advantages. Many important questions on the sources of national economic growth have been raised. Theoretical refinement and precise statistical measurement are lacking at the present time. But further thought and research may well produce answers to critical problems that to date remain unsolved. In the area of microeconomics, the human-capital approach has gone beyond the standard theory by taking account of long-run expectations that affect allocation decisions by owners of labor services. Rather than attempting to explain the supply side of the labor market in terms of responses to current wage rates (returns of the moment, so to speak), the human-capital formulation of supply has rightfully emphasized the long-run nature of employment choice and change.

Important for our purposes is the effect this analysis has upon labor supply curves utilized in the preceding chapters. It might appear that the predominance of subjective factors renders the supply curve useless or "incorrect." But this is not so. Rather, the analysis suggests that there are additional conditions that must be taken as constant when considering a given supply curve for a defined type of labor. First, a *type* of labor is normally defined in terms of an occupation. Consequently, as more members of society choose one occupation over others, basing their choice on a long-run investment decision, the supply curves for this type of labor to industries generally will shift to the right—and to the left as occupational membership declines. Second, recall that an expected income stream is formulated for a given current wage rate. An increase in labor demand will tend to raise the current wage rate and therefore shift upward an entire income-stream curve like the one drawn in Fig. 23.2. Other things being the same, the expected stream will rise and cause additional people to choose this employment opportunity over others. So it still follows that labor supply curves to industries will be positively sloped. Furthermore, any one industry is affected by a rise in the wage rates paid in other industries; e.g., as expected income streams increase elsewhere the labor supply curve will shift to the left for the industry in question.

What, then, is the outcome of the analysis? Holding constant the wage rates paid in other industries on the labor supply curve to one must be regarded as an approximation—an approximation to holding constant the expected income streams elsewhere. It remains true that an increase in the wage rate paid in one industry relative to those paid in others will increase the quantity of labor supplied to that industry. But this conclusion holds only so long as all other pecuniary and nonpecuniary characteristics of employment remain unchanged. To put it another way, the response of labor supplied to changes in wage rates remains unaltered as far as the direction of movement is concerned. Still, there are other aspects of employment that will influence labor allocation among industries. Though we cannot, at the present time, identify each of these separately and objectively (as we can the wage rate), their effects on the wage and employment equilibrium for different industries can nevertheless be traced. With these reservations in mind the labor supply curve remains an extremely useful tool of analysis.

APPLICATIONS

Applications to education and to regional labor migration will illustrate the extent to which the human capital analysis contributes to our knowledge of resource allocation and economic growth. These applications will be presented in terms of empirical studies. Since many public policies have a bearing upon human investments, the broad social implications of these studies should be apparent.

Several efforts have been made to measure the rate of return to investments in education. Common to all these efforts is the basic method of estimating returns by contrasting the lifetime earnings of those who have had more education with the lifetime earnings of those who have had less. One variation on this theme is a computation of the present value of the future stream of earnings differentials. To obtain the present value it is necessary for the investigator to choose some "objective" discount rate which is presumed to reflect what is essentially the result of people's subjective judgments.

Granted that the average earnings at each age (among all persons of that age with that level of educational attainment) are a sufficiently close approximation to expected earnings, then the present value depends upon the chosen discount rate. Using as data average earnings before taxes, drawn from the 1950 Census of Population, Professor H. S. Houthakker[4] has shown how sensitive present values are to the discount factor. For a person 14 years of age, the present value of the earnings differentials resulting from four or more years of college is $106,269 at a 3 per cent discount rate and only $47,546 at a 6 per cent discount rate. Because there is no easy answer to the question of what is the appropriate discount rate, empirically estimated present values are only rough approximations to the "average" economic worth of additional education. Choice of the long-term market rate of interest (recently about 5 to 6 per cent) seems reasonable if publicly financed education is at issue, because the government can borrow funds at that rate. However, for individuals contemplating an investment in additional education, a higher rate would be required to reflect the greater risk connected with a loan to a single person.

Table 23.1
Internal Rates of Return to Investments in Education

Increment of Education	Return
From 0 to 2 years	8.9%
From 2 years to 6 years	14.5%
From 6 years to 8 years	29.2%
From 8 years to 10 years	9.5%
From 10 years to 12 years	13.7%
From 12 years to 14 years	5.4%
From 14 years to 16 years	15.6%

Another variation of the same basic method, using earnings differentials between levels of educational attainment, computes what is called an internal percentage rate of return. A value of r is obtained by estimating the series

[4] H. S. Houthakker, "Education and Income," *Review of Economics and Statistics* (February 1959).

of R's and setting the present value equal to the cost of education, O. Using this approach, Professor W. Lee Hansen[5] has estimated the marginal rates of return to successive increments of schooling shown in Table 23.1.

It is apparent from the table that the rates rise over the first few years of education, through the elementary level. Thereafter, the rates are lower. Completion of high school and completion of college both carry higher rates of return than partial education in either category. Estimates such as these can be compared with returns from other forms of investment. For comparative purposes, it is noteworthy that the estimated average rate of return on private investments in nonhuman capital is about 9 to 10 per cent.

Regional Labor Migration

Regional labor migration can also be posed in terms of an investment decision. For two different regions, let P_t denote annual expected earnings in year t from employment in the region of present location. Let Q_t signify annual expected earnings in year t from employment in the other region. Then the difference, $R_t = Q_t - P_t$, is the expected gross gain in one year resulting from a migration investment. The present value of the expected stream (the discounted sum of R_t over n remaining working years) constitutes the gross return to migration in the present. One can postulate that migrants respond to this variable rather than to the current wage rate differentials.

Again, varying empirical approaches are possible. By using average earnings by age as an approximation to expected earnings, and by selecting some discount rate, the present value can be estimated empirically. Alternatively, having approximated gross returns by the same method, the present value can be set equal to the cost of movement to find an internal rate of return to migration. The costs include the worker's transportation cost, cost of transporting his dependents, cost of moving his personal property plus (minus) the loss (gain) from sale and repurchase of real property, and his income foregone during the time spent in migrating.

Empirical studies have shown that geographic mobility is directly related to educational attainment and inversely related to age. Mobility is inversely related to the number of a worker's dependents and to the value of his personal property holdings. These latter two variables may reflect in part the nonpecuniary determinants of migration—reluctance to move if ties are firmly established in the community of his present location. Education and age appear to be the most important demographic variables affecting mobility.

Table 23.2 records interstate migrants by education and age. Number of migrants is expressed as a percentage of the population with a given number of school years completed. For each level of educational attainment in a

[5] W. L. Hansen, "Total and Private Rates of Return to Investment in Schooling," *Journal of Political Economy*, Vol. 81 (1963).

given row (holding education constant), the percentage of migrants decreases as more advanced ages are considered. For each age group in a given column (holding age constant), it is seen that the percentage rises with educational attainment.

Table 23.2

Interstate Migration, 1955–1960
(Per cent of educational attainment population)

EDUCATIONAL ATTAINMENT	AGE GROUP			
	25–34	*35–44*	*45–64*	*65 & over*
No School	4.8	4.2	2.7	2.2
Less than 5 years	7.9	5.6	3.1	2.5
5–8 years	10.7	6.1	3.6	3.7
9–11 years	12.5	7.0	4.5	5.2
12 years	14.1	8.5	5.5	5.6
13–15 years	19.2	13.2	7.1	6.4
16 or more years	30.6	17.7	9.2	7.8

Source: U.S. Department of Commerce, *U.S. Census of Population*, 1960.

If, in fact, migration decisions are viewed as long-term investment decisions, these results should not be surprising. We have already seen that more education brings greater income. A prosperous region of the country (a higher average income in the region) will offer even greater financial rewards than a depressed area or low-income region. The absolute size of the differential in expected earnings will be larger at higher levels of educational attainment. Therefore, gross returns to migration will be larger and the rate of return to migration will be greater. Older people have a shorter work horizon than younger people. As a consequence, for a given differential in expected annual earnings, the older worker would be able to enjoy the differential over a shorter future period. Thus, the present value of the stream is smaller (n is smaller) and the rate of return is lower for a given cost of movement.

SUGGESTED READING

M. Blaug, *Economics of Education 1*. Middlesex: Penguin Books, 1968.

C. S. Benson, *The Economics of Public Education*. Boston: Houghton Mifflin Co., 1961.

M. Brennan, M. Schupack, and P. Taft, *The Economics of Age*. New York: W. W. Norton and Co., 1966.

G. S. Becker, *Human Capital: A Theoretical and Empirical Analysis*. Princeton: Princeton University Press, 1964.

24

General Equilibrium
and the Distribution of Income

The theory of price has so far been centered on a single industry. The objective, both in product and resource pricing, has been the attainment of equilibrium conditions for one industry. Economists describe this approach as *partial* equilibrium analysis—partial because it refers to one industry among many in the economy. By concentrating on the market for one commodity much is learned about the forces that allocate products and resources. Nevertheless, a single market is an incomplete picture, for the theory has clearly shown that the equilibrium price and quantity exchanged of one product or resource depend upon the price-quantity conditions existing for other products and resources. Another approach, which takes into account simultaneously all product and resource markets in the economy, is called *general* equilibrium analysis. The study of general equilibrium is concerned with the way in which movements from one equilibrium point to another in a given market will in turn generate movements in other markets.

INTERRELATED MARKETS

Product and Resource Markets: One Industry

To simplify matters, assume pure competition in both product and resource market. The results are easily extended to noncompetitive cases without any essential alteration regarding the way in which changes in one market affect the other. Furthermore, assume that the industry produces a commodity X using two resources A and B, both variable. The supply curves of A and B to the industry are positively sloped, and the product supply curve of the industry is likewise positively sloped.

Given an initial long-run equilibrium, it is desirable to trace the effects of change. Suppose first that consumer demand for the product increases because of any one of a number of causes: a rise in consumer income, a change in the price of some other good, a change in population or tastes. Regardless of the source, the market demand curve for commodity X shifts to the right.

The immediate effect, before firms can adjust output, is a rise in price. Since the product price exceeds marginal cost, each firm expands output by moving upward to the right along its marginal cost curve. Thus, the industry expands output along its short-run supply curve up to the point at which this short-run supply curve intersects the new product demand curve. The existence of profits attracts new firms, and the short-run industry supply curve shifts to the right. A new long-run equilibrium is reached when each firm once more has zero profit and the long-run industry supply curve intersects the new product demand curve.

What effect will be transmitted to resources employed by the industry? The expanded output of previously established firms along with the entry of new firms increase the demand for inputs. The industry demand curves for A and B shift to the right. Resource owners respond to the price rise by moving upward and to the right along their respective supply curves to the industry. When a new equilibrium is reached at the intersection of the supply curves with the new industry demand curves, resource prices will be higher and employment greater. Observe that these higher resource prices are "built into" the long-run industry supply curve of the product; the rise in resource prices is the pecuniary external effect making the industry one of increasing cost. The final long-run results of an increase in product demand are (1) a higher product price, (2) greater industry output and greater consumption of the product, (3) higher resource prices, and (4) expanded employment of both resources.

We turn next to a change originating in the resource market. Assume that the supply curve of resource A shifts to the right, and that the supply curve of resource B and the demand curve for the product do not change. The greater supply of A causes its price to fall. This drop in the resource price shifts cost curves downward for the firms producing X, so marginal cost is less than the product price and firms expand output. If A and B are complements in production, the marginal physical product curve of B will shift upward as more of A is used. Then it is certain that the industry demand curve for B will shift to the right, because the complementarity effect enforces the output-expansion effect. On the other hand, expanded use of A may reduce the marginal product of B, tending to reduce the demand for B. If this holds true and if the substitution effect outweighs the output-expansion effect, then A and B are defined as substitutes in production. And the demand curve for B will shift to the left in response to the lower price of A.

Regardless of whether A and B are substitutes or complements in production, the lower price of A will increase the supply of the product. As marginal costs curves of firms shift downward, the industry supply curve of the product shifts to the right and, given product demand, the product price will fall. The net long-run results of an increase in the supply of A are (1) a lower price and greater employment of A, (2) a larger supply and lower price of the product so output and consumption of the product increase, (3) a higher price and greater employment of B if A and B are complements in production, or (4) a lower price and smaller employment of B if A and B are substitutes in production.

From these illustrations we can derive some general conclusions regarding the relationship between resource and product markets. Putting aside any possibility of technological change, the effect of a change in the product market upon the resource market must originate on the demand side of the product market. A change in product demand will in turn affect resource prices by means of a change in the industry demand for resources. The effect of a change in the resource market upon the product market must originate on the supply side of the resource market. For a change in resource supply will affect the product price by means of a change in the industry supply curve for the product. In brief, changes in product demand affect resource demand and changes in resource supply affect product supply.

Changes in technology affect both resource and product markets simultaneously. A technological innovation that raises the marginal products of all resources employed in the industry will reduce average and marginal cost of production. Cost curves shift downward even though resource prices are initially unchanged. The reduction in cost increases product supply and therefore lowers the product price. It also increases the demand for all inputs, thus raising their prices and expanding employment. Not all technological innovations are of this nature, however. Certain types of technological change may reduce the marginal products of some resources, decreasing the industry demand for them. The prices of these resources will fall and their employment in the industry will contract.

Product and Resource Markets: Two Industries

In order to shed more light on how the price system allocates resources and products, let us take the analysis a step further. Rather than a single industry, we shall consider two related industries. For the sake of simplicity we concentrate on one resource employed by both industries, call it A. Although other resources are also used, we ignore them because the effects on these other resources can be inferred from the previous section. The two commodities, denoted by X and Y, are assumed to be substitutes in consumption. Product and resource markets for both industries are purely competitive.

An initial equilibrium is depicted in Fig. 24.1, where four diagrams are presented. The two on the left represent the product market for commodity X (upper diagram) and the resource market for A (lower diagram). Consumer demand for X is shown as D_x and the industry supply of X as S_x in the upper diagram. Hence, the equilibrium price of X is p_6 at which x_6 units of X are exchanged per unit of time. In this same industry equilibrium the price of resource A is p_3 and a_3 units of A are employed, the resource price-quantity combination yielded by the intersection of the industry demand curve for A, D_a^X, and the supply curve of A to the industry, S_a^X.

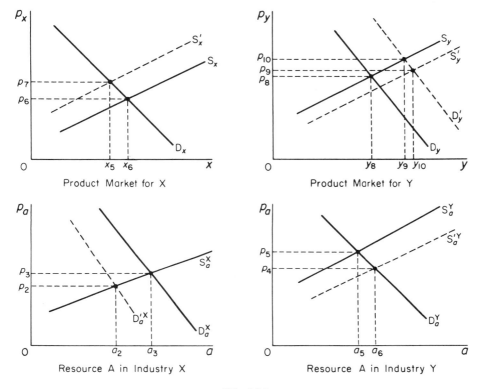

FIG. 24.1.

At the same time, there exists an equilibrium in the product market for the industry producing commodity Y. In the upper right diagram consumer demand for Y is labeled D_y and industry supply is represented by S_y. These demand and supply curves intersect at a price of p_8 and a quantity of y_8 units of Y per unit of time. Corresponding to this product-market equilibrium is the industry equilibrium in the resource market, shown in the lower right diagram. The industry demand curve for A, D_a^Y, and the supply curve of A to the industry, S_a^Y, intersect at a price of p_5 and employment of a_5 units of A per unit of time.

Before considering any change, we should pause briefly to examine the equilibria. There are several points that deserve emphasis. First, commodities X and Y are substitutes in consumption. One of the constancy conditions under which the curve D_x is drawn is a constant price of Y. Therefore, D_x lies in this position only as long as the price of Y is indeed p_8. Similarly, the curve D_y holds constant the price of commodity X and lies in its given position as long as the price of X remains p_6. Second, the industry supply curve for X takes as constant the supply curve of A to this industry (and, incidentally, the supply curves of other resources to this industry as well as the state of technology). Likewise, the supply curve of Y assumes as given the supply curve of A to the industry producing Y—in addition to the supply curves of other resources and the state of technology in this industry. Third, the demand curve for A by industry X holds as stationary the product demand curve D_x, while the demand curve for A on the part of industry Y takes as stationary the product demand curve D_y. Both resource demand curves also hold constant the prices of other resources employed in the respective industries. Finally, note that the price of A is not the same in both industries. Units of A are paid a price of p_3 in industry X and a price of p_5 in industry Y. Granted that the product and resource markets are competitive, the price of A would be equalized between the industries if resource A were perfectly mobile, i.e., if resource owners were aware of any price differences, if there were no nonpecuniary differences in employment conditions in the two industries, if there were no other institutional barriers to movement, and if the costs of migration were zero. In actuality, these phenomena prevent exact equalization of resource prices among industries.

Introduction of a sales tax by the government is a convenient way to disturb this equilibrium. Suppose an excise tax is levied on commodity X. We already know the effect on the industry producing X. In the upper left diagram the curve S_x shifts to the position denoted by S_x', raising the price of X to p_7 and decreasing output and consumption to x_5 units. The impact upon the price and employment of A in industry X is shown in the lower left diagram. The demand for A decreases as firms attempt to shift the tax backward. The industry demand curve shifts from D_a^X to $D_a'^X$, lowering the price of A to p_2 and reducing employment from a_3 to a_2 units.

So much for industry X—at least for the moment. What repercussions will be felt in the other industry? In the product market the tax has raised the price of X, which is now more expensive relative to Y as compared to the initial equilibrium. Therefore, consumers substitute Y for X in their consumption patterns. The movement upward and to the left along the curve D_x, in response to the higher price of X, is accomplished by a shift to the right in the consumer demand curve for Y. The demand curve for Y shifts to the position D_y', expanding consumption to y_9 units and raising price to p_{10}. At the same time, something is happening on the resource market. Since the demand for A in industry X has decreased and the price of A is lower there, resource owners transfer to industry Y. Before there existed a ratio of the price of A in industry X to that in industry Y at which no migration occurred. Now the ratio is lower and there is an incentive to move. Consequently, the supply curve of A to industry Y shifts to the right, to the position denoted by $S_a'^Y$. The effect is to reduce the price of A from p_5 to p_4 and to increase employment from a_5 to a_6 units.

But notice that this increased supply of A has another impact on the product market. The shift of the resource supply curve in turn causes the product supply curve of Y to shift from S_y to S_y'. Thus the price of Y falls to p_9 and consumption increases to y_{10} units.

There are even tertiary effects not shown in the diagrams. When the price of Y falls below p_{10}, the demand curve for X is affected. The curve D_x shifts to the left, causing the industry to contract output by moving down and to the left along S'_x. Then this once more affects the demand for A in industry X, with a consequent change in the supply curve of A to industry Y, and yet another shift in the supply curve of Y. These tertiary effects, however, merely modify the changes depicted in the diagrams; it is very unlikely that they would reverse the direction of change. In the final outcome we can expect the tax on commodity X to have the following effects as compared to the initial equilibria: (1) the price of X will be higher and consumption and production of X will be reduced, (2) the price of commodity Y will be higher and consumption and production of Y will be greater, (3) the price of resource A will be lower and employment smaller in industry X, (4) the price of A will be lower and employment greater in industry Y.

In focusing on a single industry a general rule was uncovered: namely, that effects of resource on product markets originate in changes in resource supply, while effects of product on resource markets originate in changes in product demand. We are now in a position to see that these "originating changes" are often traceable to something that is changing in *another* industry. Since different industries are related by virtue of the fact that their products enter the consumption patterns of households or that they employ the same types of resources, the allocation of resources in line with consumer wants is accomplished by the price mechanism.

GENERAL EQUILIBRIUM

Consideration of interrelated markets brings out one very important point. Partial equilibrium analysis is no more than an approximation to a full explanation of pricing and allocation. Even treatment of two industries is provisional because it ignores all other industries affected by any given change. In general, all prices are connected by a whole network of links to form an integrated price system. Some of these connections are weak enough to be ignored. No significant connection can be found between the price of raisins and the price of costume jewelry or between the wage rate of demolition experts and the wage rate of librarians, for example. These weak connections are the justification for using partial analysis in practice. By ignoring the remoter links and including in the analysis only a few dominant ones, it is usually possible to provide an adequate explanation of the pricing and allocation of particular commodities or resources. Still, it is important to recognize the fact that the price system is a whole made up of interrelated parts.

General equilibrium analysis attempts to display these interrelated parts in the form of a single abstract model. Though such a model has little empirical applicability at the present stage of economics, it does provide insight into the functioning of the economy. In sketching general equilibrium theory we shall be guided by the system Leon Walras introduced as long ago as 1874. The theory is necessarily algebraic because many simultaneous relationships cannot be handled precisely in words and a geometric treatment would be misleading. Nevertheless, no detailed knowledge of mathematics is necessary in order to understand the outline presented here. We shall sacrifice mathematical rigor for the sake of economic understanding, and to this extent we depart from the Walrasian theory. In place of mathematical equations let us limit ourselves to the symbolic functional notation already put to use in previous chapters.

The first step is to define the symbols. There are, in general, n products in the economy denoted by capital letters: $X_1, X_2, X_3, \cdots, X_n$. Used to produce these n commodities are m resources represented by $A_1, A_2, A_3, \cdots, A_m$. It should be noted that in dealing with many products or resources one letter with different subscripts is more convenient than many different letters. So subscripts refer to different products or resources, whereas formerly we have used a numerical subscript to denote a given amount of some product or resource. The quantities per unit of time and the prices of these commodities and resources are represented by lower-case letters as follows:

$x_1, x_2, x_3, \cdots, x_n$ are quantities of products per unit of time,
$p_1, p_2, p_3, \cdots, p_n$ are their respective product prices,
$a_1, a_2, a_3, \cdots, a_m$ are quantities of resources per unit of time,
$q_1, q_2, q_3, \cdots, q_m$ are their respective resource prices.

The Product Markets

Market demand for commodities is based upon the utility theory of consumer choice. For the quantities $x_1, x_2, x_3, \cdots, x_n$ the utility function of a consumer may be written

$$u = f(x_1, x_2, x_3, \cdots, x_n)$$

which states that his utility is a function of, or depends upon, the quantities of all commodities he consumes. The consumer is assumed to maximize utility subject to his budget constraint:

$$p_1 x_1 + p_2 x_2 + p_3 x_3 + \cdots + p_n x_n = I$$

As before I designates the consumer's income. Given that the consumer maximizes utility, it was shown in connection with the theory of product demand that this demand function can be expressed as follows for, say, the commodity X_1:

$$x_1 = d_1(p_1, p_2, p_3, \cdots, p_n; I)$$

From our earlier examination of the theory of resource pricing it now becomes obvious that I, previously taken as given, is dependent upon the resource market. That is, a person's income is determined by the quantity of each resource he supplies multiplied by the market price of that resource:

$$I = q_1a_1 + q_2a_2 + q_3a_3 + \cdots + q_ma_m$$

Of course, for any one person some of the a's may be zero. In fact, all but one will be zero if he, as resource owner, supplies only one resource, such as one type of labor. Regardless of how many resources he does supply, the foregoing expression of income can be substituted in his demand function for commodity X_1:

$$x_1 = d_1(p_1, p_2, p_3, \cdots, p_n; q_1, q_2, q_3, \cdots, q_m)$$

The response of x_1 to changes in some resource prices will be zero if the resource owner supplies none of those resources.

A similar expression of individual demand can be obtained for each of the other products entering into a household's consumption pattern. Aggregation of all individual demand functions in the economy yields a market demand function for each product. Assuming population and consumer tastes are both constant, the product demand functions are written:

$$x_1 = D_1(p_1, p_2, p_3, \cdots, p_n; q_1, q_2, q_3, \cdots, q_m)$$
$$x_2 = D_2(p_1, p_2, p_3, \cdots, p_n; q_1, q_2, q_3, \cdots, q_m)$$
$$x_3 = D_3(p_1, p_2, p_3, \cdots, p_n; q_1, q_2, q_3, \cdots, q_m)$$
$$\cdots\cdots\cdots\cdots\cdots\cdots\cdots\cdots\cdots\cdots\cdots\cdots\cdots\cdots\cdots$$
$$x_n = D_n(p_1, p_2, p_3, \cdots, p_n; q_1, q_2, q_3, \cdots, q_m)$$

The capital letter D denotes the aggregate or market demand function as opposed to the individual function. The entire demand set includes n product demand functions, one for each commodity and each containing n product prices and m resource prices as explanatory variables. It is immediately apparent that the demand for any one commodity depends upon the prices of other products *and* upon resources prices. This link between resource and product markets is provided by the fact that changes in resource prices affect consumer income and thus affect product demand.

We turn next to product supply, for which purpose we assume pure competition throughout the economy. Bringing to bear the principle of profit maximization, it is known that the quantity of any one product offered for sale depends upon the product price and the prices of all resources employed by the industry. Assuming the state of technology is constant, we can write symbolically a supply function for each of the n commodities:

$$x_1 = S_1(p_1; q_1, q_2, q_3, \cdots, q_m)$$
$$x_2 = S_2(p_2; q_1, q_2, q_3, \cdots, q_m)$$
$$x_3 = S_3(p_3; q_1, q_2, q_3, \cdots, q_m)$$
$$\cdots\cdots\cdots\cdots\cdots\cdots\cdots\cdots\cdots\cdots\cdots$$
$$x_n = S_n(p_n; q_1, q_2, q_3, \cdots, q_m)$$

The capital letter S represents the industry supply. If any one industry does not utilize a particular resource in production of its commodity, the response of quantity supplied to that resource price will be zero. But in general the supply set contains n product supply functions, each including its product price and all resource prices.

The Resource Markets

These product demand and supply functions are not sufficient to determine equilibrium. The reason is that they include resource prices and no relationships as yet exist to determine the resource prices. It is to the resource markets that we must turn to complete the economic blueprint. Industry demand for any one resource depends not only upon its price but also upon the prices of other resources employed by the industry. In addition, resource demand depends upon consumer demand for the product of the industry. With only slight oversimplification we can write the resource demand functions in the economy as follows:

$$a_1 = R_1(q_1, q_2, q_3, \cdots, q_m; p_1, p_2, p_3, \cdots, p_n)$$

$$a_2 = R_2(q_1, q_2, q_3, \cdots, q_m; p_1, p_2, p_3, \cdots, p_n)$$

$$a_3 = R_3(q_1, q_2, q_3, \cdots, q_m; p_1, p_2, p_3, \cdots, p_n)$$

$$\cdots\cdots\cdots\cdots\cdots\cdots\cdots\cdots\cdots\cdots\cdots\cdots\cdots\cdots$$

$$a_m = R_m(q_1, q_2, q_3, \cdots, q_m; p_1, p_2, p_3, \cdots, p_n)$$

The symbol R represents the market demand function for a resource on the part of all industries combined.

A word of explanation is in order. First, in general all resources prices are included in the demand function for any one resource. If two resources are unrelated, as a special case a change in the price of one will have no effect upon employment of the other. Second, all product prices are included in the demand function for any one resource because the function represents the demand by all industries. In place of the separate consumer demand functions for output, inclusion of product prices will suffice. And the reason is that each product demand function includes all product prices.

Finally, the resource supply functions are needed to establish prices and employments in the resource markets. It will be assumed that each resource owner varies his offering of resources on the basis of the resource price and all commodity prices. This assumption yields the following aggregate supply functions:

$$a_1 = T_1(q_1; p_1, p_2, p_3, \cdots, p_n)$$

$$a_2 = T_2(q_2; p_1, p_2, p_3, \cdots, p_n)$$

$$a_3 = T_3(q_3; p_1, p_2, p_3, \cdots, p_n)$$

$$\cdots\cdots\cdots\cdots\cdots\cdots\cdots\cdots\cdots\cdots\cdots$$

$$a_m = T_m(q_m; p_1, p_2, p_3, \cdots, p_n)$$

The capital letter T designates the market supply function of a resource.

The inclusion of commodity prices as well as the resource price is based upon utility analysis of choice. Essentially, resource owners supply resources with a view to their *real* income earned—or, to put it another way, with a view to the purchasing power of the money income earned, which in turn depends upon the prices they must pay for commodities as well as the price received per unit of the resource employed.

Overall Equilibrium

The set of functions can be made more specific by putting the model into the form of mathematical equations. Then the system is comprised of $2n + 2m$ simultaneous equations in $2n + 2m$ unknowns. Under certain conditions simultaneous equations can be solved to yield the values of all unknowns—in this instance the equilibrium product prices and quantities and the equilibrium resource prices and quantities. The solution takes into account the dependence of any one market upon all others in a way determined by consumer and producer behavior. Moreover, given this equilibrium solution, a change in any one market will necessitate a resolving of the entire system, so that the new equilibrium values of the variables will be different.

Obviously, a general equilibrium model includes more variables than can be handled for empirical purposes. Electronic computers are of little help, since merely collecting and recording all prices and quantities would be an immense task. As a consequence, general equilibrium analysis is of limited practical use. Statistical measurements usually ignore some prices in attempting to identify particular demand or supply functions. Nevertheless, besides contributing insight into the working of the price mechanism, general equilibrium analysis provides a guideline that helps in choosing the variables to be included in applied studies. It also spotlights the dangers hidden in incomplete analyses.

INCOME DISTRIBUTION

The theory of general equilibrium provides an answer to the question of what determines the distribution of income in society. Each person who sells resources receives a price per unit of the services sold. How much income accrues to him in his capacity as the owner of a particular resource depends upon how much he supplies at the established market price—that is, how many hours he works at the market wage rate per hour or how much machine service he offers at the price per unit of machine service. But this may well be only a part of his total income. If he owns other resources as well, he will receive income from their sale, the amount depending upon the quantities sold and their prices. In addition, he may be the recipient of residual income in his capacity as an entrepreneur.

There is implicit in this explanation two distinct notions of income distribution. One is called *functional* income distribution: the shares of total income going to different types of resources. The other notion is that of *personal* income distribution: the distribution of income among individuals in the economy.

Functional Distribution

Of the total income generated in any one year the shares paid to various resources hinge upon two basic economic forces: their relative productivities and the structure of demand for output. The greater is a resource's marginal productivity the larger will be its marginal revenue product and the higher its equilibrium price. Of course, the marginal product of a resource declines as more of it is employed relative to other resources. If the supply of labor increases relative to that of capital, for example, its price will tend to fall relative to the price of capital. But the total share of income paid to labor may still rise because of the greater quantity employed. Given the available quantities of labor and capital in the economy, and assuming all units are employed, their relative marginal products will influence the income shares allocated between them.

The marginal revenue product of a resource also depends upon the price of the commodity it produces. To this extent the income paid to a resource in a given employment is affected by the value consumers attach to the product, as reflected in product demand. If labor-intensive industries face weak product demands and low product prices, then (other things being the same) the income share going to labor will tend to be lower. The same argument applies to capital. Capital intensive industries with weak product demand will tend to cause the income share of capital to be small.

Actually, treating functional income distribution in the form of a dichotomy consisting of labor and capital is something of an oversimplification. There are many kinds of labor and a variety of nonhuman capital services. Within the category "labor," a primary cause of income dispersion is the existing structure of occupations, for various occupations bring different financial rewards. A second important cause of variance in income in this category is the age structure of the labor force. As we have seen in Chapter 23, annual earnings vary with age. Still a third contributing cause of intra-labor income variability is the distribution of employment among industries. Because of nonpecuniary differences in employment conditions, factors affecting mobility, and the structure of consumer demand for the output of different industries, it is not surprising that wage rates and annual earnings vary from one industry to another.

Returns to capital, called property income as opposed to labor income, also show considerable dispersion. Property income is made up of interest income, dividends, rents and royalties, and entrepreneurial or self-employment income. To some extent the economic forces that explain dispersion in labor income also contribute to dispersion in property income. Probably the industry and geographic location of employment of nonhuman capital services is quite important. But in addition to the variables common to labor and capital income dispersion, there are others peculiar to the returns on capital. Since property of various kinds can be accumulated to a much greater degree than labor skills, since it can be passed on through inheritance, and since people have different attitudes toward risk, property incomes understandably show more dispersion than do labor incomes.

Comparisons of the distributive shares going to labor and capital over long periods of time have been made.[1] Professor I. B. Kravis reports that the share of U.S. national income allocated to "employee compensation" has increased rather steadily since 1900. In the period 1900–1909 the proportion was 55 per cent, while in 1949–57 the labor share was somewhat greater than 67 per cent. The corresponding share allocated to "property income" dropped from 45 to 33 per cent. Part of the explanation lies in relative factor supplies. Despite a great rise in hourly earnings, the quantity of capital has nearly doubled in relation to total man-hours. Shifts from agriculture to manufacturing, restrictions on immigration, and development of more capital-using innovations in turn lie behind the changes in total capital and labor supplies.

The expanded share of national income paid to labor conceals dispersion in the incomes of different types of labor. Table 24.1 summarizes the distribution of earned income by selected occupations in 1959. Annual average earnings vary from $2,169 to over $10,000 for the occupations included in the table. But even this degree of refinement does not reveal all the dispersion, for within any one occupation earnings vary with age, sex, color, industry of employment, and geographic region. For example, among lawyers only about 20 per cent earned the average income for the group as a whole, while approximately 6 per cent earned annual incomes of less than $1,000 and 12 per cent earned over $14,000.

Table 24.1

Median Earnings of Males in 1959 by Selected Occupations

Occupation	Median Annual Earnings	Occupation	Median Annual Earnings
Lawyers and Judges	$10,000 +	Bus Drivers	$4,411
Aeronautical Engineers	9,059	Barbers	3,716
Accountants and Auditors	6,611	Laborers (Manufacturing)	3,623
Electricians	5,959	Farmers and Farm Managers	2,169

Source: U.S. Department of Commerce, U.S. Census of Population, 1960, U.S. Summary.

[1] See D. G. Johnson, "The Functional Distribution of Income in the United States, 1850–1952," Review of Economics and Statistics (May 1954), pp. 175–82; I. B. Kravis, "Relative Income Shares in Fact and Theory," American Economic Review (December 1959), pp. 917–49.

It should be noted, although empirical evidence will not be presented, that property incomes show an even greater degree of dispersion. As far as the trend of its components is concerned, available data indicate that since 1900 in the United States rent, interest, and entrepreneurial income as percentages of national income have declined while corporate profits have risen.

Personal Distribution

Charles Dickens notwithstanding, the old adage that wage earners are low-income families and property income recipients are high-income families is misleading, to say the least. The personal distribution of income, the distribution of national income among households, is indeed closely connected with the functional distribution of income. But the connection is rather complex because some families in each income class receive household income from more than one (functional) source. Even the proportions of family income obtained from different sources vary among households in the same income class. In addition, besides the accumulated wealth of the household, which can be "invested" in many ways to yield property income, household income depends upon the number of employed family members working for wages and the wage rates they receive. In this section we shall concentrate on the personal distribution of income and consider only incidentally its relation to the functional distribution.

Table 24.2 is a means of comprehending at a glance the personal distribution of income in the United States for the year 1959. In column 1 are recorded the income classes. Column 2 shows the number of households in each income class expressed as a percentage of the total number of households reporting income. It is interpreted in the following way: 15 per cent of the households reported an income under $2,000 per year; 11 per cent of the households reported an income between $2,000 and $3,000, and so forth.

Table 24.2

Incomes of Households After Taxes, 1959

Income After Tax	*Number of Households as Per Cent of All Households*	*Income as Per Cent of Total Income*
Under $2,000	15	3
$2,000 to $3,000	11	5
$3,000 to $4,000	12	7
$4,000 to $5,000	13	10
$5,000 to $6,000	12	11
$6,000 to $7,500	13	15
$7,500 to $10,000	12	17
$10,000 to $15,000	9	17
$15,000 and over	4	15

Source: U.S. Department of Commerce, *Survey of Current Business* (May 1961). Households are defined here as families and unmarried persons.

In column 3 the aggregate income of all households in a given class is expressed as a percentage of total income. That is, for all households with incomes falling within a given class, their incomes were summed and the sum was divided by total income for all classes. This means that households reporting incomes under $2,000 comprised collectively 3 per cent of total income; households reporting incomes between $2,000 and $3,000 together comprised 5 per cent of total income, etc.

What is immediately obvious from Table 24.2 is the inequality in personal distribution of income. On the lower end of the income scale, 15 per cent of the households earned only 3 per cent of total income. The first and second income classes, 26 per cent of the households, received only 8 per cent of the total. On the upper end of the scale, as little as 4 per cent of the house-

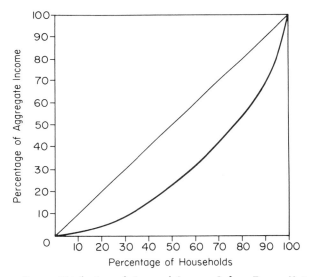

FIG. 24.2.   Lorenz Curve, Distribution of Personal Income Before Taxes, United States, 1960

holds reported incomes of $15,000 or more. Yet these 4 per cent collectively received 15 per cent of total income.

A graphic means of measuring income inequality is a Lorenz curve, such as that depicted in Fig. 24.2. On the horizontal axis is shown the percentage of households, i.e., the number of households as a percentage of all households. Of course, the range is from zero to 100 per cent. On the vertical axis is measured the percentage of total personal income. The straight 45-degree line from the origin represents an equal distribution of income, for if each household had the same income, it would follow that 10 per cent of the households received 10 per cent of total income, 20 per cent of households received 20 per cent of total income, etc., and all combinations of cumulative households and cumulative incomes would lie on this straight line.

The actual income distribution in the United States for the year 1960 is shown as the curve concave upward. This Lorenz curve indicates that 20 per cent of all households collectively earned about 5 per cent of total income. That is, the lowest income classes comprising 20 per cent of all households received only 5 per cent of aggregate income. Approximately half of all households collectively received about 23 per cent of national income, which is to say that the 50 per cent in the lower income brackets earned only 23 per cent of aggregate income. Following the curve, when we reach 90 per cent of all households, it is seen that they received less than 70 per cent of income. This is another way of saying that the remaining 10 per cent in the highest income classes were recipients of over 30 per cent of total income generated in the economy.

The closer an actual Lorenz curve approaches the straight line, the more equally is income distributed. The more it diverges from the line, the greater is inequality. For example, a Lorenz curve lying very close to the horizontal axis up to, say, 80 or 90 per cent of all households and then rising sharply, almost vertically, would represent an extremely unequal distribution. If one person had all of total income and everyone else had no income, the curve would coincide with the horizontal and right vertical axes.

Given the fact of inequality, how has the distribution been changing in the United States? From 1929 to 1946, average per capita income after taxes rose from $690 to $1,116. Over the same period average per capita income for the top one per cent fell from $13,168 to $8,994. The percentage of total income received by this same one per cent fell from 19 to about 8 per cent, while the share of the upper 5 per cent fell from 34 to 18 per cent. Although both the middle and the lowest income recipients acquired a greater share, the major beneficiaries of the income redistribution were the middle income groups.

During the past twenty years the share of total income going to the top 20 per cent of income receivers has been virtually unchanged. Neither has the share going to the bottom 20 per cent altered appreciably. In other words, poverty remains as a crucial social problem in an affluent economy.

PROBLEMS

1. The following table shows the average incomes of nonsalaried physicians, lawyers, and dentists after deduction of business expenses in 1929 and 1951.

Net Income of Nonsalaried Physicians, Lawyers, and Dentists

Year	Average Net Income for U.S. as a Whole Before Taxes		
	Physicians	Lawyers	Dentists
1929	$5,224	$5,534	$4,267
1951	13,432	8,730	7,820

Source: U.S. Department of Commerce, *Statistical Abstract*, 1953.

(*a*) List the factors that are most important in determining the structure of incomes in 1929 and explain how each one operates to establish the distribution of income among these occupations.

(*b*) From 1929 to 1951 the income of physicians rose relative to that of both lawyers and dentists. Also the income of dentists rose relative to that of lawyers. List the factors that may have caused these changes and explain how each operates to change the structure of incomes.

SUGGESTED READING

I. M. Kirzner, *Market Theory and the Price System*, Chap. 11. Princeton, N. J.: D. Van Nostrand Co., Inc., 1963.

G. Malanos, *Intermediate Economic Theory*, Part 4. Philadelphia: J. B. Lippincott Co., 1962.

A. R. Oxenfeldt, *Economic Principles and Public Issues*, Chap. 6. New York: Rinehart & Company, Inc., 1959.

W. D. Grampp and E. T. Weiler, *Economic Policy*, 3rd ed., Part 3. Homewood, Ill.: Richard D. Irwin, Inc., 1961.

H. P. Miller, *Rich Man, Poor Man*, Chaps. 1–4. New York: Thomas Y. Crowell Company, 1964.

Part VII

Normative Economics

Elements of
Welfare Economics

Since the days of Adam Smith, when economics as a systematic discipline is said to have been born, economic theory has been used and misused as a guideline for public policies. Aside from a few digressions, our inquiry up to this point has been restricted to positive economic analysis. Normative economics was touched upon only by implication. Now it is time to raise explicit questions of the socially *best* organization of the economy. Our inquiry will be based upon the theoretical welfare system introduced by the Italian economist Vilfredo Pareto late in the nineteenth century and developed more extensively over the past thirty years. Though the "Paretian" system is not the only approach to welfare economics, it is the one most frequently employed by today's economists.

THE SOCIAL WELFARE FUNCTION

In order to pose the problem and appreciate its implications, the social welfare or well-being of society can be expressed in terms of a general and abstract function. Let W denote social welfare, and let all the forces that influence welfare be represented by a set of variables represented by w's with subscripts. Then

$$W = W (w_1, w_2, w_3, \ldots)$$

asserts the proposition that social welfare is determined by an innumerable set of other variables. These variables are sometimes called social states or situations: a state of war or peace, a distribution of income, a family structure, a set of laws, a level of education, etc.

Obviously, the proposition is so general that it is virtually meaningless. If inferences possessing more concrete content are to be derived, the social welfare function must be specialized by successive assumptions.

The first assumption adopted by welfare economists is that the welfare variables, the w's, can be divided into two subsets, economic and noneconomic. The economic variables are defined as produced goods and services: all others are deemed to be noneconomic variables.[1] The non-economic variables are conceptually held constant, so the social welfare function becomes the *economic* welfare function. No generality is lost by assuming there are only two goods in the economy, X and Y. Letting r's represent noneconomic variables, economic welfare, E, is written

$$E = E(x, y; \bar{r}_1, \bar{r}_2, \bar{r}_3, \cdots)$$

The bars over the noneconomic variables indicate the assumption of constant noneconomic determinants of social welfare. Thus economic welfare is said to rise with an increase of x or y, given no decrease in the other economic variable. So that meaningful empirical conclusions may be drawn, variations in x or y must not entail variations in the r's. Otherwise, an increase of x or y can increase E but decrease W because the rise in x or y causes a decrease in some of the r's.

A second assumption restricts the definition of economic variables even further. Economic variables are not just produced goods and services, but only those goods and services that are separately assignable to individuals. Assuming for convenience two people in the economy, the economic welfare function becomes

$$E = E\ (x^1, y^1; x^2, y^2)$$

where the *superscripts* refer to amounts of X and Y consumed by persons 1 and 2. When restricted to this degree the economic welfare function excludes goods and services consumed collectively, such as military defense, public parks, police and fire protection, etc.

Third, an ethical or value assumption postulates that individual preferences are to count. Rather than some alternative (e.g., that a minority or a single wise man knows what is best for society) it is assumed that each person is the best judge of how his economic welfare is affected, and that the aggregate of individual preferences determine what is to be preferred for society as a whole. Since utility functions are indexes of individual preferences regarding economic variables, the economic welfare function in final form is written as

$$E = E\ [u^1\ (x^1, y^1),\, u^2\ (x^2, y^2)\,]$$

where u^1 denotes the utility of person 1 and u^2 the utility of person 2.

These utility functions are assumed to have the usual properties. Therefore, if the amount of X, of Y, or both consumed by one person increases, his utility will likewise increase. Moreover, if the utility of at least one person increases, given no decrease in the utilities of others, then economic welfare will increase. Finally, a rise in economic welfare will also raise social welfare as long as the first and second specializing assumptions are satisfied.

[1] More generally, economic variables also include resources. The definition has been limited to goods and services for simplicity.

THE PARETIAN WELFARE MODEL

The objective of welfare economics is to discover the conditions under which economic welfare is maximized. By postulating a direct relationship between the economic well-being of society and the utilities of individuals, the maximization of E is tantamount to maximization of the joint utilities of all individuals. But because utilities in turn depend upon the amounts of goods and services produced, maximization of utilities is constrained by the total resources available and the way resources are allocated. Two necessary conditions underlie maximum welfare: (1) efficient *production* conditions that determine the maximum output obtainable from given resource totals, and (2) optimum *exchange* conditions that determine the distribution of maximum output among different consumers.

Optimum Production Conditions

For purposes of exposition, we shall assume the two goods X and Y are produced by two resources A and B. Though a production function could be specified for each firm, suppose instead that there is one production function for each industry. Finally, let the total amounts of A and B in the economy be fixed. Then the determination of maximum output reduces to the problem of allocating resources between the production of X and Y.

In Fig. 25.1, the production isoquants for commodities X and Y are set back to back. Consider first those for X. From the entire set, three isoquants are drawn: for x_1, x_2, and x_3 units of X respectively. The origin is 0 in the lower left corner. So quantities of A used in the production of X, a_x, are measured on the lower horizontal axis, while quantities of B employed in the production of X, b_x, are measured on the left vertical axis. The total amount of A in the economy is given as a^* and that of B is b^*.

Three production isoquants for good Y are labeled y_1, y_2, and y_3. Now they have simply been turned on their heads. The origin for these isoquants is 0' in the upper right corner. Movements to the left along the top horizontal axis measure greater amounts of A used in the production of Y, a_y. And movements down from 0' along the right vertical axis measure greater quantities of B used in the production of Y, b_y. By turning the book upside down it is easily seen that this is a conventional set of isoquants.

The fixed totals a^* and b^* establish the location of the two sets of isoquants. Any point in the space determines an allocation of A and B between the two industries. If the economy is at point P_2 for example, a_1 units of A are used to produce X and the rest of A, $(a^* - a_1)$ units, are employed to produce Y. Since b_1 units of B are allocated to the pro-

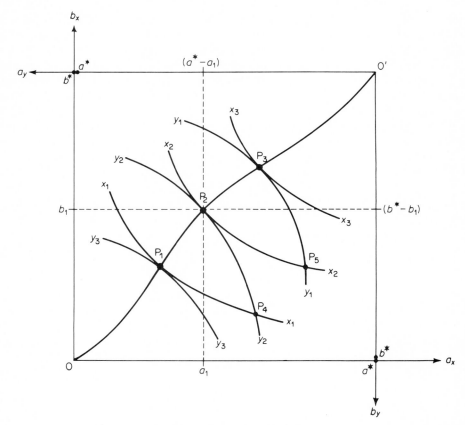

FIG. 25.1. Production Possibilities

duction of X, then $(b^* - b_1)$ units are devoted to Y, which exhausts the total amount of B.

The largest possible combined outputs of X and Y are those output combinations lying on the diagonal curve 00′, where the isoquants are tangent to each other. Suppose resources are allocated such that the economy is at point P_4, producing x_1 units of X and y_2 units of Y. By reallocating A and B and moving to point P_1, the output of X is unchanged. Yet the quantity of Y rises from y_2 to y_3 units. By moving from P_4 to P_2, the output of Y is not altered, but x rises from x_1 to x_2 units. Any point on 00′ between P_1 and P_2 expands the outputs of both X and Y as compared to P_4. The same argument applies to point P_5. A reallocation of resources that moves the economy to P_2, to P_3, or between these two points raises the output of at least one good and possibly both.

In general, given any allocation of resources such that the economy is off the curve 00′, an expansion of aggregate output is possible by a movement toward 00'. By reading off the quantities of X and Y along 00', the efficient output combinations can be found. In Fig. 25.2 the curve y^*x^* is a plot of the output combinations lying on 00' of Fig. 25.1.[2] The quantity x^* is the maximum output of X that could be produced if all resources were devoted to its production. Likewise y^* is the greatest quantity of Y if no X were produced. Points P_4 and P_5 in Fig. 25.2 correspond to P_4 and P_5 in Fig. 25.1 and are said to be inefficient. All such points inside the boundary given by y^*x^* are inefficient in the sense that a reallocation of resource totals can move the economy to the outer

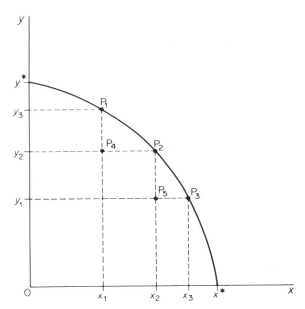

FIG. 25.2.   Efficient Combinations of X and Y

boundary. Points like P_1, P_2, and P_3 are all superior to P_4 or P_5; they entail more of at least one good and no less of the other.

What conditions must be satisfied in order that the economy produce an efficient output combination? In the theory of the production function the marginal rate of substitution of one resource for another was shown to be equal to minus the slope of an isoquant. But at each point of tangency the slopes of the two isoquants are equal. Therefore, the marginal rates of substitution must be equalized. Symbolically, let $\mathrm{MRTS}_{ab}(X)$ denote the marginal rate of substitution of A for B in the production of X, and let $\mathrm{MRTS}_{ab}(Y)$ denote the substitution rate in the production of Y. Then along the curve 00' (or along y^*x^*) the following

[2] The curve in Fig. 25.2 is drawn concave to the origin, reflecting diminishing returns to scale in both production functions or diminishing returns in one and constant returns in the other. Constant returns to scale in both production functions would generate a straight line, while increasing returns would make the curve convex.

condition prevails:

$$\text{MRTS}_{ab}(\text{X}) = \text{MRTS}_{ab}(\text{Y})$$

Furthermore, in the mathematical appendix it is demonstrated that each marginal rate of substitution is equal to the ratio of marginal products. The optimum production conditions become

$$\frac{\text{MPP}_a(\text{X})}{\text{MPP}_b(\text{X})} = \frac{\text{MPP}_a(\text{Y})}{\text{MPP}_b(\text{Y})}$$

The ratio of marginal products must be the same in both employments. More generally, for many resources and products, the ratio of marginal products of any two resources must be equalized in all uses.

Optimum Exchange Conditions

In order that the economy be anywhere on the outer boundary of production possibilities the ratio of marginal products must be equalized. But the optimum production conditions do not determine a particular output combination. Rather, an entire array of points lies on the curve y^*x^*, all of which are superior to any point within the boundary. Yet the theory does not provide a criterion for stating that any one *efficient* point is better or worse than any other, e.g., that P_1 is preferable to P_2 or P_3.

For any one efficient output combination another question arises. How shall the total output be distributed between the two consumers in the economy? The distribution of any (maximized) output is determined by optimum exchange conditions that maximize the joint utilities of the two (all) consumers. The formal process of utility maximization is the same as that of output maximization. In Fig. 25.3 the production frontier of Fig. 25.2 is reproduced. We assume that the point P_2 has been chosen, so x_2 units of X and y_2 units of Y have been produced.

The utility indifference curves of persons 1 and 2 are set back to back. The origin for person 1 is shown as 0^1 in the lower left corner. Quantities of X consumed by person 1, x^1, are measured on the lower horizontal axis, while quantities of Y, y^1, are measured on the left vertical axis. His indifference curves carry the superscript 1, and larger subscripts denote greater amounts of utility for this person. The maximum of X and Y that could be distributed to 1 is x_2 units and y_2 units respectively, the total quantities of each produced.

The origin for person 2 is labeled 0^2. Greater quantities of X consumed by 2 are represented by movements to the left along the top horizontal axis, up to the limit of x_2 units. Larger consumption of Y, up to a limit of y_2 units, is measured by greater distances from 0^2 down along the right vertical axis. The utility indifference curves u^2 with larger subscripts denote more utility for person 2.

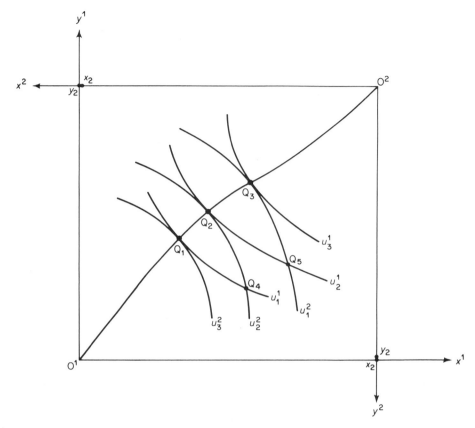

FIG. 25.3. Utility Possibilities

The combined utilities of both consumers are maximized along the curve $0^1 0^2$, a locus of points at which the indifference curves are tangent to each other. One distribution of the output total is represented by point Q_4, at which person 1 enjoys a utility of u_1^1 and person 2 a utility of u_2^2. Movement to Q_1 leaves the utility of person 1 unchanged but raises the utility of 2 to u_3^2, so their combined utility level must rise. Movement to Q_2 does not affect person 2, but it boosts the utility of person 1 from u_1^1 to u_2^1. Between Q_1 and Q_2 on $0^1 0^2$, the utilities of both consumers are larger as compared to Q_4. At point Q_5 or any other point off the locus $0^1 0^2$ the same argument applies.

In general, given any distribution of total output not on the curve $0^1 0^2$, it is possible to increase the utility of at least one person (or both) without decreasing the utility of the other by a movement toward the locus $0^1 0^2$. Once the output total has been distributed such that the economy is at a point on $0^1 0^2$, the utility of one person cannot be raised without doing so at the expense of the other. Any movement upward to the right along $0^1 0^2$ entails a shift to a higher indifference curve for consumer 1 and a lower indifference curve for consumer 2. An opposite movement benefits consumer 2 at the expense of consumer 1.

The conditions necessary for attainment of the curve $0^1 0^2$ are derived from the utility analysis of consumer choice. In Chapter 5 it was shown that the marginal rate of substitution of X for Y in consumption is equal to minus the slope of an indifference curve. But at the tangency points of Fig. 25.3, the slopes of the indifference curves are equal. Let $\text{MRS}_{xy}(1)$ denote the marginal rate of substitution of X for Y by consumer 1, and $\text{MRS}_{xy}(2)$ that by consumer 2. Symbolically, the optimum exchange conditions are

$$\text{MRS}_{xy}(1) = \text{MRS}_{xy}(2)$$

One important aspect of the optimum exchange conditions should be noted. These conditions do not determine a single distribution of total output; any point on $0^1 0^2$ satisfies the optimum exchange conditions. The distribution of X and Y among individuals is nothing other than the personal distribution of real income in society. The welfare theory stipulates that all distributions that satisfy the optimum exchange conditions are superior to distributions that do not. However, the theory presents no criteria for judging that one optimum distribution is better or worse than any other optimum distribution, e.g., that Q_1 is better than Q_2. Determination of the best among all optimal distributions requires ethical or value postulates that extend beyond the boundaries of economics.

WELFARE AND THE PRICE MECHANISM

The Paretian welfare theory concludes that there is a set of efficient output combinations. For any one of these combinations, there is a set of optimal distributions among consumers. The theory makes no direct references to degrees of competition, pricing policies, or even to prices themselves. Nevertheless, by a mathematical proof it can be shown that the Paretian welfare model and the purely competitive model lead to exactly the same results if the Paretian model assumes there are no increasing returns to scale over the relevant range of product outputs. If all resource and product markets are purely competitive, if firms maximize profit and consumers maximize utility, then the economy will settle at some point on the curve 00' of Fig. 25.1 and at some point on a curve like $0^1 0^2$ of Fig. 25.3. Since the mathematical proof is beyond the scope of this book, let us examine a more intuitive explanation of this result.

Pure Competition and the Paretian Optima

Assume first that the economy is purely competitive. The profit-maximizing conditions for firms in both industries (as shown in Chapter 20) are set out as follows:

Firms in Industry X   *Firms in Industry Y*

$$\frac{p_a}{\text{MPP}_a(\text{X})} = \frac{p_b}{\text{MPP}_b(\text{X})} = \text{MC}_x = p_x \qquad \frac{p_a}{\text{MPP}_a(\text{Y})} = \frac{p_b}{\text{MPP}_b(\text{Y})} = \text{MC}_y = p_y$$

By rewriting the two ratios on the left for each industry,

$$\frac{p_a}{p_b} = \frac{\text{MPP}_a(\text{X})}{\text{MPP}_b(\text{X})} \qquad \frac{p_a}{p_b} = \frac{\text{MPP}_a(\text{Y})}{\text{MPP}_b(\text{Y})}$$

Since the ratios of marginal products in each industry are equated to the same (net) price ratio in any given resource market, these ratios must be equal to each other:

$$\frac{\text{MPP}_a(\text{X})}{\text{MPP}_b(\text{X})} = \frac{\text{MPP}_a(\text{Y})}{\text{MPP}_b(\text{Y})}$$

Geometrically, the isocost line faced by each firm has the same slope, namely p_a/p_b, so their isoquants have the same slope *at the point of equilibrium*. The economy will reach some point on the curve $00'$, the precise point depending upon relative demand-supply forces in both product and resource markets. In equilibrium, each resource owner is paid the value of the marginal product of that resource.

On the product market each firm equates marginal cost to price, and all consumers pay the same price for a given commodity. Each consumer maximizes utility by equating his marginal rate of substitution to the established price ratio (see Chapter 5):

Consumer 1   *Consumer 2*

$$\text{MRS}_{xy}(1) = p_x/p_y \qquad \text{MRS}_{xy}(2) = p_x/p_y$$

Since the rates of substitution equal a common price ratio, they are equal to each other:

$$\text{MRS}_{xy}(1) = \text{MRS}_{xy}(2)$$

Geometrically, all consumers face a budget line with the same slope equal to p_x/p_y. *At the point of equilibrium* each indifference curve has the same slope as the budget line, and so the indifference curves have identical slopes. Equilibrium in the commodity market places the economy somewhere on $0^1 0^2$, the particular point depending upon the free play of market forces. Moreover, the MRS_{xy} (identical for all consumers) is equal to the ratio of the marginal cost of X to the marginal cost of Y. The reason is that marginal cost equals price for each good under competition. The ratio of marginal costs may be thought of as the cost of transforming one good into the other. Consequently, in equilibrium the marginal rate of substituting one good for the other in consumption equals the cost of transforming one good into the other in production.

Any elements of monopoly or monopsony generate different equilibrium conditions, which deviate from the optimum conditions of the welfare theory. For example, a monopolist in the product market may engage in price discrimination. When different consumers pay different (net) prices, marginal rates of substitution are not equalized in equilibrium, and the utility of one or more consumers can be increased without a decrease in the utilities of others by equalizing the prices paid for a given product. Even when a monopoly does not discriminate prices among consumers, the optimum production conditions are violated and resources are misallocated. Resources are not paid the value of their marginal products, marginal revenue product is less than the value of marginal product, and marginal cost is below the product price, forcing the economy inside the production frontier of Fig. 25.2. Monopsony in any resource market has the same effect. If resource A is purchased monopsonistically in the industry producing X, profit-maximizing conditions for the firm may be written

$$\frac{\text{MFC}_a}{p_b} = \frac{\text{MPP}_a(X)}{\text{MPP}_b(X)}$$

Since MFC_a is less than p_a, the ratio of marginal products are not equalized in all uses.

The arguments against monopoly or monopsony powers in any resource or product market hinge upon the assumption of nonincreasing returns to scale. If production functions show increasing returns to scale over output ranges that the market will take at positive prices, the industry is called a "natural" monopoly, because average cost declines. Given that monopoly cost would be lower than cost under competition, profit maximization by the monopoly would still leave marginal cost less than price. Compared to the profit-maximizing equilibrium of the natural monopoly, price could be lower and output greater if the firm were forced to charge a price equal to marginal cost. But since average cost is declining, marginal cost and thus price would be below average cost. In order that the good be produced at all, the monopolist would have to be compensated for the difference so that long-run profit is zero. Based upon the Paretian welfare theory, it has been argued that all markets, except where natural monopoly exists, should be made purely competitive. Natural monopoly should be controlled and required to charge prices equal to marginal cost, any losses being repaired by lump-sum transfers that do not disturb the optimum production and exchange conditions.

Income Distribution and Pure Competition

The personal income distribution generated by a competitive price mechanism need not be the distribution that society deems best. To the extent that free markets determine prices, resources are paid in accordance with productivity, so resource owners must rely on their productivity for earned income. Under these conditions a national hero, for example, who has lost an arm and a leg in defense of his country may have scant earnings because of his low productivity. But society may feel that his income should not be determined solely by his changed economic efficiency. Or, more generally, if the price system results in an unequal distribution of personal income, redistribution might be advocated on humanitarian grounds.

There are many arguments—economic and noneconomic—over the optimal distribution of income. Those in opposition to large inequality claim that it leads to waste in consumption, that the rich play with frivolous trinkets while the poor munch on coarse bread. Also, some have alleged that inequality contributes to political instability, which arises from the resentment of the poor, and that it facilitates the growth of monopolies and exploitation, which is a consequence of centralized ownership by the rich. On the other hand, few seem to accept an absolutely equal distribution of income as best. The reasons include a contention that equal retained incomes would destroy the monetary incentive for leadership and the claim that equal distribution would dry up many sources of saving that finance capital accumulation so necessary for over-all prosperity and growth.

The fact of the matter is that the optimal distribution of income cannot be determined by consideration of economics alone. Nevertheless, there is one important distinction to be kept in mind. Acceptance of free competitive markets and the price mechanism on the grounds that they efficiently allocate products and resources does not mean that one must accept the resulting distribution of earned income as final. The income distribution generated by an efficient price system can be changed in two ways. One is by direct intervention, by administered prices. The price of a resource might be "artificially" raised in an attempt to raise the incomes of the owners, a product price might be supported to benefit the producers, or a product price might be prevented from rising as a subsidy to poor consumers. The severe disadvantage of any such direct intervention is that it interferes with the efficiency of the system. Alternatively, personal income can be redistributed by lump-sum transfers. The income tax is one convenient device. The advantage of executing income redistribution "outside" the price system, so to speak, is that it does not impose undue inefficiencies that distort allocation. At least these distortions are kept to a minimum. In this sense free competitive markets are consistent with any personal income distribution that society regards as desirable.

SUGGESTED READING

J. F. Due and R. W. Clower, *Intermediate Economic Analysis*, Chap. 23. Homewood, Ill.: Richard D. Irwin, Inc., 1961.

A. P. Lerner, *The Economics of Control*, Chaps. 1-6. New York: The Macmillan Company, 1949.

I. M. D. Little, *A Critique of Welfare Economics*, Chaps. 1-7. Oxford: Clarendon Press, 1950.

Foundations of
Economic Policy

Welfare theories, such as the Paretian theory outlined in the previous chapter, are presumably designed with an eye toward policy recommendations. This exposition of economic theory will be concluded by raising issues connected with the relation of theory to policy, indicating the advantages and limitations of welfare economics as a foundation for public policy.

LIMITATIONS OF THE WELFARE MODEL

Whereas positive economic analysis can treat assumptions as useful simplifications and can judge a theory by its ability to predict observable behavior, normative analysis must regard assumptions in a different light. A successful transition from theory to policy advice hinges upon acceptance of the theoretical assumptions. Unless general acceptance of the key assumptions (some of them value assumptions) can be guaranteed, application of the theory as a policy guide is unlikely to occur.

Though an economist (or some economists) may be willing to take economic welfare as the variable to be maximized, others may not. Economic welfare maximization is primarily a criterion of efficiency, and members of society may be quite willing to accept economic inefficiency because of greater importance attached to other aspects of social welfare. Within the framework of a more general social welfare theory, it is not inconceivable that points like P_4 or P_5 in Fig. 25.2 are in fact preferred to points like P_1 or P_2 if a movement to P_1 or P_2 would entail a sacrifice of (enough) psychological security, group unity, or any other noneconomic variable that affects social well-being. Ideally, policy actions should be based upon social welfare and not just economic welfare. The economic and noneconomic determinants of social welfare might not be independently variable, so satisfaction of the optimum production conditions could produce noneconomic effects left undetermined by current welfare economics.

In addition, collective consumption does not enter individual utility functions. Although more individually assignable goods and services may in truth be preferred to less by each consumer, *ceteris paribus*, to the extent that citizens affect their budget constraints by voting, a smaller equilibrium quantity may be preferred to more under some conditions. Everyone might voluntarily prefer a smaller disposable income (hence less utility and less economic welfare as defined) in order to have more collective goods and services. How many and what kind of resources should be allocated to this purpose remains an unanswered question.

Third, each utility function and production function is assumed to be independent of each other function. Smith does not try to keep up with Jones, for Smith's utility depends only upon what he consumes and not at all on what Jones consumes. Nor does Smith benefit from his neighbor's new lawn or freshly painted house. Likewise, another factory's soot that falls upon Smith's factory windows, his flowerbeds at home, or his wife's laundry is assumed to affect neither the production function of his firm nor his utility as a household member. These *external effects* can in principle be taken into account in the welfare theory. But the resulting optimum production and exchange conditions become much more complex, less amenable to practical interpretation, and more remote from the world view of public officials.

Finally, the welfare theory incorporates the value assumption that individual preferences shall determine social welfare—an assumption that many democratically oriented people would question on grounds of social ethics. In the last analysis, the Paretian welfare economics is a specialized welfare theory. A more general theory of social welfare cannot ignore the political structure and processes of society, the non-economic aspects of social welfare, and the way in which individual well-being is related to the well-being of society and its subgroups. It is at this point that economics shades into sociology, political science, psychology, and philosophy. Nevertheless, policy actions must be taken, with or without the ideal social welfare theory. The remainder of this chapter is devoted to certain areas in which applications of the Paretian theory appear to have common-sense justification as guides for public policy.

RESOURCE AND PRODUCT ALLOCATION

In matters of resource and product allocation, foremost among the issues of public concern are (1) monopoly, (2) government intervention in the price mechanism, (3) promotion of greater resource mobility, and (4) conservation of resources.

Clearly, both monopolistic labor unions and monopolistic firms violate the optimum conditions and misallocate resources. The question of whether monopoly (or oligopoly) elements in the economy are ultimately "better" than a competitive economy may be debatable. But certainly the alternative of pure competition is not to be confused with the primitive notion of a jungle environment in which the weak are downtrodden. The Paretian welfare theory at the least can be said to bring out explicitly the consequences of monopoly elements upon resource allocation, and thereby to contribute to the formulation of an enlightened economic policy. The existence of antitrust laws in the United States, in spite of inadequate enforcement, does perhaps reflect a more intuitive similar feeling by the public itself.

Government intervention in the operation of the price mechanism is well illustrated by farm price supports and tariff policies. In some cases the effects upon efficiency in resource allocation soon become obvious, while in others the inefficiency is less dramatic and receives less attention. For years economists have advocated free international trade on the Paretian grounds that consumers would benefit even though protected (relatively inefficient) industries would be adversely affected. Moreover, the gains would exceed the losses, permitting a compensation of the minority for losses and a net gain for society. And for years economists have won the arguments while lobbyists won the legislation, not entirely because of the existence of noneconomic welfare from tariffs but because those who would benefit from free trade (consumers) were not politically organized. More recently, movements for a gradual relaxation of farm price supports and a loosening of trade barriers have appeared. The welfare theory can aid in establishing an overall feasible set of policy actions by determining the effects of specific alternatives upon aggregate output and product distribution.

Assuming mutual tariff reductions expand trade among nations of the so-called free world—that something along the lines of the American Trade Expansion Act is pursued on a larger scale—industries formerly protected by tariffs will experience a decline in output and employment (even though other industries benefit from a larger foreign market). A slow but definite relaxation of farm price supports would have similar effects. As marginal farms are made unprofitable, the existing trend of farm to nonfarm migration would be increased. Unless alternative employment opportunities are available and resources are mobile enough to take advantage of them, an expansion of aggregate output and consumer utilities cannot be guaranteed. Also, much unemployment in the United States is structural unemployment rather than cyclical unemployment. The solution to structural unemployment is to a very large extent dependent upon greater geographic resource mobility in the face of a changing structure of demand for output.

The Paretian welfare theory assumes perfect resource mobility. Comparison of the theory with a world in which mobility is not perfect makes known the economic consequences of immobility and shows how promotion of greater mobility affects aggregate output and consumption.

Public dispensation of information about alternative employment opportunities, perhaps low-interest loans to facilitate capital transfers and federal aid to retraining programs for displaced workers, are within the realm of feasible policy actions. The costs and benefits of such actions can be compared to the costs and benefits of greater public investment in depressed economic areas. If policies intended to aid depressed areas, to ameliorate the income and employment problems of older workers, to expand international trade, and to avoid the waste inherent in farm price supports are not to be ill conceived or poorly executed, the Paretian model can be used to introduce alternatives and to provide a method for evaluating their relative merits.

Conservation of resources applies partly to natural resources: forests, rivers, oil and mineral deposits, seashores, etc. Natural resources have been steadily depleted over a number of years by private interests. Restocking of fish, prevention of erosion, establishment of parks to prevent spoliation by commercialism are all part of an effort to conserve these resources as a source of utility through recreation and other goods and services. Conservation refers to human resources as well—the maintenance of a healthy and productive labor force as opposed to deterioration through forced retirement at too early an age, emotional instability, and unfulfilled education. In all facets of conservation, costs are incurred, resources used to maintain other resources, and benefits are expected. Though not purely a matter of economics, the economic aspects are of first-order importance. Efficiency in the Paretian sense cannot be ignored if conservation policies are to be effective.

The consumer is the focal point of economic welfare theory. Since everyone (regardless of other functions performed) is a consumer, economic benefits flowing from policy actions are judged by their broadest social impact. If gains to all consumers as a group outweigh losses to any industry or other private interest, the losers can in principle be compensated for losses and a net gain prevails. Then the policy is judged to be sound. Logical and philosophical limitations of the theory prohibit iron-clad inferences, but the theory does contribute to enlightened policy formulation in areas where the economic effects are significant.

INCOME DISTRIBUTION

Chapter 25 emphasized the sad conclusion that the Paretian welfare model can say little about the most desirable distribution of income among persons. The theory provides no basis for choosing between any two income distributions, both of which are among the many optimum distributions. Moreover, movement from a point off the locus of optimum distributions—such as point Q_4 in Fig. 25.3—to a point on the locus can be said to improve welfare only if the relative distribution of income is in fact left unchanged.

The actual distribution of income in the United States is indicated in Table 26.1.

Table 26.1

Distribution of Income by Families and Unattached
Individuals, 1950 and 1962

Family Personal Income Before Taxes	*Per Cent of Families and Unattached Individuals*	
	1950	*1965*
Under $2,000	25	9
$2,000 to $ 2,999	18	8
$3,000 to $ 3,999	20	8
$4,000 to $ 4,999	14	8
$5,000 to $ 5,999	9	9
$6,000 to $ 7,499	5	9
$7,500 to $ 9,999	6	24
$10,000 to $14,999	2	17
$15,000 and over	1	8
Total	100	100

Source: *Statistical Abstract of the United States*, 1967.

Although these statistics do not take account of taxes or income in kind earned outside the market system, it is apparent that the rise in total income between 1950 and 1965 was accompanied by a more equal distribution among families. In 1965, nevertheless, 17 per cent of all families had incomes below $3,000 per year—a level which has been suggested as constituting poverty—and one-quarter of all families received incomes below $4,000 per year.

What are some of the factors that underly the distribution of income? In an exchange economy, earned income is derived from the sale of resources in the market. The market puts a valuation on each resource, and the total income of a resource owner depends upon the quantity of his resources employed and the price per unit. Different individuals possess different quantities of employed resources. Variations in quality of a given type of resource are found among individuals as well. Tables 26.2 and 26.3 show the distribution of income by age and occupation.

Table 26.2

Per Capita Income by Age, the United States
(Medians for those who earned income)

Age	*Per Capita Income, 1950 (dollars)*	*Per Capita Income, 1960 (dollars)*	*Per Cent Increase 1950–60*
20–24	1,521	2,202	44.8
25–34	2,295	3,827	66.8
35–44	2,539	4,249	67.3
45–54	2,453	4,009	63.4
55–64	2,097	3,299	57.3
65 and over	955	1,282	34.2

Source: U.S. Department of Commerce, *U.S. Census of Population*, 1960.

Table 26.3

Median Money Income of Male Persons with Income,
by Occupation Group, 1950 and 1964

Occupational Group	1950	1964
Professional, technical, and kindred workers	4,073	7,950
Farmers and farm managers	1,496	2,376
Managers, officials and proprietors, except farm	3,814	7,463
Clerical and kindred workers	3,103	5,719
Sales workers	3,137	5,764
Craftsmen, foremen, and kindred workers	3,293	6,268
Operatives and kindred workers	2,790	5,130
Service workers, except private household	2,303	4,665
Farm laborers and foremen	854	1,300
Laborers, except farm and mine	1,909	3,259
All employed male civilians	2,831	5,587

Source: *Statistical Abstract of the United States*, 1966.

There appears to be an "income problem" at both age poles of the labor force: those entering and those approaching departure. For several reasons, a relatively low income at the youngest ages is to be expected. Experience normally enhances productivity and earnings; promotions occur only after some time on the company payroll; apprenticeships and on-the-job training (with the consequence of a lower income) are customary at this age. To the extent that low income in any given year is the result of these "natural" processes, the youngest age group is not experiencing an income problem. However, the relative income of the youngest has declined over the decade. Probably this decline reflects the effect of delayed entry into the labor force because of extended education. If a greater proportion of the young remain in school longer, thus expanding their earnings in later years, the income of those entering the labor force at an earlier age is more heavily weighted by dropouts from school.

The relative decline in income at the upper ages presents a more serious social problem. Not only does income decline beyond the age of 44; the rate of increase over time also declines. Moreover, the oldest group shows the smallest rate of increase. Any income-earning problems created by school dropouts among the young are carried along through the age groups with the passage of time, to be added to the other factors that produce the income distribution by age.

Table 26.3 records the distribution of income by occupation. Since occupations have different educational requirements, this table reflects in part income variations due to differences in educational attainment. As one might expect, the highest incomes accrue to professional workers and managers. Farm workers, service workers, and unskilled laborers receive the lowest incomes.

Table 26.4 exhibits the distribution of income by color and sex. Although the number of occupations in which women engage has vastly increased as a result of World War II, and the emancipation of women in terms of variety of income-earning activities began in the United States at that time, there is still considerable disparity between the incomes of men and women in the same general field of work. Even when it is acknowledged that women display greater dexterity than men in some lines of work, women do not usually command the same wages as men.

There are several reasons for this disparity. Women are not so well organized or so willing to fight for better pay. A money-earning occupation is often an interim activity before marriage or a part-time activity after marriage. Since 60 per cent of the women in the labor force are married, they frequently look upon their wages as supplementary income. Consequently, they are less dissatisfied than men with lower wages. Women, of course, do not possess the same physical strength as do men, and they may therefore be unfit for some of the heavy work performed by men. Whatever may be the reasons for disparity of income between men and women, they can only be determined by careful study of each occupation in which both sexes are employed.

Table 26.4

Distribution of Individual Wage or Salary Income
by Sex and by Color, 1950 and 1965

PER CENT WITH WAGE OR SALARY INCOME

	MALE			FEMALE		
	1950	1965		1950	1965	
		Total	*Nonwhite*		*Total*	*Nonwhite*
$999 or less	20.7	13.8	22.8	51.8	37.5	44.3
$1,000 to $1,999	16.4	10.4	15.8	23.6	18.9	22.6
$2,000 to $2,999	21.6	9.3	15.4	18.1	12.6	12.2
$3,000 to $3,999	20.9	8.9	12.6	4.5	10.9	8.2
$4,000 to $4,999	9.6	9.0	10.4	1.2	7.9	4.9
$5,000 to $5,999	4.6	10.3	9.1	0.3	5.3	3.3
$6,000 to $6,999	2.0	9.5	5.5	0.1	2.7	2.4
$7,000 to $9,999	2.0	17.4	6.5	0.2	3.2	1.7
$10,000 and over	2.0	11.3	1.8	0.2	1.0	0.7
Total	100.0	100.0	100.0	100.0	100.0	100.0
Median Income	$2,570	$4,824	$2,672	$953	$1,564	$1,213

Source: *Statistical Abstract of the United States*, 1967.

A problem of even greater significance is the disparity of income between white and nonwhites. Our table shows that even as recently as 1965, when only 24.2 per cent of all males were in the two lowest income categories, there were still 38.6 per cent of all nonwhite males in those two categories. At the other end of the income ladder, a very small percentage of the non-whites were in the higher income brackets. Furthermore, the median income of all male workers was nearly double that of the nonwhite male workers. A somewhat similar pattern existed between the total number of females in the labor force and the nonwhite females.

These statistical data provide some indication of the numerous factors that contribute to the distribution of income generated by an exchange economy. A review of the evidence shows that incomes differ by age, occupa-tion, educational attainment, color, and sex—reflecting differences in *both productivity and employment opportunity*. In addition, income derived from property is a component of family income. For decades, perhaps centuries, property income has been more unequally distributed than wage and salary income. Microeconomic theory can help to identify the causes of poverty and provide guidelines for improving productivity in order to raise income. Economics acknowledges the constraints imposed by the market system and offers a mechanism for tracing the consequences of alternative measures designed to increase welfare. In the last analysis, however, issues of income redistribution cannot escape considerations of politics and social justice as well as economic efficiency.

WELFARE THEORY AND POLICY

It is tempting to conclude a discussion of normative economics by simply admitting that the relation between welfare theory and policy is extremely complex. First, there are disagreements among economists in the area of positive economic analysis. Certainly, virtual unanimity can be found in broad areas of theory. As a consequence, most economists accept an exchange economy as basically more desirable than a centrally controlled economy. They would argue that the price mechanism should be left free to allocate particular products and resources. Nevertheless, in specific aspects of economic theory differences of opinion remain—such as disagreements on the relative importance of different determinants of changes in technology. Therefore, policy makers cannot rely upon a unified body of positive economic theory to which all experts would agree in detail.

Second, adequate statistical measurements of some important rela-tionships are not yet available. Either the necessary data are not collected and published in enough detail or cross classification, or the statistical theory upon which estimates are based is not sufficiently refined to permit unambiguous quantitative predictions. Thus measurements of the causes and effects of technological change, of income redistribution, and geographic migration, for example, leave something to be desired. And effective policies often require information not only about the directional changes in economic variables to be expected from policy actions but also the degree of change.

Third, many "practical" considerations stand as obstacles in the way of an application of theory to policy, even in instances where the theory and measurements are unassailable. Given the prevailing political processes and institutions of society, theory in itself may be misunderstood or suspected as "too academic." It is not surprising that many economic policies in American history have been founded more upon political power distributions than economic sense.

Even if these difficulties were overcome, another rears its head. There does not exist at present a theory of social welfare that would be accepted by members of society to the same degree as, say, the principle of representative government. Actually, American macroeconomic policies (and those of other nations) that have been beneficial in the Paretian sense have likely been based upon some intuitive sense of social well-being rather than a formal system of thought.

In the light of these comments, it is obvious that both positive and normative economics must be regarded as a developing organ, continually subject to revision and improvement, rather than a once-and-for-all closed system of ultimate truth. Great strides have been made over the past fifty years, more in the areas of positive than normative economics because the problems have been of the "technical" type in which disciplined intelligence and analytical rigor have produced dramatic results. Probably this advancement has contributed to a tendency of withdrawal from normative economics where broad philosophical issues plague the theorist. Yet in recent years attempts have been initiated to widen the framework of economic welfare theory, integrating the methods and objectives of economics with those of other disciplines. The success or failure of social welfare theory as an effective guide for policy will very likely rest in the hands of the next two generations of economists.

SUGGESTED READING

W. D. Grampp and E. T. Weiler, *Economic Policy*, Parts 3 and 5. Homewood, Ill.: Richard D. Irwin, Inc., 1961.

J. Tinbergen, *Economic Policy: Principles and Design*, Chaps. 1 and 2. Amsterdam: North-Holland Publishing Co., 1956.

F. H. Knight, *On The History and Method of Economics*, Chaps. 9 and 11. Chicago: University of Chicago Press, 1956.

Mathematical Appendix:
Geometric Relationships

Total average, and marginal magnitudes will be illustrated for product curves, but the principles apply equally to cost and other variables. Figure A.1 shows a total physical product curve. For any quantity of A, such as a_1, that quantity is shown geometrically as the distance $0a_1$ on the horizontal axis. The corresponding product is equal to the vertical distance a_1P_1. Average product of A is therefore $a_1P_1/0a_1$. A line drawn from the origin to the TPP curve forms an angle α at the origin. The size of this angle when a equals a_1 can be measured by $a_1P_1/0a_1$, or conversely $a_1P_1/0a_1$ is a measure

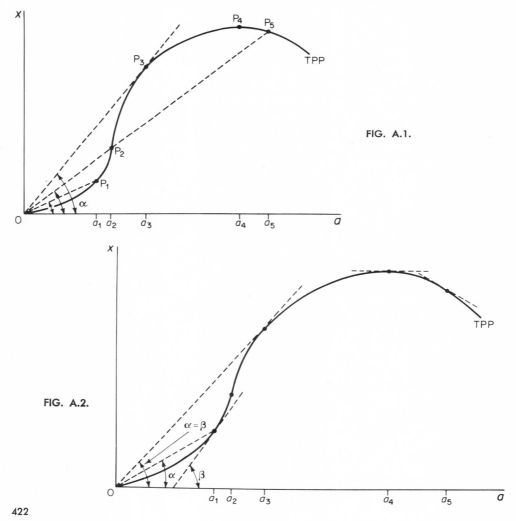

FIG. A.1.

FIG. A.2.

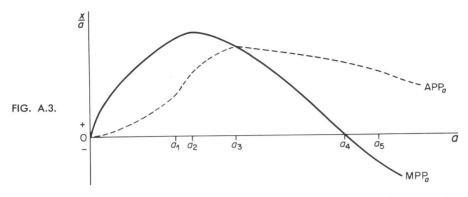

FIG. A.3.

of α when a equals a_1. The average product of A at a_1 units is plotted as a point in Fig. A.3.

For a_2 units of A, total product equals distance a_2P_2, so average physical product is $a_2P_2/0a_2$. The size of α is larger at a_2 than at a_1 units of A, so the APP_a curve is rising from a_1 to a_2 units in Fig. A.3. If the average product is computed for every quantity of A and all the points are connected in Fig. A.3, the APP_a curve is obtained.

Notice that α is largest for a_3 units of A, so the APP_a curve is at its maximum point. The line out of the origin is tangent to the TPP curve at this quantity of A. No other line can be drawn from the origin to the TPP curve to form a larger angle. Notice also that the size of α when a is a_2 is equal to the size of α when a is a_5. That is, the line from the origin to the point P_2 is the same line that joins the origin with point P_5. Hence, the average product when a_2 units of A are used equals the average product when a_5 units of A are used.

The marginal physical product curve for A can also be derived geometrically from the total physical product curve. The angle β in Fig. A.2, formed by a line from the horizontal axis and *tangent* to the TPP curve is a measure of the marginal physical product of A. That is, the marginal product is equal to the slope of the total product curve, measured by the size of β.

From zero to a_2 units of A, the size of β becomes larger with larger quantities of A, so the MPP_a curve is rising in Fig. A.3. It is also above the APP_a curve because β is larger than α (e.g., compare the size of α with that of β at a_1 units of A). The MPP_a curve is at its maximum point for a_2 units of A, where the TPP curve changes from concave upward to concave downward. At the point where the APP_a curve reaches its maximum, at a_3 units of A, the size of α equals the size of β. Indeed, they coincide (a line tangent to the TPP curve cuts the horizontal axis at the origin). It is easy to see, by comparing the size of α and β for various quantities of A that the MPP_a curve must be below the APP_a curve at quantities of A in excess of a_3. The slope of the TPP curve is zero for a_4 units of A, so the marginal product is zero. For quantities in excess of a_4 the slope of the TPP curve is negative, so the MPP_a curve dips below the horizontal axis in Fig. A.3.

Chapter 4

(1) $x_d = a - bp$ $p > 0, x_d > 0, x_s > 0$

(2) $x_s = c + dp$

(3) $x_d = x_s$

where x_d denotes quantity demanded, x_s quantity supplied, p the price of good X, and a, b, c, and d are positive constants. Substitution of (1) and (2) into (3) yields

$$p = \frac{a - c}{d + b} > 0 \quad \text{for} \quad a > c, \qquad x = \frac{cb + da}{d + b} > 0$$

Parallel shifts in the demand and supply curves are represented by

$$\frac{dp}{da} = \frac{1}{d + b} > 0 \qquad \frac{dx}{da} = \frac{d}{d + b} > 0 \qquad \frac{dp}{dc} = -\frac{1}{d + b} < 0 \qquad \frac{dx}{dc} = \frac{b}{d + b} > 0$$

Chapter 5

Assume the continuous utility function

$$u = u(x_1, x_2, \cdots, x_n)$$

where x_i denotes the quantity of the ith commodity, is to be maximized subject to the budget constraint

$$I = \sum_{i=1}^{n} p_i x_i$$

for p_i the constant price of the ith good and I constant income.
  Form the function

$$z = u(x_1, x_2, \cdots, x_n) + \lambda(I - p_1 x_1 - p_2 x_2 - \cdots - p_n x_n)$$

where λ is the undetermined Lagrange multiplier. Differentiating partially and equating the partials to zero,

$$\frac{\partial z}{\partial x_i} = \frac{\partial u}{\partial x_i} - \lambda p_i = 0 \qquad i = 1, 2, \cdots, n$$

$$\frac{\partial z}{\partial \lambda} = (I - p_1 x_1 - p_2 x_2 - \cdots - p_n x_n) = 0$$

are the necessary conditions for utility maximization.[1] Letting $\partial u/\partial x_i$ be

---

[1] The sufficient conditions are guaranteed by the forms of the functions as described in the text.

represented by u_i, the goods are consumed in quantities that satisfy

$$\lambda = \frac{u_1}{p_1} = \frac{u_2}{p_2} = \cdots = \frac{u_n}{p_n}$$

The multiplier λ is the total derivative of u with respect to income, called the marginal utility of money. For any two goods, say j and k, note that

$$\frac{u_j}{u_k} = \frac{p_j}{p_k}$$

The variable u_i is defined as the *marginal utility* of the ith good. Moreover, by definition

$$\text{MRS}_{x_j x_k} = -\frac{\partial x_k}{\partial x_j} = \frac{u_j}{u_k} = \frac{p_j}{p_k}$$

Chapters 6 and 7

Let

$$x = a - bp_x$$

be a linear demand curve where a and b are positive constants. Then

$$e_{p_x} = \frac{dx}{dp_x} \cdot \frac{p_x}{x} = -\frac{bp_x}{x} = \frac{x - a}{x}$$

which varies with x. Instead suppose

$$x = ap_x^{-b}$$

Then

$$e_{p_x} = -\frac{ab}{p_x^{b+1}} \cdot \frac{p_x}{x} = -b \cdot \frac{ap_x^{-b}}{x} = -b$$

a constant. More generally, let $p_x = f(x)$ be any demand curve. Total revenue (or total expenditure) $R = xp_x$.

$$\frac{dR}{dx} = p_x + x\frac{dp_x}{dx}$$

$$= p_x\left(1 + \frac{x}{p_x} \cdot \frac{dp_x}{dx}\right)$$

$$= p_x\left(1 + \frac{1}{e_{p_x}}\right)$$

Rather than a demand curve, consider the demand function

$$x = d(p_x, p_y, p_z, I)$$

where p_y denotes the price of good Y and p_z the price of good Z. Then the elasticities are defined as

$$e_{p_x} = \frac{\partial x}{\partial p_x} \cdot \frac{p_x}{x} \qquad e_{p_y} = \frac{\partial x}{\partial p_y} \cdot \frac{p_y}{x} \qquad e_{p_z} = \frac{\partial x}{\partial p_z} \cdot \frac{p_z}{x} \qquad e_I = \frac{\partial x}{\partial I} \cdot \frac{I}{x}$$

If the demand equation is

$$x = a p_x^{-b} p_y^{-c} p_z^{d} I^{e}$$

for a, b, c, d, and e positive constants, then

$$e_{p_x} = -b$$

$$e_{p_y} = -c \qquad \text{thus Y is a substitute for X}$$

$$e_{p_z} = d \qquad \text{thus Z is a complement of X}$$

$$e_I = e \qquad \text{thus X is a superior good}$$

Chapter 9

Assume a continuous production function

$$x = x(a_1, a_2, a_3, \cdots, a_m)$$

where a_i denotes the input of the ith resource. Profit maximization implies that any output is produced at least cost or, alternatively in this case, that for any given cost outlay total product is to be maximized.

Thus x is to be maximized subject to

$$C = \sum_{i=1}^{m} q_i a_i$$

for q_i the constant price of the ith resource and C constant total cost.

Form the function

$$y = x(a_1, a_2, \cdots, a_m) + \lambda(C - q_1 a_1 - q_2 a_2 - \cdots - q_m a_m)$$

where λ is the Lagrange multiplier. Differentiating partially and equating the partials to zero:

$$\frac{\partial y}{\partial a_i} = \frac{\partial x}{\partial a_i} - \lambda q_i = 0 \qquad i = 1, 2, \cdots, m$$

$$\frac{\partial y}{\partial \lambda} = (C - q_1 a_1 - q_2 a_2 - \cdots - q_m a_m) = 0$$

Letting $\partial x / \partial a_i$ be represented by x_i, inputs are employed in quantities that satisfy

$$\lambda = \frac{x_1}{q_1} = \frac{x_2}{q_2} = \cdots = \frac{x_m}{q_m}$$

yielding in turn a total output. The multiplier λ is the total derivative of output with respect to cost, the reciprocal of marginal cost.

For any two resources, say j and k, note that

$$\frac{x_j}{x_k} = \frac{q_j}{q_k}$$

The variable x_i is nothing other than the *marginal physical product* of the ith resource. Moreover, by definition

$$\mathrm{MRTS}_{a_j a_k} = -\frac{\partial a_k}{\partial a_j} = \frac{x_j}{x_k} = \frac{q_j}{q_k}$$

For given $x = x(a_1, a_2, \cdots, a_m)$ and any constant ϕ, if

$$x(\phi a_1, \phi a_2, \cdots, \phi a_m) = \phi^t x$$

then x is said to be a homogeneous function of degree t. The function

$$x = k a^\alpha b^\beta \qquad 0 < \alpha < 1, 0 < \beta < 1, k > 0$$

where k, α, and β are constants, shows diminishing returns to each resource:

$$\frac{\partial x}{\partial a} = \frac{k \alpha b_0^\beta}{a^{1-\alpha}} \qquad \frac{\partial x}{\partial b} = \frac{k \beta a_0^\alpha}{b^{1-\beta}}$$

where b_0 and a_0 are any constant values of b and a. Furthermore, it is a homogeneous function of degree one (constant returns to scale) if $\alpha + \beta = 1$. That is

$$k(\phi a)^\alpha (\phi b)^\beta = k \phi^{\alpha+\beta} a^\alpha b^\beta$$

$$= \phi k a^\alpha b^\beta = \phi x$$

The function exhibits increasing returns to scale (degree greater than one) or decreasing returns to scale (degree less than one) as $\alpha + \beta > 1$ or $\alpha + \beta < 1$ respectively.

Chapters 10 and 11

The necessary conditions for a constrained output maximization are tangency points between isoquants and isocosts. These tangency points can be expressed as an implicit function

$$f(a_1, a_2, \cdots, a_m) = 0$$

Let $p_m a_m = b$, a constant, which is total fixed cost in the short run. The system of equations

$$\text{I} \begin{cases} (1) \quad x = x(a_1, a_2, \cdots, a_{m-1}) \\[2ex] (2) \quad C = \sum_{i=1}^{m-1} q_i a_i + b \\[2ex] (3) \quad O = f(a_1, a_2, \cdots, a_{m-1}) \end{cases}$$

can be reduced to a single equation

$$C = g(x) + b$$

stating total cost as an explicit function of output as follows: select any input combination satisfying (3) and obtain the corresponding output from (1); then find C from (2).

For long-run cost let the amounts of "fixed" inputs—the scales of plant—be represented by the parameter s. Assume s is continuously variable and introduce it explicitly into system I above:

$$\text{I}' \begin{cases} (1) \quad x = x(a_1, a_2, \cdots, a_r, s) \\[2ex] (2) \quad C = q_1 a_1 + q_2 a_2 + \cdots + q_r a_r + h(s) \\[2ex] (3) \quad O = f(a_1, a_2, \cdots, a_r, s) \end{cases}$$

Fixed cost is an increasing function of plant size: $h'(s) > 0$. Eliminate variables as before to obtain

(4) $C = g(x, s) + h(s)$

The long-run cost curve is the envelope of the short-run curves. Write the equation for a family of short-run cost functions in implicit form:

(5) $C - g(x, s) - h(s) = j(C, x, s) = 0$

and set the partial derivative with respect to s equal to zero:

(6) $j_s(C, x, s) = 0$

The equation of the envelope curve is found by eliminating s from (5) and (6) and solving for C as a function of x:

(7) $C = C(x)$

Example: Assume

(1′) $x = k a^\alpha b^{1-\alpha}$

(2′) $C = p_a a + p_b b$

where p_a and p_b are constant prices of resources A and B. Therefore

$$\mathrm{MPP}_a/p_a = \mathrm{MPP}_b/p_b$$

gives

(3') $(1 - \alpha)\,p_a a - \alpha p_b b = 0$

Solving (2') and (3') for a and b,

$$a = \frac{\alpha\mathrm{C}}{p_a} \qquad b = \frac{(1 - \alpha)\mathrm{C}}{p_b}$$

Substituting these values into (1'):

$$x = k\left(\frac{\alpha\mathrm{C}}{p_a}\right)^{\alpha}\left[\frac{(1 - \alpha)\mathrm{C}}{p_b}\right]^{1-\alpha}$$

The total cost function is

$$\mathrm{C} = tx$$

where

$$t = \frac{p_a^{\alpha} p_b^{1-\alpha}}{k\alpha^{\alpha}(1 - \alpha)^{1-\alpha}}$$

Chapter 12

Total revenue $= \mathrm{R} = p_x x$ where p_x is a constant. For the total cost function

$$\mathrm{C} = \mathrm{C}(x) \qquad \frac{d\mathrm{C}}{dx} > 0, \qquad \frac{d^2\mathrm{C}}{dx^2} > 0$$

total profit

$$\mathrm{P} = p_x x - \mathrm{C}(x)$$

is a maximum at the output that satisfies

$$\frac{d\mathrm{P}}{dx} = p_x - \frac{d\mathrm{C}}{dx} = 0$$

Chapter 15

$$\text{Total Revenue} = \mathrm{R}(x) \qquad \frac{d\mathrm{R}}{dx} > 0, \qquad \frac{d^2\mathrm{R}}{dx^2} < 0$$

$$\text{Total Cost} \quad = \mathrm{C}(x) \qquad \frac{d\mathrm{C}}{dx} > 0, \qquad \frac{d^2\mathrm{C}}{dx^2} > 0$$

$$\text{Total Profit} \quad = \mathrm{P}(x) = \mathrm{R}(x) - \mathrm{C}(x)$$

The profit-maximizing output satisfies

$$\frac{dP}{dx} = \frac{dR}{dx} - \frac{dC}{dx} = 0$$

Assume the market demand curve is given by

$$p_x = a - bx \qquad a > 0, b > 0$$

Hence:

$$R = ax - bx^2$$

$$dR/dx = a - 2bx$$

Assume

$$C = cx^2$$

$$dC/dx = 2cx$$

Then

$$\frac{dP}{dx} = a - 2bx - 2cx = 0$$

gives

$$x = \frac{a}{2(b+c)}$$

$$p_x = a - b\left[\frac{a}{2(b+c)}\right] = a\left[1 - \frac{b}{2(b+c)}\right]$$

Chapter 20

Solution of the profit maximizing equations (see Chapter 9):

$$\frac{x_1}{q_1} = \frac{x_2}{q_2} = \cdots = \frac{x_m}{q_m} = \lambda$$

where $\lambda = 1/\mathrm{MC} = 1/p_x$, for each a_i in terms of the other variables yields the firm's demand functions for resources.

Example: Assume the production function

$$x = ka^\alpha b^\beta \qquad 0 < \alpha < 1, \qquad 0 < \beta < 1$$

$$\alpha + \beta + e = 1, \qquad e > 0$$

The firm's equilibrium conditions may then be written

(1) $p_a = \mathrm{MPP}_a \cdot p_x = kb^\beta \alpha a^{\alpha-1} p_x$

(2) $p_b = \mathrm{MPP}_b \cdot p_x = ka^\alpha \beta b^{\beta-1} p_x$

Letting capital letters denote the natural logarithms of the variables and primes the logarithms of the constants, and solving (1) and (2) for a and b, the demand equations are

(3) $A = M - \dfrac{(1-\beta)}{e} P_a - \dfrac{\beta}{e} P_b + \dfrac{1}{e} P_x$

$M = \dfrac{K + \beta\beta' + (1-\beta)\alpha'}{e} > 0$

and

(4) $B = N - \dfrac{(1-\alpha)}{e} P_b - \dfrac{\alpha}{e} P_a + \dfrac{1}{e} P_x$

$N = \dfrac{K + \alpha\alpha' + (1-\alpha)\beta'}{e} > 0$

Chapter 21

For a monopoly producing X, $\lambda = 1/MC = 1/MR_x$ in contrast to Chapter 20.

Example: Assume the same production function given in Chapter 20, but let the market demand for the product be given as

$$x = \sigma p_x^{-1/\theta} i^\phi \qquad \sigma > 0, \quad 0 < \theta < 1, \quad \phi > 0$$

for i represents consumer income, and σ, θ, and ϕ are constants. The equilibrium conditions are

(1) $P_a = MPP_a \cdot MR_x = \mu\alpha a^{\alpha(1-\theta)-1} b^{\beta(1-\theta)} i^{\phi\theta}$

(2) $P_b = MPP_b \cdot MR_x = \mu\beta a^{\alpha(1-\theta)} b^{\beta(1-\theta)-1} i^{\phi\theta}$

$\mu = (1-\theta)\sigma^\theta k^{(1-\theta)} > 0$

Using the notation of Chapter 20, the demand equations are

(3) $A = \dfrac{1}{e + \theta(\alpha+\beta)} \{M - [1 - \beta(1-\theta)]P_a - \beta(1-\theta)P_b + \theta\phi I\}$

$M = \mu' + [1 - \beta(1-\theta)]\alpha' + [\beta(1-\theta)]\beta' > 0$

and

(4) $B = \dfrac{1}{e + \theta(\alpha+\beta)} \{N - [1 - \alpha(1-\theta)]P_b - \alpha(1-\theta)P_b + \theta\phi I\}$

$N = \mu' + [\alpha(1-\theta)]\alpha' + [1 - \alpha(1-\theta)]\beta' > 0$

For monopsony selling in the resource market MFC replaces the resource price, and the derivation of demand follows the same principles.

Chapter 25

Optimum Production Conditions:

Assume

$$x = x(a_x, b_x) \qquad \text{and} \qquad y = y(a_y, b_y)$$

Maximize

$$(x + y) \quad \text{subject to}$$

$$a = a_x + a_y$$

$$b = b_x + b_y$$

Form

$$H = \pi_1 x + \pi_2 y + \lambda_1 a + \lambda_2 b$$

where the π's and λ's are the Lagrange multipliers, and maximize H. Differentiating and equating the partials to zero (see Chapter 5), after elimination of the multipliers the first-order maximum conditions are

$$\frac{\partial x/\partial a_x}{\partial x/\partial b_x} = \text{MRTS}_{ab}(X) = \frac{\partial y/\partial a_y}{\partial y/\partial b_y} = \text{MRTS}_{ab}(Y)$$

or in equivalent form

$$\frac{\partial x/\partial a_x}{\partial y/\partial a_y} = \frac{\partial x/b_x}{\partial y/\partial b_y} = -\frac{\partial x}{\partial y}$$

where the common factor of proportionality $(-\partial x/\partial y)$ is equal to the marginal cost of good X in terms of the displaced amount of good Y.

Optimum Exchange Conditions:

For two consumers, 1 and 2, maximize $(u_1 + u_2)$ subject to

(1) $x_1 + x_2 = x$

(2) $y_1 + y_2 = y$

If the level of utility for either consumer is arbitrarily specified, it is a necessary condition that the utility of the remaining consumer be a maximum. Thus maximize $u_1(x_1, y_1)$ subject to (1), (2), and

$$u_2(x_2, y_2) = \bar{u}_2$$

where $\bar{u}_2$ is an arbitrary constant. Following the usual procedure of constrained maximization already described, the first-order conditions emerge as

$$\frac{\partial u_1/\partial x_1}{\partial u_1/\partial y_1} = \text{MRS}_{xy}(1) = \frac{\partial u_2/\partial x_2}{\partial u_2/\partial y_2} = \text{MRS}_{xy}(2)$$

Index